M000097013

Caught on Camera

CRITICAL AUTHORS & ISSUES

Josué Harari, Series Editor

A complete list of books in the series is available from
the publisher.

CAUGHT ON CAMERA

Film in the Courtroom from the Nuremberg Trials
to the Trials of the Khmer Rouge

Christian Delage

Edited and translated by

Ralph Schoolcraft

and

Mary Byrd Kelly

PENN

UNIVERSITY OF PENNSYLVANIA PRESS

PHILADELPHIA

Cet ouvrage publié dans le cadre du programme d'aide à la publication bénéficie du soutien du Ministère des Affaires Etrangères et du Service Culturel de l'Ambassade de France représenté aux Etats-Unis. This work received support from the French Ministry of Foreign Affairs and the Cultural Services of the French Embassy in the United States through their publishing assistance program.

Originally published as Christian Delage, *La Vérité par l'image: De Nuremberg au procès Milosevic* (Paris: Éditions Danoël, 2006), copyright © Éditions Denoël 2006.

English translation copyright © 2014 University of Pennsylvania Press

All rights reserved. Except for brief quotations used for purposes of review or scholarly citation, none of this book may be reproduced in any form by any means without written permission from the publisher.

Published by
University of Pennsylvania Press
Philadelphia, Pennsylvania 19104-4112
www.upenn.edu/pennpress

Printed in the United States of America on acid-free paper

10 9 8 7 6 5 4 3 2 1

Library of Congress Cataloging-in-Publication Data

Delage, Christian.
  Vérité par l'image. English
  Caught on camera : film in the courtroom from the Nuremberg trials to the trials of the Khmer Rouge / Christian Delage ; edited and translated by Ralph Schoolcraft and Mary Byrd Kelly. — 1st ed.
      p.   cm. — (Critical authors and issues series)
  Includes bibliographical references and index
  ISBN 978-0-8122-4556-1 (hardcover : alk. paper)
  ("This American translation . . . has been entirely revised by the author. In addition, Chapter 14 has been added to the volume and the bibliographical materials have been updated."—Editor's note.)
  1. Mass media and criminal justice. 2. War crime trials. 3. Criminal justice, administration of. 4. Evidence, documentary. I. Title. II. Schoolcraft, Ralph W. III. Kelly, Mary Byrd. IV. Series: Critical authors and issues.
  P96.C74 D4613   2013
  341.6'90268   2013022776

CONTENTS

IV. THE ERA OF JUSTICE ON FILM (1945 TO THE PRESENT)

Illustrations follow pages 60 and 164

EDITOR'S NOTE

This American translation of *La Vérité par l'image: De Nuremberg au procès Milosevic* (Paris: Éditions Denoël, 2006) has been entirely revised by the author. In addition, Chapter 14 has been added to the volume and the bibliographical materials have been updated.

Where published translations were available for citations, we have preferred to use those to facilitate the task of readers and researchers who may wish to pursue such source references. All other translations are our own.

Mary Byrd Kelly translated Chapters 1–9. She wishes to dedicate her contribution to the memory of her father, C. W. O. Edwin L. Byrd, who proudly served in the U.S. Army from 1935 to 1961.

I translated Chapters 10–14 and have revised 1–9 to assure consistency in terminology and tone. I have also edited the text to compensate for its change in readership (the French edition needed to explain a certain number of American institutions to European readers) and provided the editorial notes. I wish to thank Mary for her excellent work, and the author for his careful reading of the manuscript.

Introduction

Spring 1945. Although President Truman had just given Robert H. Jackson the responsibility of setting up the judicial body sought by the Allies for bringing the main Nazi criminals to justice, Justice Jackson simultaneously took two entirely original initiatives: presenting motion pictures as evidence in court and filming the trial to make it a historical archive. Already faced with the novelty of an international tribunal, the exercise of justice would also discover that the fleeting nature of oral courtroom debate was altered considerably. The conditions, the unfolding, and the consequences of these experimentations lie at the heart of the research whose results we present here.

This double jurisprudence born of the Nuremberg trials (using film in the courtroom, filming the trials), which falls in the context of immediate treatments of World War II, is of singular concern to historians. In this exceptional situation, it is not the historian who first and foremost institutes the historicity of the collected archives (be they written or audiovisual) and determines their truth value. Rather it is in a public venue, the court, whose authority would be critical to the citizenry of the nations represented by the judges.

Today this question is inscribed in the framework of a rapidly growing historiography centered on, among other issues, the role of the judicial hearing and film at the conclusion of wars, the terminology for qualifying mass violence, and the memory of World War II and of the genocide of the Jews of Europe.[1]

How was Jackson, a magistrate trained in the culture of the written word, led to place so much importance on film? It might seem only natural in the country that was home to Hollywood, the most powerful movie industry in the world, that motion pictures should benefit in all quarters from an unequaled socialization. The United States certainly fed on fictions produced by the big studios to celebrate national pride and seize on countries' mythologies. But as for news and documentaries, it was often in the contact with the future allies of their country (Russia and England in particular) that the young directors called by Roosevelt's administration to participate in mobilizing the New Deal learned their trade in the 1930s. Thanks to the German artists and intellectuals who had sought refuge in New York or California, this reflection on the social and political role of film was then carried out on the motion pictures produced by the Third Reich and the means of counteracting their influence. These two realms, fiction and documentary, constantly enriched by the contributions of new immigrants, came together at the historic moment of the Allied landing in Europe. From distant observers of "Nazi atrocities," Americans were now transformed into witnesses. Cameramen from the army and intelligence service, directed by John Ford, constructed an initial account of the end of Nazism and the discovery of the camps. They did so as professionals, respecting the terms and conditions necessary for the eventual validation of their films as evidence.

It was with this legacy in mind that Justice Jackson determined the role of motion pictures in the gathering of evidence and construction of the charges against the Nazis. His desire, however, was "to establish incredible events with credible evidence" by putting together a trial in which the "documents" would be the deciding factors in proving the guilt of the accused.[2] In fact the massive and unprecedented character of the crimes committed and their authors' attempt to cover them up made it necessary to go beyond mere attestation of their reality and to make them the object of a confrontation inside the courtroom. This is how we must interpret the role of the inaugural projection, barely nine days into the trial, of a compilation of images filmed by the Allies in the camps in the West. One of the goals was to subject the defendants to viewing these crimes but also to promote public awareness of their scale and gravity. The effect was gripping. The Soviets, who in turn presented in February 1946 a film devoted mostly to the Majdanek and Auschwitz-Birkenau camps, made a lesser impression, due to the lack of care taken to evoke what had been their daily backdrop throughout the war: mass death.

To maintain the standard of a fair trial even though it was a justice emanating from the victors, Jackson also asked that the images the Nazis had filmed and shown throughout occupied Europe be collected in Germany. *The Nazi Plan*, a four-hour documentary montage, would allow people in the courtroom to hear the words uttered in the exercise of their power by those now on trial.

It was logical that in continuity with the screenings organized in the courtroom, the lessons of Nuremberg should take a cinematographic form. We will consider in detail the difficulties of the American party in the writing, making, and distribution of their film on the International Military Tribunal (IMT). In fact, to the premises of the Cold War were added the disputes over jurisdiction between Washington and the American military government in Berlin. The Soviets took advantage of this quibbling to produce their own documentary on the trial, which they presented in New York with a particularly offensive advertising slogan. In Hollywood the big studios were content to let the independent directors deal with the stakes of the IMT. Even before the Nuremberg trial was held, Orson Welles thus had the idea of presenting the power of projecting archival pictures of the Nazi camps in a movie entitled *The Stranger* (1946). Samuel Fuller, rich with his experience as a soldier in the famous artillery unit known as the "Big Red One," worked instead on the role played by film in Germany's de-Nazification. Finally, Stanley Kramer reconstituted the day at Nuremberg of November 29, 1945, during which *Nazi Concentration Camps* was presented.

The IMT is the impetus for the recent formation of tribunals for judging crimes committed in Rwanda (the International Criminal Tribunal for Rwanda, ICTR) and in the former Yugoslavia (the International Criminal Tribunal for the former Yugoslavia, ICTY), as well as a permanent International Criminal Court.[3] In a final, more diachronic part of this book, we raise the question of the cinegenic character of these trials, in the double mediation ensured by the projection of films in the courtroom and the audiovisual recording of court sessions. In the latter case, film directors, who were urged to respect often constrictive terms and conditions, were the first to perceive the tensions between historical time and courtroom narrative. In Jerusalem the Israeli state was particularly preoccupied by the immediacy of the publicity of the court sessions of the Adolf Eichmann trial. In France it was in anticipation of constituting a historical archive and by force of law that the trials of Klaus Barbie, Paul Touvier, and Maurice Papon became the objects of audiovisual recording and even of abridged television broadcasts some time later. Jurists and historians wondered then about the effects produced by the elimination of statutory limitations on crimes against humanity when it creates a contemporaneousness that is twice removed with respect to the facts being judged: in addition to the trials being held at forty years' distance, the present saw the televisual narration organized as a daily soap opera. For their part, with the concept of an "open court,"

Americans have since the 1980s been following up the experiments begun in Nuremberg by extending them to ordinary courtrooms, civil and criminal.[4]

Through the examples of depositions filmed in Nuremberg (Marie-Claude Vaillant-Couturier), Jerusalem (Holocaust survivors), and Lyon (parents and educators of the Izieu children), we will revisit the role of witnesses and the importance of the face of history they embody in the courtroom and even more on the screen. It is often with respect to them (and the jurors, if need be) that judges' reservations concerning cameras are the strongest. Moreover is it necessary to impose on the defendant the lasting recording of his image and allow public consultation of it, at the risk of freezing forever what belongs only to a moment in an individual's history?

Today it is a matter not only of knowing how the court protects itself from mediatization but how the court itself is capable of organizing it. In requiring that films of the camps be shown in closed session, the judges at the Eichmann trial failed to appreciate fully the system of mediation set in place in Nuremberg. On the other hand, the public screening at the ICTY on June 1, 2005, of a film showing Serbian militia executing young Muslims from Srebrenica compelled Serbian authorities to react that very evening and to order the arrest of several suspects identified in the footage.

Does it need to be spelled out? These film images—the ones captured by the people in charge of summary executions in 2005, like those recorded by the first visual witnesses of the situation in the camps in 1945—do not screen us from reality and they are not an obstacle to the distanced analysis to which the historian must give priority. This does not mean that simply reading them enables one to prove absolutely the sequence of decisions and behaviors that led to the crimes. We share Georges Didi-Huberman's idea that "the image is characterized by *not being all*. And it is not because the image gives what Walter Benjamin called a *flash* rather than the *substance* that we must exclude it from our inadequate means of broaching the terrible history in question."[5]

In the research that led to this book, we have come across several types of archive, many of which had never been consulted until now. It was first a matter of locating the various films presented as evidence in court sessions, then of reconstituting the path that took John Ford's team to Nuremberg.[6] Next we immersed ourselves in the IMT archives.[7] It was also fitting to observe from the inside how Justice Jackson lived this venture; we compared the minutes of the meetings of his team with the journal he kept during the preparation of the IMT and the oral interview he gave in the early 1950s.[8]

Some new information thus came to light, in particular on the dialogue initiated very early on with representatives of Jewish organizations, usefully putting into perspective the place given in the trial to the extermination of European Jews. The Telford Taylor archives also allowed us to assess the evolution of the thinking of one of the most brilliant prosecutors of the Nuremberg trials.[9]

Among specialized sources, we should mention the archives linked to the activities of the Museum of Modern Art and in particular of Siegfried Kracauer, as well as those of Leo T. Hurwitz and of Guy Saguez, both unpublished.[10] The corpus of filmed archives of the IMT, which we consulted at the National Archives and Records Administration, are now available at the Mémorial de la Shoah's documentation center.[11]

From image to text, from text to image: the movement back and forth among archives, organized with an eye to respecting the specificity of what cinematographic language contributes to the knowledge of history, is in itself enough to explain the richness of inscribing film into a judicial process.

PART I

Film as Evidence: An American
Jurisprudence (1920–1945)

CHAPTER 1

The Filmmaker, the Judge, and the Evidence

In 1936 the German filmmaker Fritz Lang arrived in the United States after fleeing Nazi Germany. With an open mind in a country where his reputation was limited to filmmaking circles, he set off by car for Arizona, spent several weeks with the Navajo, and immersed himself in comic strips to familiarize himself with American slang.[1] In keeping with his old reflexes, however, he focused daily attention on small news items in the press, hoping always to find in them a sort of social revelation. Lotte H. Eisner tells us, "He had continued in his habit of noting everything that seemed different and important to him. He read everything he could lay his hands on—particularly newspapers, to learn English and also to understand the mentality of the people."[2] In Hollywood he was forced to come to terms with a production system dominated by the majors, studios reluctant to allow him the freedom he had enjoyed in Germany to conceive and put together his films. In the files of Metro-Goldwyn-Mayer, he discovered a four-page synopsis about a lynching written by Norman Krasna entitled *Mob Rule*.[3] He decided to propose an adaptation of it to Bartlett Cormack, a screenwriter who had worked with Cecil B. DeMille and Will Rogers and had become known for a play about the underworld called *The Racket* (1928), banned from being performed in Chicago for two years.

Fritz Lang's Intuition

Lang wanted to tell the story of the lynching of a black man accused of raping a white woman. With MGM refusing to give the lead role to an African American actor so as not to offend the southern states, it would be a white man, an ordinary American citizen, Joe Wilson, who would play the hero. Unjustly accused of kidnapping and pursued by a hateful crowd all the way to the prison where he is jailed, the hero makes it seem as if he has died in the fire set by the protesters, when actually he has escaped it. Thirsty for revenge, he lets his supposed executioners be brought to court on murder charges. To deny any responsibility, they swear that they were not present at the site of the lynching. They are then confronted with the screening of news film footage made at the time of the lynching that establishes not only that they were there but that they contributed in various capacities to setting the prison on fire.

With this first American subject, entitled *The Mob*, then *Mob Rule*, and finally *Fury*, Lang was confronting well before they were really put to the test two major stakes in the future cinematographic coverage of World War II: the film account of violence and the legal recognition of the film image as evidence.

Lang arrived in Hollywood at a time when controls on films set by the profession itself were being made stricter, in the wake of polemics sparked by violent or sexually explicit movies.[4] The Studio Relations Committee, which in 1934 became the Production Code Administration, was from then on placed under the control of Joseph Breen, a conservative of Irish descent. All scripts had to be submitted to him, with any code violation subject to sanction as high as a $25,000 fine. The script of *Fury* prompted Breen to send Louis B. Mayer, head of MGM, a five-page letter in which he states, among other things, "The scenes showing the violence of the crowd outside the prison, which leads to its complete destruction by fire and especially to Joe's burning alive, are in our opinion clearly too realistic and must be toned down."[5] The inspiration for this scene is directly drawn from the book by Arthur F. Raper, *The Tragedy of Lynching* (1933).[6] This study, conducted in the framework of an investigative committee on the practice of lynching in the American South, showed that of one hundred blacks who were lynched, a third were innocent of the acts imputed to them. In half the cases, the police had actively participated in their executions. Among the cases mentioned was a lynching in Marion, Florida, at which a photojournalist from the *News-Press* was present. He had taken a series of pictures showing the crowd gathering around the already beaten and chained black victim and his hour-and-a-half walk to the school building where his execution was to take place. When the black man worriedly asked his assailants what they were planning to do to him, the leader answered, "Well, nigger, we're going to burn you." Raper then tells how the photographs taken by the journalist were destroyed: "The *News-Press* photographer's collection included pictures of the mob around the building, and of the two men on the roof pulling the Negro after them. Then the 'man in the red coat' saw him, rushed angrily at him, called for some men to assist, and they seized the camera. The rolls inside were destroyed, and the photographer had difficulty in getting them not to smash the camera itself. Several pictures were made by the photographers, however, showing the fire in progress."[7]

As shown by the presence in the filmmaker's files of a six-page typewritten note with the same title as Raper's book, Lang had available to him the pages dealing with the story of this lynching.[8] In order to film in journalistic fashion the fire at the prison where Joe Wilson is held, the director first thought of showing three technicians: a head cameraman situated on the balcony of a building facing the entrance to the prison; a first assistant with a lightweight Bell and Howell camera responsible for following crowd movements; and a second assistant, taking instantaneous pictures near the drama's agents. After some hesitation, as revealed in the corrections Lang made in the plotting of the sequence at the time of filming, only the first camera, which was supposed to film fixed shots captured in a frontal axis, was set up and shown (Figure 1).[9] Given that the camera was installed before the event even unfolded and that the place it occupied had been chosen to ensure the broadest coverage of what was going to happen, it could be said that the pictures thus captured take in the reality of the event in all its scope, without a point of view coming in to alter the frame. However, once projected at trial, they would be precisely paired with shots corresponding to what the first assistant and photographer could have done, allowing for individual incriminations of the whole group of accused persons (Figure 2).

Lang was very aware that a single axis and a single focal length cannot possibly suffice to capture an event, even a foreseeable, prepared, premeditated one, as this lynching was. While adhering to the overall style of fiction, he interspersed in the film's basic story some sequences, borrowing their form from the newsreel genre. These images correspond, in fact, to the audiovisual version of what Joe's testimony could have been if he had decided to attend the trial of his assailants. For the most part, the former rely on shot angles of the lynching that can only be the subjective ones of the field of vision of the condemned man, looking from his prison cell window (Figures 3 and 4). "At that moment who sees the scene from that angle?" asks Jean Douchet. "Joe, in his cell. The evidence comes to light. These eight newsreel shots are nothing but the projection of memorized traces of Joe's emotional experience during his lynching. These are flashes of vision all the more deeply engraved for their having been captured in a state of extreme tension."[10] Reappearing at the home of his brothers, who thought him dead, Joe says to them, "Do you know where I spent the day? At the movies. Watching the news to find out how I was burned alive. I saw it again ten, maybe twenty times, over and over, I don't know how many times. The theater was packed. They loved it. It's great to watch a man being set on fire!"

Programmed death is thus not enough. Seeing it must constitute a morbid spectacle. The history of lynching has indeed always been accompanied by this dimension of group excitement. Anne Chaon writes, "The crowd, always present, posing, radiant or indifferent, at the feet of the hanged men, satisfied with the job well-done. Shameless hunters, sure of their impunity. . . . A savage celebration for southern Whites, united in their fear and hatred of the newly emancipated 'negro.' Sometimes they take away souvenirs: photos, a fistful of hair, a phalanx, a strip of skin removed from their trophy. A notion of the law in which racism is coupled with sadism and cruelty."[11] By concerning himself with the subjective vision an individual can have of his or her own situation, then examining the reactions of the public that takes in these images, Lang was foregrounding not the factual value of news reporting but rather the social construction that structures it.

The film director had thought a lot in the 1920s about the truth status of cinematographic language. Lang recalled that his producer, Erich Pommer, had told him, "You have to tell a story with your camera. Therefore, you have to *know* the camera and what you can make the camera do." Having learned the lesson, Lang reports, "I always tell my cameraman, 'I don't want fancy photography—nothing "artistic"—I want to have newsreel photography.' Because I think every serious picture that depicts people today should be a kind of documentary of its time. Only then, in my opinion, do you get a quality of truth into a picture. In this way, *Fury* is a documentary. *M* is a documentary."[12]

To the first innovative idea of *Fury*, representing an atrocity and the "spectacle" it can constitute, a second was added, giving concrete expression to the way film can be shown as evidence in trial proceedings. Even though MGM had been reluctant to produce this first American film by Lang, the director had nevertheless benefited from the studio's great professionalism.[13] He had at his disposal a substantial file entitled "Corpus Delicti Reference Cases" compiled by Morris Lavine, several documents on American legislation concerning specific crimes, and a copy of the "Bill of Indictment" form, which allowed him to give ample support to his demonstration.[14] He combined it with his own knowledge of the role of the media and the powers of image and word in cinematographic language. Hence the importance of the use of stop action, crucial in that it in a way qualifies the probative tone characteristic of the court: it is a matter of confronting the defendants with the pleasure they took in their hideous crime, their own images having been recorded without their knowing it, by a third party (a team of news reporters) not implicated in the case at hand. Legally the value of the confrontation lies in the contradiction that it brings out in the account given by the defendants before the bench; it appears that they have indeed lied since the newsreel shows their active presence on the night of the lynching. The screening in court thus replaces the spectacle of the vision of the lynched man—at the scene and, later, in movie theaters—with that of the criminal, satisfied attitude of the lynchers. The defendants' reaction of consternation at the projection attests to the effect produced by such a device (Figures 5 and 6).

Thanks to his experience as a film director, Lang succeeds in showing in a fictional story that film of an event cannot constitute "objective" proof. Rather it always proceeds from a point of view that puts it in the same category as testimony. Once the criteria for honesty and authenticity have been verified, the film assumes all its force at the heart of the trial's arguments, in the crisscrossing of views and the confrontation of points of view which its projection organizes in the courtroom. In the temporality of the trial, the projection of film constitutes a sort of obstacle that the participants as a whole must get beyond in order that justice be done. For the judges, after the brevity of the event, the details of which must be presented, especially when the incriminating act is only partially filmed, an effort must be made to understand the motivations behind it and to bring to light its determining social, personal, and collective factors. The image does not precipitate a superficial reading of the offense committed by making it visible, or even transparent. On the contrary, it requires that one read what in it exceeds its merely factual dimension and relates back to a social behavior.

The Jurisprudence of Film as Evidence

With *Fury* Lang was synthesizing a jurisprudence built around the truth status of the still image as established by the mid-nineteenth century.[15] At that time, the court acknowledged "as obvious the necessary concordance between an image and its object, thus confirming the current notion: photography finds in automatic exactitude a quasi-absolute strength of *probation*."[16] Be that as it may, with the cinematographer's additional ability to record life's movement in continuity, the filmmaker was then subject to specific recommendations concerning its "historical" value and perpetuity.

Boleslaw Matuszewski was the first to become concerned about this. Born in 1856 in the region of Poland then annexed to Russia, he became the tsar's official photographer in 1897. In a pamphlet penned in 1898 he writes, "This simple celluloid ribbon constitutes not only an historical document, but a parcel of history. . . . A section of a museum, a library shelf, or a cabinet at the archives will have to be allotted to cinematographic prints which have historical character. Its official depository will be set up either at the National Library, or at that of the Institute, under the watch of one of the Academies that deal with history, or at the Archives. . . . A qualified committee will accept or reject proposed documents after evaluating their historical value."[17]

In 1887, when Félix Faure came to Petersburg, Matuszewski had the opportunity "to record on the fly, like a cinematographer, the important scenes and events of the French president's visit (among other curious spectacles). It was even thanks to these documents that it was possible to refute Bismarck's claim that upon disembarking Faure had failed to remove his hat in front of the Russian flag."[18]

If the truth value of these images lay in their objective neutrality alone, did that mean they were anonymous? In France jurists were quickly flooded with requests concerning the status of film shot from real life, with a view toward distinguishing film produced by "makers" (*fabricants*) and that shot by "cameramen" (*opérateurs*). Lawyer Fernand Izouard wrote in 1908:

> In the beginning, the makers of cinematographic filmstrips thought only about capturing nature and everyday life such as they presented themselves to the camera lens trained on them. They thus obtained "animated photographs" and their works indisputably had to be protected in the same way as any work of photography. Such was the case even when cameramen "composed" the scene somewhat, arranging certain accessories and prompting certain gestures. This was already common practice in photography. It was even through these details that the artistic character of the work was often revealed.[19] So up until this time, no new difficulties were encountered. . . . Soon they would arise. . . . Little by little, the action that unfolded . . . would

constitute a veritable play in several acts, with no spoken words (that invention comes later), but implying, the same as in a ballet or pantomime, the existence of a script or a libretto, and thus of an author, and thus of a copyright. And suddenly its character as literary property was established.[20]

These astute observations underscore one of the singularities of cinematographic writing, whether it takes the form of news, a documentary, or a fictional picture: the borrowings from reality—or links to it—do not prevent the film from being carried by the directing or choices in writing, framing, and editing. The film's realism lies precisely in the manner in which the director, drawing on an event or an object, creates a system of representations borrowing from the original at the same time as they free themselves from it. In this reconstruction, fantasy and imagination are not in contradiction with the desire to elucidate reality. Both of these qualities are required by the person using the film as a source of knowledge. It is striking to see how this question was the subject of a 1927 speech given before the French National Assembly itself. Minister of Public Instruction Édouard Herriot stated, "What is interesting about filmmaking, and where it contributes and will certainly continue to contribute to science (a form of continuous analysis) and to education (itself an effort oriented towards analysis) is that in putting us in control of observations that we can decompose, renew and slow down, filmmaking allows us to replace the scientific observation of things with a means of observation that is constantly worked, maneuvered, directed, and broken down into parts."[21]

How was the shift made from acknowledging the status of film images as historical truth to acknowledging their probative value? If, at the beginning of the twentieth century, no specific mention of an audiovisual document being admitted as evidence was recorded in common and civil law nations, neither does anything seem to have prohibited it. In the United States it was possible as of 1901 to find mention that "A map or a photograph, if proved to be correct at the time to which the issue relates, is competent evidence, even though made for the purposes of the trial."[22]

In general, priority is given to "real evidence," as defined by Richard Lea Kennedy in 1935: "The real evidence (sometimes called 'immediate,' 'autoptic,' or 'demonstrative' evidence) is that presented directly to the senses of the tribunal (court or jury) without an intervening medium of proof. It is based upon the principle of *res ipsa loquer*. As a general rule it may be stated that when evidence of any observable quality of a person or thing is relevant and material, real evidence, that is, the object itself, may be submitted to the senses of the tribunal. The exception to this rule, most generally recognized, is where the exhibition would involve immodesty or indecency."[23]

"Representative real evidence" comes in only secondarily in the hierarchy of evidence that is admissible and presentable in the courtroom. Considered as such, "photographs, including X-ray photographs, maps, charts, plans, models, diagrams, sketches, etc., are admissible (subject usually to rules governing secondary evidence) where evidence of the physical characteristics of the person, place or thing they represent is relevant and material, if they are duly authenticated, by anyone having knowledge, as being correct representations."[24]

In examining the most significant case in the matter (issues of personal injury in which plaintiffs use forensic film), a lawyer named Pierre R. Paradis reconstituted the evolution of legal rules of the admissibility and trial presentation of cinematic documents. The legal specialist enumerates in the following way the specific precautions that need to be taken:

1. Authentication
   a) Guarantees
   b) Identification
   c) Accuracy
   d) Speed
   e) Discretion of the court
   f) Preview in chamber
2. Projection
3. Best evidence rule
   a) Notice to the opposing party
   b) Enticement
   c) Continuity of film
   d) Continuity of action
   e) Cumulative evidence
   f) Weight
   g) Hearsay
   h) Gruesomeness
   i) Uses
   j) Tactics[25]

The items in section 1 (authenticating the film) are known as "The Foundation," that is, "the series of questions which are put to the authenticating witness, usually the photographer, which establish the accuracy of the film and tie the person or thing portrayed to an issue in the case." It turns out in general to be preferable for the filming to have been done by a professional, but this is not obligatory. On the other hand, it is imperative that its author be able to appear in court to testify (as "authenticating witness") or, failing that, any person having been present during the filming.[26] Paradis continues, "Medical Trial Tech. Q. suggests the use of a very brief series of questions that may be put to the witnesses." The following is the author's own suggestion of a typical, adequate, and technically sound series of authenticating questions to be asked after the photographer's qualifications have been established:

"Did you take these rolls of film, which I now hand you, marked Defendant's Exhibit 12 and Defendant's Exhibit 13?"

"*Yes.*"

"Would you tell us when and where you took them?"

"*I took them at various intervals on June 26 and 27 of this year at the site of the new Bedrock Medical Center construction.*"

"And what did you take these pictures of?"

"*I photographed Mr. Frederick Flintstone performing various odd jobs.*"

"That man sitting on your left at the plaintiff's table?"

"*Yes.*"

"Have you seen these films projected?"

"*I have.*"

"Do they accurately represent the activities of Mr. Flintstone which you observed on June 26 and 27?"

"*Yes. They do.*"[27]

A witness's affirmation of the authenticity of the origin of the pictures presented is a crucial factor. It is aimed first of all toward examining the reels brought to court in order, if need be, to determine whether, in the process going from the development of the negatives to the printing of one or more copies for distribution, they were altered in any manner. Other parameters germane to the film itself also come into play. One needs to look at everything in the filming that could modify the characters' appearance (the scale of shots), the rhythm of their footsteps (the speed of the unwinding of the film inside the camera or the use of dolly shots), or the continuity of an event in which they are implicated (ellipses, link shots). Judges are, of course, aware that cinematographic technique alters the qualities of people and objects represented. A facial close-up projected on a screen renders feelings and attitudes in a more accentuated or visible way.[28] The Chesterfield Borough police (Derbyshire, England), who in 1935 were trying to obtain evidence through films of trafficking carried out by street bookies, installed a hidden camera in a car to catch the offenders in the act. When asked if they were interested in this new technique used by their colleagues, Scotland Yard said that it had considered the idea but discarded it as impractical. The article concludes, "There certainly would appear to be many technical snags. If the police car is travelling at high speed, the vibration would almost certainly reduce the picture to a blur. And who will check the camera speed? The most innocuous driving looks dangerous when the camera is turning slow!"[29] On the other hand, the camera presents no viewing problem when it records people unbeknown to them and helps in their identification— hence the FBI's recourse to hidden cameras to spy on the German Embassy in Washington before the start of World War II. By examining these images, it was able "to obtain automobile licenses, peculiarities of dress and other possible leads." Kept secret, the information was revealed shortly before the release in movie theaters of a spy film about the infiltration of Nazi agents in the United States, *The House on 92nd Street* (dir. Henry Hathaway, 1945).[30]

Added together, the various cases pinpointed by Paradis result in a kind of jurisprudence, based generally on the observation that film must not be "redundant evidence" and that, through the movement that characterizes it, it contributes something more than a still image does: "The general rule . . . is that . . . motion pictures are admissible in evidence, within the sound discretion of the court, where such pictures are relevant to the issues, and are an accurate reproduction of persons and objects testified to in oral examination before the jury."[31]

CHAPTER 2

The Camera: An Impartial Witness
of Social Relations?

At first glance, the U.S. initiative to bring news film into the courtroom might not seem unusual, considering the American public's familiarity with cinematographic language and the essential role of motion pictures in creating social cohesion. Indeed in the early 1930s, eighty million viewers went to the movies every week in theaters with more than 1,200 seats, located for the most part either downtown or in suburban shopping areas. Fiction movies benefited from this very working-class audience, for such films possessed a significant box-office draw. Although subject to intense pressures, the artistic and even educational intent did not conflict with the need to entertain, in accordance with the wish expressed by one of the pioneers of the American movie industry, D. W. Griffith, who encouraged American movies to become a sort of university for the working class. To appreciate the cultural value of these films, one need only recall that they became one of the presentations offered to immigrants, with the idea of familiarizing them with their new home, thus refuting the rumors spread by puritanical, moralizing associations who claimed that the movie industry had insidiously extended "its grip on the nation and produced a new generation of children literally fashioned by it ('our movie-made children')."[1] Audience studies like the one entitled *The Movies on Trial* draw a more balanced picture of the influence of film on young people: "Identification during a short period from flight-from-every-day-life does not mean assuming the role permanently *in* everyday-life. Reality is too overpowering for this to occur."[2]

The status of documentaries and news films was notably different, since they occupied a position of secondary importance in the arrangement of the staple program offered to moviegoers. The film bill unfolded in hierarchical fashion, from charity appeals to noncommercial announcements, next to songs, then on to short subjects, and finally to "A" or "B" feature-length films.[3]

In these package offerings, the public's attention was not significantly invested in the news, which itself was divided into four sections (newsreels, screen magazines, travelogues, and exploration films). But first the Great Depression, then international events like the Spanish Civil War and the Russian-Japanese conflict led to giving greater prominence to news reports and documentaries. By the close of the 1930s, two-thirds of America's 16,500 movie houses were showing newsreels from one of five national syndicators (Paramount News, Twentieth Century Fox's Movietone News, RKO-Pathé News, MGM's News of the Day, and Universal Newsreels). RKO and then Twentieth Century Fox also distributed the independent magazine *The March of Time*. In *Citizen Kane*, Orson Welles renamed *The March of Time* to poke fun at the formatting of this new mode of communication, calling it *News on the March*, and in an emphatic tone caricatured the highly recognizable voice of the narrator, Westbrook van Voorhis. Welles's critique needs nuancing, however, since the magazine had often broken new ground by, for example, injecting dramatic elements into the presentation of the traditional news report. Welles himself participated in the radio version of *The March of Time*, in which remarks by Franklin D. Roosevelt, Al Capone, and Hitler were interpreted by actors.[4]

Finding a Realistic Objective for Cinematic News

In addition to news relayed by the majors, photographers, film directors, and essayists from the liberal and radical left sought to develop the cinematographic tool as a means of raising political awareness by taking inspiration from Soviet examples, such as the politically committed thinking of Dziga Vertov and his theory of the "kino-eye" (the cinema-eye).[5] Assembled in 1930 in New York within the Workers' Film and Photo League (WFPL), their initiative spread to other cities affected by the economic crisis, unemployment, and poverty.[6] Young apprentice filmmakers began recording the distress of workers, themselves often deprived of all access to film. With camera in hand, they also accompanied protest movements, marches, and strikes. Shown during popular rallies or in union meeting halls, these pictures drew part of their dynamic effect from the opportunity thus given to the farmers or workers filmed to see themselves projected onto the screen and, due to their attendance at the screenings, to attest in the midst of their comrades to the veracity of the facts reported. At a remove from the situation filmed, the workers who saw these reels appreciated them all the more when their contents were thus validated. Often of mediocre technical quality because they had been made on the spot and without artificial lighting, they conveyed an impression of truth that also derived from the freedom afforded by the absence of synchronous sound, allowing cameramen to move freely, the use of the new portable Eyemo camera making it easier to track the scenes as they unfolded.[7]

Following the example of their European colleagues, American union officials understood early on the particular advantages of motion pictures in the edification of the masses. In 1925 the secretary of the Workers' International Relief (an organization with communist leanings) praised the "great revolutionary possibilities" of these reportages:

> Its tremendous revolutionary possibilities, among precisely those elements difficult of access by our ordinary propaganda weapons—the primitive-minded inert working masses who never go to meetings and never read anything better than a capitalist comic page—as well as special elements like the scattered rural proletariat and semi-proletariat; the oppressed and often illiterate subject peoples; the children, and similar groups. These vast masses hold the future of the revolutionary movement in their hands—they will determine the outcome of our struggle against imperialism—we must win them. Every weapon used by the masters to hold them we must seek to turn to help set them free. And the film is by no means the least of these. We must win it for the working class.[8]

One of the benefits of the screenings organized by the WFPL had to do with the ability of the moving picture to visualize the progression of the social protest movement, with cameramen present in every major city. This was a considerable help given the scale of the North American continent. The event that laid the groundwork for this collective adventure was the Ford Hunger Massacre, which took place on March 7, 1932, in Dearborn, Michigan, the Detroit suburb where one of the large automobile factories had been built. Jean Heffer reports, "Henry Ford had let go three-quarters of his workers, reducing his workforce from 128,000 in March 1929 to 37,000 in August 1931. . . . Ford, who believed that 'the depression was due to laziness,' had just announced the manufacture of a new eight-cylinder model and declared himself ready to risk his entire fortune to revive the automobile industry."[9] The WFPL then made two film reports, *The Detroit Workers News Special: Ford Massacre* and *Hunger: The National Hunger March to Washington*. For the latter, an animated map showed how the three hundred delegates from the National Unemployment Councils flocked to the nation's capital. Meanwhile, in London during a conference organized by the Left Book Club in 1937, one of the participants, Dr. John Lewis, praised the WFPL films, less for their political intent than for their ability to bear witness to a social movement without aestheticizing it. A WFPL bulletin reports his remarks this way:

> Because of the easier assimilation of facts presented through the eye, social education by this means can . . . prepare the way for the appeal of literature. [Lewis] would like the League's film *March against Starvation* to be shown to every one of the six hundred of the Left Book Club branches throughout the country. . . . In the documentary sphere, the land or factory worker, seeing things from his own angle, can contribute more for our purpose than the most expert professional artist approaching the same subject lyrically and from the outside. Such effort must be enthused, trained and assisted in a way that only such a society as the League can do.[10]

However, the question would soon arise as to whether it was necessary to stick to this type of reporting or to devise new structures and conditions of production.

Leo T. Hurwitz and Ralph Steiner, two very politically engaged WFPL cameramen, thought it best to consider "revolutionary film" as the "next step."[11] Hurwitz was particularly insistent on the inadequately explored potential of documentary films: "For this great and rich medium the bourgeois filmers have had little use, since they cannot face the truths that the documentary camera can report."[12] If the reality of social struggles was masked by the big studios acting to protect the business community's interests, it could also be covered up by those who believed that all it took was to turn on a camera and it would mechanically record a univocal reality. Hurwitz advanced the idea that there were two types of film construction: "external editing" (*montage externe*) and "internal editing" (*montage interne*). The former consists of "the creative comparison, contrast, and opposition of shots, externally related to each other, to produce an effect not contained in any of the shots." The leading example of this was *The Man with a Movie Camera* (dir. Vertov, 1929). Internal editing is understood above all else as being "a re-creative analysis and reconstruction of an internally related visual event in terms of shots of film, to reveal best the meaning of the event." It was necessary to try to blend these two approaches, for example, by filming a jobless man returning home after an exhausting day of looking for work, sitting down worn out and hopeless, then the landlord coming to tell him his possessions were being seized for nonpayment of rent. Thus one worked "internally" on the shooting script of the story while "externally" giving it a political meaning at the same time.[13] The story was to be told by nonprofessional actors playing themselves. In an appendix to his article, Hurwitz included the program for the International Film Bureau, which had just been established in Moscow. One of the proposals mentions the possibility of taking existing documents and adding to them film images expressing a different sociopolitical view. Thus seemingly "neutral" films would then carry a "revolutionary vision."[14]

For his part, Ralph Steiner said that the documentary or the newsreel "genres" generally favored by revolutionary film directors were not necessarily a guarantee of truth: "This form has been adopted because of the immediate need for incontrovertible visual evidence of what is actually taking place in the struggles of the workers. . . . There is no truth in the idea that the documentary film is simple to make or that it is necessarily simpler than the acted form."[15] He called for the director to take a script written beforehand and to search for examples of social situations that were accurate, true and powerful, which would add to the film's statement. If certain occurrences were difficult to film—because they belonged to a bygone past or were unique to an event or of a visibility too complex to be easily interpreted or understood, three working hypotheses were considered: (1) reusing newsreel images broadcast by studios in order to undo their propagandistic nature; (2) filming new shots on worksites; or (3) inventing fictitious scenes showing what neither the official newsreels nor activist reporting could reveal about social reality. With respect to the fiction alternative, the Russians were more reserved. For his part, director and theorist Lev Kuleshov speaks about "acted" films, as opposed to documentaries and newsreels, characterized as "non-acted": "Due to ignorance concerning the foundations of filmmaking and the lack of culture in the leaders of the profession, the craze for acting, performance, or re-creations has reached the greatest heights in our country. . . . The triumph of our non-acted films is teaching our cinematographers how to properly understand the material. Now, the material of films is real events, real things, true man and his behavior in everyday life."[16]

Seeking to form an elite corps of directors capable of conceiving different sorts of documentary fictions, Hurwitz and Steiner created a dissident group within the WFPL, the Nykino (New York Kino). At the same time, their attention was drawn to the necessary consideration of the viewers' tastes and habits during an important meeting with Lee Strasberg, the head of the Group Theatre: "[Strasberg] made us conscious that every step in film making is *theatrical*—that is, it communicates its meaning by the recreation of dramatic situations in filmic time and space, and depends for its effectiveness on the emotional involvement of the audience in these situations."[17]

While a movement focusing on the struggle against fascism was taking shape on the left, the federal government clearly wanted to bring artists and intellectuals together in the context of the New Deal for a project providing a documentary testimonial about the economic and social crisis that the United States had been going through since 1929.

Film as Social Connection

The first organization put in place was the Resettlement Administration, created in 1935. Its goal was to locate funds to assist small farmers. The idea was to use broadcasts, brochures, and photo-reportage to make taxpayers in big cities aware of the desperate situation in certain rural areas.

This desire to tell what was going on allowed artists and intellectuals of different perspectives to meet and sources and documentary interventions to crossbreed. For Olivier Lugon, the gestation of this artistic production sprang from wanting not to separate the aesthetic gesture from the necessity to bear witness.[18] Though working in the framework of publicly commissioned works, these creators nevertheless asked themselves questions going beyond the merely political. For them, it was a matter of transforming into objects of knowledge elements that people do not necessarily pay attention to in everyday life and of detaching moments of social life from their overly informational conspicuousness. Asked by *Fortune* magazine to write an article about the small tenant farmers of Alabama, novelist James Agee engaged the collaboration of photographer Walker Evans, who had worked for the Farm Security Administration. Their pairing up developed around the aesthetic formulation of a project first conceived as a subject for reportage. The people in charge at *Fortune* just wanted a "good story," centered on a typical family that was supposed to be representative of all the situations experienced by the small farmers exposed to the economic and social crisis. Instead Agee and Evans applied themselves to transmitting what they had seen, perceived, or even experienced during their stay in Alabama, taking deliberate care to be "true" to the people they encountered. In the end the book was built around the tension between the "ordinary camera" and the "printed word":

> Actually, the effort is to recognize the stature of a portion of un-imagined existence, and to continue techniques proper to its record-ing, communication, analysis, and defense. More essentially, this is an independent inquiry into certain normal predicaments of human divinity.
>
> The immediate instruments are two: the motion-less camera and the printed word. The governing instrument—which is also one of the centers of the subject—is individual, anti-authoritative human consciousness.[19]

However, Agee's complex writing would end up overriding both his self-imposed demand for simplicity and the balance of text and image.

In a similar endeavor, photographer Dorothea Lange and economist Paul Taylor pooled their talents even more closely, no doubt because their text re-mained in a purely scholarly style, while the photographic reportage was shaped by editorial constraints. In 1939 they presented their book, *An Ameri-can Exodus: A Record of Human Erosion*, in the following terms: "We use the camera as a tool of research. Upon a tripod of photographs, captions, and text we rest themes evolved out of long observations in the field. We adhere to the standards of documentary photography as we have conceived them. Quotations which accompany photographs report what the persons photo-graphed said, not what we think might be their unspoken thoughts. Where there are no people, and no other source is indicated, the quotations come from persons whom we met in the field."[20]

How was one, without forsaking the freedom of creation or the value of aesthetic choices, to come to terms with that which comes from observed reality, the men and women who, often in a state of great misery, graciously allowed themselves to be photographed or filmed? Lange's first reaction was to assemble 150 of her best photographs in a series of notebooks in which she added Taylor's essays in order to convince the federal and California state governments to release emergency funds for the transit camps of families seeking work. During the making of *American Exodus*, she would give great importance to the captions of the photographs, incorporating phrases spoken by the people photographed, in a language whose style and accent had been preserved. When the book came out, she wrote, "The method which we developed is on the way to true documentary technique."[21]

Certain photographers in the WFPL, such as Paul Strand, were as adept at using a camera for still photography as they were for filming. Strand thus participated with Hurwitz and Steiner in the shooting of the first great film that Pare Lorentz directed in 1936 as head of the WFPL's film production program.[22] *The Plough That Broke the Plains* depicted the Dust Bowl's impact on farmlands in the American Midwest. Hurwitz and Steiner were indignant, though, that the final cut omitted an explicit critique of the unbridled capitalism that had concentrated landownership in the hands of a few. Lorentz then turned to Willard van Dyke on camera for the movie he wrote and directed the following year, *The River* (a sort of justification of the Tennessee Valley Authority's project to build dams).[23] After seeing the film at a private screening in Washington, President Roosevelt established the U.S. Film Service in August 1938, with Lorentz as its director.[24] For their part, Hurwitz, Steiner, Strand, and numerous other artists, such as Henri Cartier-Bresson, Sidney Meyers, and Irving Lerner, joined together in a production cooperative, Frontier Films.[25] However, the "revolutionary" program outlined earlier was implemented at the expense of abandoning the avant-garde experimentation of the 1920s for a traditional narrative style.[26]

Stuart Liebman rightly points out that most of the WFPL directors, from Nykino and Frontier Films, were children of Jewish immigrant workers from Eastern Europe:

> Their support of progressive social causes was often a reaffirmation of a family tradition in which radical socialism had taken the place of religious practice. Lack of opportunity and poverty reinforced their political convictions. Several of those destined to become influential in the movement, however, had already begun to rise in the American social hierarchy because of their prestigious college educations. Harry Alan Potamkin was graduated from the University of Pennsylvania; Leo T. Hurwitz received his degree *summa cum laude*

from Harvard; Ralph Steiner went to Dartmouth; Ben Maddow was a graduate of Columbia.[27]

They also worked in New York rather than Los Angeles, thereby gaining critical recognition in the big daily newspapers rather than in Hollywood's corporate or specialized magazines. As Europe's perils grew graver, these figures were joined in their initiatives by Herman Shumlin, Lillian Hellman, and Dorothy Parker, who created a production company called Contemporary Historians, in order to raise funds and take action in the Spanish Civil War on European turf.[28] They financed Joris Ivens's production of *The Spanish Earth* (1937), in which Ernest Hemingway and Soviet filmmaker Roman Karmen also took part.[29]

At the end of the 1930s, most of the documentary filmmakers working in the framework of the New Deal or for Frontier Films thus had theoretical or practical production experience in putting the truth status of film into play, either due to the personal intellectual and aesthetic demands they put on themselves or through confrontations with "official" news. All went on to find themselves engaged (to a greater or lesser degree) by the U.S. government in one of the many production organizations created during World War II. Meyers collaborated with the Office of War Information, editing and writing commentary for *The Cummington Story* (1945), as did van Dyke (*Steel Town*, 1944) and Lerner (*The Autobiography of a Jeep*, 1943). Cartier-Bresson directed *Reunion* for the U.S. Information Service, and Ivens participated in writing the script for *Know Your Enemy—Japan* (1945), one of the pictures supervised by Frank Capra for the U.S. Signal Corps, the U.S. Army's photographic and film service.[30] The two most charismatic leaders in these adventures, Lorentz and Hurwitz, were also going to be involved in two major projects undertaken after the war: on behalf of the Department of War, Lorentz would be charged with producing the film on the Nuremberg trials directed by Stuart Schulberg in 1948; as for Hurwitz, he would oversee the filming of the Eichmann trial in 1961.

CHAPTER 3

══════

Learning to Read Enemy Films

How Do You Screen *Triumph of the Will*? New York's Museum of Modern Art Film Program

In a special edition entitled *Inside Nazi Germany—1938*, presented as a sneak preview in New York on January 20, 1938, the film magazine *The March of Time* provided special reporting on Hitler's Germany. The mere fact of showing Hitler in the act of giving a speech posed a problem, particularly for Jewish owners of movie theaters, who did not want to give him a forum in the United States. At the same time, the idea of dismantling the mechanisms of Nazi propaganda seemed ever more useful by the day. The film images used in the feature essay had been shot in part by a special envoy, Julien Bryan, for all practical purposes nearly the only American authorized to film in Germany in 1933. However, when the head of *The March of Time*, Louis de Rochemont, viewed the rushes brought back by Bryan, he felt that, despite how interesting they were, they failed to expose in a critical fashion how the Nazi regime operated. It was more than a problem of reediting, since Rochemont decided to add in some scenes re-created in the studio. (One, for example, shows a German couple listening to the Reich's official radio broadcast, performed by German Americans living in Manhattan.) Moreover a voice-over commentary made the magazine's anti-Nazi stance explicit. In order not to distort the overall picture and take into account U.S. opinion, Bryan had obtained a film interview with Fritz Kuhn, the pro-Nazi head of the German American Bund. Reactions split between people who saw the reporting as endorsing the Nazi regime and those who viewed it as a warning against the regime. Otis Ferguson, a critic for *The New Republic*, wrote, "Working under Louis de Rochemont . . . on the shots Julien Bryan brought back from Germany, the majority of this staff seems to have been working on something it believed in. And in making any good thing, belief tells in the end."[1] For the *Motion Picture Herald*, though, he asked, "How can *The March of Time* offer this newsreel as inside information? . . . Can anyone see from this film how Germany's anti-Hitler citizens are suffering? The whole is a flaming pro-Nazi story, if ever there was one. What do you really see? Youth marching, singing and working. Iron factories and other plants going full blast. Babies cared for, people fed, soldiers and brown shirts well clad and well fed, marching happily, and dictators orating and people cheering."[2]

Indeed Bryan had filmed a certain number of demonstrations arranged by the Nazi Party, the Hitlerjugend, or the Work Service, but without ever granting them the force of expression that Leni Riefenstahl's work would. At times they were simply shown in the banality of their preparation or unfolding. He had also trained his camera on anti-Semitic signs and had put together brief reports on the life of Jewish communities. Many of his studio scenes were later reused as actual newsreels.[3]

In 1939, while New York's Museum of Modern Art (MoMA) was opening its doors on Fifty-Third Street in Manhattan, boasting a 450-seat auditorium for daily film showings, the director of the Film Study Department, Iris Barry, and her husband, John E. Abbott, the assistant director of the museum, had managed to make film a central part of the museum. When the other departments were created, the question of the potential disparity between the more exclusive taste for modern art and the general expectations of American society had not always been satisfactorily addressed. Peter Decherney writes, "Over the next few years, MoMA's staff realized that film possessed something far more valuable than a means of reaching a greater share of the middle class. Rather than refining public taste in films, MoMA embraced Hollywood cinema whole, as already a quintessentially democratic, American modernist art form."[4] If cinema was legitimized as art by way of recognition of its Americanness, this did not keep the public from being interested in productions from other countries, be it Russia and its avant-garde or Germany and its Nazi propaganda.

In spring 1933, having organized the first exhibit of German contemporary art in New York, MoMA's young director Alfred H. Barr was in Berlin. Barr was a Princeton graduate and the author of a thesis on Piero de Cosimo. He had taught art history at Harvard and Princeton before expanding his interests to architecture and film. On April 3, 1933, he attended a lecture by Joseph Goebbels at a meeting of German movie industry professionals in the Kaiserhof Hotel. The tone was clearly set: Goebbels wanted to make German film "a world force the limits of which are today not yet visible." However, unlike the Hollywood film industry's canon, which insisted on creating myths unshackled by patriotic constraints, Goebbels felt that "The sharper the national contours of a film, the greater will be its possibilities of conquering the world."[5] In Barr's written reaction, he stated, "But to even the superficial observer the German film of the past two years seems to have needed no spur to its patriotism."[6] This article from May 1933 provides one of the very first analyses of the militaristic German narrative films of the early 1930s and of documentary productions heralding the birth of Hitler's Reich. An attentive spectator, Barr proves to be equally lucid on the blending of economic and ideological interests that characterized the configuration of German film. Taking aim in particular at the films treating the war of liberation against Napoleon, he observes, "But it is doubtful whether they could have been released in such quantities were it not for the fact that [Alfred] Hugenberg, head of the Nationalist party and chief supporter of the Stahlhelm also has an important interest in the UFA [Universum Film AG, Germany's major studio at the time]. Heavy industry has rarely been opposed to war."[7]

Following in Barr's footsteps, Iris Barry and John E. Abbott went to Germany in 1935 and succeeded in acquiring a number of Nazi films to add to the museum's collection and to make available to American authorities for educational purposes.[8] The most famous of these, *Triumph of the Will*, covered the Nuremberg meetings of the National-Sozialiste Deutsche Arbeiter Partei (NSDAP, National Socialist German Workers' Party, or Nazis) in 1934. Only a smattering of critics and professionals had had occasion to see Riefenstahl's film, which was screened at meetings like the one in Berlin in 1935 organized by Goebbels.[9] In agreeing to make *The Victory of Faith* in 1933 and then *Triumph of the Will* in 1934—both commissioned by the Nazi Party—Riefenstahl participated in shaping political events whose staging was inseparable from their cinematographic transmission. As she herself explained in a book on the making of the film, "The preparations for the party congress were made in concert with the preparations for the camera work—that is, the event was planned not only as a spectacular mass meeting but as a spectacular propaganda film. . . . The ceremonies and precise plans of the parades, marches, processions, the architecture of the halls and stadium were designed for the convenience of the cameras."[10] That is why, when Riefenstahl came to the United States in 1938 to present her work, a warning published by the Hollywood Anti-Nazi League in *Daily Variety* on November 29 helped instigate a boycott of her visit: "In this moment when hundreds of thousands of our brethren await certain death, close your doors to all Nazi agents. Let the world know there is no room in Hollywood for Nazi agents."[11]

In addition to Riefenstahl's *Triumph of the Will*, Barry and Abbott chose *Flieger, Funker, Kanoniere* (Pilots, Radiomen, Gunners, dir. Martin Rikli, 1937), which dealt with German aviation at the start of the war, and *Feuertaufe* (*Baptism of Fire*, dir. Hans Bertram, 1940), which gave the Nazi perspective on the invasion of Poland. Since the total running time of this trilogy was rather long (207 minutes), Abbott asked the film library's technical supervisor, Ed Kerns, to consider abridged versions of the films. Begun in September 1940, the reediting required six months of work. The documentaries were viewed and entirely indexed on descriptive note cards. The speeches were transcribed and everything was translated.[12]

Triumph of the Will was reduced from 110 to 42 minutes. Comparing the two versions reveals how MoMA wanted to make Americans understand the political system implemented by the Nazis while remaining mindful that the representation offered was in part propaganda and that, independent of any reference to reality, it was capable of seducing viewers other than just Germans. The problem was not easy to manage. On the one hand, shortening a work generally requires eliminating whatever does not seem essential for its comprehension. In its edited version, therefore, *Triumph of the Will* lost its secondary scenes about, for example, the preparation of the NSDAP congress in Nuremberg. (Almost six minutes were cut, during which youths of the Sturmabteilung [Stormtroopers, SA] and Work Service are seen in their encampments, washing up, cooking, and entertaining themselves before the big day.) If, from a strict political point of view, these scenes were not essential to inform the American populace of the dangers posed by Hitler's Reich, their anodyne character did create a counterpoint that enabled viewers to appreciate more fully the exceptional character of the Nuremberg parades and the degree to which they were dominated by an "official" staging. One could object that the banal scenes embodied the transformation of a society able to believe that its collective force had been revitalized, but then retaining only the spectacular aspect of the event merely reinforces this impression rather than calls it into question. Another example is found in the first part of Riefenstahl's film, where a very fluid link is created between shots of the citizens of the old medieval town in traditional costume and shots of Nuremberg's visitors for the day (the SA, the Work Service, the Hitler Youth). The revised version entirely omits the "folkloric" images, a sign that the editors did not recognize the general function given such elements in the flood of documentary films offered to the German public. In the end, the only people present on the screen embody the new *Volksgemeinschaft* (people's community) that Nuremberg supposedly prefigures.

As early as 1933 Goebbels set the propaganda goal of having explicit political films coexist with those in the tradition of the UFA *Kulturfilme* (culture films), known for their pedagogical seriousness. Engaging viewers in order to intimidate or win them over required taking into account their expectations, tastes, and general desire for state acknowledgment of an existence whose feeling of well-being was grounded in *Heimat* comfort.[13]

Indeed in a country whose unity was late in coming and centrifugal, the *Länder* (states) had constituted the hearth of consolidation of national identity on a regional scale. In cinema, *Landesbildstelle* (a state-level precursor to today's media libraries) had been established to collect films directed in or about each *Land* and to create productions rooted in the land. The Nazis always had celebrations of the conquering Reich follow those of returns to one's family home and one's roots in the ancestral soil. The end of the *Länder* system brought with it the reassertion of an identity and a sociability extending beyond traditional social and political structures and addressing itself to the more intimate realm of the village and family circle. While the *Heimatfilm* preserved traces of a time long past, revitalizing them via the power of projecting it on the big screen, an almost abstract representation of the age-old Reich was attempted, with the various sectors of the state as its primary audience. Every week Germans saw numerous films produced under Nazi direction, and it was only within this larger stream of productions that the most political ones surfaced, *Triumph of the Will* being the most exceptional of these.

Another choice made by MoMA concerning Riefenstahl's film was aimed at not adding explanatory commentary that would provoke critical distance. Certainly cuts made within certain sequences made it possible not to allow Riefenstahl's aesthetic to be fully displayed, but the idea was still to try to show the spectacle of the meeting filmed as its organizers had conceived it. At the conclusion of notes written after seeing the original version, Schuyler Bradt wrote, "The picture ended. It left you with a feeling that a great force was at work which called out the unrestrained emotions of many people.

The show was without equal, in any event."[14] It was nevertheless decided that the new version would be preceded by the following warning:

> The motion picture was officially recognized as a powerful instrument of propaganda by the Nazis as early as 1933. This documentary film of the Nazi Party Meeting at Nuremberg in 1934 was "produced by command of the Führer." Actually, the entire political rally at Nuremberg was staged like some colossal movie production. Ceremonies, processions, even the architecture of the halls and stadiums were designed for the convenience of the vast battery of cameras trained on every event. Millions of feet of film were shot, and the work of editing, recording and completing the picture lasted over a year. The film served to publicize and affirm the power of the Nazi Party and to familiarize the German public with figures like Hess, Himmler and [Julius] Streicher, then almost unknown. It also recorded the official attitude regarding the "blood purge" of June 1934, and painstakingly featured Germany's new ruler and his henchmen as patriotic yet formidable saviours.[15]

In his memoirs, as in most of the interviews he gave, Luis Buñuel, director of *Un chien andalou* (*Andalusian Dog*, 1929) and *L'Âge d'or* (*The Golden Age*, 1930), recounts that he was put in charge of reediting *Triumph of the Will* in the late 1930s. Iris Barry supposedly told him they would "have some screenings, just to show the so-called experts what a movie can do." Two filmmakers, René Clair and Charlie Chaplin, eagerly went to see the edited versions and, as Buñuel tells it, had completely opposite reactions: " 'Never show them!' Clair said, horrified by their power. 'If you do, we're lost!' Chaplin, on the other hand, laughed, once so hard that he actually fell off his chair. Was he so amused because of *The Dictator*?"[16] Buñuel never got a response to his query. Moreover nothing in MoMA's archives allows us to confirm Buñuel's participation in this endeavor. He was in fact working for the Office of the Coordinator of Inter-American Affairs, one of whose tasks was producing documentary films intended to strengthen ties between the United States and Latin American countries during World War II. He and Helen van Dongen supervised the organization's two editing teams. This program, the Latin American Contract, was run by the museum, not the film department. Headed by Nelson Rockefeller and John Hay Whitney, it was administered by John E. Abbott. It is not impossible, however, that, in the few months preceding Buñuel's official hiring, Barry had him sit in informally on deliberations about how to reedit Riefenstahl's film.[17]

What is certain, though, is that President Roosevelt, to whom the shortened version was shown in early 1942, was so struck by the film's power of conviction that he eventually determined "not to have any public screenings, for fear that this brutality and display of force might produce an effect contrary to what was desired."[18]

How Do You Interpret Nazi Newsreels?
Siegfried Kracauer's Contribution

Convinced of the need for continued vigilance against the possibility of a backlash, MoMA opted for prudence and commissioned Siegfried Kracauer to draft a report on "propaganda and Nazi war films."[19] On May 3, 1937, while on a stay in Paris, Kracauer received a letter from Max Horkheimer, who drew his attention to the recent creation of MoMA's film library and, like Meyer Schapiro, encouraged him to familiarize himself with its collections and to contact Barry. This meeting occurred a year later, when the Jeu de Paume museum in Paris hosted an exhibition called "Three Centuries of Art in the United States." Barry contributed a retrospective on the history of American cinema to this show and took note of the laudatory review it received from Kracauer.[20] The Rockefeller Foundation, one of MoMA's principal financial supporters, wanted its collection to be the first worldwide center for "the preservation and distribution of historically significant films." One of the people in charge of the Humanities Department, John Marshall, advised Barry to pair the revision of *Triumph of the Will* with "a serious historical survey" of film as a propaganda weapon.

Enzo Traverso writes that Kracauer "had been living in a state of utter poverty since his exile to France, and he was physically and emotionally drained. During the second year of his stay in New York, he learned from the Swiss Red Cross that his mother and aunt had been deported to the Theresienstadt camp, where they eventually perished. The same fate awaited most of the people he knew in Frankfurt."[21] Soon after his arrival in the United States on April 25, 1941, Kracauer sent his curriculum vitae to John Marshall, with a list of the aspects of his work devoted to film: "I introduced the first serious film critique and film analysis in Germany. My interest led me to make extensive research about movies, in continuous touch with directors, cameramen and other specialists. I was regarded as an authority in those fields."[22]

In an article published in 1932, "The Task of the Film Critic," Kracauer was insistent in emphasizing that, in his contributions to the *Frankfurter Zeitung*, his interest extended beyond the works of creative auteurs to everyday productions as well: "In fact, the poorer the majority of musical and military films, dramatic entertainments, etc., are in holding their own against strict aesthetic judgment, the weightier becomes their social significance, which can by no means be overestimated. Today the smallest village has a cinema, and every halfway passable film passes through one of a thousand channels to the masses in city and countryside alike. What do these films convey to their mass public and in what sense do they influence it? These are the cardinal questions, the ones that any responsible observer must ask of mainstream products."[23] Kracauer was thus as interested in narrative films as he was in news films and documentaries. Without displaying the same militant mind-set as the members of the Film and Photo League—without, in fact, even knowing they existed—he shared a common interest in the social role of movies and took up Vertov's legacy of attention to montage and the heterogeneous while also extolling film's technical value in recording (e.g., continuity, flow of life). In 1931 he took issue with the UFA monopoly in Germany and denounced the formatted, repetitive character of the newsreels it produced, an "artificial continuum" imposed on the public week after week: "If things were shown as they are or as they usually happen today, viewers might develop some concern about them and begin to doubt the excellence of our current social order."[24] Yet he did not identify with the documentary trend associated with *Neue Sachlichkeit* (New Objectivity), which filmmakers like Hans Cürlis and Wilfried Basse embodied. With respect to their films, Kracauer observed, "They could be produced at low cost; and they offered a gratifying opportunity of showing much and revealing nothing. . . . Its inherent neutrality is corroborated by Basse's indifference to the change of political atmosphere under Hitler. In 1934, as if nothing had happened, he released *Deutschland von Gestern und Heute* (Germany from Yesterday and Today), a cross-section film of German cultural life that also refused 'to penetrate beneath the skin.'"[25] While in this first, essential phase of his critical work Kracauer never sees film as an object disconnected from all reference to reality, neither does he restrict it to its ideological content alone.[26]

In the same curriculum vitae presented to Marshall, Kracauer also summarizes his initial contacts with the United States:

3 March 1933, I left Germany for Paris.
   . . . For the International Institute of Social Research at Columbia University, New York, I prepared an extensive study on the methods of totalitarian propaganda.
   Through all these years I continued my research on moving pictures and collected material for a book on *History and Sociology of Moving Pictures*; my material includes notes on extensive research in the Paris Film Library.
   In 1938, I was invited by the Film Library of the Museum of Modern Art to come to New York and to write at this institute a study on the *History and Sociology of German Moving Pictures*.
   But I could not leave France before 24 February 1941.
   I arrived 25 April 1941, and entered this country with an Immigration Quota Visa.
   I am married; I have no children.
   References: Miss Iris Barry; Prof. Meyer Shapiro [*sic*]; Prof. Hans Speier; Dr. Ernst Kris; Mr. Donald Slesinger; Dr. Paul Lazarsfeld; Mr. Thomas Mann.[27]

As a result of his newly established American contacts, Kracauer was asked in spring 1941 to do a "study of German wartime communication through film." To carry out his work, he used access to the film library's recent acquisitions: Nazi narrative films, nearly eight hours of newsreels, including the most important subjects treated by Goebbels's propaganda since 1934, and, last, the best Soviet productions from 1922 to 1938, some of which served as models—or, at the very least, inspirations—to German directors.[28] With this corpus at his disposal, he conducted methodical viewings and took notes resulting in detailed descriptive records. Thus he was able to base his analyses on a documented reading of films and not on subjective memory of their screening in a movie theater. He also had access to the collection of *Deutsche Wochenschauen* (German weekly newsreels) assembled at the Library of Congress in Washington, the inventory and summary of which he helped compile. He benefited from the collaboration of John Grierson, a founding figure of the British documentary school, and of Sidney L. Bernstein, in charge of the film production unit of the British Information Ministry established at the beginning of the World War II.[29] Moreover he was put in contact with Ernst Kris and Hans Speier, directors of the research project on "totalitarian communication" conducted at the New School of Social Research. Kris and Speier were already studying radio alongside a team led by Harold Lasswell that was covering print media. As indicated by a note sent by Kris and Speier to Marshall, Kracauer's participation was the subject of strongly worded directives: "Only if Mr. Krakauer (*sic*) fits into that team to some extent will it be possible to achieve smooth cooperation. The whole of Monday mornings is taken up by a staff meeting in which every member reports what he is doing and in which we all criticize each other and try to detect the weak points in what the other is doing. We should like Mr. Krakauer to attend these meetings. We also suggested to him that his intercourse with ourselves and with our staff should be regular, so that he might be in constant touch with all the topical and methodological aspects of our work."[30]

Kracauer willingly complied with the expectations of the New School's directors, being careful to infuse the analysis of films submitted to him with the same rigor he had used as a critic for the *Frankfurter Zeitung*, and no doubt he was happy to be working on a team once again. His diligence was mocked by some of the colleagues reading his reports, in particular those in War Department offices concerned with counterpropaganda.[31] However, the transcription of a Kris lecture on war imagery published in 1942 indicates that Kracauer's works prevailed, at the risk even of seeing his conclusions copied more often than cited.[32]

Before concentrating on documentaries and news, Kracauer began by analyzing Nazi films.[33] He consulted a large number of books and articles whose inventory the library regularly kept up to date. He spent so much time in the reading room that Iris Barry nicknamed him "the Reader." The bibliography accompanying the study written for MoMA gives an idea of the scope of his reading.[34] While German film historians dominate with their works (Arnheim, Béla Balazs, Oskar Kalbus, Rudolf Kurtz), the great British documentary specialist Paul Rotha is quoted several times. Two journals, probably available at the Film Study Center of MoMA, were systematically consulted: *Close Up*, published first in Switzerland and then in England, and *La Revue du Cinéma* from Paris. There are also a great number of film screening notes written by MoMA collaborators such as Barry and Jay Leyda on Russian films.[35]

Far from instrumentalizing the films he was analyzing in order to draw quick political conclusions, Kracauer constantly took pains to pick out the

singular qualities of the screen images, voices, and sounds, together or separately, in particular in the effects related to editing. In *Victory in the West*, he
thus remarks on the ellipses: "The announcement of an action is immediately followed by its result, and long developments are supposed to have been
consummated in the tiny period between two verbal units. Thus a great deal
of reality and enemy resistance disappears in the 'pockets' of the commentary, giving the audience a sense of ease of accomplishment and increasing
the impression of an indomitable German blitz. Actually, the blitz has flashed
through an artificial vacuum."[36]

He also shows how certain seemingly harmless techniques can make an
insidious impression on the viewer. Drawing on a study written by Speier in
1941, Kracauer cites the use of maps that "seem to illustrate, through an ar-
ray of moving arrows and lines, tests on some substance. Resembling graphs
of physical processes, they show how all known materials are broken up,
penetrated, pushed by, and eaten away by the new one, thus demonstrating
its absolute superiority in a most striking manner." Likewise he observes
that from May 1940 onward, the running time of news journals gets considerably longer, allowing one to reproduce on screen "much the same effects as
those obtained through steady repetition in speeches."[37]

Beyond these few notations, however, he elaborates a veritable grid of
reading and interpretation, a structural analysis arising from the viewing of
the films in his corpus and not an abstract semiological schema. Nazi propaganda films thus appear to him to be constituted by three modes of expression:

> commentary—including both verbal statements and occasional cap-
>   tions;
> the visuals—including camera reality and numerous maps;
> the sound—composed of sound effects and music, including songs
>   (words spoken by characters on the screen are so rare that they
>   can be ignored).[38]

So there are three fundamental elements: the verbal, the visual, and the
acoustic. They can be analyzed separately; in *Baptism of Fire*, "the statement
about the German character of Danzig [Gdansk] . . . and the picture unit
representing old Danzig houses . . . are accompanied by a sound unit."[39] It is
fitting, however, to see how these elements of content are organized in and
of themselves and then, on the level of the film as a whole, how they are

subject to a "synchronization" and/or to "cross-linkages." Several examples are given to illustrate this analytical schema.

In his study of newsreel films—documentaries like *Baptism of Fire* and *Victory in the West*, made from recent footage tied to the beginning of World War II—Kracauer observes that instead of being less shackled to the flow of events, directors frantically resorted to filming unstaged reality. While the Soviets constantly mixed these with reconstitutions, the Germans systematically stuck to news images filmed in real time: "It is not easy to understand why the Nazi film experts obstinately insisted upon composing their campaign films from newsreel shots. The average spectator, of course, believed their loudly proclaimed desire to be true to reality. But actually the wholly staged bombardment in the British film *Target for Tonight* seems more real—and is aesthetically more impressive—than any newsreel of a similar bombardment in the Nazi films."[40] This remark might seem paradoxical. Confronted with the genre of the propaganda film, and responsible in particular for measuring its impact so as to foresee its influence on viewers, Kracauer resorts to putting himself in his adversary's shoes and imagining better solutions for the mise-en-scène. Convinced that the usual force of the topical film derives from the possibility of direct recording, he thinks the Nazis, whose aim was not "realistic," should or could have done without this constraint when it detracted from the desired effect. Perhaps this was also a way of distinguishing these films (the *Deutsche Wochenschauen*) from works by auteurs, whose materialistic quality he sought out, thereby sharing the preoccupations that Panofsky was developing at the same time at the Princeton Institute of Advanced Studies: "It is the movies, and only the movies, that do justice to that materialistic interpretation of the universe. . . . The movies organize material things and persons, not a neutral medium, into a composition that receives its style, and may even become fantastic or pretervoluntarily symbolic, not so much by an interpretation in the artist's mind as by the actual manipulation of physical objects and recording machinery. The medium of the movies is physical reality as such. . . . The problem is to manipulate and shoot unstylized reality in such a way that the result has style."[41]

In the language of those in charge at MoMA, the films that took into account this physical reality were called "Films of Fact." In 1939 Richard Griffith had already extolled the merits of the year's American documentary production by entitling his article "A Big Year for Fact Films," which he followed in 1942 with a brief work coauthored with Barry entitled *The Films of*

Fact.[42] As Decherney reminds us, "The label primarily designated documentary films but it also included narrative feature films, animation, and any film out of which they could squeeze sociological merit."[43]

With German newsreels being very much under government control (Hitler himself watched them regularly in his private screening room), they indeed usually consisted of on-the-spot reports. The German camera crews were extremely professional. They had long been able to shoot events far from Berlin and get their film delivered in a very short time. Even though certain clichéd sequences were reused out of context, atemporally (parades, shots of Hitler, well-crafted shots of soldiers in training or of use of military hardware), the news was well covered wherever it occurred, at least while the Wehrmacht was winning. While the films recovered by MoMA constitute within Nazi propaganda a full-fledged genre in their own right, they nevertheless were never shown unaccompanied to German viewers. Kracauer, in restricting himself to these news film montages, was unable to compare these sources with examples from other contemporary documentary production. Such a cross-check would have enabled him to discover Nazi propaganda's other face, its celebration of *Heimat*. Between 1933 and 1945, if the masses saw themselves in the mirror held up by Nazi propaganda, it was not in the single image of the huge Nuremberg rallies but in the Janus face of a Reich promised to last for ages *and* of an archaic land preserved in the Heimat films.

One should therefore nuance the famous remark made by Walter Benjamin: "Mass reproduction is aided especially by the reproduction of masses. In big parades and monster rallies, in sports events, and in war, all of which nowadays are captured by camera and sound recording, the masses are brought face to face with themselves."[44] In fact the image conveyed by the *Heimat* films is in no way comparable to the abstract one reflected in the films of Riefenstahl or in the "realism" of war reporting. The *Heimat* films certainly do not show the masses such as they "really" are but rather as members of miniature "fatherlands" which, taken together, constitute the German people. However, they were widely shown all over the country, thanks to an enormous network of simultaneous distribution.

The technical means implemented to show these films went far beyond the territory of the Great Reich. In another study for the New School, Kracauer thus examined the multidistribution system for certain Nazi documentaries that were translated into as many as sixteen different languages. Depending on the country, these films underwent cuts or additions according to the target audience. For example, Kracauer tells how previously in France he had seen *Olympia*, Riefenstahl's film about the 1936 Olympic Games, which allowed him to catch variants in its "American" copy:

> So far as I remember, the French version—but I attended only part of it—did not include so many scenes dealing with American *and* Japanese victories. Perhaps, the whole overseas part was less accentuated, in favor of the European events. It also seems to me that particularly the French came somewhat more into existence; but this would be quite natural. My reminiscences are not entirely trustworthy, though, because I exceptionally refrained from taking notes in this case.
>
> In my opinion, by the way, it would be highly important for the Army morale film makers to study the whole behavior of the Japanese fighters—their almost religious ambition, their indomitable energy and their attitude in cases of failure. However, I imagine that the *Olympia* film has already been looked through for these ends.[45]

At the completion of his study, Kracauer was able to pinpoint two major flaws in wartime production. One had to do with anti-Semitic propaganda and the other with the account of human losses sustained on the battlefield. On the first count, he very deftly exposes one of the singular features of the cinematographic images: their resistance to the will to degrade human figuration. Comments Kracauer, "While the Nazis continued practicing, printing, and broadcasting their racial anti-Semitism, they reduced its role in the war films, apparently hesitant to spread it through pictures. On the screen, anti-Jewish activities were almost as taboo as, for instance, concentration camps or sterilizations. All this can be done and propagated in print and speech, but it stubbornly resists pictorial representation. The image seems to be the last refuge of violated human dignity."[46]

Indeed while it was possible for the Nazis to proceed by using assertions or incantatory turns of phrase in order to prolong the illusion of the pertinence of the regime's racial doctrine and to promote its political and administrative implementation, the same cannot be said for the cinematographic translation of this theory. Being unable to create genetically a master race, Nazism tried to materialize it by representing it on film. However, it proved unfeasible to feature the too uniform bodies of the SS and the SA in the creation of any kind of movie with genuine fictional potential. It was indirectly, through the denunciation of their "evil" counterparts, the Jews, that form would be given to Aryans' existence and that their superiority would be suggested to the viewer.

The imagery crafted in this way loaded the people doomed to extinction with a much stronger metaphorical content, all the while claiming to base it on the truth emanating from documentary film. If the promise of creating an elite race entailed promoting the refusal of otherness, it meant sharing this figuration with the Jews, who supposedly were parasites upon its purity. However, insistence on the degradation of the Jews in the Polish ghettos went far beyond the intentions of its propagandists. Viewers felt uneasy looking at the distress of men, women, and children racked by misery and hunger. Although they were ready and willing at the beginning of the regime to accept a discourse comparing the amount of money spent to care for the handicapped with the estimated cost of houses built by the state for the well-being of the rural population, it was a different story when they were confronted with a racist typing of a people, the negative connotation of which was overzealously solicited.[47] This poor reception of the filmic representation of Nazi anti-Semitism allows us to gauge one of film's singular contributions: realistic in essence, the cinematic narrative cannot harm human dignity without repudiating itself, a point that Kracauer underscored remarkably.

As to the second flaw identified in German wartime movie productions, Kracauer comes back to a question already underlying his analyses related to representations of World War I. He rightly observed that the Russians did not hesitate to show corpses of civilians and soldiers, and he wondered about the nearly total absence of death in German films.[48] In a manuscript version of his study, he reports the criticisms on this subject heard on the Reich's radio programs: "We know from shortwave radio that there have been mutterings and criticism, for instance, within Germany about the newsreels dished out to the people. They complained that the newsreels never showed any dead soldiers. . . . The propaganda bureau had its answers, but even in Germany one wonders if they were very effective—the people were told that it was impossible to show any dead in the films because this would be offensive to the German soldiers. Presumably German soldiers do not like to be seen dead."[49]

So the true reason for this censorship did not reside in some sort of consideration for people's dignity but in the fact that Nazi film techniques, whose manipulative dimension was not usually visible, functioned well as long as the German army was victorious. At the first setbacks, it became much more difficult to disguise a tragic reality that German families were discovering even in home and hearth.

Finally, Nazi diplomats had turned to certain films in order to undermine the resistance of foreign peoples and governments. In Bucharest, Oslo, Belgrade, Ankara, and Sofia—to mention but a few—official showings of these pictures served as psychological holdups. Thus on October 11, 1941, the *New York Times* reported that Franz von Papen had left Istanbul with a film of the German invasion of Russia, and that he "will have a large party at the German embassy during which he will show the film to Turkish leaders." Propaganda films as a means of blackmail—the gangster methods of the Nazis could not be better illustrated.[50]

Triumph of the Will, as well as German newsreels as a whole, figured among the documents given priority by the IMT in its investigation prior to the Nuremberg Trial. No one doubts that the analysis done on these films by MoMA and by Kracauer contributed to their visibility in the United States and facilitated their reading when they were considered as evidence in judgment of the "Nazi plan."

CHAPTER 4

Face-to-Face with Nazi Atrocities

A Backdrop of Violence and Death

At the turn of the twentieth century, most of the nations involved in wars had laid out some ground rules for photographic and then film coverage of the conflicts. In order to be able to respond quickly to situations largely beyond their control, it was best to prepare for them by giving cameramen orders allowing them to deal with unforeseen or extraordinary events. Two types of constraints, technical and political, came together. On the one hand, filmmaking equipment was not lightweight and mobile enough to follow soldiers in combat up close. On the other hand, military and political leaders of warring countries were reluctant to acknowledge openly the number of human losses sustained on the battlefield; internalized or simply accepted, this abdication quickly slipped the dead bodies from the spectators' view.[1] Death on the battlefield, however, is altogether different from deliberate murder, whose photographic and cinematic recording is disturbing to both the people who order it and to those such as family members of the victims, professional witnesses, judicial authorities, and historians who are led to preserve and value the trace of it.

In the collection recently put together by Tomasz Kizny of rare period photographs that attest to the reality of the gulag, detainees and their guards occasionally pose for the camera.[2] The effect is often gripping, as in the picture taken at the Slovoki monastery, transformed into the camp infirmary; the photographer has chosen to capture the worried faces of the ill set against the backdrop of an Irenic tapestry that depicts the care given by monks to their patients in earlier times.[3] Another striking shot in Kizny's collection is that of the wounded piled up on a cart, one of them clearly in

great pain, no doubt a result of the terrible conditions imposed on the workers of the Belomorkanal (Stalin's White Sea Canal).[4] Here photography plays
an important role in recording and preserving the traces of the violent acts
experienced. In the course of the World War I, warring parties had also confronted each other via white papers in which they accused each other of
committing atrocities. Driven, of course, by a political agenda but hoping to
establish his International Anti-War Museum on a solid documentary foundation, Ernst Friedrich published in Frankfurt *Krieg dem Krieg* (1924), a
sort of picture book in which photographic documentation of war's violent
acts was a central part. Each photograph had a caption and was contextual-
ized from the perspective of its production or reception.[5] The trace thus
preserved not only bore witness to the fate of the victims but attested to the
point of view of the executioners, often proud to pose before their victims.
One encounters this attitude again in the unauthorized pictures taken by
certain members of the Einsatzgruppen (Special Task Forces, the SS death
squads) on the Eastern Front in 1941.[6]

In this respect, the account by one of the accredited Nazi camera operators is revealing. Born in 1907, Walter Frentz had been chosen by Leni Riefenstahl to participate in filming the Nazi Party meeting in Nuremberg in
1933 (*The Victory of Faith*) and then in 1934 (*Triumph of the Will*). He then
became one of Hitler's regular cameramen, while continuing to make documentaries, both for his own body of work and as commissions accepted for
propaganda purposes. On August 15, 1941, Frentz wrote in his journal,
"With SS Reichsführer Himmler in Minsk. 10:00 hours: prison camp. Noon:
execution. 13:00 hours: lunch at the Lenin House. 15:00 hours: insane asylum, then *kolkholzy* and SS children's home. The SS Reichsführer takes two
young Russian boys to Berlin. Film the SS Reichsfürher when the two boys
from the *kolkhoz* change clothes."[7] Against this backdrop of violence and
death depicted by the story of an execution in Minsk on August 15, 1941,
Frentz gives the following account fifty pages later:

> Nobody watched over me. I did what I wanted. I attended an execu-
> tion only once, in Russia. Himmler had been good enough to take me
> in his plane. It was purely out of curiosity. I wanted to go to Russia,
> get out of the headquarters. We never went to the front. It was for the
> birthday of the most senior SS officer, Sepp Dietrich. But we learned
> unexpectedly that the next day we would go see an execution. So we

went. Ditches had been dug. Later, trucks arrived, full of very simple people, probably peasants. They were ordered to lie in the ditches, headfirst. The SS circled around them. Each SS took aim at a single person. At the signal, they killed them. The man accompanying me, a guy from the Ministry of Culture, said to me, "Good God, Frentz, it's going to end badly for us, too. . . ." I filmed that on purpose, for I didn't know such things existed. I wanted to see if I could get something positive out of it. Alas, I was forced to conclude that even our superior officers at headquarters were cowards. One evening, I was alone with one of our highest ranking officers—I don't want to give his name—and I said to him, "Sir, I saw something I'd like to tell you about. It is very disturbing to me." I had taken a slide showing officers with guns, shooting at the ditches. I showed it to him and I asked, "What is a person to make of this?" He answered, "A word of advice: don't talk about it to anyone!"[8]

It was also forbidden to photograph or film the concentration and extermination camps. However, photography was part of the administrative routine and management of deportees.[9] A few films were also made during convoy transfers. Thus one camera recorded Jews being transported from central Franconia. Sybil Milton reports, "On police orders, the Würzburg electricity company had installed in advance a special 20,000-watt system at the assembly center to facilitate this filming. Enlarged photographic stills from the film were later exhibited in the windows of the [newspaper] *Mainfränkische Zeitung*; afterwards the photos were returned to the Nazi party district office."[10] With no moving picture having been shown until summer 1944, the job of allied cameramen would prove to be all the more difficult and counted upon when they entered the Polish camps.

Upon arriving at Auschwitz-Birkenau, the Red Army soldiers were every bit as stunned as the remaining deportees. This suspended moment prevented the liberation from being filmed live.[11] Before they fled, the Nazis destroyed part of the camp installations and cut off the electricity. The first glances exchanged in the barracks took place in the dark, which is why most of the filming was done outdoors, tracking the movement of the most able-bodied as they exited. The head of the camera crew poignantly relates that, whereas they themselves were in a state of shock upon arrival, most of the seven thousand or so detainees showed no reaction.[12] A fair bit of time elapsed before the cameramen felt ready to film—too much, in fact, for the deportees to show what the Soviets were expecting of them: the awareness—for want of joy—of being liberated. Sometimes, when the survivors were finally ready to go on camera, the film crew had already left. Envir Alimbekov, a sergeant in the Red Army, reports, "Late in the afternoon, a few who were still crying began to hug us, to murmur a few words in languages we didn't understand. They wanted to talk, began telling what had taken place. But we were out of time. Night was already falling. We had to leave."[13]

Later it would also be necessary to consider the reception and believability of the images captured as the camps were liberated—not because viewers doubted the honesty of military reporters but because the number and intensity of the acts of brutality committed went beyond all prior experiences of wartime violence.

Stories of Atrocities

On April 26, 1945, when *Nazi Atrocities*, a single-reel film compiled from Soviet footage, was shown at the Embassy Theatre in New York, censors refused to license it for distribution for all audiences, on the grounds that it was being released by a commercial agency, Artkino.[14] In the United States skepticism concerning reports about Nazi camps was coupled with wariness toward anything that the Soviets might say about them. This disbelief also stemmed from the difficulties of measuring from afar the gravity and magnitude of the acts of violence perpetrated against the Jews. However, in September 1933 an "anti-Hitler" film project was announced in Hollywood, the theme of which would be "the persecutions suffered by the Jews since Hitler came to power."[15] Apparently Will Hays, the man in charge of enforcing the film code, prohibited it from being made because it was directed against the chancellor of Germany as an individual.[16] In 1938 Kristallnacht (the Night of Broken Glass) had seemed terrifying, but the yardstick for judging this violence was a "barbarity" thought long past. In a note to the U.S. ambassador in Berlin, the American consul in Stuttgart, Samuel W. Honaker, thought the presence of creditable witnesses had been essential to certifying the reality of this night of horror: "I have the honor to report that the Jews of southwest Germany have suffered vicissitudes during the last three days which would seem unreal to one living in an enlightened country during the twentieth century if one had not actually been a witness of their dreadful experiences, or if one had not had them corroborated by more than one person of undoubted integrity."[17] At the time, news journals told of the Nazis' anti-Jewish acts of brutality. In the *Universal News* on November 15, 1938, one of the items was entitled "FDR Leads Nation in Protest Against Nazi Persecutions." On November 21, 1938, another report dealt with the "Madison Square Garden Protest Meeting Against Persecutions," where "22,000 jam[med] Garden in protest against nazi persecutions."

Moreover the use of the word *atrocities* for crimes committed by the Nazis echoed World War I memories in which myth, propaganda, and war crimes were so interwoven that it was difficult to know what to believe about reports on the German army's campaign of brutality that resulted in the deaths of some 6,500 French and Belgian civilians in fall 1914.[18] There were reports early on establishing the facts of these crimes, but false information, such as Germans putatively crucifying some of their enemies, was also spread.[19] In the end, all of this was mixed together in the dragnet of the opposing forces' politics of communication. Alan Kramer recalls that in the interwar period marked by pacifist opinion, "'German atrocities' were considered, at least in the Anglo-Saxon world, to be the very example of falsifications specific to war propaganda."[20] The Nazis kept the memory of this confusion alive, going so far as to make people believe in the so-called model camps that were supposed to refute the *Greuelpropaganda* (propaganda about atrocities).[21] The future organizer of the International Military Tribunal, Justice Robert H. Jackson, recognized that he himself had been one of those "who received during this war most atrocity tales with suspicion and skepticism."[22] However, by early 1945 some publications had drawn their readers' attention to these "atrocity stories." Among them, *Collier's* magazine must be mentioned for a particularly detailed editorial it published on January 8:

> We suppose a lot of Americans simply do not believe the stories of Nazi mass executions of Jews and anti-Nazi Gentiles in Eastern Europe by means of gas chambers, freight cars partly loaded with lime and other horrifying devices. These stories are so foreign to most Americans' experience of life in this country that they seem incredible. Then, too, some of the atrocity stories of World War I were later proved false.
>
> The Government's War Refugee Board, however, is convinced that these World War II atrocity reports are true in the main. Says a

recent WRB report: "It is a fact beyond denial that the Germans have deliberately and systematically murdered millions of innocent civilians—Jews and Christians alike—all over Europe. . . . So revolting and diabolical are the Germans that the minds of civilized people find it difficult to believe that they have actually taken place."

Whether the estimate that "millions" have been exterminated is true or exaggerated, it follows logically from Hitler's philosophy that such things would happen under a Nazi regime. Hitler hates the Jews, as set forth at length in *Mein Kampf,* and considers them unfit to inhabit the earth along with those whom he considers "superior" peoples.[23]

Nevertheless it took seeing film images recorded by their own cameramen for Americans to lend credence to those distributed by Artkino. At one time observers from afar of events in which they were not involved, American cameramen found themselves in the middle of the European battlefields. The screening of the Soviet film occurred the day after the American War Department sent a directive to Signal Corps officials, urging them to ensure "an immediate and complete coverage, by motion pictures and still pictures, of atrocities, enemy prisoners of war, concentration camps and persons who were there at the time of liberation." These pictures were for use in the following cases:

a) Evidence for the Judge Advocate General of the War Crimes Commission
b) Screenings for American troops
c) Possible distribution in U.S. movie theaters
d) Movie screenings by the Bureau of Psychological Warfare
e) Movie screenings organized by the Office of War Information[24]

Thus on May 1 a short montage of film images shot by the Signal Corps on April 5–12, 1945, in camps liberated by the Western allies—Ohrdruf, Nordhausen, Buchenwald, and Hadamar, an "asylum" where more than ten thousand Germans considered mentally ill (among others) were killed—was inserted into the newsreels of Fox Movietone News and Universal News for distribution in first-run and neighborhood movie theaters. Fox introduced them with a warning: "These scenes of horror are an awesome indictment of

Nazi bestiality. To the civilized mind such inhuman cruelty is incredible. We show these films as documentary evidence and warn you not to look at the screen if you are susceptible to gruesome sights." But for Ed Herlihy, the commentator for Universal, it was a matter of urging the spectator, "Don't turn away. Look."[25] Guy S. Eyssell, director of Radio City Music Hall, New York's biggest movie theater, disagreed, however, and omitted the document from his programs. He believed the risk of "shocking and sickening any 'squeamish' persons in the audience" needed to be avoided, given that the venue was frequented mainly by women and children; he felt obliged to protect them from seeing these films.[26] The *New York Times* reports that the audience fell silent but also that there were some murmurs of indignation at seeing shots of corpses stacked in piles and of survivors more dead than alive. The fact that apparently very few spectators closed their eyes during the film was attributed in part to the fact that "General Eisenhower and the Army want you to see [this]."[27]

Indeed following a visit he made to camps in April 1945, Gen. Dwight D. Eisenhower took a number of initiatives so that members of the U.S. Congress and the press corps could go on site and report on the situation of the deportees. States Eisenhower in a letter:

> The things I saw beggar description. While I was touring the camp I encountered three men who had been inmates and by one ruse or another had made their escape. I interviewed them through an interpreter. The visual evidence and the verbal testimony of starvation, cruelty and bestiality were so overpowering as to leave me a bit sick. In one room, where [there] were piled up twenty or thirty naked men, killed by starvation, George Patton would not even enter. He said he would get sick if he did so. I made the visit deliberately, in order to be in position to give first-hand evidence of these things if ever, in the future, there develops a tendency to charge these allegations merely to "propaganda."[28]

In another *New York Times* article from spring 1945, Representative John C. Kunkel of Pennsylvania says, "No one could visualize these horrors without seeing them. It's hard to believe that such brutality existed anywhere in the world, but it certainly did here. It is incredible that some people were able to survive such an awful ordeal. This is a sight I hope never to see again."[29] Renée Poznanski writes, "The emotion that swept over all these new witnesses to the horror of the concentration camps, when they had read and sometimes published information on extermination camps during the war years, speaks volumes about the blindness of the past."[30]

It is not certain that the "emotion" felt in 1945 was the consequence of a "blindness" displayed during the war. As indicated earlier, American diplomats who witnessed Kristallnacht had already admitted to being at a total loss before the horror of which they had direct knowledge. When key American figures came to view the Nazi camps firsthand in 1945, it did not prompt any introspection on their attitude during the war. The viewing phase of the camp visit, necessary for realizing the extent of the crimes committed, usually immediately provoked the desire to determine the responsibility of the first torturers arrested or what ordinary Germans living nearby had known.

What had been shown only in the form of short reports in weekly newsreels was thus pieced together to compose a six-reel film. The projection of this approximately hour-long document constitutes the third phase of the U.S. cinematographic discovery of the camps. However, this movie was not shown by itself but in tandem with a fifteen-minute documentary called *Your Job in Germany*. Director Ernst Lubitsch, who left Germany after the Nazis came to power, was first commissioned to do this film after Pearl Harbor. Known initially by the title *Know Your Enemy Germany*, the film was revised as *Here Is Germany* in 1944 to better instruct occupation forces in the European arena. In the end, *Your Job in Germany* is actually the title of the third version, directed by Frank Capra and Theodore Geisel for the Signal Corps and the Office of War Information.[31] It had been designed to prepare American troops who entered Germany after the Allied invasion for the task of implementing de-Nazification.[32]

The film's deliberately simplistic, virulent commentary was motivated entirely by fears about the danger to young soldiers of contact with a country whose whole history was a demonstration of warmongering and political immaturity. Within every ordinary German lurked a past or future Nazi, hence the need to be constantly on guard and not get too closely involved with any of the population. The only major warring country that had not had to suffer the war on its own soil, and whose very distance from old Europe, where the genocide of the Jews occurred, could explain the relative indifference to their fate until 1945, seemed inordinately worried about the hidden presence of Nazi sympathizers. Foreseeing this reaction, James Agee refused to see the first film on Nazi atrocities, shown in the United States in early May, thinking that it was in part only "an ordered and successful effort to condition the people of this country against interfering with, or even questioning, an extremely hard peace against the people of Germany."[33]

At the same time, the *St. Louis Post-Dispatch* publisher, Joseph Pulitzer II, who had been part of the group of journalists and congressional members who answered Eisenhower's invitation to go to Europe and visit the camps, decided on his return to St. Louis to organize a photography exhibit, show the two films (*Your Job in Germany* and the one-hour documentary), and print spectators' reactions in his daily paper.[34] Pulitzer felt that this action was both "civic" and "patriotic": "My thought is that in St. Louis, for example, Mayor [Aloys P.] Kaufman might well sponsor the first showing of these films in a large hall, perhaps the Kiel Auditorium, with an invited audience representing all elements in the community."[35] On May 12 he applied to the Department of War for authorization to show the film about the camps throughout the entire United States, but with a minimum viewing age set at sixteen. According to newspaper correspondent Alvin H. Goldstein (who drew attention to the effect that would be produced by the repetition of brief scenes from Dachau and Buchenwald, similar from one camp to the next), Pulitzer said, "Anyone who has seen these films will have seen more than we newspapermen saw, as our inquiry was limited to two camps." It seemed to Goldstein that the viewer, at the sight of the terrible state of the camp survivors, would turn back with relief to the images of the deceased.[36]

On May 13 the mayor of St. Louis submitted to President Truman an official request to show the two films. Between then and May 30, Pulitzer arranged fourteen free showings to forty-nine thousand spectators. These screenings led to several observations: there were twice as many women as men; the shows transpired in silence; only a few spectators looked away from the screen; one woman cried (on investigation, the paper managed to identify her and record the impressions of Mrs. William J. Schnitker, 2108-A, Ann Avenue); one out of twenty viewers professed to being against such a screening; and the audience broke into applause at "a scene showing a reluctant German medical officer being forced by an American M.P. to enter a woodshed where bodies of slave laborers at Ohrdruf were stacked like cordwood."[37]

The majority of viewers concluded that the German people needed to be punished. One discordant voice was that of Pastor E. H. Dickbernd: "They will not affect persons who are already aware of the horrors of Europe, but they may drive others into the wrong camp—the uncritical haters. However, I was gratified to hear the audience applaud when the German officer was forced to go into the shed and see the prison dead. I feel that we Americans are arriving at a more intellectual appraisal of the facts, and are outgrowing the first emotional reactions."[38] In comparison, German filmmaker Billy Wilder, who had immigrated to the United States after 1933, was in charge during his return to Berlin in 1945 of rescripting the shoot for the first film about the Nazi camps made specifically for Germans, *Die Todesmühlen* (*The Death Mills*, dir. Hanus Burger, 1945). Philippe Despoix recounts, "Arriving first in Hamburg, [Wilder] arranges for previews of the projected film in order to test its effect on the German people. In essence, he turns this Hollywood practice into a veritable ethnographic investigation. The reaction to the part about the camps added to the traditional program is unequivocal: the vast majority of the German audience leaves the movie theater in a state of shock, without filling out the questionnaire distributed. Wilder commits the experience to memory in the form of an anecdote: 'Not one form filled out, but every pencil stolen!' "[39]

Like the Americans and the French, the British also organized showings of films on the "Nazi atrocities" in German movie theaters. On May 29, 1945, military commanders decided that the little Westphalia town of Burgsteinfurt would get a week-long history lesson by film on what had gone on in Berlin and at Buchenwald.[40] Since almost no one came to the first showings, it was decided the next day to make them obligatory. A military cameraman, Sgt. Charles Stiggins, followed people to the movie house, capturing how they looked before and after the screening. Commentary on the principal shots was written by the reporter himself (Figures 7–10).

Signal Corps cameramen also filmed the reactions of Germans confronted with the first reports given by the Allies. Thus on May 20, 1945, camera operator Morris J. Ratick of the 163rd Photo Signal Detachment was in Munich, where he jotted down what he saw on a note sheet accompanying his footage: "At the Feldherrnhalle on Odeon Platz, an exhibit of photographs taken in a camp of atrocities and asking the question, 'Who is to blame?' Civilians see the truth. On a wall, a German wrote that he was ashamed to be German. Above, he put the names of the worst atrocity camps (three camps). Many civilians were stunned, appearing not to know anything about this. Directly in front of the Portico, 16 Nazis were killed by the Bavarian police on November 9, 1923. The story goes that Hitler was hidden behind one of the statues and thus escaped death."[41]

The Tone of the Archives

It was not only difficult to depict the experience of deportation in front of the Allied forces' cameras. Those among the survivors who were led to testify in a pretrial setting also ran the risk of seeing their person "disappear behind the few facts whose 'truth' it was a matter of reconstructing."[42] In this initial footage, several gazes converge: those of the liberated deportees, their liberators, the eyewitness reporters, but also the torturers forced to view their victims and the local populations led inside the camp confines in order to (re)acknowledge their existence. Far from being univocal or merely frontal, the camera's eye captured the complex interplay of apprehending a reality that required the simultaneous presence of most of the protagonists to guarantee that it was true.

Jorge Semprún was one of the deportees present at Buchenwald when the Allies arrived. A few weeks after being liberated, in December 1945, he went to a movie theater in Locarno, Switzerland, for a matinee showing of John Ford's *The Long Voyage Home* (1940)—"a story of sailors on a long, rather rough passage," he recalls. However, instead of letting the movie sweep him along, he was plunged "almost in a daze. The images went by in a staccato rhythm, without much internal cohesion, despite their undeniable power. . . . It wasn't the film itself . . . that had put me in this stupor, of course. It was what had come first, the newsreel they had shown before the feature."[43] Without any forewarning, Semprún had found himself a spectator of film of the camp he had left a short time earlier: moreover it was not via one of the postwar documentaries made by Americans to be shown in Europe, but by way of a mere news magazine.

Few survivors have spoken of the effect produced by recognizing in cinematographic news the camp where they had been held. It took time and the mediation of producing a literary work for Semprún to be able to evoke in the form of a reconstruction the competition that could be played out between personal memory and cinematographic representation:

Until that winter's day—somewhat by chance, much more through a spontaneous strategy of self-defense—I'd managed to avoid filmed images of the Nazi camps. I had the ones in my memory, images that sometimes burst forth cruelly into my consciousness. Images I could also summon deliberately, even giving them a more or less structured form, organizing them into a course of anamnesis, a kind of narrative or intimate exorcism. That's exactly what they were: intimate images. Memories that to me were as consubstantial, as natural (despite their unbearable element) as those of my childhood. Or those of happy adolescent initiations of all kinds: into friendship, reading, the beauty of women.

All of a sudden, though, in the silence of that movie theater in Locarno, where whispers and murmurs died away into a rigid silence of horror and compassion (and disgust, probably), these intimate images became foreign to me, objectified up on the screen. They also broke free of my personal procedures of memory and censorship. They ceased being my property and my torment, the deadly riches of my life. They were, finally, nothing more than the externalized, radical reality of Evil: its chilling yet searing reflection.[44]

Semprún first considers these images as being outside himself. This was probably the impression he had upon seeing them for the first time. It seems that over time, they had come to prevail over his personal memory: "The gray, sometimes hazy images, filmed with the jerky motions of a handheld camera, acquired an inordinate and overwhelming dimension of reality that my memories themselves could not attain."[45] Indeed in this type of cinematographic account, the images were rarely framed the way Margaret Bourke-White's photographs were.[46] Not that there was no "staging" of the opening or liberation of the camps by the Allies (be it Western Allies or the Soviets), but for the person holding the camera it served first of all as protection. The act of holding it in one's hands, of entering the camp while filming, explains the jerky movements, which moreover usher in a method of filmmaking soon facilitated by the launching of the first lightweight 35 mm Cameflex camera in 1945.[47] Because camera operators were removed from what had taken place at the camp and, at the same time, confronted very closely with its terminal context, they were probably torn between assuming the proximity inevitably maintained with the living and the dead and the necessity of establishing some distance. Hence the feeling evoked by Semprún of perceiving an "exteriorized" reality, as refracted by "the eye of the camera," revealed almost impersonally and yet empathetically. As Jean Breschand rightly reminds us: "Filming is not watching what goes on via the camera's eyepiece. On the contrary, it is being present to what you are filming, being sensitive to the presence of the person filmed, being receptive to his breathing in a way that is instinctive and raw. The other is not behind a window; he is in the same space and in the same time as the filmmaker. . . . In all cases, the art or secret of direct filmmaking is to be attentive to the singularity of the moment, to its 'fracture,' as [French film critic André] Bazin says."[48]

What was captured on film was also caught in a "gray tonelessness" that was both that which the deportee had lived and the cameraman felt. For Semprún, this cold tonality of film no doubt helped make it an upsetting reality. Unlike recollections in memory, film would keep the texture of its contemporaneousness intact. Is this because Semprún, like most people of his generation, gradually got used to equating the gray and jerky character of the original filming with that related to the poor state of preservation of the physical medium of archives? The fact remains that today the war archives' major attribute of realism—and of the proximity that it can maintain with viewers—is not to be found in blacks and whites washed out by multiple copies, but rather in the particular rendering given by color.[49] It is true that shots recorded in color by German camera crews during the filming of Fritz Hippler's movie *Der Ewige Jude* (The Eternal Jew, 1940), accentuate the visibility of the distress and death of children left to themselves in the Warsaw Ghetto. Our attention is all the greater given that the cameraman purposely filmed these children in a manner to make German viewers believe the Jews abandoned them to die of starvation. Likewise the images recorded in 1942 at the execution by hanging of hostages in the suburbs of Belgrade make a very strong impression, as do those made by an American soldier in June 1944 in Saipan, in which one sees the corpses of Japanese soldiers who had attempted a suicide attack: blood and marks of strangulation and burning are much clearer than in black and white.[50]

These film images are sufficiently rare for their rediscovery to have constituted a minor event, hailed as offering an unofficial and more realistic view of the war. Since they did not emanate from any governmental authority and had not been elevated to the rank of historical archive, these bits of unusual amateur film were recently seen to be more capable of revivifying a much too faded past. The U.S. Army had not overlooked professional use of color film, however. In 1941 it was used for training films (learning camouflage techniques and the identification of weapons, sectors in which visual precision was indispensable).[51] Then a sort of division was made between films made in Europe (almost exclusively in black and white) and in the Pacific (often in color). However, the format of this film was not 35 but 16 mm. In 1935, when Kodak first introduced Kodachrome film, it was marketed as being for amateur cameras, and its use spread in conjunction with that of movie projectors that allowed for home viewing.[52]

How did people, be they amateurs or professionals, react to the increased clarity and ease of viewing that color afforded? In January 1942, when John Ford was put in charge of directing a movie about the Japanese attack on Pearl Harbor, he had just tried Technicolor for the first time, in *Drums Along the Mohawk* (1939). At first he tried to go about reconstructing the battle with models of boats and explosions filmed in color (Figure 11). In Washington, D.C., the effect was deemed too flashy, and Ford had to start over from scratch in black and white.[53] Asked later about the difference between black and white and color, he answered:

> [Color] is much easier than black and white for the cameraman; it's a cinch to work in, if you've any eye at all for color or composition. But black and white is pretty tough—you've got to know your job and be very careful to lay your shadows properly and get the perspective right. In color—there it is; but it can go awfully wrong and throw a picture off. There are certain pictures, like *The Quiet Man* [1952], that call for color—not a blatant kind—but a soft, misty color. For a good dramatic story, though, I much prefer to work in black and white; you'll probably say I'm old-fashioned, but black and white is real photography.[54]

The use of black and white cannot thus be considered a default choice. Lawrence Douglas says that the U.S. Army, "fearing that the three-track projectors necessary for showing Technicolor films would be unavailable in courtrooms and movie houses, decided to rely exclusively on monochrome for its documentaries, a decision that proved instrumental in shaping persistent cultural images of the Holocaust as an event that unfolded in black and white."[55] As McKahan astutely explains, the technical argument would be pertinent were it not implicitly tied to the supposition that color represents aesthetic progress with respect to black and white: "Color footage may modify the visual memory of the Holocaust. However, any study of archival color Holocaust footage must take into account the extent to which producers, critics and consumers participate in a technological and presentist discourse that comprehends color footage as 'progress' towards a medium of representing the Holocaust 'more realistically' than black-and-white."[56]

A few days before the end of the war, the camera crew in the Army Pictorial Service that had developed a technique for long-distance transmission of color stills succeeded in sending the shot showing Truman, Clement Attlee, and Stalin at the Potsdam conference to the United States in twenty-one minutes (seven for each of the three colors). But it was not this technical feat that would earn them recognition for their professionalism. In 1944 nearly 50 percent of the Signal Corps photographs appeared in the press and commercial publications. A year later President Truman chose a photographer from the Signal Corps to do his official portrait, in black and white.[57]

The example that best embodies the successful color-amateur combination is doubtless the 1944 movie *D Day to Berlin*, put together from footage shot by the famous director George Stevens. But to my mind this example comes from an entirely different situation. In 1944 Stevens was put in charge of U.S. film shot in Nazi concentration camps.[58] He took along a 16 mm color camera for strictly personal use. He took impromptu footage throughout his unit's advance, from the Normandy landing to its arrival in Berlin. Once he was back in the United States, he put these films away in his attic like souvenirs, rarely if ever to be looked at again.[59] Stored under good conditions, these fourteen 16 mm reels maintained their incredibly crisp colors; since it was reversal film, there were no generations of copies between the negative and the positive print. Strictly speaking, these are amateur films, but shot by a great professional. Confined neither to his role as team leader nor to that of cameraman on assignment, Stevens did not have to compose sequences ready to be edited and turned into "subjects." Hence the impression of time suspended, with the camera dwelling on the simple facts of the soldiers' everyday life yet still changing registers when the unit experienced exceptional events. Such was the case during the arrival in Paris (an unforgettable moment, often reused in documentary montages, including by Marcel Ophuls in 1991's *November Days*) and during the "detour" via Dachau and Buchenwald. Famed French film critic Serge Daney wrote in 1992, "What I understand today is that the beauty of Stevens' film is not so much having found just the right distance as it is the *innocence* of the gaze. Accuracy is the burden of he who comes 'afterwards'; innocence, the terrible grace given to the first one on the scene—to the first who simply goes through the motions of filmmaking."[60]

One of the interesting aspects of these images stems from their complementarity with those filmed in 35 mm black and white by Stevens's team. These latter works were dictated by the need to provide the most accurate account possible of the size of the camp, its functioning, the number of deportees still there in 1945, of the living and the dead. It did so by inscribing on film and in the narrative immediately composed the presence of the liberators, the search for those responsible, and the assembling of the local population to be shown the results of Nazi atrocities.

Figure 1. In *Fury* (1936), Fritz Lang films an imitation newsreel report of a mob attacking the jail in which an American everyman, "Joe Wilson," is being held for a kidnapping that he did not commit. A single camera is set up to record a static frontal shot. Photo taken on the set. Copyright MGM.

Figure 2. During the trial in *Fury*, the prosecution presents this footage as evidence of the crowd's intent to lynch Wilson. Additional close-ups make it possible to incriminate individually each of the defendants. Photo taken on the set. Copyright MGM.

3

Figures 3 and 4. This close-up of one of the assailants in *Fury* (3) corresponds to the line of sight from Wilson's cell, as the next shot—of the bars on his window—implies (4). The view of the assailants is thus subjective; the audience sees the witness's account that Joe would have provided had he participated in the trial. Photos taken on the set. Copyright MGM.

4

5

Figures 5 and 6. In *Fury* footage of the violence allows Lang to place at the very heart of the trial scene the lynch mob being confronted with its own image. Unable to bear images of her participation in the riot (5), "Sally Humphrey" in the courtroom (6) eventually faints. Copyright MGM.

6

Figures 7–10. Still frames and their captions from the film *Nazi Atrocities* screened in Germany in 1945: "The citizens of Burgsteinfurt head to the movie theater" (7); "Above the entrance, large signs announce the presentation, stating in German: 'Proof of atrocities in the concentration camps of Belsen and Buchenwald'" (8); the German audience sees the irrefutable evidence (9); and, "Visibly upset, civilians leave the movie theater after the showing" (10). The original caption provided by Sgt. Charles Stiggins for these scenes was "'The Village of Hate' sees the film of horror (Burgsteinfurt, May 10, 1945)." Copyright Imperial War Museum.

9

10

Figure 11. In charge of the U.S. Office of Strategic Services in 1941, Gen. William J. Donovan names John Ford to head the Field Photographic Branch, a team of professional photographers and filmmakers. Ford is first sent to Pearl Harbor in order to reconstruct the narrative of the Japanese attack of December 7, 1941. Field Photographic Branch, photo taken on the set of *December 7th*. Copyright National Archives and Records Administration.

Figure 12. On the eve of D-Day, Ford switched to the European theater of operations, as shown in this photo, taken in the company of Adm. Harold "Betty" Stark in London. Field Photographic Branch, 1944. Copyright National Archives and Records Administration.

Figure 13. American prosecutor Robert H. Jackson during his opening statement. Photo by Charles R. Alexander, 1945. Copyright National Archives and Records Administration.

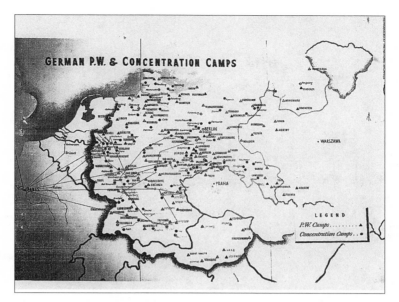

Figure 14. Directed by Ray Kellogg in 1945, *Nazi Concentration Camps* begins with a map and a legend: "German P. W. [Prisoner of War] & Concentration Camps." Prepared by the Field Photographic Branch, it is accompanied by a handwritten document, annotated with corrections, which serves to establish the initial thread of the film's commentary. 1945, photocopy. Copyright National Archives and Records Administration.

narration over map.

These are the locations of the largest Concentration and prison camps maintained throughout Germany and Occupied Europe under the Nazi Regime.

~~The following~~

This film report, covering a representative group of such camps, illustrates of the general conditions which prevailed.

Plug for National Biscuit Co.

Heaving chest

Montrose

Culva – Bulva

A custom obscure + unsavory

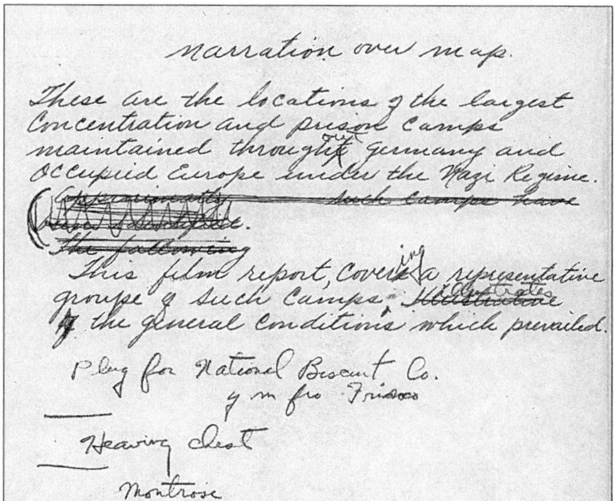

Figure 15. In this detailed view of a draft of the film's commentary, we see that a sentence—"There are approximate identifications for these camps"—has been eliminated, thus suppressing mention of Belsen. Copyright National Archives and Records Administration.

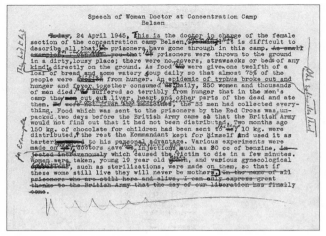

Speech of Woman Doctor at Concentration Camp
Belsen

Today, 24 April 1945, This is the doctor in charge of the female
section of the concentration camp Belsen. Gentlemen, it is difficult to
describe all that we prisoners have gone through in this camp. As small
examples I can tell you that the prisoners were thrown to the ground
in a dirty, lousy place; there were no covers, strawsacks or beds of any
kind, directly on the ground. As food we were given one twelfth of a
loaf of bread and some watery soup daily so that almost 75% of the
people were dieing from hunger. An epidemic of typhus broke out and
hunger and fever together consumed us daily, 250 women and thousands
of men died. We suffered so terribly from hunger that in the men's
camp they men cut, eat liver, heart and other parts of the dead and ate
them. We were not given any medicines; the SS men had collected everything. Food which was sent to the prisoners by the Red Cross was un-
packed two days before the British Army came so that the British Army
would not find out that it had not been distributed. Two months ago
150 kg. of chocolate for children had been sent to only 10 kg. were
distributed, the rest the Kommandant kept for himself and used it as
barter to his personal advantage. Various experiments were
made on us, doctors gave injections, such as 20 cc of benzine, in-
jected intravenously which caused the victim to die in a few minutes.
Women were taken, young 19 year old which, and various gynecological
experiments, such as sterilizations, were made on them, so that if
these women still live they will never be mothers. In the name of all
prisoners who are still here and alive, I can only express great
thanks to the British Army that the day of our liberation has finally
come.

16

17

18

Figures 16–18. On April 24, 1945, the British chose to have a woman doctor provide eyewitness testimony on camera concerning the living conditions endured by the deportees of the Bergen-Belsen camp. In order to insert this account into *Nazi Concentration Camps* (1945), the doctor's words were transcribed and then edited to condense them. The result produced an impersonal, abstracted text, as this annotated typed Field Photographic Branch document attests (16). The two accompanying still frames were taken on the set. In the first, just before the doctor received the "clap" announcing the beginning of the filmed interview, she is smiling and relaxed (17). Once the interview was under way, however, the contrast is striking between her and the women assembled behind, the latter being quite thin and visibly uncomfortable (18) with their spokesperson. Copyright National Archives and Records Administration.

Figures 19–21. In order to attest to the veracity of the images they were filming, the Signal Corps camera operators often placed American soldiers in the frame, as demonstrated by these three shots documenting deportee corpses at Buchenwald. Still frames from *Nazi Concentration Camps*, 1945. Copyright National Archives and Records Administration.

19

20

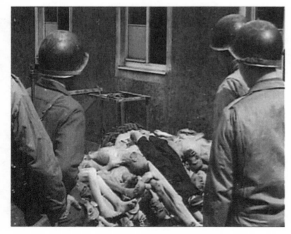

21

Figure 22. The city of Nuremberg was in ruins when the Allies chose it as the site for the IMT. As this aerial view shows, however, the Hall of Justice itself had not been damaged. It presented the additional advantage of having a prison adjacent to it. Anonymous photo, 1945. Copyright National Archives and Records Administration.

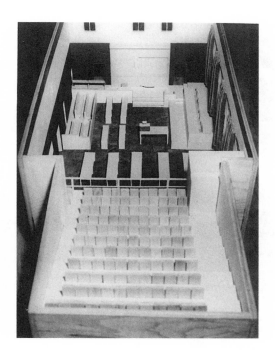

Figure 23. As we see in this scaled model designed by American architect Dan Kiley for his renovation of the Nuremberg Hall of Justice, the screen occupies the central position in the room, marking the symbolic line separating the Court and the accused. Field Photographic Branch, 1945. Copyright Imperial War Museum, London.

Figure 24. In Kiley's completed version of the IMT courtroom (shown here in session), the movie screen does indeed occupy the symbolic axis separating Court and accused. Field Photographic Branch, 1945. Copyright National Archives and Records Administration.

Figure 25. During this first-ever filmed trial, the sound technician (Ralph Lovell) and camera operator (Julian Blakely) had to work as discreetly as possible. Photo by Ray D'Addario, March 20, 1946. Copyright National Archives and Records Administration.

Figure 26. The movie screen was installed very early on during the Nuremberg courthouse renovations. Photo by Charles R. Alexander, 1945. Copyright National Archives and Records Administration.

Figure 27. Fritz Lang's *Fury* had already shown how the in-session screening of filmic evidence entirely reorganizes the ordinary functioning of the judicial floor plan. However, in this instance, the judge—the only spectator placed in the perfect line of sight for the viewing—remains in the center of the courtroom. Lang hung a large white canvas behind him, a sort of replica of the screen toward which the audience would alternatively turn. Photo taken on the set, 1936. Copyright MGM.

Figure 28. In the Nuremberg courtroom on November 28, 1945, the day before the in-court projection of these film documents, John Ford's team decided to install a row of neon lights above the defendants so that the latter's facial expressions would be visible during the screening. Anonymous photo, 1945. Copyright Imperial War Museum, London.

Figure 29. Psychologist Capt. G. M. Gilbert (shown here with some of the accused) interviewed Nazi authorities during the trial and recorded their remarks in writing. Anonymous photo, 1945. Copyright National Archives and Records Administration.

PART II

The Stakes of the International
Military Tribunal
(Nuremberg, 1945–1946)

CHAPTER 5

"Establishing Incredible Events by Means of Credible Evidence"

In the United States the showing in April 1945 of the first footage of concentration camps made Congress increasingly agitated by "the lack of authoritative information about the government war crime plans."[1] In part to respond to this expectation, President Truman issued an order on May 2 giving Justice Robert H. Jackson the responsibility in "preparing and prosecuting charges of atrocities and war crimes against such of the leaders . . . as the United States may agree with any of the UN [member countries] to bring to trial before an international tribunal."[2] Jackson, who was close to the Democrats and particularly to Roosevelt, had been named attorney general in January 1940, then associate justice to the Supreme Court in July 1941.[3] He had shown interest on several occasions in putting Nazi war criminals on trial. In a speech delivered to the Inter-American Bar Association in Havana in 1941, he denounced as violations of international law the Axis powers' "wars of aggression." But the central question focused on the judicial body that could, when the time came, indict those responsible for these acts.[4]

Jackson was aware that American judicial authorities were not very keen on the notion of an international justice system. In 1919, however, President Woodrow Wilson had spoken of "the passion for justice" that was then emerging "throughout the world," readily explaining that "this enthusiastic aspiration for just solutions would turn into cynical skepticism if people thought we were remiss in following the rules of justice that we ourselves had set forth."[5] During the thirty-ninth annual meeting of the American Society of International Law, Jackson had spoken in defense of the first Permanent Court of International Justice, the creation of which had been set

forth in Article 14 of the Pact of the League of Nations. He felt legal experts
had not fully appreciated the few but important actions undertaken by the
Court. However, he warned, "We must not use the forms of judicial proceedings to carry out or rationalize previously settled political or military
policy. Farcical judicial trials conducted by us will destroy confidence in the
judicial process as quickly as those conducted by any other people."[6] Pursuing this line of reasoning, Jackson concluded that there could be no truly
international justice without its being possible, where necessary, to take legal action against any of the countries that had agreed to its very principle:
"We cannot successfully cooperate with the rest of the world in establishing
a reign of law unless we are prepared to have that law sometimes operate
against what would be our national advantage."[7]

Justice Jackson's first concern was not to fall back into the errant ways
of the Leipzig trials held after World War I in the Reich's High Court.[8] As
he would explain explicitly in his opening statement at the trial, "Either
the victors must judge the vanquished or we must leave the defeated to
judge themselves. After the First World War, we learned the futility of
the latter course. . . . We must never forget that the record on which we
judge these defendants today is the record on which history will judge us
tomorrow."[9]

At the time, the French and Belgians had taken it upon themselves to
conduct trials in absentia in military courts, with more than 1,200 Germans
declared guilty by late 1924.[10] Between 1939 and 1945 the attitude of the Allies engaged in combat against the Axis forces seemed early on to be driven
by a common desire to punish those responsible for the crimes and atrocities committed. And yet the choice of a judicial (rather than extrajudicial)
solution was slow to materialize. Certainly, even before entering the war, at
the signing of the Atlantic Charter, the Americans had agreed with the British to put Hitler and the principal Nazi leaders on trial for their crimes when
the time came. This was thus already established as one of the war's objectives. But, for different reasons and due to the intense sacrifices made for the
war effort and its cost in human lives, the Soviets and the British favored
summary execution of major Nazi criminals over judicial prosecution.

In the United States the choice to take the judicial path was set by two
officers, Colonels Murray Bernays and William Chanler. They proposed
devising a specific procedure for judging Nazi officials, basing indictment
on the illegality of the war of aggression and the demonstration of a conspiracy.[11] Roosevelt's death occurred just as his special envoy to Europe, Judge

Samuel Rosenman, was trying to win over support for the judicial approach. President Truman quickly took on the issue with the same determination. Within six months, continuing on the path laid out by the group of experts to which he belonged and which had been put in place by Secretary of War Henry L. Stimson, Jackson therefore had to convince the British and the Soviets of the necessity of putting together the IMT, even though the war was barely ending in Europe and continued on in Asia.[12] He also insisted on the need to free the future international court of overly direct political or military control by the victors. Jackson did, however, have to compromise with the U.S. military in Europe and respond to criticism from those in Washington who felt it was not the place of a Supreme Court justice to lead such a mission. In order to hold a fair trial, the quality of the search for and presentation of documentary evidence against the accused was going to be paramount.

Competing War Crimes Investigations

Quickly assembling his team, Jackson enlisted the services of the former Office of Coordination of Information, created in 1941, which had become the Office of Strategic Services (OSS) in 1942.[13] Under the influence of its head, Col. William J. Donovan, the Field Photographic Branch (FPB) run by John Ford had been added to the OSS. A few weeks before Pearl Harbor, Ford was called back to active duty and named to command the Navy's 11th Photographic Section. He would go on to produce and sometimes direct wartime news coverage and documentaries which would earn him not only recognition from political and military authorities, but honors from Hollywood.[14]

In the bimonthly reports of the OSS, under the heading "War Crimes," the question of gathering written and audiovisual evidence regularly came up. Several organizations were successively or simultaneously in charge of this work: the United Nations War Crimes Commission (UNWCC); the office in charge of "War Crimes" in the U.S. War Department (United States War Crimes Office, USWCO), connected with the judge advocate general; and, based on the same model, the OSS's own War Crimes Office.

The UNWCC, composed of fourteen nations, was created at a meeting at the Foreign Office in London in October 1943. Its mission was to investigate Nazi atrocities by collecting information and evidence that would allow them to be proven in a court of law. In the early stage of its activities, the

Commission was confronted with the difficulty of intervening in countries still under German occupation, with the danger of eventual retaliation if the people responsible for the crimes were arrested. After the Nazi capitulation, national offices connected to the Commission but acting within the framework of the liberated countries' regained sovereignty drew up their own policies of investigation. The reports thus drafted had then to be submitted for approval by the Commission. Within the confines of the information at its disposal, the Commission took pains to ensure the respect for impartiality and the seriousness of the task performed in order to establish official lists of persons accused of crimes and to transmit the former to each country's military authorities so that the requisite arrests could be made.

There was also the question of which courts were going to be declared qualified to try persons acknowledged as guilty. On May 6, during a session of the Commission over which he presided, Robert Alderson Wright, Lord Wright of Durley, emphasized the difference in nature between concentration camps and extermination camps. Concerning the latter, he stated, "There is no precedent in history for these atrocities and if there is no international law which covers these dreadful acts, it is up to us to make one. I, personally, am quite convinced that the existing international law, the customary law of nations, is quite sufficient."[15] Jackson did not disagree with this position, but whether it be the UNWCC, the USWCO, or even the OSS, the American judge's assessment of the results of their work was harsh: "It is plain that our case will have to be built from the ground up, that despite the large talk there has been little done to really dig out evidence, which makes our task a more difficult one but nonetheless challenging."[16]

By April 27 the War Department had given the Signal Corps precise instructions to make the audiovisual coverage of "liberated prisoners of war and concentration camps" its top priority, and then to see to it that the footage, duly accompanied by an affidavit certifying its authenticity, get to London and be made available to the USWCO and the judge advocate general.[17] The USWCO contacted John Ford and the FPB unit to discuss the possibility of their participation in the audiovisual recording of the war crimes trials (Figure 12). It appears that the army wanted exclusive coverage of the liberation of the camps and of the ensuing initial interrogations. But following Jackson's intervention, it was decided to give the OSS priority in collecting audiovisual evidence of war crimes: "This involves not only atrocities themselves, but the larger picture of conspiracy by the Nazis to dominate first Germany, then Europe, then the world."[18] On June 9 the FPB joined

forces with the Office of War Information (OWI, which, as a civilian organization, would be made responsible for the de-Nazification of Germany) to
get some benefit from the work the Film Division had just carried out in editing eight reels of film from footage that had been censored by the Supreme
Headquarters Allied Expeditionary Force.[19] These turf wars between the
Signal Corps, the OWI, and the FPB would intensify after the summer and
culminate with the question of who would be in charge of distributing and
showing the Nuremberg trial films.

Even though Jackson was critical of all three of these organizations, it
was easier for him to turn to the OSS to line up the search for evidence with
the main counts of the future trial and to best manage the recovery of information. He felt, in fact, that military intelligence had shown "woeful inade-
quacy" in postwar preparation for trying Nazi war criminals.[20] Cognizant
of the confusion that might exist between the different authorities dealing
with war crimes, the OSS prepared a note specifying the responsibilities for
each of them. It was pointed out that the UNWCC was not a tribunal; it
could neither prosecute nor judge war criminals, these latter functions being the domain of civil, military, or international jurisdictions.[21]

On June 1 Jackson was received by Truman and presented him with a
progress report on the mission the president had given him. This document
was then made public on June 7. The reasons and motives that were to prevail at the constitution of the IMT were expressed this way:

> The groundwork of our case must be factually authentic and consti-
> tute a well-documented history of what we are convinced was a grand,
> concerted pattern to incite and commit the aggressions and barbari-
> ties which have shocked the world. We must not forget that when the
> Nazi plans were boldly proclaimed they were so extravagant that the
> world refused to take them seriously. Unless we write the record of
> this movement with clarity and precision, we cannot blame the fu-
> ture if in days of peace it finds incredible the accusatory generalities
> uttered during the war. We must establish incredible events by cred-
> ible evidence.[22]

This last remark bears emphasizing: finding *credible* evidence to establish *incredible* events. Jackson worried about the future trial's power to educate and whether it would have a lasting impact. Once peace had returned,
how could you keep the "general accusations voiced during the war" alive in

collective memory? Let us note that there is no allusion here to the edifying value of witness testimony but to the "facts," which it is not only a question of uncovering but of establishing through judicial work. The IMT could not operate like an ordinary court.[23] In addition to the factuality, authenticity, and veracity of the documents that were to be part of the prosecution's case, they needed to take into account their "credibility," that is to say, the assurance that their probative capacity would be affirmed as much in the "internal" phase of the investigation as in the necessarily public phase of the hearing. The proceedings would employ inquisitorial procedure—"We accept the duty of proving the criminal acts and the responsibility of these defendants," Jackson explained in his opening statement—but it would also apply accusatorial procedure: in keeping with common law tradition, the courtroom would be considered a workshop or a "workroom" (to borrow Antoine Garapon's notion), where sources would come into play *de vivo* (to use Luigi Ferrajoli's phrase).[24] Given the considerable mass of written documents assembled, the presence of films would certainly be a major event; if the "incredible" could be visibly demonstrated, then the "injustice" of the Nazi atrocities would not be irreconcilable with a chain of legal and then historical discourse.

June 12, 1945, would prove to be a telling day with respect to Jackson's method and will to prepare the IMT to take these "atrocities" into account. That morning he received representatives from Jewish organizations, and by the afternoon he had assigned John Ford the job of finding the film evidence.

Justice Jackson and the Jewish Organizations

At 10 a.m. Jackson met with Judge Nathan D. Perlman, Alexander Kohanski, and Jacob Robinson, all three of them appointed by the American Jewish Congress (AJC) and the World Jewish Congress (WJC). The meeting had been preceded by letters exchanged throughout the month of May. Jackson first received a letter from Perlman, and, as soon as he was nominated to the IMT, he answered it on May 5 by proposing to the AJC and the WJC that they send him the archives in their possession. He made a second request that same day, specifying, however, "What we need against the top Nazis is evidence of the general pattern of conduct more than of specific instances of brutality." Perlman confirmed to him, "The data in our possession go exactly to the point you mention in your letter: —the general pattern of conduct, proving the concerted action, the criminal conspiracy of the top leaders. We shall be glad to submit our data to you."[25] The initiatives taken by Jackson anticipated recommendations issued by the Department of War and were laid out in the "Memorandum on Trial Preparation of 16 May 1945," which delineated procedures for contacting religious organizations, in particular Jewish ones, in search of evidence of war crimes.[26]

After congratulating Jackson on the report he had submitted to President Truman at the beginning of the month, Perlman, Kohanski, and Robinson presented their view of the fate the Nazis had wrought upon the Jews of Europe. They asserted first that the Jewish people were "the greatest victim of the war." They readily recognized that in absolute numbers more people had died in the Soviet Union. However, the Jews had not been killed by acts of war but as a result of a deliberate and meticulously implemented decision to persecute them. The example of the Armenians massacred by the Turks was brought up as a historical reference, not so much to establish a comparison between the two genocides as to warn of the dangers of an inadequate judicial response. The injustice of the lack of sanctions against Turkish authorities had led to a wave of terrorist attacks across Europe; this precedent, argued the three Jewish representatives, should serve as a warning. The delegation then explained that the desire to obtain specific consideration of crimes committed against the Jews in the indictment of Nazi war criminals was not motivated by vengeance or even the hope of redress proportionate to the losses suffered. The Tribunal needed to cast light on this policy so that these crimes would be made known to the general public and never again occur. Moreover, even though two-thirds of the Jews of Europe had been exterminated, those who survived must not suffer again the torments of an anti-Semitism encouraged far and wide by the Nazis. The delegation therefore asked to be represented in the form of an amicus curiae at the trial and, more immediately, as part of Jackson's team. Being associated with the preparation of the IMT would facilitate access to the general archives of the Reich the United States and Britain were going to collect to build the prosecution.

In his responses and observations, Jackson started off by asking for an evaluation of the total number of Jewish victims, which the delegation quickly set about to provide him. The figure of five to six million was put forth. To the question of how this number had been determined, Robinson answered that it was the result of official estimates of Jewish populations established in 1933, 1939, and 1945 in European countries that suffered Nazi domination. The wartime and postwar figures had been compared thanks to available information on the number of Jews still alive in 1945. But, as the three Jewish leaders stressed, far from overestimating the number of the deceased, "We record the lowest possible figures in the faint hope that more survivors may show up as conditions in Europe become stabilized. And our hand trembles even in writing these lower estimates."[27]

On the question of the specificity of the acts of violence inflicted on the Jews, Jackson responded that he intended to build the trial around the general Nazi plot for triggering the war and committing a certain number of crimes, among them those that targeted the Jews.[28] With respect to this, those who were talking with Jackson had themselves used the expression "Nazi plot" to characterize the Third Reich's overall project and to emphasize that it was directed not only against the Jews subject to their condemnation but also against civilization and democracy as a whole. At the same time, Jackson also insisted on the possibility of incriminating both groups and individuals recognized as guilty of having participated in one way or another in these crimes, unless they could prove they had acted under duress. The request for an amicus curiae did not seem acceptable to him, considering that approving it could lead to similar demands from other groups. Finally, as for allowing Jewish representatives to be part of the team preparing the trial, Jackson preferred to enlist their help for documentary assistance, namely for judicial expertise on legal conditions, including those pertaining to German law, that would allow them to proceed to indictments for crimes committed against Jews.

A table summarizing Jewish population statistics was submitted to Jackson and discussed at a meeting of representatives of the British Ministry of War and the American team (based in London at the time). The chart had been drawn up by the Institute of Jewish Affairs (IJA) headed by Robinson and on whose advisory board Perlman sat. Created in February 1941 under the leadership of the WJC and the AJC, the New York–based IJA sought as its mission "to analyze fundamental aspects of Jewish life since the first World War in order to establish the facts of the present situation and to formulate the basis on which Jewish rights and freedom may be secured in a general post-war reconstruction." In November 1941 the IJA published an initial report on the subject of the situation of the Jews in Europe.[29] On all points considered—the declining number of Jews in Europe, the deterioration of health conditions, the uprooting of old communities, the spoliation of property, the religious discrimination, the psychological distress—the findings were very pessimistic. However, four reasons for hope in a better future were presented: the belief that Hitler's fall from power could be imminent; the notion that the generally tolerant attitude of national populations in countries where the Nazis had imposed their rule would prevail over the spread of anti-Semitic hatred; the idea that the fate of the Jews could not be separated from that of all of Europe and of civilized humanity; and the desire to take up arms in self-defense alongside those fighting Nazi Germany. Three months later another booklet presented the IJA's aims and methods, with its leadership team meeting regularly from then on in order to assemble information on the situation of the Jews in Europe.[30] Prof. Jerome Michael, in a piece entitled "The Jews Have an Added Problem," emphasized that the Jews "are not only exposed to the hazards to which other people are exposed but to a special set of hazards arising out of the Nazis' determination to exterminate them, if possible."[31] Then came the brutal moment of tallying up, country by country, the results of the Nazi policy of extermination: in 1943 the IJA published a work coordinated by Boris Shub, *Hitler's Ten Years War on the Jews*. The figure of five million victims was put forth. In the introduction, Robinson writes, "The full story of what happened to European Jewry under Hitler and the rule of the Axis cannot be told at this time. Some of its most terrible pages are still being written, from day to day, wherever the power of the Axis has not been broken. An interim balance is possible, however, of the effects of Hitler's war against the Jewish people since January 1933, and more especially since September 1, 1939, when his armies invaded Poland."[32]

At the close of the June 25 meeting, and with the announcement of five million Jewish victims, the British proposed that the tallied results of the concentration camps be presented as exhibits at the trial. However, the evidence would comprise first and foremost testimony by the Allied armies who liberated the camps. Jackson felt that the IJA's estimates were certainly "dramatic but they were not authenticated and could not be used as evidence."[33] Justice Jackson proposed that they be examined by a statistics expert from London. The IJA, however, had already submitted the document to Sheldon Glueck, a renowned professor of criminology at Harvard University.[34] Starting in the early 1940s, the scholar had thought about the proper judicial means to use for punishing those responsible for war crimes, and he had donned the historian's mantle to remind the UN that the errors of 1918 must not be repeated.[35] What is in fact remarkable in these studies by the

IJA is their quasi-scientific—or, at the very least, highly nonpolemical—desire to show immediately the scale and gravity of the policy of extermination led by the Nazis against the Jews, based on documentary sources gathered in Europe by local correspondents.[36]

The statistical table established in 1945 was corrected and honed throughout August.[37] Despite everything, the man in charge of setting up the IMT favored prudence. Keeping the Jewish organizations at arm's length must first be understood as Jackson's desire to remain in control of the investigation prior to the trial and of the definition of the principal charges to be filed. However, the pressures put on him by the WJC and the AJC were in no way contradictory to the logic of conspiracy charges, as the letters exchanged show; there was not, at least not in the minds of the Jewish figures with whom he was in contact, any calling into question of the deliberate plan linking specific mass crime to their general aggression.[38] Nevertheless Donald Bloxham thinks that the preeminence given to the notion of conspiracy led Jackson to a distortion in the representation of Nazi crimes: "The American jurists created a distorted representation of Nazi crimes by the very act of trying to standardize the prosecution of an unevenly distributed cruelty. Over and above this, they also diminished the real, specific crimes by attempting to cram them into the space left after the consideration of the theory of aggressive war within the broad and imaginary conspiracy framework."[39] The criticism certainly merits discussion if it is referring to how the trial was conducted, but it does not seem founded if aimed at pretrial reflections. At the very least, the overall picture must be considered from three angles: Jackson's personal feelings about the situation of the Jews; the general policy of the United States since 1938; and the intellectual construction of the IMT.

Less than two weeks after the pogroms organized by the Nazis in 1938, the League of American Writers sent a letter to a number of well-known people to ask that they speak out on anti-Semitism in the United States. The question was asked as follows: "What do you know about anti-Semitism in this country? What would you do to stop it if you were chosen to lay down a program? . . . The Twentieth Century which opened with the promise of light, threatens to close in great darkness. Flames may again climb about the victims at the stake. So dreadful is the danger that we feel privileged to make this claim upon your time. Speed is essential, for the wave of revulsion sweeping the country against the new Nazi excesses will result in the formulation of a new national policy."[40]

Having been contacted, Jackson answered on December 12, "I abhor anti-Semitism, as does every straight-thinking person." He adds that he trusts three influences to save America from this blight: respect for the rights of all minorities (which he sees as a core component of American society); the American nation's spirit of tolerance as a shield against any idea of persecution (despite the existence of alien and sedition laws, groups like the Ku Klux Klan, and "Red" hunts); and the ability, remarkably displayed by the Roosevelt administration, to correct social inequalities and the economic frustrations generated by the Depression (which Jackson credits with being responsible for a large part of the flare-up of anti-Semitism in the 1930s).[41] Part of these arguments reappears in a speech given at the National Conference on Palestine taking place in Washington, D.C., on January 15, 1939. Jackson says that "the plight of the Jews in the world today is a challenge to the Christian conscience to make good the promise of a National Jewish Home in Palestine."[42] Vaunting the merits of America's multiracial society— without much worrying about the plight of the Indians or the status of blacks—did not represent a very original stand. The defense of the Zionist project was more audacious, or at least less frequent, as Peter Novick reminds us.[43] The legitimacy of this claim was presented as being as much about religion (realizing the biblical prophecies of Isaac, Ezekiel, and Amos) as it was about politics (facilitating the emigration of Jews from Europe, a question made all the more urgent since the Évian Conference and the ongoing British preparation of a white paper setting very restrictive quotas).[44] Skirting the problem of dividing up Palestine between Jews and Arabs, Jackson extolled the eminent positions in American society held by Jewish jurists Louis D. Brandeis and Benjamin N. Cardozo and expressed the conviction that the establishment of a Jewish national homeland would in part draw inspiration from the democratic precepts that Brandeis and Cardozo had continually promoted in the United States.[45]

In the files he prepared for the indictment, Jackson had gathered a certain number of official documents stating American or international positions on the situation of European Jews. He had, for example, the two communiqués written by Roosevelt in which the president spoke of Nazi crimes. While on October 7, 1942, the victims are mentioned only as "civilian populations," the March 24, 1944, communiqué forefronts "the wholesale systematic murder of the Jews of Europe."[46] In the meantime, the manifesto launched on November 17, 1942, from London by the eleven Allied nations and the Gaullist resistance group Comité de la France Libre (Committee of the Free French) mentioned the deportation of tens of thousands of Jews from different countries in occupied Europe and denounced "in the strongest possible terms this bestial policy of cold-blooded extermination."[47] As for the Senate, a resolution dated March 18, 1943, solemnly called for a halt to and the imminent judgment of "atrocities inflicted upon the civilian population in Nazi-occupied countries, and especially the mass murder of Jewish men, women, and children."[48] Jackson also had in his possession an editorial from the *Washington Post*, which argued, "It is a mistake, perhaps, to call these killings 'atrocities.' An atrocity is a wanton brutality. There were unspeakable atrocities at Auschwitz and Birkenau. But the point about these killings is that they were systematic and purposeful. The gas chambers and furnaces were not improvisations, they were scientifically designed instruments for the extermination of an entire ethnic group. On the scale practiced by the Germans, this is something new. And it is this purpose which human beings find it difficult to believe or to understand."[49]

The *Post* cited Raphael Lemkin, whose recent book defined which crimes might be called "genocide."[50] Barely two days after Jackson assumed his post, Lemkin personally sent him another, more recent text on the same subject.[51] Of Polish origin, Lemkin had made a plea in Madrid in October 1933 during the Fifth Conference for the Unification of Penal Law to ask that new crimes be taken into account, such as "the actions of extermination directed against ethnic, religious or social groups regardless of the motives (political, religious, etc.)." Lemkin included in this category "the massacres, pogroms, and actions undertaken so as to ruin the economic existence of members of a group."[52] But it was not until 1944 that he qualified these crimes as "genocide" in connection with Hitler's "plan" to invade Eastern Europe and to annihilate the Jews.[53] Now, however, having joined Jackson's team on May 18, he was clearly anxious to see the word *genocide* appear in the bill of indictment. The British, as well as the Harvard University jurists consulted on this point, were basically against it, finding the word not very appropriate in regard to penal law.

It is clear that Jackson had at his disposal relatively precise firsthand sources for determining the numbers and scale—but not for understanding the genesis—of the policy of exterminating the Jews of Europe. At that time, most Americans imagined the number of people who died in the camps to be one million, with this figure including all victims, Jewish or not.[54] Nevertheless U.S. Chief of Counsel Jackson did not want to turn the trial into a "Jewish matter."[55] The judge stated, "The Jewish people felt almost a proprietary interest in the trials because they had been the chief victim of Hitler's atrocities. I tried to point out to them the very great damage they would do to their surviving people if they let this trial become a Jewish trial. I pointed out to them that what we must do was to get away from the racial aspects of the situation. We were prosecuting these Nazis not because they had killed Jews, but because they had killed men and women. We didn't want to exaggerate racial tensions."[56]

He mentions that certain representatives of Jewish organizations agreed with him, such as Joseph Proskauer of the AJC and Rabbi Stephen S. Wise of the WJC, who was close to Roosevelt. Chaim Weizmann, who presided over the World Zionist Organization (WZO), proposed that he choose someone to represent him (which Jackson refused) or that Weizmann himself appear as a witness during the trial (which Jackson accepted). At that moment in September, it seems that Jackson's team was ready to accept testimony at trial and presentation in court of estimates of the number of victims. Sydney S. Alderman writes, "We had a further discussion of the Jewish problem. The Justice thought that Weizmann would be better able to testify and would make a good witness, probably far better than anybody Joe Proskauer could turn up. The Justice and we all agreed that there was no reason why we could not use Weizmann's estimate as to the numbers of Jews destroyed. I suggested that the Germans would hardly put themselves in the position of arguing that they did not murder five million Jews, but only murdered four million."[57] Weizmann was considered by several Jewish organizations as being the best placed to speak at the IMT. A team made up of Robinson (IJA), two lawyers (from the WJC and Anglo-Jewish Association of London), and Lewis B. Namier, a history professor at Lancaster University (Jewish Agency), was created to help prepare Weizmann's testimony, estimated to last about three hours.

In Berlin on October 18, the day of the official opening of the IMT, Weizmann sent a letter to Jackson to ask for assurances about the conditions of his testimony. The WZO's director wrote of his fear that, in light of the aspect the Belsen trials had taken on, his court appearance as a Jewish witness would be greatly undermined unless all of the prosecutors (or, at the very least, the American and British ones) had approved it.[58] Jackson, who was in the process of leaving London for Nuremberg, did not learn of the letter until later and thus did not answer it until January 1946, when the trial had already started. Justice Jackson reaffirmed his choice of a trial in which the mass of documents would predominate. In his opinion, the persuasive power of the documents would be owed to the fact that there could be no doubt about their authenticity or the truth of their terrible content. It was not possible to claim that they were tainted by a desire for vengeance. Jackson believed that the future position of Jews in Europe depended on building the case in this manner rather than attempting to support it with testimony that would be vulnerable to attack.[59] In conclusion, Jackson stated, "I think that in the trial, which I conducted, the Germans found very little of that to complain about. On the other hand, we did use, in presentation of the case, at least one Jewish lawyer, because we thought it would be just as bad to let it appear that we were not willing to let any appear as it would be to let too many appear. We tried to steer a course that would cause no greater anti-Semitism that would eventually be taken out on a few surviving Jews in Europe."[60]

The priority shown by the U.S. chief of counsel was thus less the declaration of the identity of the principal victims of the Nazi policy of extermination (which, according to him, risked stirring up racial hatreds) than it was the organization of a judicial mechanism capable of subjecting the accused to viewing their crimes and fostering awareness outside the courtroom of the radical inhumanity of the acts they had ordered and/or carried out. Under this strategy, motion pictures were going to play a major role.

Putting Together a Trial-by-Documentary

On that same day (June 12), Jackson assigned one of his assistants, Cmdr. James B. Donovan, to send a memo to John Ford outlining the tasks the justice wanted completed by the FPB prior to the opening of the IMT.[61] Shortly thereafter Commander Donovan received travel papers drawn up by his immediate superior, Sydney S. Alderman. He was reminded in this document that specialists were hard at work pouring over German newsreels and films captured from the enemy. The FPB correspondents were performing the same tasks in London, Paris, and Germany.[62] Negotiations were additionally under way with the Soviets for easier access to their archives. Commander Donovan thus proposed six objectives for Ford's unit to accomplish:

a) To collect, evaluate, integrate and present all photographic evidence of war crimes, with such assistance from other Departments and agencies of the Government as may be required;

b) To make a one-reel short within the next 45 days, according to the plan approved by Justice Jackson;

c) To prepare for the filming of the international trial;

d) To prepare a documentary film, following the trial, concerning the entire prosecution;

e) To film the interrogation of certain prominent Nazis, per the Justice's directions;

f) Such other photographic projects as the Justice may approve.[63]

Budd Schulberg, the son of one of Hollywood's great scriptwriters, was in charge of film research.[64] With two members of the team, Joe Zigman and Karl Jacoby, he began by traveling to New York in order to consult the holdings at Fox Movietone News. On average, they watched six thousand meters of film per day. Within two weeks they put together a 20,000-meter rough cut, carefully recording reference notes and descriptions of each reel. Among the notable moments included were the speech by Hermann Göring (as Prussia's minister of the interior prior to the Nazis' rise to power) when he called for getting rid of all opposition, as well as Joseph Goebbels' morning address to the SA on the day that the first anti-Semitic act of violence was organized. Budd Schulberg focused on finding images having an explicit political character and, if possible, showing early on the programmatic intentions of the highest Nazi officials. Most of this news footage appeared only in reedited versions with supporting commentary from journalists of American broadcasting companies. To everyone's great surprise, it was discovered that Hearst Metronome News treated reports of the first anti-Semitic measures—the 1933 book burning and the last big gathering of the NSDAP before the Nazi rise to power—quite superficially, indeed even ironically. Clearly, in the early days, Nazi Germany had not been taken very seriously by some major media in America.[65] Unfortunately, when they finally did adopt a more vigilant attitude, there was a lack of subject matter, exportation of German newsreels having ceased in 1939. Though the American public was no longer able to view Nazi film footage, President Roosevelt and his administration nevertheless continued to be able to watch it thanks to the OSS, which every week delivered the *Deutsche Wochenschau* news journal via Switzerland, Portugal, or Spain, only one or two days after its release in Germany.

Among the other sources available were Nazi documentaries. Some had already been analyzed by the OSS Film Library Group, others were held by

MoMA, and still others had been picked up by the Alien Property Custodian, which had confiscated propaganda films (including *Triumph of the Will*, *The Poland Campaign*, and *Victory in the West*) shown in Yorkville and other German expatriate enclaves at the start of the war.

This initial work was followed up in July and August 1945 by locating film storage sites set up under the German Reich. Films needed to be found, analyzed, and annotated in conformity with an indictment that had not yet been formally drawn up by the team of lawyers brought together for this purpose. It is clear that one of the priorities was the discovery of images made in the camps by the Nazis themselves. In Ford's absence, Ray Kellogg, formerly of Twentieth Century Fox, was put in charge of directing operations. In Bayreuth he discovered the Wehrmacht's photographic library, containing millions of shots that John Bott, Stuart Schulberg, and a team of German translators began identifying at their Wiesbaden headquarters. The team then turned its attention to the Berlin region. In Rüdersdorf, fifty kilometers east of Berlin, they discovered a cache of films in an underground shelter dug into a granite quarry: "Burrowing down to the bottom we found some footage only partially destroyed that clearly indicated Nazi coverage of concentration camps. . . . We found a second film archive site in a salt mine at Grasleben, near the Belsen concentration camp. But here also the film was burned."[66]

The team grew concerned but took solace in thinking about the documents found in the United States. Commander Donovan then stepped in, among other things to see that the films presented at trial were in keeping with the indictment. The IMT had warned him that no documents brought from the United States could be admitted. Only films printed in Germany would constitute evidence. It would otherwise be too easy for the defense to maintain that the German subjects reshown in American news footage had been falsified, and the IMT did not want to waste time authenticating them. After a moment of dejection, the unit got back to work and in Babelsberg ended up finding the most complete film archives in Nazi Germany. Next they set up in Nuremberg to make themselves available to the IMT, taking on overall responsibility for the Documentary Evidence Section.

The films collected were going to be added to the evidence supporting the prosecution. In July 1945 Jackson went to Wiesbaden to see the initial results compiled by the teams he had set up. He consulted important written documents that had been found and participated in oral interviews concerning key figures involved in anti-Nazi actions. Allen Dulles arranged for him to meet Fabian von Schlabrendorff, legal counsel for the German army who had rebelled against his superiors; Hans Gisevius, one of the leaders of the July 20, 1944, attempt to assassinate Hitler; a Lutheran pastor arrested and persecuted by the Nazis; and Fritz Kolbe, a diplomatic courier in the German Ministry of Foreign Affairs who smuggled compromising documents to Switzerland.[67] Interrogated and cross-examined, these witnesses enabled investigators to track back to the source of certain important pieces of information. Jackson, however, considered their contributions to be a delicate matter. The recollections of some differed from those of others. Their point of view depended on the position they held in German society or on the network of connections they had built up. Their anti-Nazi involvement prevented them from being impartial, even though it guaranteed their credibility. In short, "Their stories, on their own admission of their activities, would be the self-serving statements of highly interested persons trying to vindicate their own past."[68] In opposition to these potential weaknesses, Jackson claimed an indisputable character for documents, whose informative value was supposedly unadulterated: "The documents, if their authenticity was established, then spoke for themselves."[69] All these reasons led him to opt for a trial wherein the mass of documents, not the mass of witnesses, would weigh the most heavily.

The superiority attributed by Jackson to the document may appear excessively positivistic, as well as oblivious to the constructed nature of any archive and the fact that some texts are merely the written transcription of accounts originally collected in oral form. But the jurist's argumentation is based less on an overestimation of the objectivity of the document than on its presumed power of conviction, in court, in an open debate where it is a matter of demonstrating at all times that the charge is well-founded and based on material evidence and not on the power and subjectivity of the victors.

The minimization of witness accounts also stems from the fact that, in the trial's preliminary investigation phase, numerous interrogations took place under military command, including for prisoners incarcerated at Nuremberg awaiting trial. Soon a conflict over jurisdiction pitted Jackson against the head of the OSS, William J. Donovan. Although named the International *Military* Tribunal, the judicial instance created by the Allies was not for military justice, as the first trials organized in the Reich had been.

Rather it was to serve civilian justice with a universal mission.[70] As already indicated, the U.S. chief of counsel chose early on to use the services of the OSS—and not those of the UNWCC, considered deficient—in the initial search for solid proof against Nazi officials.[71] In return, Maj. Gen. Donovan thought he would be able to influence how the upcoming trial would be conceived. In particular, it seemed to him that the presence of witnesses in the courtroom would be an important asset for sensitizing the press and thus, in turn, public opinion, by giving a human dimension to the proceedings. Jackson disagreed and pleaded his case directly with President Truman. The major general was furious and withdrew from the team. Beyond the clashes between individuals, the choice of what ratio to establish between documents and witnesses was discussed up until the very start of the trial, sparking broad debate on an essential question. Moreover the topic was continually rekindled in subsequent trials of a similar nature, from the one that brought Adolf Eichmann to court to those that sent Klaus Barbie, Paul Touvier, and Maurice Papon to appear before circuit courts.

In a memo addressed to Jackson on November 3, 1945, Telford Taylor very aptly suggests how to go about selecting and presenting evidence.[72] Most important, the selection of documents must be adapted to the particular point under discussion that day in court. However, with the trial expected to go on for months, "The type of proof used must also be selected with an eye to the course of the case as a whole, so that continuity is preserved and variety and interest maintained."[73] As to the roles of documents and witnesses, Taylor identifies two important factors. The first is of a practical nature and concerns problems of language: while it is possible to translate a document ahead of time and to distribute it to all parties involved before it is discussed, oral testimony cannot be translated until it is pronounced, and this in the always difficult conditions of simultaneous interpreting.[74] The second concerns the political significance of the Nazi officials on trial and the gravity of the actions for which they are blamed. In this respect, the atmosphere during Nuremberg court testimony risks being exceptionally tense: "Many witnesses will be under extreme emotional pressure and nervous tension, and their behavior will be unpredictable."[75] Taylor offers a nuanced conclusion, though. To his mind, it is not a question of deliberately limiting the number of witnesses called to the stand but of being certain of the necessity and relevance of their presence. As for the documents, unlike Jackson, he does not believe they constitute, in and of themselves, a model of objectivity and impartiality:

To be sure, the testimony of a witness is subject to attack, but so is the testimony of a document. A document cannot talk, and therefore cannot be cross-examined, but it can, of course, be attacked other ways—it can be explained away or contradicted by witnesses, by other documents, or by any other kind of evidence. There is, I believe, no more reason to attempt to try this case with documents alone than to try it with witnesses alone—either process would be like trying to box with one hand tied behind the back. We must pursue a flexible policy in this case of using the best and most telling evidence available, whether it be a witness, a document, a chart, etc. Any other approach will deprive us of one of the proceedings.[76]

Written a few days before the trial, these remarks complete and at the same time shed light on Jackson's reasons for justifying the "documentary" aim of the preliminary investigation and of the case in court. In the short run, Jackson was concerned with the ability of the Allies' legal system to make the IMT an equitable judicial body, offering the accused the right to defend themselves without giving them a platform for their propaganda. There was the chance that certain Nazi officials would find the means to justify their acts or, conversely, that ordinary citizens who had been victims of Nazi violence would fail to reproduce the incriminating force of their testimony sworn to previously in a less intimidating context. In this setting, written and audiovisual proof would constitute a trail of evidence emanating from Nazi power itself or originating in reports the Allies made in the aftermath of particular segments of the Nazi politics of aggression, which could be called voluntary eyewitness accounts.

However, exhibits presented by the prosecution at Nuremberg cannot be considered more objective than the eyewitness testimony deposed orally at the trial. For simple reasons of time, the search for documentary proof could not be an exhaustive one. Moreover it was carried out after the main counts of the indictment had been determined, thus conditioning the work of the archivists dispatched to Europe to conform to a predefined set of issues, which did not, nonetheless, preclude interest in information found by chance or on the advice of intermediaries brought in to help on site. We must also take into account the temporal doubling that occurs in consideration of the Nazi policies of concentration and extermination: in addition to the information obtained during the war and by the usual diplomatic channels, there was also direct confrontation at the time of the Allies' arrival at the camps. In most cases, the charges concerning decisions, actions, and events were constructed before collecting the relevant documentary material. This approach turns out to be very close to that of the historian who knows quite well that he cannot remove himself from the facts before him and remain passive, but that on the contrary he must establish the facts in accordance with a preliminary questioning of them. It is not only the "obligation of conscience" that famed French historian Marc Bloch talked about that brings the judge and the historian together here in the same heuristic honesty. It is the obligation to make choices, by causing only a certain number of putatively instructive facts to spring forth from a memory that is still quite fresh.

At the close of his memo, Taylor wonders about the role of the technique of iconographical display of certain items of evidence and, consequently, about the presence of film within the courtroom. He declares himself favorable to projecting onto a screen maps, charts, and models consisting of evidence previously photographed and enlarged to make it more legible. As for motion pictures, he takes note of their numerical and qualitative importance as exhibits and proposes that they be treated in both a specific and ordinary way: "Motion pictures should be treated as a normal and legitimate type of proof, and used at those points in the case where they best fit and are most helpful in establishing what we want to establish."[77]

On the eve of the trial's opening, Jackson's team had not merely integrated motion pictures into the totality of evidentiary exhibits assembled in support of the charges. It had prepared for their projection in court, knowing full well that, given the unbelievable nature of the facts that were progressively going to build the proof of the genocide of the Jews in Europe, a strictly "documentary" case would not be sufficient. On no occasion should film get in the way of knowledge of the politics of concentration and extermination. Rather it was supposed to allow everyone, inside and outside the courtroom, to begin to understand it.

CHAPTER 6

Getting Film into the Courtroom

The Visibility of the Crime

The presentation of film documents at Nuremberg was going to play a role in a context devoid of any previous censure or historiographical tradition. This precedent would enable the motion picture to fully display its unique and only seemingly contradictory qualities: the mechanical recording of a current event with a place assigned nevertheless to the future viewer. Because a film is always intended for someone and because authors know full well that they can portray only whatever they are fortunate enough to see, the faithfulness of the filming lies less in some technical attribute than in assuming this subjectivity while at the same time guaranteeing its truth value.[1] Recalling the descriptions made by Herodotus in his *Histories*, François Hartog points out that they "make things seen and known. Their focal point is the eye; it is the eye that organizes them (what is visible), that restricts over-proliferation (the field of vision), and that authenticates them (witness). It is thus the eye that makes the reader believe that he sees and knows; the eye produces *peitho*, persuasion: I have seen, it is true."[2]

In the history of court proceedings, the visibility of the truth of the crime has at times been organized directly within the court itself. In Roman times, when a trial concerned affairs of state, only the sentence—the death penalty—was public. But most of the time the trial was a spectacle, like circus acts or theatrical performances. On a large canvas hung laterally between the court, the prosecution, and the defense, the incriminated deeds were painted as they were revealed.[3] In contrast, Michel Foucault notes that from the Middle Ages up to the French Revolution, "Written, secret, subjected, in order to construct its proofs, to rigorous rules, the penal investigation was a machine that might produce the truth in the absence of the accused."[4] During the Revolution itself, the orality of debates was the guarantee of their transparency: "In the case of testimony, rediscovered speech and debate proclaimed society's newly acquired sovereignty. Everyone can stand, at least ideally, and face his judges—or stand in place of his judges—and tell with the full awareness of a free man the reality of a fact or an act."[5]

In viewing the pictures (which Budd Schulberg's team had gathered) made by the Nazis themselves in the exercise of their power and propaganda, Justice Jackson quickly understood how difficult it would be to locate and put forward against these officials films that illustrated their crimes. In fact this task mobilized the FPB as much as it did the U.S. Army Signal Corps. However, it was not a matter of building proof a posteriori of said crimes, nor of acting as if the troops had simply captured a written, oral, or visual trace of the criminal actions whose results they were recording. An ambitious federal policy had been implemented during the war to give the U.S. Army high-performance tools that would allow, among other things, for training film professionals, designing short "orientation" films, and filming combat.[6] Close ties with the film industry had been forged thanks to the intervention of producers such as Darryl F. Zanuck. In July 1941 Gen. George Marshall put Zanuck in charge of doing a report on how films were used in training soldiers. Zanuck uncovered "a complete absence of coordination between the production, distribution, and use of training films."[7]

In June 1942 the government published an information manual defining the central role that movies could play in the war against the Axis Powers. One of the priorities at the time was to convince the public of the necessity and legitimacy of American military engagement: "Public opinion polls indicate that some confusion still exists as to the issues for which this war is to be fought. Unless every American clearly understands how much he has at stake, the nation cannot gear itself to the all-out effort necessary for Victory. The motion picture should be the best medium for bringing to life the democratic idea."[8] This manual was written in the same spirit as the manual of the cultural policy put in place in the 1930s under the New Deal.[9] Although presented by its editors as a response to questions formulated by Hollywood, the idea that the federal government could bring pressure to bear on the politics practiced by the motion picture profession was more or less well received, even in an exceptional context.[10] This did not discourage some of the most renowned actors, directors, and technicians in the profession from signing up to do battle or to film it.[11]

Participating in mobilizing public opinion and in the war effort was one thing; reporting war crimes was another. Thus a specific operating plan was issued to officers and soldiers who were members of the FPB or were working with the OSS so they could react judiciously if they became aware of such facts:

> In the performance of normal duties, officers and men frequently encounter evidence of war crimes and atrocities that should be preserved for future consideration. Because human memory is faulty and because objects constituting physical evidence decompose, change, or are lost, it is important that a contemporary record be made of the event in such form that it will constitute an acceptable proof of occurrence, identify the participants, and afford a method of locating principals and witnesses so far as may be possible at some future time. To record such evidence in a uniform manner and in a form which will be acceptable in military tribunals or courts, it is essential that the instructions herein be followed closely. Study them and carry the manual with you in the field to serve as a guide.[12]

The flyer did not start off with a preliminary statement revealing the novelty, scale, and gravity of the major crimes committed by the Nazis in the concentration and extermination camps, despite information that American authorities had had in their possession since 1942. Neither did it consider that the war "crimes" and "atrocities" were so rare that their discovery would concern only a small number of soldiers and the even fewer specialists or teams of people psychologically prepared for such contexts. It was presented as "in the exercise of their usual missions" that U.S. military forces would putatively come across these crimes, be they committed against civilians, prisoners, or deportees.

The first paragraph is specifically directed to "atrocities," that is to say, "crimes against persons." The recommendations first address camera shots: How do you photograph or film a corpse? The answers are very precise. You must show the signs of the brutal treatment endured (hands tied behind the back with electrical cord, marks left from being tortured, kicked, beaten with a bayonet or saber, stabbed with a knife). If the body is in an advanced state of decomposition and it is dangerous or uncomfortable to get close to it, it is recommended that a gas mask or some other protection be worn.

Whatever the circumstances, though, the important thing is to record close-ups. If it is better to capture the person on the ground from several angles in order to highlight the visibility of the abuse suffered, it is also advisable to show the whole body, keeping in mind the distortions of perspective that can result from this. If there are several bodies—an eventuality that is touched upon only in passing—one needs to show the number of persons (wide-angle shot) but also to choose particularly representative shots of the brutality of the methods used. In addition to "killing," the guide groups cases of "torture, rape, physical violence, interment, mistreatment" under the heading "Atrocities." Deportation appears along with the execution of hostages and forced work as a case of "interference in the economic and social life of occupied territories."[13] The manner of comprehending these atrocities is clearly based on the international accords defining war crimes as shown later in the pamphlet (even though in that instance it will be dealing with other types of crimes) through the reference to The Hague and the Geneva Conventions.

In connection with this visual groundwork, two series of eyewitness reports are required: that of the person who took the picture and that of the persons who were in a position to "see" or "be familiar with" the event reported. The witness who can be deemed "official" must fill out a form ("Certificate to Accompany Any Photographs Taken as Evidence") on which he gives his name, position, technical expertise, and address. He must also specify the time, date, and location of the event reported, before certifying that he carried out this work while on assignment for the FPB/OSS and that the "photograph is a true, accurate, untouched, unchanged, undistorted picturization of the scene." These characteristics are the very ones American jurisprudence established in the 1920s, with the certificate in question playing the role of "Witness Authentication."[14] This certificate must also be corroborated by eyewitness testimony received on site or by other reports. These accounts, from victims if they are alive, from persons who were present as events unfolded or who had heard about them, but also from executioners under arrest, are in turn the subject of a standard description ("How to Make Written Statements of Witnesses").[15] It begins by recalling that in countries of common law, written transcriptions of testimony are not generally admitted as evidence in a penal court. However, since the first trials held after the war had demonstrated some leeway in the definition of the rules of admission of evidence, the editors were hoping to be able to give these transcriptions an eminent role. The argument put forth was directed at the advisability for a prosecutor to use the written document in order to determine whether the information it contained made it worthwhile to summon the witness to trial. In the forms filled out by the FPB based on film images it had (or not) made itself, there thus appear accounts of filmed interrogations offering a sort of second reading of the results obtained. For example, document 12, dated June 20, 1945, synthesizes the result of answers given to the U.S. Army by two German civilians:

SCENE	DESCRIPTION
1	Medium shot interviewing Ger. Civilian by U.S. Army.
2	Officers ask prisoner to identify pictures.
3	They ask a variety of questions—When did you join the Hitler Youth? Who was your leader?
4	The Ger. Youth is finally dismissed.
5	The officers now interview an older Ger. Fellow.
6	They ask him a variety of questions. When did you join the Nazi Party? *1932.* Who is Skinner? Who shot him? *I did.* Officer produces gun—Whose is it? Etc.

Maj. Gen. William J. Donovan's influence can be felt here, even if one knows what the general orientation of the IMT was in the end. The importance that Jackson gave film was nevertheless a major subject of agreement and cooperation between the two men and reinforced one of the specific traits of this source.[16] No doubt more so than other types of evidence or exhibits, film requires in its fabrication and in its showing all variety of mediation that prevents it from presenting an absolute truth, thus leaving open to argument the conclusions and then decisions determined in court.[17]

At the Nuremberg Trial, films could be considered exhibits (objective physical trace), evidence (a demonstration of truth), and testimony (affidavits attesting to the good faith of the filming or editing) because the IMT had specifically stated in Article 19 of its rules, "The Tribunal shall not be bound by technical rules of evidence. It shall adopt and apply to the greatest possible extent expeditious and non-technical procedure, and shall admit any evidence which it deems to be of probative value." While not excluding preliminary review of sources (Article 20 states, "The Tribunal may require to be informed of the nature of any evidence before it is entered so that it may rule upon the relevance thereof"), this spirit of openness was going to be especially germane to admitting into the courtroom motion pictures projected on a big screen.

In his opening speech, in which he speaks at length on "Crimes against the Jews," Chief of Counsel Jackson explained to those present, "If I should recite these horrors in words of my own, you would think me intemperate and unreliable. Fortunately, we need not take the word of any witness but the Germans themselves" (Figure 13).[18] Indeed he cited as evidence adduced in support of the case a host of orders and reports written by the Nazis. However, the films presented during the trial hardly entered into this framework, if at all. Those emanating from Nazi executioners were rare and always shot outside the camps, generally without authorization; they revealed a few of the Nazis' brutal actions, particularly in the ghettos. The majority came from pictures made by the Allies when the camps were opened. Jackson therefore added, "We will show you these concentration camps in motion pictures, just as the Allied armies found them when they arrived, and the measures General Eisenhower had to take to clean them up. Our proof will be disgusting and you will say I have robbed you of your sleep. But these are the things which have turned the stomach of the world and set every civilized hand against Nazi Germany."[19]

American Film and the Camps: Evidence and Testimony

The first film projected in court on November 29, 1945, *Nazi Concentration Camps* (PS-2430), was made under the direction of Lt. Ray Kellogg, John Ford's assistant at the FPB/OSS. Col. George Stevens, serving at the time in an Allied Expeditionary Forces unit attached to General Headquarters, is often cited as the film's director, but he appended his affidavit only in his capacity as the person in charge on May 1–8, 1945, of filming in the Nazi concentration camps liberated by the Allies.[20] These responsibilities fell to him in light of his official duties in the Signal Corps. The film presented at Nuremberg, produced entirely under the tutelage of the FPB, is in truth a reediting of the Signal Corps document established in late May, known by the name *Army Signal Corps Atrocity Film*, whose narrative construction followed the chronology of the discovery of the sites where "Nazi atrocities" had taken place. After perusing this material, Kellogg's team then examined in July 1945 reels of raw Signal Corps footage from the camps and carefully read the filming notes written by the military cameramen. Respect for the cameramen's initial choices did not mean they did not depart from the camera operators' written account, preferring instead a simple synthetic description of the shots.

Nazi Concentration Camps is indeed presented as a "report" whose commentary draws from the cameramen's notes in its summary. Pushing this logic to the limit, the copy projected at Nuremberg was silent; a representative of the FPB read the commentary aloud as the images passed on the screen. It was extremely important not to alter the source images in order to comply with the rules guaranteeing their status as evidence. Logically it was not possible to add after the fact a commentary giving an Allied interpretation of Nazi concentration camp policy. "The accompanying narration is taken directly from the reports of the military photographers who filmed the camps," stated James B. Donovan during his presentation of the film in the Nuremberg tribunal courtroom. Once again, that does not mean that modifications were not made. The FPB did make changes in the set comprising images shot in spring 1945 with documentary description to produce their own version.

The spirit of the FPB project may be summed up by the map shown at the beginning of the film: the extermination camps appear on it without their being mentioned. In the OSS archives, we found the first map available to the FPB as the film was being prepared. Entitled "German P. W. & Concentration Camps," this map did not include geographic indications of the camps found in Poland, the latter having been liberated or opened by the Soviets (Figure 14). An altered manuscript text figures along with this earlier map; it constitutes the initial broad outline of the commentary of the film. The phrase "There are approximate identifications for these camps" has been crossed out (Figure 15). This bears witness to the confusion that reigned in the minds of the FPB team with respect to the nature of the Nazi camps. Mention—no doubt in extremis—of the location of death camps did not require modification of the map's legend or the addition of any relevant images. Moreover, if one refers back to the Signal Corps' compilation film made in May, cuts were made. The FPB eliminated the first reel, which dealt with the massacres committed against Italians in the Ardeatine caves, the French Forces of the Interior in Paris, American soldiers in Gambsheim, and Belgians in Stavelot. In the fourth reel, the sequences on the death of political and Russian prisoners are omitted as well.

Despite its title, the film did not retrace the history of the Nazi camps, understood as the history of the "Final Solution." Rather it showed "a representative group of such camps [to illustrate] the general conditions which prevailed."[21] The camps presented were ones liberated or discovered by the Americans and the British. There was one near Leipzig, where attention was directed to the fact that "200 political prisoners were burned to death in this concentration camp" and where the few survivors "relate how 12 SS troopers and a Gestapo agent lured 220 starving prisoners into a big wooden building in this camp, sprayed the structure with an inflammable liquid and then applied the torch." Next was Penig, where young Hungarian women "showed scars of miserable existence under Nazi prison rule. American doctors examine the victims," who "are able to smile for the first time in years." Then came Ohrdruf (filmed during Eisenhower's visit) and Hadamar (scenes of the exhumation and autopsy of bodies that were poisoned or subjected to bad treatment). For the latter, the commentary does not dwell on the fact that "20,000 are buried here. 15,000 who died in the lethal gas chamber were cremated and their ashes interred." Instead it focuses on the interrogation of the Nazi in charge of the facility, "Dr. Waldman," and the head nurse, "Karl Wille": "As many as 17 at a time died from the morphine injections. The investigating officers were told that the Nazis never bothered to determine whether a victim may have survived the overdose."[22] Then came Breendonck (reconstitution of torture techniques used against Belgian resistors), Nordhausen (a very few weakened survivors among thousands of dead), Harlan (first meal in a long time for the deportees), Arnstadt (exhumation of bodies of deportees), Mauthausen (account by an American officer held prisoner), Buchenwald (forced visit by 1,200 citizens of Weimar; pictures, including those of crematory ovens, related to the report of the American Commission for Prisoners of War and Displaced Persons), Dachau (aerial views giving an idea of the size of the camp; a series of close shots of the survivors), and Bergen-Belsen.

Speaking in the Name of the Victims

It is possible to see how the FPB put together the film's commentary by examining the account given by the woman doctor from Belsen. With the camera rolling, she tells about the conditions of everyday life in the camp and the various medical experiments conducted on the detainees. Since the majority of images filmed in the camps were silent, the few accounts filmed live on site have a particularly powerful emotional charge. Yet they were rarely spontaneous, usually having been prearranged by the Signal Corps cameramen. Generally what is said should be concise and informative; in the case of deportees, they must not forget to address a word of thanks to their liberators.[23] As for the liberators themselves, they usually talk of the horror they have seen with their own eyes, thereby adding to its confirmation for the viewer. In the memoranda sent by the War Department to the judge advocate general concerning "the punishment of war criminals," tracking down the people responsible for the death or mistreatment of American soldiers was a stated priority.[24] As a result, the first witnesses talking on camera for the Signal Corps cameramen were American soldiers who had been held prisoner among racial or political deportees in the Nazi camps. Their presence and their words most surely helped their fellow citizens to feel concerned by these events and, through their accounts, by the fate of European detainees.[25]

The doctor's remarks were supposed to last at most three minutes, corresponding to the standard length of a reel of 35 mm film. No single take ever went on this long, however, as it would have been tedious to the eye. Therefore there are two shots, going from a wide axis to a narrow framing, the first, one minute five seconds, and the second, one minute forty-three seconds. All the doctor's comments were transcribed by the FPB and translated from German to English. The archives display the evolution moving from simple transcription to rewriting. In the original version, the first sentences are spoken as follows:

> Today, 24th April 1945, this is the doctor in charge of the female section of the concentration camp Belsen speaking. It is difficult to describe all that we prisoners have gone through in this camp. As [a] small example, I can tell you that we prisoners were thrown to the ground in a dirty lousy place; there were no covers, strawsacks or beds of any kind.[26]

At first this account seems to be delivered in accordance with a certain number of rules of speaking established by the interviewer. Indeed there is the matter of clearly specifying the date, the person's position, and the place, all of which are elements indispensable for authenticating what is said. Next, it is fitting to warn the viewer of the extraordinary character of life in a concentration camp. How could one do otherwise than to say that words are going to be insufficient to describe the atrocities committed or that there is no precedent for them? This is generally what is heard in the words spoken on site and to start with. However, following this introductory line, examples must be given, which the doctor does. In the FPB handling of her account, one passes from direct to indirect mode, with her words now relayed by a commentator:

> ~~Today,~~ 24th April 1945. This is the doctor in charge of the female section of the concentration camp Belsen, ~~speaking.~~ **She says that** it is difficult to describe all that ~~we~~ **the** prisoners have gone through in this camp. ~~As [a] small example, I can tell you that we~~ **For example, the** prisoners were thrown to the ground in a dirty lousy place. (Figure 16)

A more impersonal mode is preferred, in principle offering a less subjective view. In a third version, the account is less detailed:

> 24th April 1945. This is the doctor in charge of the female section of the concentration camp Belsen. ~~She says that it is difficult to describe all that the prisoners have gone through in this camp. For example, the prisoners were thrown to the ground in a dirty lousy place;~~ **she says that** there were no covers, strawsacks or beds of any kind.

The fourth version differs even more in its concision:

> 24th April 1945. This is the doctor in charge of the female section of the concentration camp **Bergen** Belsen. **She was a prisoner at this camp.** She says ~~that~~ "there were no covers, strawsacks or beds of any kind."

In the film's definitive version, the commentary features a mixture of the doctor's voice fully heard in certain segments and the voice of the commentator superimposed over hers, the latter fading out, allowing us to hear:

> This is the woman doctor of the concentration camp Bergen-Belsen. 24th of April 1945. This is the doctor in charge of the female section of the concentration camp Bergen-Belsen. She says there were no covers, strawsacks or beds of any kind.

On film, the contrast is striking. On the one hand is the woman doctor who, dressed all in white and apparently in good health, seems to be reciting a rehearsed text: no letting up, no silences, no hesitations.[27] On the other are the women assembled behind her: physically wasted, with emaciated faces covered by gray scarves, and seeming not to understand German as they constantly look away from the camera and doctor or toward what is going on off camera (Figures 17 and 18). The doctor can no longer appear as a spokesperson, given that what she says has been modified in its oral expression, and even more so in its collective status. For reasons of language or emotional shock, it seems the reporters preferred not to have the deportees themselves speak and found in the doctor a mediator between what could be said about the concentration camp experience in a slightly distanced way and what the liberators felt conformed to their communication objectives and the constraints of getting these film images admitted as judicial evidence.

British Film and Images of Belsen

The British filmed the Bergen-Belsen sequence. In it, a soldier is seen declaring, "I am the officer commanding the regiment of the Royal Artillery guarding this camp. Our most unpleasant task has been making the SS, of which there are 50, bury the dead. Up to present we have buried about 17,000 people and we expect to bury about half as much again." Indeed since thousands of dead bodies were strewn about the camp grounds, for sanitation purposes the British had to put them quickly into common graves and then burn the camp with flamethrowers after its evacuation. Several scenes from this sequence were presented "as 'principal witnesses' during the trial of the Belsen executioners, the first courtroom screening of this kind, before a British tribunal established in Lüneburg on September 20, 1945."[28] It was in this context of great urgency and in the perspective of the approaching trial that one must situate the work of collecting information carried out by British forces, described in a first interim report written on June 22, 1945, by two officers of the Royal Infantry, Lt. Col. Leopold John Genn and Maj. Savile Geoffrey Champion.[29] This document allows us to understand how the British War Crimes Investigation Commission worked at Belsen to reconstitute the history of the camp, establish precise statistical data on the people who were there in April, proceed to interrogations of the people presumed to be

in charge, gather accounts by survivors, and prepare the trials of the criminals. The authors first emphasize the huge difficulties that confronted them
and which they feel that they only partially overcame to fulfill their mission.
They then estimate the number of potential witnesses who, sick or healthy,
were present at the various sites of Bergen-Belsen, to be fifty-five thousand:
"The general administrative task of reducing the various Belsen Camps to
something like order was Herculean." Lacking personnel, the Commission
had to wait several days before a group of interpreters arrived at Belsen. The
translators spoke only German and English, however, which was valuable
for interrogating camp authorities but not for the "considerable number of
witnesses who spoke only Czech, Polish, Russian, or other languages."

Two objectives were then set: first, to collect all evidence of guilt of the
camp commandant, Josef Kramer, then of those responsible for crimes
committed against British victims of whom it could be proved that they had
been deported to Belsen, and finally of forty-eight SS men and twenty-nine
SS women. Subsequently it was appropriate to gather evidence concerning
other camps, like the one at Auschwitz, for which information was lacking
"in relating to mass extermination in Gas Chambers." It is understandable
that the films shot at Belsen cannot at the same time show the state of the
camp at the moment of its liberation—in particular its necessary sanitary
treatment—and explain in detail what required fourteen pages of report on
the crimes that had been committed there. However, if one studies the commentary spoken at Nuremberg, isolating it, for example, from the viewing of
the film, the remarks seem in all their concision to be reporting the essential, though probably at the price of work similar to and much more ardu-
ous than that carried out on the words of the woman doctor.

Before being edited into *Nazi Concentration Camps*, the sequence on
Belsen was supposed to be part of a movie produced for German viewers
that was not broadcast until the early 1980s, when it aired on British television under the title *Memory of the Camps*.[30] We must make no mistake as to
why this movie was not shown in either Germany or England in 1946. If the
images captured by the British cameramen had been released immediately,
in the form of newsreel items, their reception would have given rise to opportunities to observe the audience's behavior, and then in turn allow for
better defining of the content as well as the conditions of this type of screening. With no such reference points, given that the collection and editing of
footage for F3080 (the code name given to the film at the time) lasted several
months, those in official British circles could not help but grow more con-

cerned, especially if one was of the opinion that it was better to roll up one's sleeves and help Germany rebuild than to crush it under the weight of the Nazis' wrongdoing.

The head of this project, Sidney Bernstein, was preoccupied with seeing his picture succeed in serving as a form of proof, even though it was not destined for the Nuremberg Trial. On April 30, 1945, he explained that this motion picture must tell about real and proven facts, and that "it should be in the form of a Prosecuting counsel stating his case. It is of extreme importance that German audiences see the faces of the individual directly responsible. Efforts should be made to secure the names. And personal background of all persons thus shown, attempting to establish that they were once 'ordinary people.'"[31] To do this, he sought advice from Alfred Hitchcock, one of his old friends who was back in England to talk to him about creating an independent movie production company. One of the film's editors recalls, "I can still see him walking back and forth in his suite at the Claridge, saying, 'How can we make that convincing?' We would try to set up the longest shots possible using camera movements. That way there was no possibility of being misleading. By panning from a group of clerics and other officials over to the dead bodies, we knew that no one could claim that the film was doctored."[32] The sequence shot, thanks to its continuous panoptic view, was therefore considered the most respectful of the event filmed, precluding any point of view or editing from altering its meaning.

In 1942, however, a directive from the U.S. secretary of war, Robert Patterson, recommended that the various teams of cameramen act in a complementary fashion in order to get cross-views of the same event: "When Signal Corps motion picture cameramen cover a news story, they should operate in collaboration with newsreel cameramen, if present, and photograph scenes to augment coverage by the latter. Thus the coverage will be complete with a variety of picture angles. This will make a complete and well rounded pictures story. Usually coverage by more than one cameraman results in a better product."[33]

Although it took a different form, the desire to transcribe into the image itself the concern for truth that drove its producers was shared by the British and American production policies. On the American side, thanks to the professionalism of the reporting teams and the need to show pictures of the soldiers who were witness to the atrocities committed, a form of editing was improvised live, with the length of shots and the size of frames having to allow for building on the spot an account inspired by the writing codes of the Hollywood system (alternation of wide and close shots, narration of a "story" centered on individuals, drama usually oriented toward an optimistic outcome). To get a good idea today of the cameramen's internalization of the normal film rules of event coverage, it is important to consult the unaltered film documents that they shot, as well as the forms filled out by them at the time. The example of the piece filmed at Buchenwald on April 1, 1945, is instructive. Four minutes and thirty-three seconds long, it includes in its final sequence a succession of three shots showing corpses surrounded by American soldiers. In the first shot, the pile of dead corpses dominates the picture. In the second shot, a pan going from left to right puts the soldiers, filmed head-on, in the center. In the last one, the soldiers have moved apart slightly so that the camera's perspective passes between them and shows the viewers what the soldiers are seeing (Figures 19–21).[34]

On the British side, the desire to ensure the greatest objectivity possible was in no way a matter of naïve belief in the transparency of the act of filming or of the liberators' occupying the sole position of impartial third party. To be convinced of this, it suffices to read the note of intent presenting the commentary of *The Memory of the Camps*: "It has been the intention wherever possible to let the picture tell its own story, consequently it must be borne in mind that large lapses of time will occur throughout this commentary and passages may seem disconnected unless they are in relation to the visuals. If facts are not pointed out at one part of the film it is perhaps because they can be explained with more force at a later point. This is done to avoid overloading the film with commentary so that an audience may have time to think, and absorb what it is hoped will be a dreadful lesson."[35]

If the viewer was not supposed to be dependent upon a commentary instantaneously and univocally giving him the meaning of the pictures with which he was confronted, it was because they already contained, sometimes explicitly, the first reaction of the liberators and the first judgment of the victors. For example, in the continuity of the famous sequence shot spoken of by Bernstein—in reality, a short panoramic shot—going from the mass grave piled with corpses toward neighboring inhabitants forced to attend this summary burial, the speech addressed to them via loudspeaker by a British major is heard from start to finish and in actual sound. The words are those of the original film, but they clearly expressed the British position with respect to the Germans' collective responsibility. Moreover this sequence was not kept for the version shown at Nuremberg, if indeed the FPB ever had access to it. (Bernstein's documentary was not available in its entirety.) It is therefore the shot of the soldier bulldozing corpses into the common grave that struck hearts and minds the hardest, beginning with the Americans themselves.[36]

In both cases, the shots filmed in the camps were conditioned in part by the necessity of collecting evidence that might be used to bring a case to trial or be admitted as evidence against war criminals. Hence the interest of the montage film made for the trial which was neither able nor willing to mask its testimonial dimension while at the same time trying to give a history lesson with the aim of getting at the truth. By finding a way to multiply examples of the modes of execution and torture that were used, and by distinguishing even minor specificities of each of the liberated camps, some near-exhaustive idea of the scope of the techniques of crime could be suggested, since it was impossible to show it outright, the Nazis having applied themselves to covering up the traces of the death camps. It was not a matter of trying to evoke a phenomenon of the scale of a genocide or even of posing the question of the limits of representation. Rather they sought to position themselves on the threshold of the inhumanity felt by the deportees, showing what there was to see and not what in a time already set off from us had been hidden from view.[37] This vision of the camps was in part adapted to public opinion, which between 1941 and 1945 was ill informed (if at all) concerning the camps' existence, while at the same time drawing full benefit from a know-how that resulted from cinematographic storytelling techniques and the formidable capacity for recording and reconstructing reality.[38]

After *Nazi Concentration Camps*, two other motion pictures were presented at trial, such as a document presented on December 13, 1945, called "Original German Film (8 mm) on the Atrocities Committed against the Jews" (PS-3502). Seized by U.S. Army forces in a barracks on the outskirts of Augsburg, this was an "amateur" document filmed by one or several SS during the liquidation of a ghetto by Gestapo agents with help from military units. It shows naked women brutalized, dragged on the ground by their hair, men beaten, others running terrorized out of buildings from which they have been violently evicted. This very short (about one minute) document was of poor technical quality. Presenting it on behalf of the U.S. attorney general, James B. Donovan insisted first of all on specifying that the situation described in the film, regardless of the fact that it had not been possible to identify its place and date, "occurred a thousand times all over Europe under the Nazi rule of terror." He then proposed to the president of the Tribunal that the film be shown several times again, which was accepted. Thus reiterated, this document undoubtedly acted powerfully as a counterpoint to the film shown prior to it, since it came from the executioners themselves, revealing their complacency toward their own wrongdoing. It also had the advantage of being situated in an urban setting whose familiarity only added to the disparity between the ordinary life of the people who lived there and the terror enacted.[39]

The Soviets and the Familiar World of Death

It was finally the turn of the Soviets, on February 19, 1946. In addressing the court, Col. and Chief Counselor of Justice L. N. Smirnov insisted first of all on situating the role of this film, entitled *Film Documents on the Atrocities of the German-Fascist Invaders* (USSR-81).[40] It was one of the last pieces of evidence "in the series of those that the USSR provided concerning crimes against civilian populations." Smirnov had previously referred to photographs taken by the Germans (a series of nineteen indexed under the call numbers USSR-100, 101, 102, 212, 385, 388, 389, 390, 391). Telford Taylor, remembering that Gen. Roman Rudenko had shown him these documents, commented, "Since the source was German and the pictures often portrayed identifiable locations or individuals—e.g., SS generals Arthur [*sic*] Gebauer and Karl Strock—their authenticity was solid. The scenes were in line with the content of the documentary evidence."[41] Nonetheless the Soviet prosecution still preferred to leave open the possibility of calling witnesses to the stand after the screening, the most important of them being Abram Sujkever, who appeared in court eight days later. Smirnov made sure to give a few details on the nature of the crimes committed by the Nazis:

> Those who are now in the dock have freed from "the chimera of the so-called conscience" hundreds of thousands and millions of criminals. They educated these criminals and created for them an atmosphere of impunity and drove their blood-thirsty hounds against peaceful citizens. They mocked at human conscience and self-respect. But those who were poisoned in murder vans and gas chambers, those who were torn to shreds, those whose bodies were burned in the ovens of crematoria and whose ashes strewn to the winds, appeal to the conscience of the world. Now we cannot yet name, or even number, many of the burial places where millions of innocent people

were vilely murdered. But on the damp walls of the gas chambers, in the places of the shootings, in the forts of death, on the stones and casemates of the prisons, we can still read brief messages of the doomed, full of agony, calling for retribution. Let the living ones remember these voices of the victims of German fascist terror, who before dying appealed to the conscience of the world for justice and for retribution.[42]

Unlike the Americans who had entitled their film *Nazi Concentration Camps*, the Soviet prosecution used the very title of the film it was presenting to emphasize the two categories of crimes committed by the Nazis, war of aggression ("The Invaders") and war crimes ("Atrocities"), thus fully legitimizing the legal construction of charges of conspiracy. Smirnov did not merely differentiate among the victims ("peaceful citizens" and those "poisoned in murder vans and gas chambers"). He thought that the deaths of the latter were an appeal to "the conscience of the world," in this way describing, without explicitly naming it, crimes against humanity. As we have seen, the Americans opted to stress their own victims among prisoners of war in order then to sensitize their fellow citizens to the fate of European populations subjected to Nazi barbarity. Since Americans had only liberated and opened concentration camps, it was understandable that there was hardly any mention of death camps. The Soviets also started off with a focus on their own dead, the difference being that the number of victims was beyond comparison with that of the other Allies, or even with that of European Jews. However, without going so far as singularizing this genocide, the film constructs its progression in horror by going from the massacres committed against the prisoners of war and Soviet civilians to those carried out in the extermination camps. It is true, though, that no mention of the Jews as principal victims of the "German fascist terror" is included in the historical reminder preceding the film's projection. Although the Soviets usually downplayed the central character of the genocide of the Jews of Europe, Chief Soviet Prosecutor Rudenko had been very explicit in his opening statement on February 8, 1946, when he described the nature of this crime:

The fascist conspirators planned the extermination to the last man of the Jewish population of the world and carried out this extermination throughout the whole of their conspiratorial activity from 1933 onwards.

My American colleague has already quoted Hitler's statement of 24 February 1942, that "the Jews will be annihilated." In a speech by the defendant [Hans] Frank, published in the *Kraków Gazette* on 18 August 1942, it is stated: "Anyone who passes through Kraków, Lvov, Warsaw, Radom, or Lublin today must in all fairness admit that the efforts of the German administration have been crowned with real success, as one now sees hardly any Jews." The bestial annihilation of the Jewish population took place in the Ukraine, in [Belarus], and in the Baltic States. In the town of Riga some 80,000 Jews lived before the German occupation. At the moment of the liberation of Riga by the Red Army there were 140 Jews left there.

It is impossible to enumerate in an opening statement the crimes committed by the defendants against humanity.[43]

Film Documents on the Atrocities of the German-Fascist Invaders was comprised of images filmed by Soviet news cameramen, Roman Karmen principal among them.[44] In the affidavit read at the beginning of the film, the director of the Central Bureau of the Order of the Red Banner of the Documentary Film Studio attests that "the filming was done immediately after the liberation of areas subjected to the yoke of German-Fascist troops." The film thus follows the chronological order, from 1941 to 1945, of the discovery of atrocities, from the barbaric acts committed against the civilian populations and massacres of Soviet prisoners of war to the extermination camps themselves. The film commentary draws on the reports by the Soviet special state commission put in place to investigate the "atrocities of the German-fascists."

When it is a question of civilians, each case is reported with great precision. First, the place and date of filming are indicated, as well as the names of the cameramen:

The town of Rostow [Rostov]. These shots were filmed by cameramen [Andrei] Sologubov, [Georgii] Popov, and [Arkadii] Levitan on November 29, 1941, on the corner of Sowjet and Nollnoy Streets.

Then the circumstances of the crimes are made known:

On the corner of Engels Street, the Germans slaughtered 50 peaceful inhabitants who had been chased from homes situated nearby. Some peasants who just happened to be passing through were led by force to the same place to be murdered also. Among the people slaughtered were intellectuals, workers, and housewives.

The victims' profession is indicated several times. On occasion the commentary even underscores the multiplicity of the professions practiced, while prominently featuring the fact that the "German-fascist" criminals targeted the Soviet population as a whole: "Among the victims were all sorts of professions: engineer, doctor, chauffeur, stenographer, accountant, waitress, watchman, housewife." No one was spared, be they parents or children, peasants or workers. If women often are seen crying over the corpses of their children or husbands, we also see men bent over their murdered wives or offspring. For example, one segment shows "the wife of an engineer, raped and tortured." The shots have been deliberately filmed frontally and as close-ups.

In comparison with American and British techniques, the Soviet approach seems rather brutal, taking very little care with precautions concerning footage of victims' suffering or the viewer's difficulty in being subjected to such scenes of violence. No Germans appear on film. The forced visits to the camps or sites of atrocities imposed on local populations by the Signal Corps and the British Army give way here to scenes where only the lamenting relatives of the victims are presented. The millions of Soviet deaths alone were sufficient for the populace to be able to believe the reality of the atrocities committed against them; no specific evidentiary strategy was needed to convince them. That is the reason why the filming serves as a simple statement of facts, a sort of visual *procès-verbal*, with no oral testimony at all, unlike in the official investigation reels. Moreover Smirnov states that since the question of the concentration camps for the civilian population "has already been extensively treated by the members of the Prosecution who presented their cases before mine, I shall try to be as brief as possible; I shall limit myself either only to absolutely new information or to the text of the documents which serve as an explanation to the movie films which will be shown today before the Tribunal."[45] For the most part, these texts are accounts given by surviving victims or by executioners.

Having addressed the fate of civilians, the Soviets then turned their attention to that of their soldiers who had been prisoners of war. They screened an archival document filmed on a caption stand that revealed an order authorizing German soldiers to proceed as they saw fit to the summary execution of prisoners of war. At the Rostov train station, more than one hundred

Soviet prisoners of war were shot by the Nazis after being tortured. The commentary states, "The faces of many of them were deformed. The Germans cut off their noses and ears."

In a second part lasting as long as the first (twenty-four minutes), the camps of Majdanek and then Auschwitz-Birkenau are shown at their moment of liberation and during the visit by the Soviet Special Investigating Committee. Aerial shots, close-ups of crematory ovens, gas chambers, piles of clothes, bundles of women's hair, and victims injured by medical experiments were all taken from two films made in 1944 and 1945. The first, *Vernichtungslager Majdanek—Cmentarzysko Europy* (*The Majdanek Death Camp, Europe's Cemetery*, dir. Aleksander Ford, 1944), was a montage of images filmed by Polish and Soviet crews. Karmen, who directed the Soviet cameramen, made another film in 1945 on Auschwitz, *Oscwięçim*.[46] *Film Documents on the Atrocities of the German-Fascist Invaders* remained ambiguous, however, as to the nature of the process that led from the crimes committed against Soviet civilians and servicemen to the crimes in extermination camps, where Jews were cited only in the enumeration of the nationalities of those deported to Auschwitz ("Poles, Russians, Jews, French, Belgians").

Film as Third Party in the Courtroom

The radical alterity of the atrocities committed by the Nazis could have created a terrifying effect and harmed the credibility of the images presented. Eyewitnesses before all else, American cameramen did not hide their initial shock but rather underlined their presence by incorporating themselves into the film's frame. Added together, these images soon formed an ensemble that effectively excluded the death camps—since those camps had been liberated by the Soviets—but that could make the proportions of the Nazi crimes perceptible. The OSS team assigned to assemble the montage of *Nazi Concentration Camps* added a narrative dimension, recounting "Nazi barbarity" in a sort of story form, constituting an exhibit whose legal pertinence was going to be put to the test during the judicial proceeding. The presence of motion pictures was thus not limited to their factual dimension but to what Pierre Legendre calls the "structural position of third party fiction, exercising as such a hermeneutic prerogative."[47] To term such a position a *fiction* might seem surprising, given the weight placed on truth in a legal proceeding. This would be taking the word solely in the sense of a hypo-

thetical construction used by convention to support an argument or a demonstration. But fiction is also the elaboration, working from raw material, of
a narrative that helps to understand the reality to which it refers and which
could not be deciphered without this mediation. If film contributes to elucidating a fact, it is not due to the recording technique's mechanical dimension but to the combination of its double status as evidence and testimony.
Renaud Dulong is right to raise cautiously the question of modification of
the "regulating ideal of the eyewitness" caused by the intrusion of film into
the judicial process: "Doesn't the use of these technical means surrepti-
tiously support the tendency to devalue witnesses as compared to filmed
representation? One is at least entitled to ask about the role played by the
impression of perfect fidelity given off by photographic images and recordings on tape in the denunciations of witness accounts' defectiveness."[48]

In a letter addressed to John Ford at the outset of the trial, Ray Kellogg
relates how impatient he was for the moment when the film that he had supervised would be shown: "I can hardly wait until we hit them with the Concentration Camps film, which, by the way, has become not only the highlight
of the Prosecution, but the main support of Count #4 of the Indictment—
which is 'Crimes Against Humanity.' Also, the film we made on Atrocities
of War Camps is the Main support of Count #3 which is 'War Crimes.'"[49]

Another member of the OSS, Dan Kiley, was selected to redo the Nuremberg courtroom to accommodate the IMT. Born in 1912 and having studied
landscape architecture at Harvard, Kiley first worked with Louis Kahn and
Eero Saarinen at the U.S. Housing Authority. He then served from 1942 to
1945 in the Army Corps of Engineers and joined the OSS as chief designer. In
the midst of a city in ruins, the building that he was to renovate had remained
miraculously intact (Figure 22). That allowed him some room to maneuver in
dealing with the constraints of the space for the judicial proceedings. Looking
back on his work, Kiley states, "What I was trying to do was to have a unified
and orderly and dignified [courtroom]—that's what the courtroom should be,
and it should reflect the scales of justice, you might say, too. We had a logo that
one of the boys in my branch designed, and it shows the typical woman with
the scales of justice. And we had shoulder patches with those on them."[50]

The rather narrow, rectangular form of the courtroom made for close
quarters in the symbolic division of the places occupied by the judges, the defense, and the prosecution. Kiley was asked not only to restructure the layout
of the room but to design and make the furniture as well (Figure 23). At first
he built the dock in such a way that the benches for the accused had no

backrest, but given the significant length of the court sessions, he was forced to improve their comfort. For the large bay windows, he selected green-colored draperies: "I wanted a neutral kind of soft color. It wasn't jazzy, but it was nice." American novelist John Dos Passos, covering the trial for *Life* magazine, wrote, "The freshly redecorated courtroom with its sage-green curtains and crimson chairs seems warm and luxurious and radiant with silky white light. . . . Great clusters of floodlights hang from the ceiling. A G.I. is smoothing out the folds of four flags that stand behind the judges' dais."[51]

One of Kiley's priorities had been to create spaces for discreetly placing cameras for film or photography and installing the OSS technical teams assigned to film the trial (Figure 24). But first and foremost he decided on the central position of the screen on which the films, photographs, maps, and diagrams that constituted the visual part of the "documentary" trial were going to be projected (Figures 25 and 26). The judges and the accused were on either side of the screen. The prosecution and, on the mezzanine, the journalists and invited guests were in proper line with the projection, but in a sort of second space, slightly set off behind the first. The screen, and therefore the films projected, occupied indeed a third party's position. In *Fury*, Fritz Lang had positioned the screen in the same perspective, the only difference being that the president of the court was himself in front of a white wall, as if the image was not supposed to compete with the symbolic space of judicial power (Figure 27).

The day before *Nazi Concentration Camps* was to be shown, the FPB team decided at the very last moment—probably with the consent of judicial authorities—to proceed with the installation of a row of lights above the benches of the accused.[52] The next day, people could turn their gaze simultaneously to the images projected and to the accused, visible despite the darkness of the room (Figure 28). The French reporter and writer Joseph Kessel, special correspondent for the daily *France-Soir*, reported, "Suddenly I had the feeling that the resurrection of horror was at that moment no longer the essential act. . . . It was not a matter of showing the members of the court a document which they most certainly knew in depth. It was a matter of suddenly putting the criminals face to face with their massive crime, of in a sense throwing the murderers, these butchers of Europe, into the middle of the killing houses they had organized and catching by surprise the movements that this spectacle, this shock, would force out of them."[53] This in fact was the reaction of many journalists present on that day. Their reports inextricably combine what the film showed of the Nazi camps and the way the accused reacted to these images. The next day, the editors of *P.M. Daily* (New York) thus titled the article by Victor H. Bernstein, "19 Nazis Look at the Face of Death: [Hjalmar] Schacht Turns Away as Film of Camp Atrocities Is Shown at Trial." The *New York Herald Tribune* emphasized, "The projection of films on atrocities at the hearing [shook] the Nazis' confidence," observing in conclusion that "when the projection was over, there was complete silence in the court. The judges retired without a word and the defendants slowly left the courtroom."[54] With a similar eye-catching title ("Nazis on Trial See Horror Camp Film"), the *Washington Post* stressed one of the prosecution's goals, quoting the U.S. Assistant Prosecutor Thomas J. Dodd's opening remarks: "We intend to prove each and every one of these defendants knew of the existence of these concentration camps and used them as instruments of terror to enforce their control on the German people, and to obliterate freedom in Germany and the invaded countries."[55]

This system of confronting the defendants with images of "Nazi atrocities" does not prove an individual's direct incrimination. From the outset, all had pleaded not guilty. However, on the subject of the camps, for the most part they simply denied even knowing of their existence. It was therefore a matter of finding the means to contradict declarations they had made before or during the trial. Still pictures were used most often to accomplish this. Alois Höllriegl was thus led to identify Ernst Kaltenbrunner as indeed the person in a photograph taken at Mauthausen showing in the background a quarry (Wiener-Graben) into which deportees were thrown from the top of a cliff (document PS-2641). Analyzing this segment of the trial, Ilsen About rightly observes that although this document is as such inconclusive as to Kaltenbrunner's criminal responsibility, the fact that he is standing next to the camp commandant and Himmler gives the image greater evocative power, that of "a certain contiguity between supreme power and crime."[56]

On a broader scale, it remains nevertheless a question of knowing, be it for film or for any other evidence, what type of document or argument can give weight to a charge inaugurated on the occasion of the Nuremberg Trial. The wavering throughout the trial between the terms *war crime* and *crime against humanity* shows how difficult this was. Indeed Yan Thomas reminds us that "the facts dealt with by law and made known to the judges have no weight of their own if they have not first received their meaning from a law. In law, the question of fact is always raised after the question of law."[57]

The reactions of the accused constituted a major stake of the film screening. To found crimes against humanity on legal grounds, perhaps the defendants needed to be led individually to *feel* the major transgression of these acts. Thus, from the beginning of the trial, all eyes were trained on them. During Jackson's opening speech, Dos Passos noted:

> When the prosecutor reaches the crimes against the Jews they freeze into an agony of attention. The voice of the German translator follows the prosecutor's voice like a shrill echo of vengeance. Through the glass partition beside the prisoners' dock you can see the taut face between gleaming earphones of the dark-haired woman who is making the translation. There is a look of horror on her face. Sometimes her throat seems to stiffen so that she can hardly speak the terrible words.... The Nazi leaders stare with twisted mouths out into the light of the courtroom. For the first time they have seen themselves as the world sees them.[58]

The defendants' behavior was observed daily by a psychologist, Capt. G. M. Gilbert (Figure 29). He arrived in Nuremberg on October 20, 1945, after working as an intelligence officer at the camp at Dachau. In his interrogations of low-ranking Nazi civil servants, he had systematically run up against denials on their part. When the same attitude was adopted by the Nazi leadership brought before the IMT, Gilbert was not fooled by their defense strategy, even if he continued to listen to them. Writes Gilbert, "A good deal of the Nazis' conversation was consumed in rationalization, self-justification and recrimination; but even in thus protesting too much, and by being more frank in their opinions about each other than about themselves, they inevitably revealed their personalities and motives."[59] On November 29 Gilbert was therefore seated near the defendants in order to observe their reactions before speaking with those who wanted to have a session with him later that evening. The psychologist recounts, "Piles of dead are shown in a slave labor camp.... [Baldur] Von Schirach watching intently, gasps, whispers to [Fritz] Sauckel.... [Walther] Funk crying now.... Göring looks sad, leaning on elbow.... Sauckel shudders at picture Buchenwald crematorium oven.... As human skin lampshade is shown, Streicher says, 'I don't believe that.'... Göring coughing.... Attorneys gasping."[60] In an account published in 1947 by Edmund Jan Osmańczyk of Poland, a rather different impression of the defendants' behavior emerges. In his opinion, the defendants were far too healthy to allow them to feel even slightly what the deportees had endured. Furthermore their fixation on celebrating Aryan beauty could only make them insensitive to seeing the inhumanity suffered in the camps. Their gestures were thus pure play-acting to make it appear as if they knew nothing of the crimes in question.[61]

After *Film Documents on the Atrocities of the German-Fascist Invaders* was shown, Göring used it as a pretext to call the Soviets' good faith into doubt, arguing:

> First of all, a film that *they* made is no proof, just looking at it from a legal point of view. They could just as easily have killed a few hundred German PW's and put them in Russian uniforms for the atrocity picture—you don't know the Russians the way I do. Secondly, lots of those pictures were probably taken during their own revolution, like the baskets of heads. Thirdly, those fields covered with bodies.— Why, such pictures are easy to get any time in a war. I've seen thousands of bodies myself. And where did they get the *fresh* corpses to photograph? They couldn't have come right in ready to take pictures. They must have shot those people themselves.[62]

Taken in isolation from the first sequence, the film images of the extermination camps of Majdanek and Auschwitz would have undoubtedly provoked a reaction of even greater stupor than was felt by all the defendants when they watched the American film, *Nazi Concentration Camps*. But by inserting the images into the litany of crimes committed by the Germans against the Soviets, it became possible for Göring, in a most cynical way, either to claim responsibility for them implicitly or to try to deprive the camp images of the specificity of their genocidal violence. In adopting this attitude, he isolated himself, and most of the others in the dock were visibly shaken.[63] Gilbert reports that when he talked with him, Göring "threw in a sop to our moral sensitivity: 'Of course . . . it is enough if only 5 per cent of all the atrocity stories are true, from all that has already been presented before—but I do not put any stock in what the Russians bring.—They are blaming their own atrocities on us.' "[64] This was an allusion to the Katyn Affair, which had almost led to a serious incident among the Allies. The Soviets were intent on raising this issue in court to pin it on the Nazis. The Americans had become convinced the Russians had massacred the Polish officers and thus tried to keep the matter out of court.[65]

During the war the Nazis, who had been extremely careful to keep control over those in a position to expose the functioning of the camps—particularly the extermination camps—seized the opportunity to reveal those atrocities that could not, or at least should not, be attributed to them. The photo volume about the massacre at Katyn published in Berlin in 1943 is striking today for its scriptural and photographic techniques.[66] It includes images of the discovery of the mass graves, views of the corpses, identification of a dead person in the presence of a high-ranking official, an autopsy performed by foreign experts, the visit of European writers gathered together at the graves, the study of photographic evidence by English, Canadian, and American members of an investigative commission, and a collection of photographs garnered from the personal effects of the murdered Polish officers. Of course, these various techniques of proof had already been used in the past with respect to accounts of such exactions, in particular during World War I. But here the Nazis were only too happy to be able to denounce to the international community crimes for which they were not responsible, using procedures that would soon turn out to be implemented by the Allies to reveal the deportees' fate.

The trial at Nuremberg was not about simply having people in attendance sit through an uncritical spectacle or giving the filmed document a merely documentary value. The aim was to force Nazi leaders to acknowledge as their own, in camera and before a court of law, crimes for which they were accountable or responsible. Because of their physical position in the room, the accused had to accept being seen juxtaposed to the images projected in the courtroom.[67] This approach was a continuation of the one initiated in the camps by the Americans, whereby the mass graves and "official" witnesses sent from the United States were shown in the same shot. In one case as in the other, it is through the filter of the image that it becomes possible to perceive the genocidal violence, both for the reporters faced with its consequences or its visible traces as well as for the viewers of cinematographic news and persons participating in or attending the Nuremberg Trial.

Discovering these films in the United States after having worked up until then on analyzing Nazi propaganda, Siegfried Kracauer thought they allowed their viewers to bear the shock of seeing the horror and of "integrating into their own memory . . . the face of things. . . . Through the visual experience . . . of tortured human bodies that appeared in the films about the Nazi concentration camps, we redeem the horror of its invisibility beyond panic and fantasy. And this experience is very liberating for it gets rid of a very powerful taboo."[68]

Aware of the novelty of using motion pictures in the courtroom and the role they were to have with respect to other documents, Telford Taylor suggested before the trial that they be shown early on: "I feel that *some* use of film should be made comparatively early in the proceedings, so that the court will more rapidly become accustomed to moving pictures as a normal part of the body of proof."[69] In the end, footage of the Nazi camps was shown first. Jackson recounts in his memoirs that scarcely had the trial begun when it started to drag on too long and the defendants appeared excessively self-assured. The mass of written documents was such that it was even difficult to display them physically before the court (Figure 30). It was soon agreed that only a synopsis of exhibits need be presented, with a copy of the complete document having been distributed to all parties (Figure 31). The prosecution wanted to shock the proceedings out of their torpor:

> The trial badly needed a shot in the arm to pep up our own staff, as well as to give the correspondents something to write about. The remedy that we sought to use was to show rather out of order, and rather before we had expected to, the films, both taken by the Americans and captured German films, on the concentration camps.... Many of the war correspondents had seen either the conditions, or the films, and they were not startled by this. But the spectators generally, the members of the court, the German Counsel and the defendants in the dock were tremendously affected by this picture. It really scored.... It was a shot in the arm that the case needed at that point and it certainly deflated the defendants in an effective manner. They never got their courage back after that picture.[70]

The cinematographic mediation of atrocities committed by the Nazis seems to have humbled all willful arrogance, whether emanating from the self-assuredness of the guilty or the justice of the victors.[71] Shaking up the logical order of the courts of indictment by showing *Nazi Concentration Camps* before the montage illustrating the conspiracy thesis, and only a few days after the opening of the IMT, the trial in a sense started at the end, on the chronological level as well as on the level of building a case. The crimes committed by the Nazis were supposed to be described as part and parcel of a politics that had begun by impacting the peace and then the laws of war. The Allies chose to present from the very start what they had just witnessed, without even taking the time to explain how the camps were the result of the "Nazi plot" or the ultimate consequence of its political project. They did this in the context of a new experiment, whose result could not be entirely controlled in advance: the screening of a film in court. Thanks to the wise counsel of John Ford's team, they nonetheless were aware that this was an inaugural moment. In the long run, this projection does indeed constitute the first stage of the collective work of elaborating and establishing some distance from which to consider the genocide of the Jews of Europe.[72] It thus constitutes as such a determinant vector in the construction and evolution of social knowledge and the work of memory in Western postwar societies.

CHAPTER 7

Catching the Enemy with Its Own Pictures

Hess Face-to-Face with His Own Image

The first film the International Military Tribunal dealt with was *Triumph of the Will*, screened in camera before the trial even opened, on November 8, 1945. This was done on the initiative of Col. John H. Amen, formerly in charge of interrogations in Paris. Since his arrival at the Tribunal, Rudolf Hess had been feigning amnesia and was therefore subjected to various medical and psychiatric analyses. He was put in the presence of Göring and Franz von Papen, but he did not recognize either one. Amen then had the idea of showing him Leni Riefenstahl's film in which he appears several times in Hitler's company (Figures 32 and 33). Hess had in fact opened and closed the Nuremberg meeting of the NSDAP in 1934. He was also responsible for warming up the crowd, in particular the Hitler Youth. In his opening speech, he addresses Hitler directly: "My Führer! Gathered around you are the flags and banner of national socialism. Only when they are worn out will the people looking back be in a position to understand truly the greatness of this moment and what you, my Führer, represent for Germany. You are Germany. When you act, the nation acts. When you judge, the people judge. To show our gratitude, we will stay by your side for better and for worse, no matter what! Under your command, Germany will achieve its goal: being the homeland of all Germans in the world. You have promised us victory and you now promise us peace."

The viewing of the film was scheduled for November 8, in a room with twenty-five handpicked viewers. Telford Taylor was present:

> When the film had finished, Amen (through an interpreter) asked
> [Hess]: "Do you remember?" to which Hess replied that he recognized

Hitler and Göring, but added: "I must have been there because obviously I was there. But I don't remember."

The experiment was not a bad idea, but had been amateurishly executed. The presence of so many kibitzers was ill calculated to put Hess at ease. The film should have been shown to him under more casual and private circumstances, with one or two knowledgeable German-speaking questioners, preferably known to Hess in a non-adversarial way, who could converse with him during the showing. Of course, this method might well have worked no better, but the chances of tripping up Hess, if he was indeed feigning, would have been much greater, and if not, his replies to factual questions and comment might have led to a better understanding of his ailment.[1]

Even though this account was given after the trial, Taylor's reaction is instructive. Riefenstahl's film had been transformed into a tool, a mode of self-recognition for one of its former actors turned into its privileged spectator. Could Hess pass through the screen and blend into the character shown by Riefenstahl, thus recovering his self-unity, so to speak, and appear in court fit for judgment?[2] To pull off such an experiment, Taylor emphasizes, it would have been necessary to be given the means to construct the viewing in a serious manner so as not to put Hess under pressure. Was this possible?

In any case, let us keep in mind the idea of the pairing up of a "passive" spectator position and a critical distance maintained during the screening. This kind of operating system is not unrealistic. In professional sound-mixing rooms, a small desk with a directional light allows for taking notes or talking with another person without interfering with watching the film. In this instance, it seems that it would have been very difficult to get a dialogue going while images of Hess giving speeches unfurled on the screen. One would have to have taken the time to watch a full reel, stop the viewing, interrogate Hess, and then return to watching the following reels. But the essential thing here was that this first film projection—within the context of, if not yet actually in, the courtroom (since it was occurring prior to the trial's official opening)—was not so much intended to produce evidence as to confront a defendant with his own filmed image, furnished, as it so happened, by the Nazi leadership itself. This unprecedented situation could not have come about without the contributions culled from the work of the

MoMA and of Siegfried Kracauer. In fact it would add to the critical exercise of reading film images, the dynamic of the live presence of Nazi authorities in Nuremberg.

The Nazi Plan

It was thus in the wake of work carried out by the MoMA that in the summer of 1945 the OSS began searching in Germany for newsreels made by the Nazis themselves for their cinematographic state propaganda. Since the Nazis had filmed themselves in the exercise of their power, the prosecution could show these documents as proof of a political doctrine and political action resolutely adopted. Eighty-four items were assembled into a four-hour film shown in court on December 11, 1945. Entitled *The Nazi Plan*, it consisted of four sequences: "The Rise to Power of the NSDAP, 1921–1933," "Bringing Germany under Totalitarian Control, 1933–1935," "Preparation for the Wars of Aggression, 1936–1939," and "The Wars of Aggression, 1939–1944." In one of the documents describing the final result, the spirit of the project was presented as follows:

Newsreels from 1933 to 1944 showing how Nazis prepared, started, and prolonged the Second World War.

Factual evidence of the PARTY, ARMY, and GOVERNMENT LEADER'S RESPONSIBILITY for the DEVELOPMENT of the NAZI MASTER PLAN also showing the COMPLICITY of the German REICHSTAG, the WEHRMACHT, and the PARTY ORGANIZATIONS.

For the first time in the history of legal procedure and jurisdiction, it has become possible to present in sound and picture the significant events of an historical period. In the case of the present war crimes trial, the International Court is in the position to found its examination of the responsibility and guilt of the Nazi leaders, their accomplices, and organized followers on the basis of factual evidence presented in the form of documentary photographs and original speeches. Newsreels, made on the spot, started and prolonged the Second World War.

At the MoMA, Kracauer had watched most of the newsreels in their entirety, without instrumentalizing them. Moreover he was interested in the reception of these films, which were supposed to provide an immediate interpretation of events occurring in Germany and, during the war, in the different theaters of operations. The constraints and unpredictability of frequent production limited the possibility of ensuring a univocal reading of their content. The OSS hardly even asked itself this question, so absorbed was it in reconstructing an intentional and explicit process, to show how Hitler and the Nazi Party moved from the attempted coup d'état of Munich to the seizure of power and preparation for war.[3] Although made by men of the motion picture world, the montage put the emphasis on the most discursive and political aspects of the German newsreels.

However, a few sequences were chosen for their particularly visual character: Goebbels showing Hitler's NSDAP membership card, mentioning the date he joined, March 21, 1925 (item 2); the May 10, 1933, book burning (item 12);[4] the Swastika adopted as a national symbol on July 9, 1933 (item 16); images of the ambiance of the Nuremberg convention filmed by Riefenstahl on September 4–10, 1934 (item 21); German troops entering Austria and Vienna on March 12–13, 1938 (item 36); the signing of the Munich Agreement, September 29, 1938, with a short scene of Göring in a belly laugh, rubbing his hands together in satisfaction (item 42); French general Charles Huntzinger and Hitler at Compiègne, June 22, 1940, where the victor of the battle of France dances a little jig (item 58); Hitler and Pétain meeting at Montoire in October 1940 (item 73);[5] and Himmler smiling in front of Soviet prisoners during his visit to Minsk in June 1941 (item 74).

The Role of Nazi Leadership

Since the choice was made not to accompany the film with commentary, even for general orientation, the meaning of the proposed narrative needed to be clear. When Frank Capra used excerpts from Nazi newsreels and from *Triumph of the Will* in his series *Why We Fight* (1942–45), he started out with the same intention: letting the enemy himself do the talking. Nonetheless he intervened insofar as he completely anchored the footage to an overall analysis of the peril that the Axis Powers represented.[6] But it was not possible to proceed in the same manner for *The Nazi Plan*. Hence an initial clever idea: the authors of the film had obtained one of the portraits of the Nazi leadership made during the war, an excerpt from a series entitled *Fil-*

marchiv der Persönlichkeiten.[7] This document on Alfred Rosenberg is doubtless one of those that Jackson had in mind when he said early in the trial, "We will show you their own films. You will see their own conduct and hear their own voices as these defendants re-enact for you, from the screen, some of the events in the course of the conspiracy."[8]

Born in Reval (today Tallin, Estonia) of German parents, Rosenberg had been one of the first to join the NSDAP after meeting Hitler and Ernst Röhm in 1919. In 1921 he was named editor of the Nazi Party's official paper, the *Völkischer Beobachter* (People's Observer). He then theorized on German racial superiority, publishing in 1930 *Der Mythus des 20. Jahrhunderts* (The Myth of the Twentieth Century). When Hitler came to power in 1933, Rosenberg was put in charge of foreign affairs for the Nazi Party, before being named minister of the occupied territories in the East in March 1941. This is the only time he appears in German newsreels in this capacity. Since he was one of the defendants and the only one to have recorded a retrospective account of the early days of Nazism, his account was placed at the beginning of *The Nazi Plan*. Filmed in his Nazi uniform while seated behind a desk, Rosenberg recounts meeting Hitler and his ensuing involvement in the NSDAP's rise to power (Figure 34): "I was introduced to the Führer. Since that time I have devoted myself completely to the NSDAP. . . . It was always being asked what points of program the NSDAP had and how they each were to be interpreted. Therefore, I wrote the principal program and aims of the NSDAP."

The first newsreel footage incorporated into the film is inserted into this story, as if it were an illustration of it. However, newspaper headlines are also shown, first in their diversity—a sign no doubt important for Americans of the democracy that prevailed under Weimar—and then in their submission to Nazi control. Thus in the unfolding footage of street battles and protests put down by police, the film's viewers could spot references to the Munich uprising:

> *Die Rote Fahne* [main paper of the German Communist Party]: "Everyone out in the streets!"
> *Der Angriff* [official newspaper of the NSDAP, founded by Goebbels in 1927]: "Goebbels settles some scores!"
> *Vorwärts* [newspaper of the German Socialist Party]: "Shots at the Feldherrnhalle!"

Vorwärts: "[Erich] Ludendorff and Hitler imprisoned. Call for party reform."

While Rosenberg was the only one to have been the subject of a documentary, other Nazi officials had regularly been filmed in studios for short subjects probably intended for internal communication in the NSDAP. The interesting thing about this set of documents is that they allowed for seeing and hearing political speeches that had not been formatted for public broadcast. Some excerpts are reused in *The Nazi Plan*. For example, after being named minister of the interior in Prussia, Göring presented his agenda in a very direct way: "I am going to clean out with an iron broom and sweep out all those who hold offices only because of their Red or Black trend and are for the subjugation of all national aspirations. To make Prussia again the first and strongest bulwark of the German nation, that is my task. I shall execute this by the commitment of all my power, with merciless decision and with iron nerves."[9]

Göring spoke in the first person even though the action he announced corresponded to a general party policy. For his part, Goebbels made himself the spokesman for the official campaign against Jews in Germany: "My fellow countrymen and women. At ten o'clock this morning the boycott began. It will be continued until the hour of midnight. It is being executed with a momentum like that of a blow, but at the same time with an impressive order and discipline. Now they have found a place of refuge in Paris and London and New York. To our party and to our Führer, 'Heil.' "[10] This anti-Semitic harangue was followed by the one accompanying the book burning: "My German men and women! The era of the over-pointed Jewish intellectualism has now finished and the success of the German revolution has also opened the road for the German way."[11]

Other members of the NSDAP—in fact most of the political and military leaders of the Third Reich—figure in the cast of those appearing in *The Nazi Plan*. Using the list of defendants in the order established at their indictment, the breakdown of the number of their appearances in the film is as follows: Göring (25), Hess (2), Joachim von Ribbentrop (15), Wilhelm Keitel (12), Ernst Kaltenbrunner (0), Rosenberg (2), Hans Frank (1), Wilhelm Frick (4), Julius Streicher (1), Walther Funk (0), Hjalmar Schacht (3), Karl Dönitz (3), Erich Raeder (9), Baldur von Schirach (2), Fritz Sauckel (1), Alfred Jodl (3), von Papen (2), Arthur Seyss-Inquart (1), Albert Speer (1), Constantin von Neurath (3), Hans Fritzsche (2), and Martin Bormann (2). The numbers for those who were not at Nuremberg are Hitler (41), Werner von Blomberg (8), Goebbels (6), Heinz Guderian (5), Himmler (4), Walther von Brauchitsch (4), and Robert Ley (2).[12]

The Führer's Aura

It was logical that authors would give special attention in their selection of subjects to the leaders and emphasize the Führer's position. The number of subjects devoted to Hitler therefore corresponds to intense German newsreel coverage of his activities, political pronouncements, and rapport with the masses. The crowd scenes filmed by German cameramen were usually framed by events organized around Hitler's travels. Sometimes they even used extras, selected and prepped, in order to give the most ostentatious signs of support and fervor before the camera. In spite of everything, though, *The Nazi Plan* tried not to revitalize the propaganda orchestrated by Goebbels. The risk of confusion was nevertheless twofold. On the one hand, the choice of images somewhat isolates the political power from the living mass of the nation, and in so doing reinforces the mythology of the creation of a new "popular community" shaped entirely by the Nazis and represented (albeit artificially) via the great Nuremberg rallies. On the other hand, as Norbert Frei, Peter Reichel, and Ian Kershaw have shown, the Hitlerian exercise of power could never have been as dynamic without strong popular support. As Kershaw writes, "The wide variety of social expectations invested in the regime, resting upon an extensive underlying consensus, had a common denominator in the image of the Führer. This in turn engendered a level of acclamation and plebiscitary support which could repeatedly be tapped, thus reinforcing Hitler's increasingly deified position as leader, and contributing to the growth of 'Führer absolutism' and the relatively high level of autonomy from the traditional ruling elites which Hitler was able to attain by the later 1930s."[13]

The Nazi Plan included segments on most of the NSDAP's major meetings in Nuremberg.[14] Starting with 1937, it was above all the results of Nazi expansion that were highlighted: the invasion of Danzig (item 53), Poland (54), Denmark and Norway (56), and Belgium and Holland (57). The invasions of Yugoslavia and Greece (71) as well as of the USSR (72) followed.[15] One can ask whether the resulting history of the Third Reich, given this strong focus on the history of Hitlerism, was not too linear and unified, logically moving from elaboration of the doctrine to the seizure of power and its consolidation, then to the launching of the wars of aggression. On the one hand, as Philippe Burrin recalls, "The centrality of Hitler is not just an artifice of Goebbels's propaganda, and rare are those historians who would question that he occupied an essential place in the regime."[16] *The Nazi Plan* does in fact show this quite clearly. But on the other hand, while foregrounding the most politicized dimensions of the regime's propaganda films and by privileging the illustration of how the conspiracy was implemented and executed, the film hardly provides any keys to interpreting "the diffusion throughout the regime of an attitude of mind that was propitious to the realization of [Hitler's] orders" or to comprehending the way that those orders "made possible the explosion of violence fermenting in Nazi ideology."[17]

Victor Klemperer speaks of the important role played by newsreels in mobilizing the German population when he describes the impact made on him in 1932 watching footage of a military parade:

> The scene took place following Papen's assumption of office; it was entitled "Anniversary of the Battle of Jutland, the Marine Guard of the Presidential Palace Marches through the Brandenburg Gate." . . . These men kicked their legs so high that the tips of their boots seemed to rise up above their noses, all in a single sweeping arc, all as one leg, and the posture of all these bodies—no, this one body—was so convulsively taut that the whole movement appeared to freeze, in a way that the faces had already frozen, so that the troop as a whole gave the impression of being utterly lifeless and frenziedly animated at the same time.

After observing similar movements being performed by the drum major, Klemperer continues his reflections:

> Comparable tension and convulsive distortions could be seen in contemporary Expressionist paintings and heard in Expressionist literature of the period, but amidst the sober life of the most sober town its impact was that of unalloyed novelty. And it was highly contagious. A bellowing crowd pushed forward until it was almost touching the troops, frantically outstretched arms appeared to want to grab hold of them, a young man in the front row with eyes ablaze bore an expression of religious ecstasy.

The drum-major was my first truly shocking encounter with National Socialism, which, despite its rapid spread, had seemed to me up until this point a trivial and passing aberration on the part of immature malcontents. It was here that I saw for the first time that form of fanaticism unique to National Socialism; this mute figure forced me to confront the language of the Third Reich for the first time.[18]

Two documents in *The Nazi Plan* held particular importance for the prosecution. The first was the speech Hitler gave at the Reichstag on January 30, 1939 (item 45), presented in these terms:

HITLER PREDICTS ANNIHILATION OF THE JEWISH RACE IN EUROPE IF WAR OCCURS (Jan. 30, 1939)
a) Hitler in Reichstag, Göring presiding. Speer seen in audience.
b) Great applause.
Hitler: "Today I want to play prophet again: if international Jewish finance in and outside of Europe succeeded in pushing people into a world war, the result would not be the Bolshevization of the world, and through it the victory of Judaism, but, on the contrary, the annihilation of the Jewish race in Europe."

This important "prophecy" recorded on film could not, of course, be connected with other footage showing its fulfillment.[19] From the outset of the pretrial investigation, the OSS was obviously aware of this dilemma. Nevertheless, in spring 1945, a procedural method had been decreed for collecting this type of evidence, be it written or on film: "Restricted films on secret weapons, Army staff reports or SS and Gestapo pictures may contain excellent evidence. A secret staff report, for instance, might report, in narration, that 'according to the orders of Reinhard Heydrich, all Jews in Prague are being systematically eliminated. . . .' Such a statement makes excellent evidence."[20]

The second document is the film footage of the trial of the individuals alleged to be responsible for the assassination attempt against Hitler on July 20, 1944. The FPB team discovered it barely two months before the trial opened. According to Budd Schulberg, the film had been stored in the basement of a small Berlin film library and comprised sixty-eight reels (approximately eleven hours running time).[21] The last sequences showed the execution of defendants filmed during a particularly cruel manner of death—they had been hung from meat hooks—that lasted fifteen to twenty minutes. Faced with spectators' horrified reactions, Goebbels pulled the movie from circulation.[22] The American prosecution included only three reels from this lengthy source in *The Nazi Plan*, which allowed it to focus attention on the behavior of the prosecutor Roland Freisler. It was important to end the screening with the presentation of the parody of justice practiced by the Nazis, as the ultimate response to accusations concerning the legitimacy of the justice of the victors—who, one must recall, agreed to let the Nazi officials choose their own lawyers and directed the IMT to cover the costs (Figures 35 and 36). As had been the case for the negative images of Jews that Fritz Hippler attempted to promote in *Der Ewige Jude*, the defendants' attitude of fear mixed with courage tended to stir the viewers' empathy (rather than make a spectacle of their humiliation; Figures 37–40). Reporting on the screening of *The Nazi Plan* for the *New Yorker* magazine, Joel G. Sayre clearly grasped the techniques used by the Nazis to belittle the accused during a trial organized to be filmed: "Every time Judge Freisler speaks, his voice thunders, and when a defendant tries to answer, his voice is smothered by timidity. The proceedings are most frequently photographed from behind the Judge, with the camera focused on the defendant, who stands before the bar flanked by two policemen seated in chairs and wearing helmets that look like inverted coal scuttles."[23]

In the first military trials in which Americans brought proceedings against Germans for war crimes such as those committed at Malmédy, Belgium, the defendants looked anxious.[24] But the context was obviously very different. Premises that were scarcely fit for such proceedings had been quickly transformed into a courtroom. However, photographs show the formal seriousness of these acts of justice, put under the protection of the book of law (Figures 41 and 42).

The Nazi Plan's Impact on the Trial

How was *The Nazi Plan* received in court? Budd Schulberg reports that it did not produce the same "sensational" effect as the film about the camps.[25] Göring and the other Nazi authorities actually appreciated the chance to see themselves again at the height of their power and to be able to escape for a few moments their situation as the defeated, prisoners, and defendants. They were all the more willing to recognize themselves in this footage because it had been sufficiently monitored at the time of its production to project an acceptable image of them, even though the decisions they were announcing were fraught with serious consequences.[26] However, this film played out its role fully when the actors in these pictures let their guard down and let slip reaffirmations of their allegiance to the person of the Führer. Von Ribbentrop, for example, explained to Captain Gilbert that the charisma Hitler exercised over him was still intact: "Even with all I know, if Hitler should come to me in this cell now, and say, 'Do this!'—I would still do it.—Isn't it amazing? Can't you really feel the terrific magnetism of his personality?" A few days later, though, on December 14, when the deportation in Poland was brought up, Gilbert reports, "The momentary flair of Nazi inspiration which flickered up after the Nazi films was smothered completely by the devastating evidence of calculated mass murders brought out in yesterday's and today's sessions."[27]

In the course of the trial, film and writing alternated in probing the crimes committed by the Nazis, putting constant pressure on the defendants and providing an ever-growing description of the verdict that the court was going to have to reach at the end of the trial. There was really no suspense to the decision even though the sentences given varied according to the defendant. In this workshop of a courtroom, the story of Nazi Germany was shown in continuity (linearity of the overall story) and through ruptures (revelation of atrocities, the uncompleted designation of crimes against humanity). The overabundance of documentation for some of the crimes being judged turned out to go against the dynamics of judicial confrontation and was detrimental to broad publicity of the courtroom debates. Film had been able to reveal little and yet too much early on (the genocide of the Jews of Europe) or a lot but too late in the proceedings (the July 20, 1944, trial of the "conspirators"). However, it would be simplistic to see *The Nazi Plan* as merely a somewhat unimaginative exercise in historical narration, a merely stacked recounting in a completely event-based format. At the time, the film was very worthwhile because it retraced chronologically a story that few people knew in its entirety. As Henry Rousso emphasizes, the Allies wanted to give "in the heat of the moment and in a somewhat haphazard manner, a first narration and interpretation of the events that had just ended with the defeat of the Reich. This unprecedented form of historical narrative *preceded* the first historical analyses."[28]

The authors of *The Nazi Plan* had been given instructions to find film footage that would support the indictment against the Nazi leadership and

the Reich's organizations. It was therefore particularly important to *see* the
Nazis among themselves in situations that proved their "agreement" on the
implementation of a "common plan," without, however, seeking out the
meaning of this footage (as opposed to still pictures, sometimes instrumen-
talized by the prosecution).[29] Their political intentions were often reconstituted in all their legibility, but since in certain cases they were more or less
hidden, the choice of certain subjects proved to be particularly judicious.
Document 13, for instance, recounts a seemingly trivial event, the inaugura-
tion of a new German civilian plane. In the written description of the segment, the Americans emphasize that the members of Hitler's cabinet present
at the event are dressed in civilian attire, including von Blomberg; it helps to
illustrate the conspiracy thesis, since, in the context of Germany's rearma-
ment plan, well before the plan was openly recognized as such, this type of
aircraft was manufactured with the intent of later converting it into an war
plane. Without having to suggest manipulations of this sort, the next news
item, number 14, enabled viewers to witness an implicit challenge of the
terms and conditions imposed on Germany after 1918. In it, Hitler explained
in a speech given at the Reichstag, "Germany has fulfilled all obligations of
the peace treaty, far beyond the limits of justice, yes, beyond any trace of
reason."

Released barely three weeks after the trial opened, *The Nazi Plan* provided support to developing the case pursued by the American and British
parties. Starting on November 21, 1945, Jackson dealt with the conspiracy
notion and acts of aggression through the war against Poland; on December
5 the British chief prosecutor Lord Shawcross began with the war in the
West, in the Balkans, and at sea. The French representative's speech, beginning January 17, 1946, about crimes committed in the West can be linked
with the film about the camps (which should have been shown at this time
but was instead scheduled for an earlier date, as we have seen). Beginning
February 8 the Russian representative, Roman Rudenko, illustrated the
atrocities committed in the East with the Soviet film *Film Documents on the
Atrocities of the German-Fascist Invaders* (shown in court on February 11).
The Nazi Plan functioned in essence as a matrix for other motion pictures.
The newsreel subjects it comprised had been completed between 1933 and
1945 and released weekly throughout Germany and then in countries occupied by the Reich. What was the effect produced by seeing them all, one
after another, but in a different time frame? On the one hand, it could be

that the montage reinforced the coherence of a political propaganda that, despite being strictly controlled, nevertheless had to make do with the subject matter provided by the news, in particular where international issues were at stake. On the other hand—and this was probably the effect sought and obtained in the courtroom—the ordinary violence of Nazism, which was not necessarily spectacular, was revealed bit by bit either through the recurrence of certain themes or, conversely, through the sudden appearance in the course of a report of what was most brutal in Nazi political discourse and practice.[30]

The film's pedagogical significance prompted the great Hollywood producer Darryl F. Zanuck to propose making a shorter version of it for distribution in theaters. On behalf of Twentieth Century Fox and with Jackson's agreement, Ray Kellogg took on the job of establishing an English version. In doing the translation, he removed a certain number of caption heads to facilitate fluidity and direction comprehension of the archival footage. He also proceeded to make some cuts, in particular in the political speeches. He added German music to the credits and improved transitions from one subject to the next with dissolves (whereas in the first version he simply ran them in their entirety, one after the other). He wrote to reassure Jackson, though: "I shall however continue to observe the straightforward factual presentation, without any dramatics or hokum used in Hollywood productions."[31]

Presented first in a private screening in Washington for a certain number of politicians and military personnel, the film met with criticism over the fact that the German news footage was included without being subjected to a critical commentary. Taken out of the context of its projection at Nuremberg in a judicial setting where other evidence and opposing arguments surrounded it, would this film speak to the public at large? James B. Donovan tried to explain these concerns to Kellogg, but the latter, who had returned to Los Angeles after spending almost five years working with John Ford and then Jackson, turned a deaf ear to him. In the end, a prologue was added to the film with footage of the Allied armies (in particular the American soldiers) advancing through Europe and of the liberation of the Continent's principal capitals. Shots of movie reels were then shown before the camera entered the Nuremberg courtroom. The affidavit of proof PS-3054 (the legal classification number of the movie *The Nazi Plan*) introduced excerpts from newsreels on Nazi parades and the German army. The commentary announced:

Close on the heels of the advancing Armies followed teams organized to search for enemy documents. One of their targets: enemy
motion picture film. From the cities, from farms, barns, and play-
grounds, caches of Nazi films were found. Then, in September 1945,
the International Military Tribunal concluded to the conspiracy to
commit crimes against peace, war crimes, and crimes against humanity. In addition to traditional evidence, there was presented a motion
picture compiled from the films found by the search team. We sought
to establish the manner in which the Nazis obtained totalitarian
power in Germany, and how the use of that power, with the aim of
war as an instrument of national policy, led Germany into World
War II.

Instead of transforming *The Nazi Plan* into an American documentary
on Nazism, Kellogg preferred, by subjecting the German film footage to a
retrospective reading, to highlight something new ushered in by the Nuremberg trial: letting the enemy's word be heard but also *seen*. This step was
possible in part because World War II had also unfolded through motion
pictures. The Nazis had challenged Hollywood's power by trying to impose
their own vision of the world, at least where newsreels and documentaries
were concerned. In this context, film is not only a *representation* of the politics
of various views, something added to a thought or an action already defined
and put into practice; it accompanies, sometimes even precedes, and often
gives shape to doctrines that first of all were supposed to unite the national
communities in question before trying to influence others. This familiarity
with the narratives offered by the movies, common to Germans and Americans, explains why during the war the Germans hid from the public news of
both military defeats and the death camps, leaving the door open to the
Americans to become the sole, or at least principal, voice bearing witness.

PART III

Nuremberg: History on Film

CHAPTER 8

<hr/>

The Un-United Nations and the Ideal
of a Universal Justice

An American Vision of a Universal Justice

In a message broadcast on October 7, 1942, the U.S. president promised to go after the people chiefly responsible for "barbarian crimes committed against the civilian populations in the occupied countries, in particular, Europe."[1] One week after the "Declaration by the United Nations," Roosevelt called for the creation of an investigative commission on war crimes.[2] Judicial sanction was thus becoming one of the key themes of the fight against the Axis forces, and this came to fruition in the organization of the Tokyo and Nuremberg trials. American public opinion was therefore expecting this moment, a fact not lost on the Hollywood film industry.

In 1943, for instance, Sam Bischoff, executive producer at Columbia, took note of a movie pitch proposed by two exiled actors—one German, probably a Jewish refugee (Alfred Neumann), the other Austrian, born of Jewish Czech parents (Joseph Than)—and got it accepted by the studio's director, Harry Cohn.[3] The idea was to make a movie about a United Nations trial of a Nazi Party official accused of atrocities committed in Poland during the war. The project was assigned to a filmmaker of Hungarian origin, also exiled in the United States, André de Toth, and was given the title *None Shall Escape*. The bosses of the major studios had always been able to spot (when they were not yet well known) or attract (when they were) the industry talents coming from Europe. Although the majority of them were Jewish, they had not been eager to put their cinematographic weapons in the service of political causes fighting Nazism.[4] The war nevertheless often led to their being the only ones capable of putting together a figuration of what was at stake internationally, indeed even universally. Released in 1944, *None Shall Escape* started off with an introductory caption that read, "This story is set in the future. The war is over. As promised, the war criminals have been led back to the scene of their crimes in order to be judged. In fact, as our leaders have announced, 'None shall escape.'"

The movie thus gave shape to a universal jurisdiction that would not materialize until fifty years later, with the creation of the International Criminal Court. With a balance of national origins represented (from Europe, Asia, Africa, America), the court depicted did not appear as emanating from the victors but as the incarnation of humanity against whom the crimes being judged had been perpetrated (even though it was defined as the International Tribunal of the Warsaw District). The presiding judge was flanked by two assessors, and twenty people represented the jury. The set design was a mix of judicial and political assemblies. There was no audience, and the presiding judge was speaking in front of the camera, as if the viewers of the film were attending the trial. To those present before him, the president of the tribunal declared, "Men and women of the United Nations, you are the jury. It will be up to you to judge all the criminals and determine their sentence. This will be your war if the final victory brings you justice and a true and lasting peace among peoples."

Because they wanted to stick as closely as possible to the facts of what had occurred during the war and to the different policy stages on the trials then being elaborated, Bischoff's associate Burt Kelly submitted the movie's script to the OWI at the State Department. Proposed modifications were accepted by the production team so as not to have the film "contain incidents, characterizations, plot, narration, or any other story elements which are contrary to international policy of both the United Nations and the United States government."[5] The president of the tribunal was thus shown describing his mission in conformity with the policy that Secretary Stimson's group had worked out:

Unconditional surrender. The Nazi leaders are now being judged in Poland and other countries in Europe. Today we are judging those who subjected humanity to unspeakable torture. We must be conscious of our great responsibility to the past but also to the future. During the Nazi occupation of the countries invaded, records of their crimes, and those of their collaborators were carefully preserved. Their names were recorded in anticipation of their day of judgment. This court will determine not only whether the defendants are innocent or guilty, but also the scope of their crimes. This court will determine the price they will have to pay.

While Hollywood alone could undertake production of fiction films about Nazis on trial, it was Justice Jackson who decided early on to have the future trial recorded on film and, prior to it, to make a short documentary justifying the tribunal's creation. John Ford's team was assigned to produce the latter, designated initially by a code name, "P.O. 158." It was going to open on October 18, 1945, under the title *That Justice Be Done*, with distribution negotiated with the motion picture industry's Committee on War Activities so that its release in commercial circuits would coincide with the trial of major war criminals in Berlin. The OWI was to handle screenings in the European theater of operations.[6] Even prior to their conflicts with Allies over the organization of the IMT, the Americans were determined to assume authorship of the court and inscribe it within the spirit of the democratic ideal of their nation's founding fathers.

The evolution of the movie's scriptwriting reveals insights as to how the desired message was modulated. Since the idea was to address first and foremost the American people, the authors hesitated between two introductory sequences, one built directly around crimes committed by Hitler's Reich, the other reminding viewers of the philosophical foundations of the origins of American justice.[7] In the script's first draft, images of Nazi atrocities open the film, without commentary but with music mounting to a crescendo as the camps are enumerated. The search for the opening shot is presented this way: "The most horrifying shot available of corpses with Germans reacting." The tone is set; the aim is to raise right away the question of the Germans' responsibility in accepting Nazi concentration and extermination policies and, for some, their participation therein. Other shots of "atrocities" follow. Then the narrator, presented as both "calm" and "angry," makes a first observation: "Murder has been committed. Not one murder—or a hundred murders—or a thousand. *Millions* of murders." The massive character of the crimes committed is emphasized by suggesting that it was not a matter of isolated acts but of a deliberate policy.

How do you sensitize the viewer to the fate of thousands, of millions of people, without showing such quantities of anonymous figures that any process of identification or of understanding the scale of the crime ends up hindered? The film's authors thought that it was probably better to show a few dead bodies with people tending to them, later weeping at the funerals;

loved ones of the deceased rather than soldiers or, as was often the case in this type of situation, Germans led by force to see the fate that had been reserved for prisoners of Nazi camps. However, the liberators knew full well that most deportees died far from their families and that most of the corpses were now only ashes. It must have seemed essential to them to reintroduce ritual, to re-create a bond, there where everything had been planned to make all traces of the dead disappear.

A listing of the origins of the victims follows, with the French, then Jews, Poles, Belgians, English, and Russians mentioned according to the chronology of the Allied stand against Nazi war crimes. Among these first declarations are the simultaneous announcements made by the U.S. president and the British prime minister on October 24, 1941, denouncing "the massive executions of innocent hostages" that the Germans had just carried out in France and the "atrocities" they had committed in occupied territories.[8] This explains why the French are mentioned first, before the Jews, with the last on the list being the Americans: "Our own soldiers, shot in the back, while wearing American uniforms—in open defiance of the Geneva Conventions that German officers quote by heart when *they* become prisoners."

Yet it was not this first sequence that was kept for the opening of *That Justice Be Done*. Instead it was the second sequence, highlighting before all else the democratic heritage of the American nation in opposition to Hitler's project. The film thus begins with the bust of Thomas Jefferson (shots of his statue in Washington, D.C.), while solemn music plays in the background and the quotation that graces his memorial is read: "I, Thomas Jefferson, have sworn upon the altar of God eternal hostility against every form of tyranny over the mind of man."

Jefferson was the obvious choice for several reasons. Passionate about classical culture and highly versed in Enlightenment Europe (he spoke Latin, Greek, French, Italian, and Spanish), he had of course written the Declaration of Independence in 1776. The future third president of the United States (1801) had become a lawyer by the age of twenty-four. His dual knowledge of politics and law along with the reputation he had acquired abroad made him a particularly fitting embodiment of the universalism, whose name the IMT was invoking, sensitive to reproaches of applying "victors' law."[9] After his image comes that of the Supreme Court, of which Jackson was a member before being called to direct the IMT. Budd Schulberg, assigned by John Ford to supervise production of *That Justice Be Done*, had obtained authorization from Harry Cohn, producer of *None Shall Escape*, to use an excerpt from another movie from Columbia, *Mr. Smith Goes to Washington* (Frank Capra, 1936) for a similar aspect of their message.[10] Schulberg borrowed the scenes in which the character played by Jimmy Stewart, having just arrived in the nation's capital, takes a bus ride through its main historical, legal, and political centers.[11] Jefferson's humanistic words were the converse of Hitler's aggressive, threatening discourse. For the latter, a note in the script's margin specified that they needed to locate the "most hysterical and vicious" shot available in the OSS archives. But, as in the case of the edited montage of *The Nazi Plan*, it was especially the speech's tone and content that mattered: "If I, Adolf Hitler, can send the flower of the German nation into the hell of war without the smallest pity for spilling precious German blood, then surely I have the right to remove millions of an inferior race that breeds like vermin." To ensure the best and broadest understanding of Hitler's words, his remarks were dubbed in English with a heavy German accent imitating the tone of his voice.

After this opening, the film connects the fate of the concentration camp victims to Lt. Telford Taylor's eyewitness account filmed at Mauthausen. Shots of dead camp deportees and people in tears at funerals are reduced to a single scene, accompanied by the question, repeated further on, "How can we rectify these crimes?" Three examples are considered: the "sadist" in charge of Buchenwald; the doctor who misused certain medicines to turn them into instruments of death; and the technician who fine-tuned the gas chamber. The commentary stresses that the first one cannot be tortured, the second cannot be poisoned, and the third cannot be subjected to the deadly gas that killed thousands.

While the film started off on the grounds of strictly American values, its development evokes a justice that goes beyond traditional national and state contexts. The spirit of Roosevelt, Churchill, and Stalin's common declaration is recalled: "Germans who take part in wholesale shootings, executions, and have shared in the slaughter inflicted on innocent people will be judged by the people they have outraged . . . in order that Justice may be done."

Still, some problems are not covered over. International law is not going to be defined and applicable in a day. In a very pedagogical manner, the film uses diagrams to show the different types of trials already held or to come. Traitors to their country will be brought before their own national courts. Members of the Gestapo, SS, SA, and generally anyone who killed or mistreated American soldiers will be tried by military tribunals placed under the supervision of Gen. John M. Weir, head of the War Crimes Branch reporting to the judge advocate general. Filmed in his office, the judge advocate general himself explains the responsibilities of his position: "In France, under General [Edward C.] Betts, and in Italy, under General [Adam] Richmond, trials are under way. As fast as we can identify, hunt down and apprehend those responsible for committing atrocities against American prisoners of war, we are going to bring them to trial and hold them accountable for their acts."

In fact the relationship between Jackson's team and General Weir was not one of great mutual confidence, although it was improving over the summer of 1945. As we have already seen, when Jackson began his job at the IMT, he felt that the work in London of the Commission for the Investigation of War Crimes, like that of the judge advocate general in the European theater, had not produced much in the way of concrete results. On May 17, 1945, John H. Amen let it be known that "the JAG had not heard a single case and had practically nothing that would make it possible to convict the principal defendants." It is clear, though, that it was easier to convince the American people of the necessity of creating the IMT by closely associating it with the fate of GIs who had been victims of German abuse than by promoting the notion of a universal justice. One of the few documents filmed with a caption stand and inserted into *That Justice Be Done* is the copy of Hitler's order from October 10, 1942, demanding the execution of soldiers of enemy commandos who were captured. With this violation of international agreements in mind, the film presented a series of shots whose continuity also evoked a history that now allowed the United States, itself founded on the affirmation of a strong bond to justice, to help in Europe redefine the common laws and relations between nation-states.[12]

Written in the summer of 1945 under the influence of Stimson's group, the film's final script still had to wear kid gloves in dealing with the staff of the European Theater of Operations. The judge advocate general had used certain passages of the report Jackson submitted to Truman in early June, and a new directive received by Eisenhower in September concerning the role of the U.S. Army of Occupation gave the former renewed initiative. The film clearly stated that the cases heard by the JAG general staff were distinct from the one being built under the aegis of the UN to put the big criminals on trial. As he watched a first cut of the film on September 6, 1945, at the OSS base, Jackson stressed that the film was a way "to educate the public as to what we are trying to accomplish."[13] He suggested removing a particularly horrible hanging scene and asked that the film be updated to include the recent signing of the London Agreement on August 8, 1945, and the progress made in preparing the IMT.[14]

The film thus concludes by underscoring that the International Tribunal's mission was to "outlaw the greatest inhumanity that man inflicts upon himself, the crime of war." While America's indignation could be immediate when it came to crimes committed against its own citizens, a concerted attempt to explain and convince proved necessary for the general population to grasp what, according to Mark Osiel, French sociologist Émile Durkeim's criminology did not sufficiently confront, "the moral complexity in much wrongdoing, even wrongdoing on a massive scale, complexity that criminal law—especially on *mens rea*, justification, and excuse—seeks to acknowledge and accommodate."[15]

The Place of German Citizens and Spectators

After having long favored an expeditious solution concerning captured leaders of the Third Reich, the Soviets had finally rallied to the idea of an international tribunal. They did so by most often taking an obstructive attitude toward Jackson's proposals in the preparatory meetings for the IMT's creation and in the definition of the charges. To the Americans, it was clear that the task of highlighting the trial's history lessons would fall to them. What they had seen of Soviet military justice, for instance, had hardly struck them as exemplary. The film *German Atrocities Committed at Kharkov* (Moscow, 1945) showed some signs of equity (a shot of defense attorneys, the presence of the press and of public figures like Soviet intellectual Ilya Ehrenburg and Leo Tolstoy's distant relative Aleksey Nikolayevich), but it ended in applause with a verdict pronouncing a death sentence by public hanging with no option to appeal.[16] As for the British, based on a memo dated June 16, 1945, and sent to Jackson by one of his principal collaborators, Francis M. Shea, it appears that they were ready to leave the filming of the trial to the Americans: "[American photographer and occasional filmmaker] Tony Muto told me this morning that he hoped you would see that the English did not interfere with American moving pictures of the Military Tribunal. I too think that pictures of the opening of the trial, and perhaps a few other subsequent activities, would be valuable historically and would show the people in the best possible way what you are doing."[17]

At the same time as *That Justice Be Done* was commissioned, the OSS was thus told to prepare to film the upcoming trial and make a historical documentary. A pool was set up, allowing the Allies to use footage by the

Americans. However, the Soviets nonetheless quickly sent Roman Karmen to the site so they could shoot additional footage with their own crew.[18]

In September 1946, while awaiting the Nuremberg verdict, the United States felt that the lessons of this unprecedented trial needed to be directed first and foremost at the German population, in the interests of de-Nazification and the politics of "reeducation." The Americans therefore proposed to the Allied Control Council in Berlin that the four occupation forces work together on a feature-length picture and distribute it in each of the zones. It seems that all agreed that the Americans would produce the film, with Gen. Robert Mc-Clure, the head of the Information Control Division of the Office of Military Government for Germany–United States (OMGUS), supervising the project.

McClure had no material means and especially no professional technicians at his disposal, so he turned to the War Department in Washington for help from a cinematographic branch of the Civil Affairs Division, directed by Pare Lorentz. There are notes in the U.S. National Archives about the question of resistance to Nazism sent by the great German playwright and scriptwriter Carl Zuckmayer (himself in the midst of writing *The Devil's General*, which premiered in 1946). As someone who knew his country's history well, Zuckmayer believed that a movie on the Nuremberg Trial was essential for Germany's "reorientation," as long as it was a true "document of justice": "We have the chance to prove to the Germans and to the world that justice is stronger than force and that the principles of right and law must be respected among individuals as well as among nations. Moreover, we have the possibility to display not only the Nazis and their system but the entire complex and fatal philosophy of German nationalism."[19]

In his presentation of the project, Zuckmayer argues that the film's message, and thus the meaning of the trial, must not be based on formulations that are too "broad or general," such as "crimes against humanity" or "against world peace." He sees it as important to focus prominently on individual responsibility, despite the defendants' pleas of not guilty, so that the actions that led some people to participate in Nazi power could be distinguished from those that led other people to fight against it. He quite articulately points out that "if we don't find the Germans to advocate and plead this picture's cause, we might hardly find the German audience that wants to see it." Indeed the place of the German spectator could not be unilaterally that of the accused, of the guilty party. It was only right to provide Germans with another option, a perspective that looked toward their future and opened a new horizon: "I could imagine a Bishop, a Protestant minister, a judge, a teacher, a workman, a woman whose husband was executed by the *Volksgericht* [people's court], a young crippled war veteran, a peasant, a mother, a poet; a premium of people who have missed the chance to try their own oppressors in time but who represent the better voice and conscience of a people which take these trials and the German defeat as a first step to a moral and national rebirth."

While Lorentz was busy in New York thinking about the film project, the OMGUS in Berlin commissioned a synopsis from John Scott, a journalist for *Time* magazine. Scott was writing a long shooting script entitled *Nuremberg Trial*.[20] The continuity proposed is structured by a series of steps. As an introduction, a selection of archival images is supposed to present the war in a very journalistic fashion, through a series of short flashes. The only sequence that identifies a precise historical reference is that of the crushing of the Warsaw Ghetto revolt. The other shots are anonymous (a sinking boat, a burning city, an artillery barrage, etc.) or interchangeable ("a road filled with hysterical refugees, France—1940 or Germany—1945"). Animated maps are interpolated to illustrate the principal phases of the war.[21] The commentary then insists, "So many millions of men, women, and children killed; so many made homeless. . . . Why?" A mention of the Moscow Conference (October 30, 1944) leads into Nuremberg and the IMT. From there, the film follows the chronology of the trial, dividing it up into what the writer terms "episodes," thirteen in all, each two minutes long, proceeding by themes or case studies: the conspiracy; the history of the Nazi Party; the annexation of Austria; the attack on Norway; Rudolf Höss's statement on Auschwitz; and so on. All these matters are tied to particular moments of the trial. The final judgment is the subject of a codicil specifying, "Eleven of the main war criminals had been executed, but many remained to be tried by future tribunals, many more were still at large. But a precedent had been established in International Law making the planning and waging of aggressive war by any nation a crime. This was the main significance of the trial at Nuremberg."

This project was carefully read by experts in OMGUS, including the assistant director of the Legal Division, Alvin J. Rockwell.[22] Rockwell believed the film could and should be destined only for Germans, to the exclusion of all other countries. Seen from this angle, it seemed to him that the project was not effective enough. It was not a question of placing the burden of guilt on all Germans but of vigorously putting the blame on the Nazi Party leaders who had contributed to establishing a policy resulting in "crimes against humanity and total war." He advised against showing too many shots of crowds cheering Hitler at party rallies and thought it unwise to show certain events which, like the treaties of Versailles, "were anything but perfect documents of fairness or justice." More generally, the question arose as to whether to retrace all the intricacies of the prosecution's case, at the risk of "putting the audience to sleep" through the repetition of technical terms that were standard in legal parlance but not always clear for the average person. In addition, Scott was criticized for dwelling on statistics and dry facts instead of on the narrative side of the case, and also of making insufficient use of the mass of documentary evidence presented in court.

These criticisms stipulate that the trial, even with its pedagogical orientation, had not given way to some sort of desire to turn it into a show. Osiel observes, "In orchestrating such a trial there may be some trade-off between the goals of didactic spectacle and adherence to liberal principle. Yet one should not exclude the possibility that the trial may fail in both respects. Nuremberg (and, even more, the Tokyo Trial) appear to have been both boring and illiberal at once, on many accounts."[23] One also has to take into account the novelty that the filming of the trial and almost immediate distribution of the film constituted for both judges and general public. Rockwell very aptly used the example of testimony from Erich Raeder (head of Germany's naval forces until 1943) and imagined the film's future viewers as being in the position of a jury. Rockwell was not convinced that, in Raeder's telling of how the attack on Norway was prepared, the German grand admiral would be perceived as guilty: "Although I recognize the fact that we do not wish this film to appear to the German mind as a biased version of the trials, I cannot help but feel that, were I a German witnessing this single instance purporting to typify Admiral Raeder's part in the trials, I would, rather than coming away with the opinion that he was a Nazi criminal, consider him a man to be well proud of and one who had been sadly put upon when sentenced to life imprisonment."

One should remember, however, that these reactions came from a population that had just lived this history and was now being summoned to make a critical evaluation of it before having had time to take stock of it personally. The trial was taking place before the events were even over, yet the IMT's organizers had in mind a trial to establish history. True, insofar as the proceedings had not allowed the victims to act jointly with the prosecutor, the arguments were established on a solid documentary foundation, and, unlike what we often see in present-day classifications, it did not set out to highlight and honor memory. The film would therefore also be judged by this yardstick, with its distribution and its impact reaching beyond German audiences and the brief lapse of time since the events themselves.

In addition to these multiple constraints there were turf wars between Berlin and Washington. Instead of Scott's OMGUS-sponsored script, the assistant secretary of war decided in fact to promote a rival project, led by Stuart Schulberg and Lorentz (who had directed the U.S. Film Service until Congress cut off its federal funding when the United States joined in the war). It was only logical that the work of writing and finding suitable footage be done in the United States; all the members of the American prosecution team had come back to Washington, and most of the films taken from the Germans, along with the rushes of the trial, were now being kept on Long Island.[24] So on January 20, 1947, Schulberg in turn presented a script project approved by Lorentz.[25] While not markedly different from Scott's script, this document had the benefit of Schulberg's experience in Nuremberg (in particular concerning the presentation of film as evidence and the follow-up of the filming of the trial) and of inside connections with Jackson.

Although the film began with archival footage, just as Scott's did, these images were less spectacular and were supposed to situate the historical, geographical, and human context in which the trial was going to take place: a Europe in ruins, with refugees, displaced persons, and deportees returning from the camps crisscrossing it in every direction. After mention of the Potsdam Conference, the reading of the indictment at Nuremberg was followed by long excerpts from Jackson's opening speech, no doubt a strong nod in his direction so that he would support Lorentz and Schulberg's project instead of Scott's. Then, in a chronological mode, the film would alternate excerpts of the filmed trial with archival images taken for the most part from films presented as evidence. When information was lacking on the existence of images that could accompany what was said in court, the elements that needed to be found were noted in the script's margins. Hence the indication regarding the speech by Russian prosecutor Roman Rudenko: "Russian film appropriate to text" or "Film on terror in Poland and USSR." For Höss's testimony, the list of archives to be tracked down was more precise and recalled how Ford's team had had to find film images for a count of the indictment prior to the trial:

CONCENTRATION CAMP MATERIAL
a) Gas chambers
b) Sprinkler system
c) Signs saying "Baden," etc.

Lawyers for the accused were given more attention than in the Scott project, and, on the whole, each of the Allies received equal treatment. In the end, the film's commentary emphasized the "lesson" of Nuremberg:

> Europe—1947, and Civilization, the real complaining party, tries to rise from the ruins, to rebuild cities, rebuild lives, rebuild peace. Today, learning the lesson of the Nuremberg Trial, Europe knows the answers. Today we know what happens between [sic] the holocaust years and why. But for Germany, there is a special lesson in the Nuremberg Trial. It warns—perhaps for the last time—that the people of Germany must turn away forever from Nazi philosophies of hate and destruction. It warns that they must replace master race theories with brotherhood, aggression and Nazism with peace and democracy. Only that way can Germany and the world find real peace—a peace based, like the Nuremberg Trial, on justice and humanity.[26]

Some rather heated discussions ensued between Washington and Berlin, which tried to thwart the Lorentz and Schulberg project by asking another journalist, Michael Gordon, to write a new script called *Nuremberg Judgment*.[27] The secretary of war came down in favor of the first project and informed General Clay, Director of the OMGUS, of his decision, made in concert with Jackson. In May 1947 Lorentz and Schulberg thus went to Berlin accompanied by an editor, taking along twelve hours of filmed archives selected from the holdings stored on Long Island. However, the other Allies did not understand why the Americans were taking so long to get the film under way and took the liberty of starting up their own production. The French made a two-reel news montage, while the Soviets took the opportunity to showcase their point of view by asking Karmen to produce a film more than one hour long, which he did in record time.

In the Name of the Martyrs and the Victims: Nuremberg as Seen by the Soviets

Nuremberg: The Trial was aimed first and foremost at German viewers and Red Army troops in the Soviet occupied zone. Yet because it had also been designed to showcase in the eyes of all the role played by the USSR in Nazi

Germany's capitulation and in the judgment of the latter's war criminals, the picture was shown at the end of May 1947 in New York's Stanley Theatre, prior to its Moscow release. The American promotion campaign made use of advertising's most hard-hitting effects for the film's preview trailer:

> SEE! The Secret Document of the Nazi Master Plan for the Conquest of the World!
> SEE! The Graphic, Terrifying Evidence of the Nazis' Most Fiendish Crimes.
> SEE! Goering, Hess, Ribbentrop, Streicher, and Other Nazi Arch-Criminals in the Greatest Roundup of Hitlers Brought to JUSTICE in a People's Court.
> SEE! *The Nuremberg Trials.*
> UNCUT! Full Length! OFFICIAL!
> Get a Ringside Seat at History's Greatest Criminal Trials.
> Photographed by Soviet Cameramen.
> An Artkino Release.

Conceived by Artkino, which two years earlier had presented the first footage of the extermination camps, the promotional trailer foregrounded a quote from Justice Jackson and downplayed the cameramen's Soviet origins. The fact that the USSR's film came out before the American version must have sufficed for Karmen, presented in the credits as a "Stalin Laureate." In the trade paper *Variety,* the heading of an article on the Americans' setbacks made clear what the stakes were in these early days of the Cold War: "[Americans] Claim Internal U.S. Army Snarl Let Reds Beat Yanks on Nuremberg Film."[28] The Soviets were thus winning the communications battle and could calmly claim the Nuremberg Trial for themselves.

In their presentation of the war's end and the creation of the IMT, the Soviets gave themselves the lion's share of credit. As Jackson quite rightly observes in a letter dated October 21, 1948, "This is done not by false pictures but by arrangement of the sequence."[29] The facts—the Red Army's arrival in Berlin, the arrest of Nazi authorities, Generalfeldmarschall Wilhelm Keitel's surrender in Karlshorst—were true. The cameramen had recorded Soviet soldiers in combat, staging scenes where necessary, but the Allies were used to this. An agreement with the U.S. military left the taking of the Reich's capital to the Soviets, though it came at a cost heavy in human losses.[30] In short, there was no real distortion of history, just a focus on the last phase of the Great Patriotic War. When the Soviets were not the sole or main protagonists, they found other ways to leave their mark on an event. For example, at the entrance to the Nuremberg courthouse, a shot of the guards allowed the film's narrator to announce, "The time for justice has come. These warriors of the Red Army fought at Stalingrad; now they are guarding Nuremberg." Similarly, when the turn came for Rudenko's first courtroom speech, his taking the floor was presented as an "event." *Nuremberg: The Trial* is less surprising for its claim that the Soviets had a decisive role in ending Nazism than for certain writing choices.

In their first cut, Lorentz and Schulberg chose to open their film with shots of the devastation of Europe that inevitably mixed Germany's fate with that of other European countries. Jackson expressed serious reservations about this sequence, similar to that which opened Roberto Rossellini's *Germany Year Zero* (1948): "The film opens with the picture of destruction and misery in Germany which at once arouses sympathy with the Germans and self-pity of the Germans. That impression is pretty firmly implanted long before it appears that their present plight is the recoil of their own aggressions. I am fearful it might stimulate their feeling that they are wronged people and tend to make them applaud the scenes of prosperity, pomp and power, and to long for the good old days of the Nazis."[31]

The Soviets avoided this pitfall by leading with the ruins of Nuremberg as the symbol of the Nazis' military and political defeat and by stating that a trial had long been slated, one that would take place "in the very lair of Nazism," devoid of any spirit of "vengeance," motivated only by a desire for "truth." Even more remarkable is the presentation of the Court during the solemn opening of the IMT: "This court of nations speaks in the name of the martyrs and the victims, those of Majdanek. One united protest issues from those mass graves, a single sigh resonates in those death camp crematoria."

The allusion to victims of the camps thus seems to legitimize the authority conferred upon the judges, now guardians of the memory of the dead and of the survivors' testimony: "This torture of all humanity must not remain unpunished. With the same prayer, each survivor beseeches human justice. The memory and dignity of these victims, their cries and their entreaties, will stay forever etched in the conscience of these judges, who will be their echo in the face of these torturers, henceforth reduced to a state of powerlessness."

This reference to universal conscience is not abstract or ambiguous, as it often was in Soviet declarations and in films made after the liberations of Majdanek and Auschwitz-Birkenau. Victims are specifically named in conjunction with their oppressors: Ernst Kaltenbrunner, who has "on his conscience those millions of murders in the gas chambers"; Hans Frank, who "swore that the Jews had to be exterminated"; and Julius Streicher, "the corruptor of young people, who nicknamed himself the Anti-Jew."

It is true that Rudenko brought to the first meeting (September 17, 1945) of the representatives of the public ministry a mass of documents from the Soviet Special State Commission on War Crimes, thereby enriching the documentary basis for the portion of the trial addressing the results of the Nazi politics of extermination. But as Michael Marrus reminds us, "Most of the Nuremberg prosecutors readily spoke about the Jews."[32] However, the apparent ease with which the Soviets broached the question of anti-Jewish politics must be placed in a broader perspective that jumbles together all of the victims, be they civilian or military, Polish or Soviet, as was done in the Red Army piece *Film Documents on the Atrocities of the German-Fascist Invaders*. Moreover the other allies had agreed that the IMT would not raise the issue of the German-Soviet Non-Aggression Pact, its ensuing policy of dividing the spoils of Poland, or still yet the invasion of the Baltic States. As we have seen, the Allies settled for tempering the Soviet prosecution's impulsive desire to demonstrate that the Germans had committed the Katyn massacres. They hailed Andrey Vyshinsky's presence at Nuremberg.[33] The narrator of *Nuremberg: The Trial* could thus flatly state that "only the Soviet Union survived the peril of fascist aggression. The Munich Accords deluded the totality of Europe's nations, which were quickly invaded. All Hitler and Keitel talked about was redrawing the map of Europe."[34] The film also indicated in no uncertain terms that Iona Nikitchenko (the Soviet judge of the IMT) held a very dim view of the court's decisions: "[Nikitchenko] did not agree with the verdicts on Schacht, Papen, and Fritzsche. He wanted to see the death penalty applied for Hess."[35] Decisions concerning the Government of the Reich and its military leadership and High Command were contested as well: "This opinion was shared by the progressive world of the time." In its evocation of "the world-wide cause of peace among peoples, a democratic and lasting peace," and the implied suggestion that the Soviets were its best safeguard, the film's conclusion used a hackneyed ideological language far removed from the arguments pitched at its outset. This only added to the bitterness of the Americans whose own film, finished late in 1949, never had the same impact as Karmen's.

The Americans Deprived of the "Lessons" of the Trial

The beginnings of the Cold War and the Berlin blockade seriously complicated the message that the War Department wanted to get across to Germany.[36] Indeed the Americans soon went from occupiers to liberators for many Germans who did not wish to be under the Soviet yoke. Already Nuremberg seemed to belong to the past, both in its intended pedagogical force and in its affirmation of universal values guaranteed by the UN. For its part, the OMGUS continued to be a thorn in the side of Schulberg's team, whereas Lorentz was caught up in a witch hunt. He was eventually obliged to open up about it to Jackson, telling him on May 12, 1947, that he was resigning from his position in the film division at the War Department because he had run up against the counterespionage services in New York. (They wanted to verify his "loyalty with respect to the government" and also to view his Roosevelt-era movies to see if they carried a "subversive" message.) Lorentz admitted, "After four years of service in the air corps, I find that rather humiliating." The creator of the IMT could only reply, "I am sorry to learn of the difficulties you have had. The investigation of your loyalty seems to one who has known you as long as I have, so fantastic as to discredit not you but the people who are engaged in such business. We seem to be passing through a period of hysteria."[37]

It ended up taking another eighteen months to finish *Nuremberg: Its Lesson for Today* (dir. Stuart Schulberg, 1948). Formally it was a well-balanced work, maintaining a good equilibrium between filmed trial archives and news subjects taken from *The Nazi Plan* and *Nazi Concentration Camps*, as well as between the respective roles of the four Allies and the prosecution and the defense. The documentary highlighted how first the Stimson group and then the Jackson team built the trial around the conspiracy charge. By condensing their account of the trial to a chronological summary of seventy-eight minutes, the interpretation of Nazi policy, anchored in its "intent," emerged even more sharply in a demonstration framed by two long clips of Jackson speaking. The excerpt employed at the conclusion was particularly effective: "At Nuremberg, the world discovered what happened and why. But Nuremberg offers more than an answer to a question. 'This trial is part of the great effort to make the peace more secure. It constitutes juridical action of a kind to ensure that those who start a war will pay for it personally. Nuremberg stands as a warning to all those who plan and wage aggressive war.'"

The film, which ends with an image of a sculpture of Christ on the cross that had visibly been damaged during the war, indicates in the credits that the OMGUS produced it and that the sound was done in Berlin's Tempelhof Studios. While Lorentz was no longer part of the film's executive direction, Stuart Schulberg oversaw the final editing before being named in 1949 head of the OMGUS Information Services Division's film unit, and then taking over that of the Marshall Plan.

In an article published in an OMGUS brochure, Schulberg seems quite satisfied with the reactions noted at the film's first showing (November 21, 1948, in Stuttgart), where it ran for three weeks. More than fifty thousand people went to see it in Munich.[38] Studies of the film's reception were conducted by the Military Government's Opinion Surveys Branch (OSB) in Nuremberg (February 3–9, 1949), as well as in Wurzburg and Bamburg.[39] The section of the OSB report pertaining to Bamberg concerned 386 viewers in all, 60 percent of whom returned completed questionnaires. This small number is an indication of an attendance index that did not allow the film to run for long. Moreover word-of-mouth did little to motivate others to see the picture. It is true that the screenings occurred mere weeks before Germany gradually regained its sovereignty, beginning in May. More than 80 percent of the sample said they agreed with the film's message, which they considered to be solidly grounded in fact. Two elements of the film were most often cited as standing out in their minds. On the one hand, they were struck by the regime's acts of cruelty committed against the Jews, prisoners of war, and various populations as a whole.[40] But, on the other, they felt the authors revealed a bias in showing only Nazi crimes and not those committed by the Allies (the Russians, in particular). In its conclusions, the OSB raises the question of the desirability of showing the Germans this type of picture, at least during the period that featured the screenings: "The audiences reached by this film were quite limited in scope, which brings up the question whether in the future documentary films of this type should not be substituted by regular feature films more subtly carrying the message to be conveyed." Another OSB query reflected upon the very nature of the spectators who went to see the film: "The film largely carried its message to an audience which by and large believed it to begin with, and it failed to reach the concentrations of those who need reeducation in this respect."

Would the picture have been better received in the United States? Even before the German release of *Nuremberg: Its Lesson for Today*, Lorentz thought he could get back in the mix early in the new year by offering the war secretary the services of his production company in the hopes of making the movie's American version and taking charge of its domestic distribution. Thus began another long soap opera in which Jackson again had to intervene. On October 21, 1948, the judge seemed resigned to the idea that the Nuremberg Trial no longer interested Americans, except perhaps "those who had friends or family in concentration camps."[41] Several solutions were considered, such as presenting the film as the last episode of the famous series *Why We Fight*.[42] Also intervening was William Shirer, a Peabody Award–winning journalist who covered the Nuremberg trials. Having watched a mediocre copy of the film furnished by the OMGUS for a press screening, Shirer contacted Jackson to tell him that the movie absolutely needed to be shown to the American public.[43] On March 11 Jackson reported in a letter to Lorentz that he had hesitated to inform high-ranking officials such as Gen. Omar N. Bradley of the blockage of the film because the justice felt that they were not very favorable toward the war crimes program.[44] In late 1950 Lorentz was still reworking the script for a revised version of the film, incorporating recent international developments and still seeking support, especially in legal circles.

Herbert Wechsler, a law professor at Columbia University, was one of the readers of this new document. A Democrat who had been involved in New Deal politics in the 1930s and served as an assistant attorney general during the war, he was part of Stimson's group and helped define the principles of the London Agreement. Judge Francis Biddle had proposed that he join him as an advisor in Nuremberg along with another law professor, Quincy Wright. Rich from this experience and familiar with Schulberg's work, Wechsler delivered interesting remarks on it at a law school convention in Chicago on December 28, 1950, just prior to the projection of the film accompanied by commentary read in English.[45] The tone was not an optimistic one. The film dealt with death and destruction, and the "sinister" mood of the day was not inclined toward reflection. The only specific event mentioned by Wechsler was the Korean War, but one can easily imagine that he had the Cold War in mind when he spoke of a dictatorship that, "no less malevolent than Hitler's, dominates large portions of the world today and holds the rest at bay." Wechsler added that perhaps it would take still more wars for institutions to be solid enough to ensure that law would prevail. Nuremberg was therefore not just a distant memory, and for Wechsler one of its principal lessons echoed what Jackson had called for ten years earlier: "Nuremberg served to stay the hand of private violence by public assumption of responsibility for judgment and for punishment. That undertaking made it possible to judge the enemy by standards we would accept for ourselves."

The "Strange Victory of 1945" as Seen by Leo T. Hurwitz

The lessons of the trial were not only drawn by filmmakers working in an official capacity. For Hurwitz, one of the founding members of the Film and Photo League (FPL), it was a personal matter, as much in the analysis he wanted to articulate as in its cinematographic writing.

Like most of his colleagues, Hurwitz worked for the federal government during the war.[46] But it is *Native Land*, codirected with Paul Strand in 1942 for the production cooperative Frontier Films, that concerns us most directly here. In the tradition of *The Plow That Broke the Plains* (dir. Lorentz, 1936), the picture opens with an exalted reminder of the first immigrants: "Here, on this stony sea-coast, we founded liberty, we built liberty into the beams of our house. We, the plain people—plowman and pioneer—lived and fought and dreamed a new kind of nation, a new kind of life, under a new sky—free of all tyranny."[47]

The lyrical accents of this ode to the pioneers won over Frank Capra when he was in the midst of producing the series *Why We Fight*. He took a clip from *Native Land* about Plymouth Rock and placed it at the beginning of the episode entitled *War Comes to America* (1945). For Capra, war needed to bring the American people together around their founding ideals. For Hurwitz and Strand, defending civil rights was a constant imperative, and citizens should not take it for granted. Whatever the context, fighting the forces hostile to basic U.S. freedoms was necessary. A text at the outset of the film clarified the authors' intentions: "Since the founding of our country, the American people have had to fight for their freedom in every generation. *Native Land* is a document of America's struggle for liberty in recent years. It was in this struggle that the fascist-minded on our soil were forced to retreat. And the people gained the democratic strength essential for national unity and for victory over the Axis."

Begun in 1938, the film was not completed until 1942 due to uneven financing coming from the activist network assembled by the FPL. It mentioned several news items that had been recorded by the U.S. Senate La Follette Civil Liberties Committee, such as the murder of a unionist in Michigan (1934) and Ku Klux Klan brutality in Florida (1935). Film archives were combined with reenacted scenes.

Paradoxically, the first difficulties Hurwitz and Strand encountered came from their own political turf. In a letter dated April 1, 1943, Joris Ivens very tactfully informed his friend Hurwitz of the unfavorable reactions from workers' organizations, representatives of the black community, and a few California activists who had participated in financing the film. The activists imposed changes because they felt that the values celebrated in the film—most likely the relation to nature, the *pastorale* of attachment to the land—"could work in favor of Hitler."[48] Little seen during the war, the film then became the object of a witch hunt.[49] By late 1947 the FPL was listed as one of the "totalitarian, fascist, communist or subversive organizations" cited in the official report requested by President Truman in order to assess the loyalty of federal agents.[50] In the course of a special meeting, the FPL's president Walter Rosenblum defended the organization's benevolent attitude toward the United States and quoted the words spoken in 1943 by Supreme Court Justice Robert H. Jackson, the future organizer of the trial of Nazi war criminals: "If there is any fixed star in our constitutional constellation, it is that no official, high or petty, can prescribe what shall be orthodox in politics, nationalism, religion or other matters of opinion, or force citizens to confess by word or act their faith therein. . . . Those who begin coercive elimination of dissent soon find themselves exterminating dissenters. Compulsory unification of opinion achieves only the unanimity of the graveyard." Rosenblum then spoke of the Nuremberg Trial and how Abraham Pomerantz, an American member of the prosecution, had characterized the U.S. political situation upon his return home: "'We are giving Nazi war criminals American justice, and American citizens, Nazi justice.' Thus did [Pomerantz] characterize the summary dismissal of federal employees under the President's loyalty purge. He said that he had seen the accused Nazis given fullest protection of civil and legal rights. He returned to find Americans fired out of jobs without hearings, or right to confront accusers or cross-examine, or even to know the charges against them."[51]

Hurwitz did not figure in the credits of the work he had done as a documentary filmmaker. While blacklisted, he directed two films that commented on the postwar period and the concentration and extermination camps, *Strange Victory* (1948) and *The Museum and the Fury* (1956).

Strange Victory premiered in September 1948 in New York. It was produced by Barnet Lee Rosset, Jr., known later as Barney Rosset, owner of
Grove Press and editor in chief of *Evergreen Review*, but at the time a young
World War II veteran who had directed a unit of combat cameramen in
China. Born into a wealthy Chicago family, he met Hurwitz and came under the sway of his political commitments to the point of joining the Communist Party during their two-year collaboration. Both of them considered
the victory of 1945 a "strange" one, insofar as the values which the Americans
had defended, the very ones constituting the underlying spirit of Nuremberg, were not (or no longer) respected in the United States. In the first half
of 1947 they combed through the cinematographic archives from which the
movie would essentially be compiled. Their screening notes attest both to
the orientation of the project and to the enormous work done to locate the
footage. The list of film libraries consulted is indicative of their extensive efforts: Artkino, the Canadian Film Board, Mayer and Burstyn, MoMA, the
State Department, the Signal Corps, and *March of Time*. Likewise the clip
selection from Allied-directed films confirms the scope of their enterprise:
Stalingrad, Ukraine in Flames (dir. Aleksandr Dovzhenko, 1944), *Moscow
Strikes Back* (dir. Ilya Kopalin and Leonid Varlamov, 1942), *Oswiecim, Liberation of Paris, Camps of the Dead, Nuremberg, We Accuse, You Can't Kill a
City, Guilty Men* (dir. Tom Daly, 1945), *Suffer Little Children* (dir. Sydney
Newman, 1945), *In the Wake of the Army, Food: Secret of the Peace* (dir. Stuart Legg, 1945), *A City Sings, The War for Men's Minds* (dir. Legg, 1943), *57,000
Nazis in Moscow, Czechoslovakia, Professor Mamlock* (dirs. Adolf Minkin
and Gerbert Rappaport, 1938), *One Tenth of a Nation*, and *Lights out in Europe*
(dirs. Herbert Kline and Alexander Hammid, 1940).

In the attention given to current events and already existing films, as in
their critical reading, Hurwitz revived the FPL's heritage and reflected on
how it not only reused but created images organized according to an event-
based frame. Although they were articulated in several segments in order to
facilitate the search for archives, the themes proposed clearly suggest the
meaning that the authors wanted to give their montage: it was due to the commitment of all, including blacks in the army and women in the war effort, that
the Nazi "infection" had been eradicated. In film images of bombardments,
destroyed cities, and concentration camps, the fight led by the Americans,
British, and Soviets was justified by the attacks on freedom in a Europe of
which "we were the children and grandchildren." Nazism had been fueled by
an "idea that made men unequal," contrary to the American ideal.

Quickly, though, the film slipped toward another message. Certainly, in order to judge these "new crimes," a "new law" had been applied at Nuremberg, but peace had not ushered in a positive evolution in American mentalities, in particular where racism and anti-Semitism were concerned. Although Hitler had disappeared in April 1945, his voice still echoed in the United States. As a narrator announces at the beginning of the film, "The loser [is] still active in the land of the winner." The "enemy's ideas" wafted around the KKK and other groups like the German-American Bund that openly proclaimed allegiance to the Nazi project. In fairly radical terms, *Strange Victory* denounced these "fascists" and the segregation of which blacks (primarily, but also Jews) continued to be victims.[52] It is useful here to recall that Jackson had intervened several times before the war to combat American anti-Semitism in the name of the nation's values of tolerance. While Rosset and Hurwitz's discourse mentions this argument in passing (doubtless because of the directors' Jewish roots), the collaborators focus above all on defending the civil rights of blacks.

The film met with little success in its brief run in theaters. It had been promoted on a modest budget through some advertising inserts in the press that failed to make the movie's intent very clear. A couple was shown fleeing a menacing dark cloud, and the caption read, "Powerful! Persuasive! Pulls no punches! The most daring and provocative story of prejudice ever shown on the screen!"

Though rather discreet, critical response was not particularly negative. Under the title "*Strange Victory* Hits Racial Bias," the *New York World Telegram* (September 25, 1948) provides a sympathetic summary of the content but considers the subject to be more convincing than its rendering. In the left-leaning *Daily Worker* (September 27, 1948), Herb Tank astutely insists on the film's poetic dimension and the way it mixes archival shots with footage of 1947 New York and surrounding areas. At the same time, though, Tank notes with regret that the production of documentaries fostered in the early 1930s and kept up during the war had now come to an end: "During the grim hour of war, filmmakers dreamed of continuing the flow of significant documentaries that marked the war years. It was hoped then that the documentary film, with its study of social reality, would turn a revealing searchlight on our times and help men to build an abundant life in peace. But *Strange Victory* has stomped on that dream."[53]

Some reviewers on the right, however, were less favorable. The *New York Journal American* of the Hearst group ran the headline "The Red Party Line in *Strange Victory*," with Frank Conniff wondering "how the industry will explain a garish little firebrand of a pamphlet on display at the Ambassador Theatre." As a result, the army's Security Division called for an FBI investigation of Rosset's "loyalty," but the response was clear enough: "No investigation by FBI pertinent to your inquiry."[54]

The movie was the big event of Italy's Mostra International Festival of Cinematographic Art, where some journalists and filmmakers interpreted its late-night slot at the Lido as a sort of censorship jointly devised by the film festival's director and the American delegation's representative. Hurwitz used this montage again in 1964, adding images (mostly photographic) of the civil rights movement and the famous 1963 march on Washington. New commentary explained, "This is where *Strange Victory* ended in 1948. But the forces this film shared with life kept moving. . . . If we want victory, we'll still have to get it."

The victory had gone from strange to bitter. Caught in the torment of the Cold War and McCarthyism, Hurwitz was led to consider his Jewishness at a time when it seemed to him that America's memory of the camps was fading. He therefore accepted a request to make a movie for Polski Films and the Auschwitz Museum, initially called *Memory at Oswiecim* and then *The Museum and the Fury*. Somewhat disappointed by the recent coproduction of Alain Resnais's *Night and Fog*, the Poles believed Hurwitz would succeed in situating the history of the genocide in a society now swept up by other historical dramas.

Opening with a shot of a human face so as to better evoke its decomposition in the camps, the film explicitly evoked the extermination of the Jews. This was significant since the makers of *Night and Fog* ultimately chose to eliminate all specific references to this.[55] The problem remained, though, of how to communicate the horror of the camps in a museum whose function it is to conserve works of art. How could the beauty of the traces left by artists since the days of antiquity be made to coexist with the inhumanity of the death camps? These issues were the point of departure for poet Thomas McGrath, whose poem-text appears against the backdrop of Hurwitz's film images. "Humanity is not a category in a textbook," writes McGrath, "but a kinship of shared experiences." Hurwitz would later explain what he had sought to do:

> I tried to make a film-poem out of the substance of facts and essences. The facts relate to the Nazi concentration camps. The essences

relate to human destructiveness and human creativity reflected in
art. The facts of the concentration camps are among the harshest
facts of our time. They are so difficult to grasp within a human context, so unbearable in their reflection on the unboundedness of human evil, that we have closed the door of memory on them, act as if
they never existed. Yet, these facts pursue us. And, unless from the
arc of our own experience in the mid-twentieth century, we grasp
these facts and relate them to ourselves, we cannot comprehend what
has followed or what has gone before.[56]

The film began by showing the close relationship that connects art and
the memory of humanity; the trajectory of a life was presented, starting
from childhood and moving on to the period of initiation, the mystery of
love, work, and old age. In counterpoint to this peaceful vision, a visit to the
Auschwitz Museum reflected upon humanity's forces of destruction. Archival footage of the war, the liberation of the camps, and Nazis brought before
the IMT in Nuremberg were followed by contemporary images of the social
administration of Warsaw, whose reconstruction nevertheless should cause
the past to be forgotten. The film's conclusion was an invitation to remembrance and celebrated the continuity of life, constantly renewed. A deeply
personal work, *The Museum and the Fury* was never released in Poland and
had to wait until the 1980s to be seen in the United States, thanks to MoMA,
among others.[57]

CHAPTER 9

Documentary Archives and Fictional Film Narratives

Faced with distrustful military authorities and caught in the tormented machinations of a political witch hunt, American documentary filmmakers were unable to complete their project (Lorentz) or get it shown to a large audience (Hurwitz). Would fiction have a better chance of popularizing the lessons of Nuremberg? Three filmmakers took up the challenge: Orson Welles and Samuel Fuller for the probative power of film, and Stanley Kramer for the staging of the trial itself.

"One Step Forward": Orson Welles and Films of the Camps

Welles was the first to think to show the evidentiary role of Nazi camp film footage in a fictional story that revealed its truth-telling power. In the summer of 1945, producer Sam Spiegel, a protégé of Columbia Pictures chief Harry Cohn, was charged by William Goetz on behalf of International Pictures with asking Welles if he would like to act in the film then entitled *Date with Destiny*. Of Jewish Polish descent, Spiegel had studied at the University of Vienna and in the early 1930s had directed the Berlin subsidiary of Universal Studios. After the Nazis came to power, he left for Paris and London, where he met John Huston. Spiegel then began a new career as a producer in the United States under the name S. P. Eagle.[1] Welles was on the outs in Hollywood since the commercial failure of *Citizen Kane* (1941) and *The Magnificent Ambersons* (1942) and his ensuing departure from RKO.[2] Goetz and Spiegel were resolved not to have Welles direct the picture, but he managed to change their minds by agreeing to harsh contractual conditions. The producer reserved the right to change the script before the shoot, but once filming began Welles himself had to respect the script as established. In addition, the legendary actor-director had to commit to reimbursing the production company if he went over budget and agree that he would not be paid until the last day of filming.[3] The initial script of *Date with Destiny*, proposed by Anthony Veiler, was soon rebaptized by Victor Trivas as *The Stranger*.[4]

Instead of depicting an American plunged into Germany's disarray after the Nazi surrender—the subject of documentary films like *Your Job in Germany* (U.S. War Department, 1945)—Welles and Trivas chose to work from the opposite premise, that of a Nazi criminal who fled to the United States under a false identity and transformed himself into an ordinary American without anyone's noticing.[5] Throughout 1944–45 Welles had given talks in the United States on "the survival of fascism" and "the nature of the enemy." Michael Denning points out that, "Like many of his contemporaries, [Welles] saw a continuum between European fascism and domestic fascism, between Hitler and Hearst, the Brown Shirts and the Black Legion."[6]

For the first time in his career, Welles, unable to use his preferred crew, had to deal with having his casting choices nullified and making compromises with an editor from the production company, Ernest J. Nims.[7] In an interview with Peter Bogdanovich, the genius behind *Citizen Kane* explains that John Huston "wrote most of the script, under the table because he was in the army at the time and couldn't take credit."[8] Huston had indeed joined Capra's team in the Signal Corps in 1942 and directed three important films: *Report from the Aleutians* (1943), *The Battle of San Pietro* (1945), and *Let There Be Light* (1946). Before he had even finished editing the second of these, Huston was assigned to do the third. *Let There Be Light* was supposed to show how American soldiers traumatized by the war were cared for at Long Island's Mason Hospital through psychotherapy, hypnosis, and narcosynthesis. The army banned the film, however, arguing that soldiers should not be shown in such a state, even if in the end they were cured of their illnesses. This is probably why Huston preferred not to be seen as Welles's scriptwriter. For various reasons (Jewish origin, participation in filming the war, political engagement under Roosevelt), the crew for *The Stranger*, diverse as it was, was very involved in the period leading up to Germany's surrender and in bringing its principal leaders to justice. It was therefore not by chance that the film pits an official of the Allied War Crimes Commission against a Nazi presented as having had important responsibilities in Germany's extermination policy planning.[9]

Even though Welles was not in favor, the choice of Edgar G. Robinson for the role of the Allied Commission official was relevant. Robinson had been very involved in Hollywood's anti-Nazi movement during the war and took part in a show at Madison Square Garden called "We Will Never Die." Conceived as a memorial ceremony for "the Jews murdered in Europe," it was followed by the staging of a "Postwar Peace Table," which prefigured the postwar trial and featured the Oscar-winning actor Paul Muni exclaiming, "There are four million Jews surviving in Europe. The Germans have promised to deliver to the world by the end of the year a Christmas package of four million dead Jews. And this is not a Jewish problem. It is a problem that belongs to humanity and it is a challenge to the soul of mankind."[10]

In *The Stranger*, Robinson's character, Inspector Wilson, convinces his colleagues in the Allied Commission of the necessity of releasing one of the Nazi war criminal's former assistants, a man named Meinike, because he could lead Wilson to the disguised fugitive. They all seem averse to taking such a risk, particularly the French commissioner, who argues that the blame would be on them if the tactic were to fail. Wilson settles the discussion emphatically, concluding, "This human filth must be destroyed."

Welles lends great credibility to his character of the Nazi villain hiding in the small Connecticut town of Harper. Known to the local population as a U.S. citizen and high school history professor going by the name of Charles Rankin, "the stranger" has successfully concealed his true identity as Franz Kindler, presented in the movie as being the one who "conceived the theory of genocide of populations in the defeated countries." Kindler "had a passion for anonymity. Newspapers have no picture of him. Before he disappeared, he destroyed all evidence linking him to his past, down to his fingerprints."

The idea that those in charge of the Nazi policy of extermination did all they could to eliminate all traces of it is not only true historically; it also explains why the Allies, whether in the UN War Crimes Commission or in the case preparation for the Nuremberg Trial, attached so much importance to finding reliable evidence concerning the Nazi camps. The work of truth on the genocide of Europe's Jews could not, however, rest solely on documents found in Nazi archives. It was necessary to interrogate the leaders arrested by the Allies to produce courtroom testimony and to subject some of them—the relevant officials of towns adjacent to the camps and, more broadly, the German population at large—to forced visits of the camps liberated in 1945.

The first script of *The Stranger* is dated August 9, 1945, and the last (which includes changes made during filming) is dated October 31, with shooting spanning from October 1 to December 1, 1945.[11] In October Welles's friend Madeline Karr sent him a long telex informing him of the creation of the International Military Tribunal and the public announcement of the indictments.[12] However, Welles had the idea of organizing a sequence of *The Stranger* around the projection of footage of the concentration camps well before November 29 (when *Nazi Concentration Camps* was shown in the Nuremberg courtroom).

In Welles's treatment, Inspector Wilson wants to convince Rankin's young wife, Mary, that she has just married a former Nazi. Wilson decides to summon her to the residence of her father (himself a judge) and to reveal to her the story of the criminal Kindler by providing background commentary while the camp footage is being viewed. In this list of the footage, we have indicated the sources for each document (Figures 43–47):

a) A pile of corpses at Buchenwald (footage from the film *Army Signal Corps Atrocity Film*).
b) Cells in the Sonnenburg Fortress, located on the Polish border, presented as gas chambers but which, in fact, housed prisoners (footage from *Film Documents on the Atrocities of the German-Fascist Invaders*).
c) Barracks at Ohrdruf, where a German doctor is being forced to enter and view the corpses found inside (*Army Signal Corps Atrocity Film*).
d) Presentation of a cudgel used as a torture instrument at Buchenwald (*Army Signal Corps Atrocity Film*).
e) As he is carried on a stretcher by American soldiers, a deportee at Nordhausen clasps his hands together in a sign of relief (*Army Signal Corps Atrocity Film*).

When asked about this "first" of inserting actual news footage of the camps into a fictional film, Welles answered:

I'm against that sort of thing in principle—exploiting real misery, agony or death for purposes of entertainment. But in that case, I do think that, every time you can get the public to look at any footage of a concentration camp, under any excuse at all, it's a step forward. People just don't want to know that those things ever happened.

I had a terrible experience. I was in a rather poor picture called *Is Paris Burning?* [1966] in which we had a scene where they were loading Jews into cattle cars in the station in Paris and sending them away. It was at exactly the same station where it actually happened, probably the same cars, and about 60 percent of the people were veterans of the experience. They kept opening up their sleeves and showing me their tattoo numbers. And a lot of the Germans were real Germans—if not from that scene, at least they were from the German army—and it was so unpleasant I really could hardly get through the day.[13]

What does this footage contribute to the movie's story? All the excerpts were filmed by American camera operators present when the camps were opened. The selections are fairly representative of the types of clips shot in spring 1945, leaving to the imagination the numerical extent of the victims of the Nazis' murderous will while at the same time showing the suffering endured, visible on the faces and bodies of survivors. These images form an ensemble that cannot be reduced to the mere horror that comes from seeing them. Not being the executioner's doing, these excerpts have already moved beyond the ordeal of immediate emotion, the effort to control one's reactions, and the obligation to respect the project specifications that each cameraman had to internalize. It was a matter of preparing evidence likely to satisfy legal standards of proof and, more generally, of gathering available archival documents in order to thwart plans by those who had thought they could erase all trace of their crimes. Of course, Wilson speaks of the "genocide of populations in the defeated countries" without specifying the particular fate reserved for the Jews. The tone is more that of "atrocities," typical of the time.

In fact, as he explains to the father of Rankin's wife, Wilson wants to provoke a feeling of shock in Mary, not by showing her horrible film footage but by creating tension between the intimacy of the relationship with the person who is closest to her (her husband) and the exteriority of the crime committed (Figures 48 and 49). In the inspector's imposing shadow, often placed in the front of the screen, Welles brings together Mary's somewhat juvenile innocence and the enormity of Rankin's crimes, which enables Welles to show the shock in the United States at the discovery of the Nazi camps. It was possible to demonstrate the responsibility of a *single* individual, Rankin, in the Germans' execution of their massive death program. But it was also necessary that all Americans, no matter how removed they might be from the death camps, could in turn become *singular* witnesses, thanks to the mediation of images. Bolstered by the experience he had already acquired with his critical inscription in *Citizen Kane* of the role of newsreels, Welles helped turn these first film images into traces, documents that allowed him to set in motion a work of memory and knowledge parallel to that of the judicial proceedings.[14]

"You Have to Watch": Samuel Fuller and De-Nazification

Where Welles resolutely set his film's action on American soil, Fuller elected fourteen years later to situate his treatment of the same operation overseas. Taking place in 1945, *Verboten!* (1959) tells the story of an American sergeant, David, who is tracking down the last of the Wehrmacht in a small German village. Wounded, he is taken in by a young German woman, Helga, whom he later marries once he is demobilized. Her teenage brother, Franz, comes under the influence of a *Werwolf*.[15] When her reasoned arguments fail to break the grip of seduction that these views have on her brother, Helga decides to take him to the IMT in Nuremberg on November 29, 1945, the day *Nazi Concentration Camps* is shown.

Accompanied by his sister, Franz sits in the courtroom balcony reserved for the press and guests. Fuller then alternates reverse angle shots between footage of the camps (isolated from the judicial framework in which it is projected) and tighter and tighter close-ups of Franz's face:

> *Helga:* Franz, I want you to see this. You have to watch, we have to watch together. Everyone should watch. The whole world should watch. You didn't believe it, did you? Look, Franz!
> *Franz:* I didn't know . . .

Not believing, not knowing: these had been the attitudes of the Allies and Germans. The Germans had been forced by Americans to look at the consequences of Nazi crimes in local, recently liberated camps. Nuremberg then made it possible to watch "together" the filmed evidence of those moments.

A journalist, writer, and screenwriter before the war, Fuller joined the prestigious 1st Infantry Division, nicknamed the Big Red One, in the weeks following Pearl Harbor. After participating in the landings in Africa, Sicily, and Normandy, he wound up in Czechoslovakia, where he helped to liberate the Falkenau camp on May 7, 1945.[16] Fuller's mother had sent him a small Bell and Howell 16 mm movie camera in 1943, and he had already been filming his unit's progress across Germany when his captain asked him to record the burial ceremony in Falkenau for the deportees. Most of them had been found deceased, and the local community leaders had been forced to carry them to their final resting place. When he was back in the United States, the former infantryman put away his film and started his career as a director.[17] Although Fuller shows a teenager discovering the reality of the camps in *Verboten!*, it was the filmmaker's belief that the generation of Germans who had lived under Nazism since 1933 did not want to know what happened during the war.

In 1959, however, a film called *Der Nürnberger Prozess* (The Nuremberg Trial) was made by Felix von Podmanitzky for München Films, the first such film to come out of West Germany.[18] It showed the central role of Hitler in the Third Reich, of course, but also pointed out the responsibility of the defendants brought before the IMT. Probably because the newsreel footage often shown in the United States of Göring and his henchmen declaring themselves at the trial's outset not guilty had remained imprinted in his memory, Fuller was also sensitive to these two distinct facets of the Nazi crimes. In the American director's instance, they were represented by the Falkenau population's claims of ignorance (which Fuller witnessed and filmed himself) and the Nazi leadership's denials of guilt (which the Signal Corps cameramen had captured on film).

In a 1988 interview filmed in the former Nuremberg courthouse, Fuller explained:

> The layout has changed a bit. Here, there used to be two rows of seats, and behind each criminal stood an American soldier from my division. I'd have given anything to be behind Göring.... Everyone could see the criminal's face, everyone.... When Jackson asked a defendant seated over there, "Were you present when such and such an atrocity was committed?"—"No."—"Where were you?"—"50 kilometers away."—"You swear that you were not there?"—"I swear it." Jackson then addresses the projectionist: "Start the movie!" Images filmed by American camera operators flash across the screen. The same questions come up over and over. After which it was again requested:

"Show the film." It was necessary to prove that these men were guilty, responsible for or complicitous in the odious crimes perpetrated. . . . It was not only a matter of the death of soldiers, but of massacres, mass executions—by gas, hunger, brutality. . . . Thanks to some film footage, generations of children are learning not to hate, not to be violent, to be appalled at pictures like the ones [of the camps] that you have just seen, because they represent inhumanity and evil. For this reason, a camera is very valuable and that is why I love cinema, for not only does it educate, it helps civilization progress. No longer will anyone be able to deny what you just saw![19]

Between 1949 and 1958 Fuller directed eleven films, in genres as different as westerns, detective films, and war films. He shot stories that unfolded during the Korean War and the conflict in Indochina but not one about his personal experience in World War II. He waited thirty-five years before venturing to direct *The Big Red One* (1980).[20] No doubt fascinated by the moment when the Nazis were confronted with their own crimes (he very much regretted not having been present at the Nuremberg Trials), Fuller directed *Verboten!* first. Of all the effects produced by the court's screening of camp footage on November 29, the American filmmaker retained two and blended them together: the possibility of demonstrating in archival footage the presence of a defendant alongside those in charge of a camp, thus contradicting the declarations made before the judges of ignorance of concentration camp policy; and the evidentiary power and force of conviction of film footage of Nazi atrocities as a bulwark against incredulity and the negation of reality.

In the sequence set in the old Nuremberg courthouse, Fuller left aside the strictly judicial mechanism of showing a film as evidence and focused instead on treating the tribunal like a movie theater, putting his characters in the balcony so as to accentuate the downward direction of their gaze upon the screen.

"How Dare They Show Us These Films?" Stanley Kramer and the Nuremberg Screening of Camp Footage

A few months later, in *Judgment at Nuremberg* (1961), it was the contrary vision of intersecting judicial and cinematographic mises-en-scène that captured the attention of another American filmmaker, Stanley Kramer.[21]

Written first in the form of a play and then again for television, the first version, penned by Abby Mann, benefited from advice from Telford Taylor.[22] In a memo sent in 1957, Taylor described the form and content of what were called the "subsequent" trials.[23] The seemingly descriptive document specified a certain number of points that Taylor thought it important to make without appearing to influence the screenwriting too much. These included the fact that the accused had obtained the right to a defense by lawyers of their own choosing (all German), whose fees were handled by the American occupation government. Moreover, while administratively dependent on Gen. Lucius D. Clay, the judges were independent as far as their legal prerogatives were concerned. Finally, Taylor drew the author's attention in particular to the change in atmosphere that came about between the beginning and the end of the trial: "Nuremberg began right after the war, when violent anti-German feelings were well-nigh universal, and when relations between the Allies and the Russians were still reasonably good, at least on the surface. But in the course of the trials the whole basis for East-West cooperation collapsed. . . . The Germans soon realized that they were being wooed competitively by the Russians and ourselves, and their attitude was markedly affected, and at times verged on arrogance."

Even before the opening of the IMT, Taylor was aware of the audiovisual stakes of the trials, of the specificities of cinematographic language. He invited Mann to meet with him at his home to view some photographs that could help the scriptwriter to visualize what had been formulated in written form. It was in the context of the relationship thus established with the author of *Judgment at Nuremberg* that Taylor was sent a copy of the movie's first screenplay. A public magistrate who failed in his reelection bid in Maine is sent to Nuremberg in 1948 to preside over the trial of four German judges accused of participating in the legalization of the policies of eugenics and deportation set forth by Hitler. The four men are found guilty and sentenced to life in prison. The story was inspired by the second of the American-run "subsequent trials" held in Nuremberg. Kramer had not sought the advice of former members—Taylor and Benjamin Ferencz—of the American legal team who were now associates in a law firm. On seeing the script, they were very irritated by writing choices they thought were contrary to the spirit of the trials they had conducted at Nuremberg. Early in 1961 Ferencz, former chief prosecutor in the Einsatzgruppen trial, let it be known that he was not happy to see the general counsel, Col. Tad Lawson, described as being motivated by a spirit of revenge arising from his discovery of the concentration camps when he was an officer in the Signal Corps: "The altruism which really prompted the prosecution in its endeavors to create new legal horizons in the areas of crime against humanity and crimes against peace, nowhere appears."[24] Ferencz was also indignant at seeing the prosecutor scolded by his superior, who thought that the war crimes trials were not the best way to foster the pursuit of friendly ties with Germany now that the time had come to ensure these relations for the security of Americans.

With the release of the film announced for December in Berlin, Taylor opted to inform General Clay of his opinion directly. He reiterated the points that he found objectionable and reminded him of his substantial exchange of letters with the president of United Artists (which was distributing Kramer's film). A revised script incorporating some of his observations had indeed been sent to him, but, without having seen the finished film, Taylor was nevertheless informed by various people who saw it that its tone was "excessively anti-German." Taylor thus concluded his letter to Clay, "If these reports are accurate, I should doubt that it will stimulate enthusiasm for the defense of West Berlin."[25]

Obviously Ferencz and Taylor's interventions had produced the opposite effect of what they had sought. The world premiere had been scheduled in Berlin even before the American release and was placed under the patronage of Willy Brandt (then mayor of West Berlin), whose words introduced the screening: "This subject is topical for us Germans and especially for us Berliners. We cannot deny the fact . . . that the roots of the present position of our people, country, and city lie in the fact that we did not prevent right from being trampled underfoot during the time of the Nazi power. Anyone who remains blind to this fact can also not properly understand the rights which are today still being withheld from our people. . . . If the film serves justice, we will welcome it and will still welcome it, even if we have to feel ashamed of many aspects."[26] Kramer himself acknowledged that the film was very poorly received.[27] Whatever the reasons for this failure, the film does not seem today as ill-intentioned as it did to the former organizers of the Nuremberg Trials.[28]

Mann and Kramer had expressly chosen the trial of German judges and incorporated into it the IMT court session of November 29, 1945. Even if this sequence alone does not suffice to sum up the script's tone or the dramatic progression of the narration, it nevertheless constitutes one of the movie's central moments. It occurs 104 minutes into the film, a little past the halfway point (it runs 178 minutes). Played by Richard Widmark, General

Counsel Lawson has just displayed Hitler's decree stipulating that "all persons accused or suspected of disorder or resistance will be secretly arrested, without their loved ones being informed and without judicial proceedings, and sent to a concentration camp." Widmark then brandishes one by one the deportation orders signed by the defendants, clearly indicating the chain of decision allowing for individual incrimination of those on trial. This touches on one of the IMT's challenges, which was to provide answers to a series of complex questions: How do you establish the individual responsibilities of each of the accused? How do you distinguish between what is a matter of decision and execution at the highest policy level (as with concentration and extermination camps), and what occurs at a more administrative level in a chain of command that leaves little room for initiative, thus leading some of the accused to hide behind the expression *Befehl ist Befehl* (an order is an order)? Finally, how does a prosecutor communicate in its entirety a "Final Solution" whose principal decision makers, Hitler and Himmler, are absent from the defendants' dock? Should one limit the exposé to elements directly imputable to the defendants? How do you avoid sliding from the direct or indirect establishment of a responsibility to the simple charge of denial of knowledge of the crimes committed?

In addition to these questions concerning both the individuals and the organizations being judged, the IMT and subsequent trials had to resolve another problem, that of the legitimacy of the judges, who needed to be distinct from their positions as victors. It is in this vexed context that one must interpret the general counsel's change in status (rather improbable in a real court). Maj. Abe Radnitz (Joseph Bernard) asks the court to authorize Lawson to appear as a witness, to which chief judge Dan Haywood (Spencer Tracy) agrees. Thus the character of Lawson combines several historical identities: Eisenhower, Robert H. Jackson, and George Stevens.

As the scene continues, panels are moved to reveal a screen, and a projectionist waits at the ready. Radnitz questions Lawson about his duties during the war, and Lawson responds that he was an active duty officer in 1945 in command of the troops who liberated the concentration camps (Figure 50). Lawson adds that he was present at Dachau and Belsen for the filming of the footage that is about to be shown. The general counsel switches roles here because, as we discussed in Chapter 1, American jurisprudence covering the first uses of moving pictures as evidence required the appearance in court of an *authenticating witness*—as it happens, the person responsible for the footage recorded at the scene of the crime or event. Having started the projection, Lawson comments first on a map showing the number and location of the concentration camps under the Third Reich. The images shown are in fact from the beginning of *Nazi Concentration Camps*, and the ensuing series of shots are taken entirely from that film as well.

For practical reasons, Kramer reconstituted the courtroom in studio (Figure 51). He therefore disposed of a flexible space that allowed him to optimize the camera axes. The chief benefit of these variable perspectives was that he could thus make the main characters' reactions visible for spectators while at the same time maintaining the freedom of fiction.[29]

Even if Lawson had already recalled the principal stages that led from the concentration policies to those of extermination, his presentation, in following the immediate logic of proof and testimony of *Nazi Concentration Camps*, drew partly on iconography that did not allow for distinguishing concentration from extermination. In the hierarchy of representations, crematory ovens were at the apex; then came the bundles of hair and gold teeth that evoked the industry of recuperating deportees' personal effects; the gas chambers; the medical experiments; and, last, the number and origin of the victims, conveyed by the infamous image of the bulldozers at Belsen.[30] The confused impression that the film gave (gas chambers were shown as having functioned at Dachau) should nonetheless be tempered by appreciating how crosscut editing revealed the courtroom's reactions to the graduated intensity of the story being told. The director first shows the presiding judge (Figure 52), then the principal defendant (Dr. Ernst Janning) and his defense attorney (Maximilian Schell). The next shot gives the impression that the camera is going to provoke a reaction in Janning: he has his head down (Figure 53), but then he raises it back up and turns toward the screen to stare at the atrocities being shown on it.

As the most powerful of the archival footage unfolds, Judge Haywood becomes the focus of attention. We see him fully engaged in his responsibilities, at least in the common law tradition that makes him a sort of arbiter and mediator. Initially the judge is very concentrated and impassive, as if he were keeping to himself his impressions as a viewer. But gradually Haywood lets the emotion get to him, and, in a movement exactly the opposite of Janning's, it is now he who lowers his head. A slow circular tracking shot establishes a kind of exchange of glances between the judge and the prosecutor Lawson, within a space no longer open to contestation between trial parties but which marks a withdrawal into the intimacy of a shared conviction. After this brief moment, a traveling shot quickly tracks in on the presiding judge to reestablish him symbolically in his central position. Maintaining the balance of shots distributed among the protagonists, the following scene returns to Janning, again with his head down until his attention is drawn almost magnetically back to the screen.

Added to these strictly visual effects is Lawson's commentary spanning the length of the camp footage. Inscribed naturally in the context of the courtroom debates where speech dominates, it nevertheless sets up another mode of listening in the courtroom. It can in fact sometimes be situated "under" the film image, like a background soundtrack, allowing the audience to concentrate on what they are seeing yet letting them be carried along by the sound of the voice. At other times, the speech is foregrounded, taking viewers out of the torpor of watching the screening and imposing on them a type of authoritative speech that is much more effective than the usual judicial rhetoric. This masterly manner is tolerated all the more when footage difficult to watch is relayed by such factual elements of information that serve to temper the frontal visual violence. Judith E. Doneson joins numerous other scholars in raising the point that the Jews are not mentioned as the main victims until the very end of Lawson's remarks:

> During the showing of the footage, there is no mention of Jews but of "these people—90,000 Slovakians, 65,000 from Greece." Only when the footage finishes does the prosecutor, Colonel Lawson, ask: "Who were the bodies? Members of every occupied country of Europe. Two-thirds of the Jews of Europe were exterminated. More than six million according to reports from the Nazis' own figures." Certainly, Colonel Lawson mentions the Jews, but along with members of "every occupied country in Europe." In so doing, *Judgment* obscures the reality of Nazi policy against the Jews and, in turn, by means of shared history, universalizes the Holocaust.[31]

In choosing to revisit this commonly expressed argument—the absence of any mention of the victims' Jewishness in the depiction at Nuremberg of the mass crimes committed by the Nazis—Doneson commits an interpretive error in her analysis of Kramer's film. It is true that Kramer has Lawson ask at the conclusion of his presentation, "Who were these corpses?" The response explicitly identifies them as Jewish. One should recall, however, that the sequence in question is supposed to occur in 1948 (the year of the judges' Nuremberg trial) or even 1945 (if one takes into account the date of production and distribution of *Nazi Concentration Camps*). As we have already noted, Justice Jackson already had in his possession at the time very precise firsthand information furnished by the Institute of Jewish Affairs, but he thought the trial should not be turned into "a Jewish matter" because it could risk reactivating discrimination. Sensitive as they were to the evolving reawakening of Jewish memory fostered by the Eichmann trial, Mann and Kramer transferred back into 1945 the preoccupations of their own day.

As for the film itself, it fostered anew the main ideas that Eisenhower had wished to communicate through the movie he sponsored after visiting the camps. It sensitized the American public to the atrocities committed by the Nazis by showing primarily GIs as prisoners of war enduring the sufferings of deportees or as liberators attesting through their presence to the truth of the film images that had been captured. The central question was not to assess what had not yet been named the Holocaust but rather to provide an account of what the Allies had seen, in the quasi-chronological order of the troops' advance on the European front. For all these reasons, with only rare exceptions where Jews were identified as such, their mention was linked to the nationality of their country of origin.

In this context, Lawson's conclusion seems to us to respect what had been said in 1945, while successfully suggesting the massive and thus premeditated character of the destruction of Europe's Jews. Certainly, evoking the issue of extermination with footage of Belsen and not of Auschwitz can give rise to confusion. But it was less a matter of proving the visibility of the death camps than of fighting against the programmed disappearance of the bodies, a scarce few traces of which had been preserved on film.

Figure 30. After collecting documentary evidence throughout Europe to be brought against Nazi officials, Robert H. Jackson's team filed them by category of charge. Photo by Charles R. Alexander, 1945. Copyright National Archives and Records Administration.

Figure 31. Göring's lawyer Otto Stahmer complained early in the trial about a lack of access to complete translations of the evidentiary exhibits, visible here in the foreground. Anonymous photo, 1946. Copyright National Archives and Records Administration.

33

32

Figures 32 and 33. In 1945 in Nuremberg, defendant Rudolf Hess (32) is confronted with his own image, as Party leader filmed during a 1934 Nuremberg rally (33) and inserted into *The Nazi Plan*, a documentary comprising German newsreel clips assembled by the prosecution and presented at the Tribunal on December 11, 1945. Photo by Ray D'Addario, 1945. Still frame from *The Nazi Plan*, 1945. Copyright National Archives and Records Administration.

Figure 34. In another still image taken from *The Nazi Plan*, Alfred Rosenberg recounts his participation in the early days of the NSDAP. 1945. Copyright National Archives and Records Administration.

Figure 35. The defendants with some of their lawyers in the Nuremberg courtroom. Anonymous photo, ca. 1945–46. Copyright National Archives and Records Administration.

Figure 36. The judge's bench. Anonymous photo, Nuremberg, 1945. Copyright National Archives and Records Administration.

37

38

39

40

Figures 37–40. The People's Tribunal of Berlin hosted the trial of the "Conspirators of July 20, 1944," and thus for symbolic reasons it was decided to hold the opening season of the IMT there as well, on October 18, 1945. In this first view, defendant Schwerin von Schwanefeld tries to make himself heard by Judge Roland Freisler (37). Seen now from the front, von Schwanefeld (38 and 39) participates in the following exchange with Judge Freisler (40). Still frames. Copyright National Archives and Records Administration.

Freisler: Whatever the facts may be, is it possible to accuse the National Socialist Party of being indecisive?

Von Schwanefeld: I was thinking of the numerous assassinations . . .

Freisler: Assassinations?

Von Schwanefeld: . . . those here and abroad . . .

Freisler: You're repugnant! Such an abomination does not even cause you to break down, to burst into tears?

Von Schwanefeld: Judge, sir!

Freisler: I want a clear answer, "Yes" or "No."

Von Schwanefeld: No.

Freisler: "No"?! You are not even distraught because you are nothing but a miserable little pile of garbage who has lost all respect for himself.

Figure 41. The military trial for the Malmédy massacre was organized by the Americans from May to July 1946 in Dachau, Germany. From left to right: defense counsel Capt. Benjamin N. Narvid, chief defense counsel Col. Willis M. Everett, Jr., and Waffen SS field officer Joachim Peiper. Anonymous photo, Germany, 1945. Copyright National Archives and Records Administration.

Figure 42. The trial for the Malmédy massacre in session. Anonymous photo, Germany, 1946. Copyright National Archives and Records Administration.

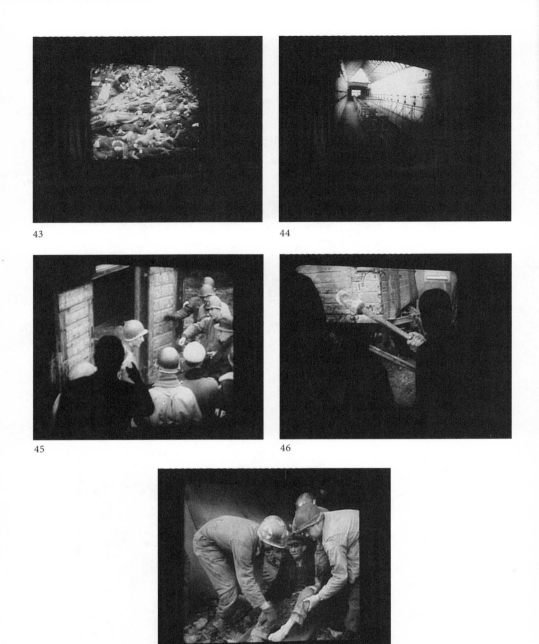

43

44

45

46

47

Figures 43–47. For *The Stranger* (1946), Orson Welles inserted archival images of Nazi atrocities: a pile of corpses at Buchenwald (43); cells at the Sonnenburg Fortress presented as gas chambers but which, in fact, housed prisoners (44); barracks at Ohrdruf, where a German doctor is forced to enter and view corpses found inside (45); a cudgel used as a torture instrument at Buchenwald (46); and a deportee at Nordhausen carried on a stretcher by American soldiers (47). Still frames. Copyright National Archives and Records Administration.

48

Figures 48 and 49. Scenes in Welles's *The Stranger* also display other types of arrangements for screening such materials. As the representative of the Allied Investigative Commission on War Crimes, "Wilson" (Edward G. Robinson) prepares a reel for "Mary Rankin" (Loretta Young) in the presence of her father, "Judge Adam Longstreet" (Philip Merivale). The scene (48) is thus placed under both paternal and judicial authority. A close-up (49) shows "Mary" quite shaken upon learning of the atrocities committed by her husband, "Charles" (Welles), a former Nazi hiding in the United States. Still frames. Copyright MGM.

49

50

51

Figures 50–53. In *Judgment at Nuremberg* (1961), director Stanley Kramer re-creates one of the trials that took place after Nuremberg. The first frame shows "General Advocate Lawson" (Richard Widmark) introducing deportation orders signed by the defendants (50). For this movie, the Nuremberg court was reconstructed in Los Angeles in an accurate reproduction of the IMT's floor plan (51). Kramer also included scenes of the courtroom projection of camp footage. "Judge Dan Haywood" (Spencer Tracy) looks intently at the images being shown (52), while one of the primary defendants, "Ernst Janning" (Burt Lancaster), lowers his eyes (53). Photos taken on the set, 1961. Copyright MGM.

52

53

54

55

56

57

Figures 54–57. These 1961 photos of the filming of the Eichmann trial in Jerusalem demonstrate the four camera angles selected by director Leo T. Hurwitz. Anonymous photos. Copyrights United States Holocaust Memorial Museum, 6527, 65289, 65274, 65286.

58

59

60

61

Figures 58–61. A powerful sequence during the Nuremberg trial was captured by American camera operators on January 28, 1946: Marie-Claude Vaillant-Couturier testifies (58 and 59), leaves the stand, crosses in front of Göring (60), and stares him down (61). Anonymous photos for 58, 59, and 61; Charles R. Alexander for 60. Copyright National Archives and Records Administration.

62

63

Figures 62 and 63. Chief Prosecutor Gideon Hausner kept the testimony of his witnesses within narrow boundaries during the Eichmann trial in Jerusalem. Anonymous photos, 1961. Copyrights United States Holocaust Memorial Museum 65275, 65274.

Figures 64–66. In Christian Delage's documentary film *La Rafle des enfants d'Izieu* (The Roundup of the Children of Izieu, 1994), a series of witnesses are shown from the 1987 Klaus Barbie trial in Lyon, France. They did not have the opportunity to testify before the accused as he refused to attend the rest of the proceedings. Swept up by emotion, Ita Halaunbrenner is supported by her children (64). In a very different register, Léon Reifman first gives an account of what he did on the day of the roundup of the children of Izieu, then of what he saw, and finally of what he thinks of the defendant (65). Last, we see Julien Favet, the only eyewitness of the roundup (66). In Favet's instance, Prosecutor Truche did not consider his testimony to be reliable, though the issue of credibility in this case concerned less the veracity of the facts that he reported than his social persona and the language used to recount his recollections. Still frames. Copyright Christian Delage.

64

65

66

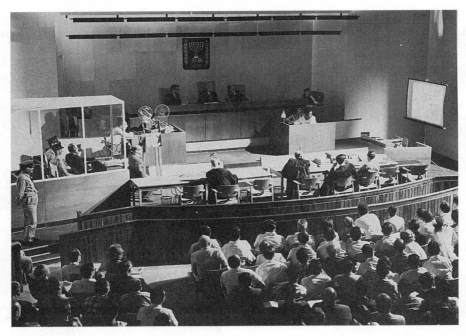

Figure 67. The screening of footage of Nazi camps during the Eichmann trial, occurring nearly two months after it began, did not have the same impact as it did at Nuremberg. Anonymous photo, Jerusalem, June 8, 1961. Copyright United States Holocaust Memorial Museum 65271.

Figure 68. The presence of film images presented as evidence has become commonplace today. At The Hague, the courtroom of the International Criminal Tribunal for the former Yugoslavia (ICTY) is fully functional: all participants in the trial have individual viewing monitors at their disposal. In this image, the audiovisual installation allows us to see the swearing-in of the judges at the Milosevic trial (http://www.icty.org/sections/Press/Gallery). Copyright International Criminal Tribunal for the former Yugoslavia.

69

70

72

71

73

Figures 69–71. At the IMT in Nuremberg, Otto Ohlendorf (right) faces Col. John Amen (center) on January 3, 1946. Copyright National Archives and Records Administration.

Figures 72 and 73. Avrom Sutzkever on the witness stand at Nuremberg (left) and Presiding Judge Geoffrey Lawrence (right), who entreats Sutzkever, "Please have a seat, if you so desire." Copyright National Archives and Records Administration.

Figure 74. Huy's mother (right) says before her son (left), "You have to tell the truth." Still frame, *S21, The Khmer Rouge Killing Machine,* 2003. Copyright Rithy Panh.

75

76

Figures 75 and 76. A former prison guard at Tuol Sleng Prison, also known as "S21," reenacts his rounds: "It stinks, and I have to clean it up by myself!" (75); "Don't budge while you sleep, whore-of-your-mother!" (76). Still frames, *S21, The Khmer Rouge Killing Machine,* 2003. Copyright Rithy Panh.

Figure 77. The Extraordinary Chambers in the Hall of Justice, site of the Cambodian tribunals. Photo by Extraordinary Chambers in the Courts of Cambodia, June, 2009. Copyright Extraordinary Chambers in the Courts of Cambodia.

PART IV

The Era of Justice on Film
(1945 to the Present)

CHAPTER 10

Trials of the Present or the Past?

History in the Present: The Eichmann Trial Televised

In a continuation of the judicial experiences undertaken by the IMT, the Jerusalem District Court agreed to allow Nazi camp footage to be shown in hearings and, most notably, the Adolf Eichmann trial to be filmed in its entirety. Despite the precedent of Nuremberg, however, these two arrangements were not adopted without discussion. While the first element hardly came into play during the trial (if at all), the second took on unprecedented importance in light of the particular stakes of this trial organized by the Israeli government. "Ben-Gurion had two goals," explains Tom Segev. "One was to remind the countries of the world that the Holocaust obligated them to support the only Jewish state on earth. The second was to impress the lessons of the Holocaust on the people of Israel, especially the younger generation."[1] In an interview granted to the *New York Times*, Israel's former prime minister also announced that he wanted to prove that the Jews had not been lambs who let themselves be led to slaughter.[2] The trial thus needed substantial media coverage in order to inform both Israeli society and international public opinion of the trial's findings.

Very early on—November 8, 1960, a full five months before the trial was set to begin—an especially bold decision on the part of the Israeli government was revealed: it had granted a contract of exclusive right to New York–based Capital Cities Broadcasting Corporation (CCBC) for the audiovisual recording of the Eichmann trial and its later distribution to movie theaters and television. The contract spelled out the goal of this operation: "It is anticipated that the said Eichmann trial will be an event of worldwide public interest, and that widespread dissemination of the trial proceedings through all available media of communication is a highly desirable social objective."[3]

Back in July of the same year, CCBC had named a thirty-four-year-old executive producer, Milton A. Fruchtman, to oversee the company's proposal extolling the merits of the technical system it had developed at the Screen Directors International videolab.[4] Motion picture cameras—whose presence, it was promised, would be fairly discreet—were to be linked up to a control room. The tapes could later be converted to film. Lacking its own national television system, the Israeli government thus justified its choice of a smaller foreign company (at the expense of the major U.S. networks) based on the attention the Capital Cities proposal paid to the public service to be rendered by this project and the professionalism of Fruchtman's team.

Hollywood, however, was not completely locked out of the Eichmann trial. A historical movie was made retracing the arrest and kidnapping of Eichmann in Argentina, with its general release timed to coincide with the trial's opening. Directed by R. G. Springsteen, *Operation Eichmann* debuted in American theaters on March 14, 1961. In light of the film's extravagant budget, critics were somewhat wary of its content: "Eichmann movie stirs suspicions," announced the *New York Times* at the time of the filming. One of the producers, David Diamond, was forced to justify at a press conference the nature of the project and the speed with which it had been completed: "We are not trying to capitalize on an opportunity. We want a picture that will be shown for a hundred years to come. The conscience of six million dead is on us." The military service of two technicians was also mentioned: "By coincidence, both the cameraman, Joseph Biroc, and one of the sound technicians, Bill Hamilton, were among the first Americans to break into Dachau. They were part of an Army combat photo team that took official pictures of the concentration camps.[5] They spoke quietly as they recalled the horrors of that camp."[6]

The producer's insistence on the burden of the "conscience of six million dead" can be explained in part by Jewish American organizations' heightened activity in the lead-up to the trial. Jacob Robinson, for instance, was called in August 1960 by Israel's Office of Public Prosecution to assist in the preliminary investigation of Eichmann. One should recall that it was Robinson who, in his role as director of the Institute of Jewish Studies, pressured Justice Jackson in the spring of 1945 to name a representative of the Jewish community to serve on the IMT. Moreover Robinson had served since the early 1950s as a legal advisor to Israel's UN delegation and as research coordinator at New York's Jewish Research Institute.

The announcement of CCBC's exclusive rights provoked hostile reactions from the American networks as well as from foreign stations. Even if Capital Cities took care to specify that it was not acting in Israel's name, NBC judged it a "bad precedent" to have a single company be the "funnel through which the TV account may flow." In this respect, conflicts were predictable. When CCBC offered to provide all interested television stations with video cassettes of the trial—putatively as a public service yet demanding payments to cover 85 percent of their total production costs (estimated at $1 million)—the major networks refused the announced rates and made counteroffers which eventually produced an agreement.[7]

In February 1961 Capital Cities hired Leo T. Hurwitz as director of the video recording and film of the trial. As in any contract, it was clearly laid out that the company retained complete control over his work. There was no discussion, however, of the specifics regarding the introduction of cameras into the courtroom, circumstance that would also engage the responsibilities of the judicial authorities.

Hurwitz's first task was to prepare Israeli cameramen for the challenges of filming live. In the absence of any national television, their prior training was oriented strictly toward the needs of movie sets. Hurwitz and Fruchtman then brought themselves up to date on the decisions issued at the March 22 special hearing, called in order for the Court to render its rulings on the general prosecutor's request for authorization to record the trial's proceedings. The Court's first remark was to state that, since there was no judicial precedent for this matter in Israel, the government's contractual stipulation asserting that recording must occur "subject to the rules of court" was without foundation. That said, Article 5717-1957 of Section 40 of the Courts Law left the determination of such considerations to the discretion of the tribunal charged with hearing the case. After an inspection of the equipment installations in Beit Ha'am auditorium (the House of the People), the Court announced that it was satisfied with the arrangements: "We have satisfied ourselves that these machines stand concealed behind netted apertures, and that the persons operating them are likewise concealed; the machines record pictures by the ordinary lighting in the room and make no noise whatsoever. In this respect, i.e., as regards the possibility of a disturbance during the proceedings, we are absolutely satisfied that there will be none."[8]

The defense objected "vigorously" to the general prosecutor's request. Dr. Robert Servatius opposed two claims in particular:

a) The knowledge that the proceedings are being recorded for television and cinema may induce the witnesses not to give their evidence truthfully, both because they may be afraid of persons outside the courtroom who may be watching their televised evidence and because of a desire to play-act before a world-wide-audience.

b) The television broadcasts are apt to lead to a distorted presentation of the proceedings, e.g., by omitting the arguments of the Defence.

The Court's response was drawn from jurisprudence on the public nature of trial proceedings and on the authority of Jeremy Bentham's instructions (as reported in an authoritative, turn-of-the-century reference work).[9] Trial proceedings are to be conducted "publicly before the eyes of all," thus putting everyone in a position to notice eventual judicial errors. The public nature of the trial is the very guarantee that justice has been well rendered, insofar as this includes communicating everything that everyone has a right to know. To satisfy fully this condition, given that not everyone has mastered legal discourse, a judge may provide a sort of explanatory speech clarifying the grounds for a decision; in this instance, the information provided must be "accurate and fair." It is from this perspective that the Court, already of the opinion that the Eichmann trial arguments should be brought to the attention of the greatest number possible, stated that audiovisual equipment records events the most faithfully of all, "far more accurately than the written word." This claim goes much further than the IMT, itself already an innovator in this area. The judges were aware of this since they based their denial of the defense's objection on the fact that the criterion of novelty cannot constitute an argument in and of itself against what the Court believes beyond any doubt to be in the interest of justice.

The second part of Servatius's request to deny cameras in court concerned the risk that witnesses would formulate their testimony in the knowledge that it was being filmed, directing their remarks more toward viewers than toward the Court. The latter reminded the defense that, while it is indeed the role of the witness in traditional penal procedure to contribute to establishing the truth, the evaluation of this truth ultimately falls to the judge. Moreover, continued the Court, witnesses are never immune to external influences because one can always discover, from written or audiovisual

sources, what was said during a hearing. Finally, one can argue that testifying would be taken all the more seriously when witnesses were aware that
their remarks could be considered again after the immediate matter at hand
was long resolved.

In the end, the only valid concern was the use that television would
make of trial footage. By what means can judges ensure that excerpts culled
from the day's filming will not "distort the picture of what happens in the
courtroom"? From a strictly legal point of view, in the event of abusive practices, one has no recourse to penal sanctions unless the offense rises to the
level of impugning the honor of the court or one of its parties. While the
judges granted that such a risk existed, it was not considered substantial
enough to warrant annulling the overall operation of filming a trial. It
would always be possible to intervene on the spur of the moment to inter-
rupt the recording in case of an incident. To this end, the Court announced
its intention to monitor the process so that the filming did not "in any way
alter the manner of conducting the trial" and expressed confidence that "the
representatives of the parties [would] conduct themselves accordingly."

After an examination of Beit Ha'am, Hurwitz proposed a sophisticated
system for filming the proceedings. Equipment was brought in from as far
as Hollywood, Montana, and Texas and Rome, Paris, and London. The primary recording device was a Marconi camera made in England, fitted with
an ultrasensitive vacuum tube requiring little artificial interior light for filming. Another of its characteristics was to be able to film through glass without any distortion to the image, especially relevant in this instance since the
defendant was going to be enclosed in a bullet-proof booth. Four of these
cameras had been acquired for the duration of the filming.

Hurwitz still had two problems to resolve, however: How could he come
up with space sufficient for camera installations that would allow his operators a variety of camera angles (which required tripods), yet keep the presence of these same cameras and operators as discreet as possible (which
meant devising means of soundproofing and invisibility)? Judging from
press accounts, these obstacles were successfully negotiated well before the
trial opened. Offered a guided visit to demonstrate that the recording would
not disrupt the serene unfolding of the trial, members of the media were
unable to detect the location of the cameras inside the courtroom: "The Hall
was normally lighted and for almost ten minutes [the reporters] wandered
about searching for the cameras. One visitor almost stumbled on one of
them. He looked into what appeared to be a ventilation vent covered by a

double screen of wire. He actually poked his nose up against the wire, but unable to see into the dark shaft, he backed away. . . . This group was firmly convinced that a system which took pictures without noise, with both cameras and cameramen invisible, and under normal lighting conditions, could not possibly infringe on the dignity of the court."[10]

Capital Cities Broadcasting Corporation's work was facilitated by the fact that the hall in which Eichmann was going to be tried, the Beit Ha'am auditorium, was of recent construction and thus more easily allowed for modifications useful for the camera installation process. A first camera was set up on a balcony of the rear wall. Its purpose was to provide straight-on views (close-ups or full-field) of the judge's bench by means of its long shots. It was intended also to allow the defendant (on the left) and witnesses as well as even a couple rows of spectators (on the right) to be included as desired within that frame. This camera angle essentially enabled operators to capture on film virtually all the trials' protagonists (including the audience), be it from the front, back, or side (Figure 54).

The second camera was placed in a hallway leading from the balcony of the left wall. Normally this corridor was kept closed, but Hurwitz obtained permission to open it, keeping it unlit for discretion and filming purposes (Figure 55). From here it was possible to film the witnesses (frontally), judges (at a three-quarter angle), accused (in profile), and lawyers (from the back).

The third camera was set more than twelve feet above the floor in an unused ventilation shaft on the right wall of the auditorium. Owing its view of the proceedings to a hole drilled into the shaft, this camera was tilted downward at a 30-degree angle, was trained on Eichmann, and remained fixed on him throughout the trial to be certain not to miss any of his reactions (Figure 56).

The final camera was installed behind the accused by means of another hole, this time in the rear wall. In this location, it was desirable to have the freedom of movement necessary for producing a variety of visual compositions; depending on the angle adopted, one could capture in the same frame Eichmann with the judges, or the witnesses and lawyers, or the spectators (Figure 57). The equipment was set on wheels, and the breadth of motion was about eight feet. This installation was more complicated, insofar as Fruchtman did not want to do anything that might disturb the judges and thereby provoke a negative reaction from them. This camera position was shielded by a mesh screen that filtered light and thereby rendered the camera and its operator invisible.

The studio from which the director was to work was set up in the upper floors of a bank opposite the courthouse. The motion images captured by the four cameras were transmitted by cable to a control room where it was recorded on 2-inch tape. The latter had two tracks for sound, one for live feed and the other for simultaneous translation. Ampex had provided the equipment, which was so new on the market that a special technician was designated to monitor quality control and maintenance throughout the trial. Stationed full time at the four screen monitors, Hurwitz saw what each cameraman had in his viewfinder and could indicate to them the shot and frame he wanted thanks to earpieces. A fifth screen monitor ("Recorder") corresponded to the image selected. The editing was done live.[11] Even if Hurwitz already had substantial television experience to his credit, he nonetheless jotted in personal notes a number of potential trouble spots for a job such as this, requiring as it did talents in the use of television technology different from those demanded for the movies. Hurwitz's notes outlined the following questions:

> Experience at the controls. What is the basis for switching?
> Dissolves or cuts.
> Use of cameramen.
> Interplay of key people.
> Content of the scene.
> Personal sustain.
> Relief.
> Concentration & work.
> Emotion and concentration.
> 2nd Wind.
> Relation of meaning to method. Use of material to method.
> History and the future?
> News and brief moments.[12]

With respect to attending the trial, journalists and special guests were given priority: 474 of 750 seats went to reporters, and nearly all the remainder were reserved for those with invitations. Another six hundred people could follow via live feed, shown on a giant screen in the main hall of the Ratisbonne, a neighboring French monastery.[13] Otherwise the general public had to content itself with the live, commercial-free broadcast on Israeli national radio, Kol Yisroel, "The Voice of Israel." Every evening CCBC also provided excerpts of the trial for the international media, who were then able to compile detailed summaries thanks to the availability of trial transcripts translated into several languages.

In a letter sent early in the trial to *New York Times* reporter Jack Gould, Hurwitz seconds the judges' call for transparency in the proceedings. In the director's opinion, filming the trial marked the materialization "of the concept of the 'Open Court,' [by] opening the four walls of the court to the public of the world." At the same time, however, Hurwitz brings up what he deems a "strange phenomenon": the major networks broadcasting trial footage thanks to the CCBC agreement systematically fail to credit the "author" of the images.[14] While it is true that capturing an event on film is not the same as producing a creative work, the tasks of camera placement, filming, and simultaneous editing all presuppose constant awareness and decision making, in addition to a great ability to improvise. The technical expertise that allowed them to gamble on using innovative technology also helps delineate Hurwitz's contributions from Fruchtman's. Doubtless in order to make Gould aware of these elements and to assist him in informing readers, Hurwitz details in this same letter what his direction contributes to the final product. For instance, he explains that by mixing camera views he can organize the play of glances exchanged between the trial's main participants or juxtapose simultaneous reactions to expose features that the spectators in attendance did not necessarily remark. What might have struck one as cold and distant, immersed as it was in the rather large space of the courtroom, takes on a different dimension in the film. The faces of the witnesses and the accused are seen up close, which reveals emotions and behaviors that were perhaps not very demonstrative. Changes in image scale enable viewers to alternate between frames to get an overall view of the proceedings (perhaps during somewhat dry procedural phases or résumés of historical context) as well as more intimate sequences of an individual placed at the focal point.

The discussion Hurwitz opens here is extremely important. It reminds us that the director does not replace the judge in organizing trial arguments. On the contrary, Hurwitz will try to render on film the trial's exchanges and confrontations. His direction aims to respect the spirit and concrete unfolding of the proceedings while simultaneously imprinting an immediate vision of them. A great amount of patience and poise are necessary to stay cooped up in a tiny space for months on end while just a few meters away the tale of the genocide of Europe's Jews is being pieced together: "Working day after day in the control room for four months, trying to express in the images and sounds of the trial the meanings of the events which were taking place, was for me an experience like being in a mine, closed out from air and sky, digging out the inexpressible terrors, brutalities, the icy adaptations of inhumanity, the consignment of other people to thingness."[15]

The Matter of Historical Archives: The French Trials

In France it took a measure being voted into law for the audiovisual recording of trials to be authorized. Before that, if we are to judge by a 1930s discussion of the intrusion of cameras into the courtroom, motion picture collaborations with the work of justice were to be restricted for fear of "compromising the dignity and seriousness of judicial halls." Magistrates had been led to "consider it—at the very least—ill-advised to turn courtrooms into arenas for public spectacle." It was *prior* to the trial that pictures—photographic ones, at the time—could eventually be used, as an auxiliary document for use by the court in its collaborations with "police forensics for reconstructing and documenting the scenes where some form of crime occurred."[16]

Photographers soon won permission to enter the courtroom, but the excesses of the Dominici trial put an end to this practice in 1953.[17] Since 1981 photographers (now accompanied by television cameras) have regained entry to the halls of justice, but their presence, strictly limited to the trial's opening (that is, prior to questioning), depends on the judge's discretion. The Security and Liberty law of February 2, 1981, specifies the terms of such arrangements: "In response to requests presented before the hearing, the presiding judge may authorize visual recording prior to the opening of debates as long as the parties or their representatives and the ministry of the Public give their consent."

As the beginning of the Klaus Barbie trial drew near in 1985, François Mitterrand's minister of justice, Robert Badinter (1981–86), introduced a bill expressing the desire "to go beyond preserving written records" and suggesting a policy of maintaining audiovisual records of the judicial archives. In submitting this proposal, he evoked a memory dating back to 1945: "I had seen the Gaumont newsreels concerning the Pétain trial. This document struck me as extraordinary, especially [the scene] where we see Laval arrive. Later on, having been myself a spectator or participant in trials, I regretted the absence of any images illustrating them."[18]

Badinter's bill was approved by the National Assembly on July 11, 1985. It decreed the "establishment of historical archives for the courts," citing their importance to national heritage and the fact that they would be especially beneficial to scholars who could use them to grasp the "true functioning" of French justice.

It was not the "public hearings before jurisdictions of the judicial or administrative orders" that were to be regarded as "historical" but rather the fact of their having been "recorded." The law was not designed for a specific category of trial and left it up to the court's discretion to assess the desirability of filming a particular hearing. In the end, however, the only prosecutions impacted by this new legislation were the Barbie, Touvier, and Papon trials held in assize court, despite the fact that the law itself applied to ordinary court cases as well as to such major events of the judicial world.[19] It would be another twenty years before the French Ministry of Justice would commission a judge to devise a general working policy on this subject.[20]

Up until the 1980s the Assize Court Code of Procedure had been very restrictive. For example, Article 308 makes no distinction between the presence of print or audiovisual media and the actual recording of the trial itself: "ART 308. As soon as the trial begins, the use of any recording or sound broadcast apparatus, television or movie camera or photographic equipment, is forbidden under penalty of a fine of no less than 300 French francs and no greater than 120,000 French francs." An initial modification of the law on February 2, 1981, granted the presiding judge of the assize court the right to authorize sound recordings of the hearings so that one could consult a transcription of the tapes in the event it was deemed necessary to reexamine the "declarations of persons who can no longer appear before the court." In the 1985 law, Article 6 is fairly vague in its discussion of the conditions for filming a trial:

> Recordings are to be carried out in a manner that does not disrupt the proper course of the proceedings or the free exercise of the rights of the defense. The former will be done using stationary installations.
>
> When the clauses of the preceding subsection are not respected, the presiding judge may, as befits his charge of maintaining an orderly trial, rule against such recordings or momentarily interrupt them.[21]

On January 15, 1986, a decree further modifying the application of the law gave greater force to pretrial regulation of any filming:

Art. 12—Recording of the hearings is to be provided by the offices of the Ministry of Justice or the Ministry of the Interior and of Decentralization or, lacking that, by one or several companies selected according to the conditions established by Book II of the Code of Public Offers. . . .

Art. 13—The placement of recording equipment inside the courtroom is determined in concert with the presiding judge charged with maintaining order during proceedings.[22]

In essence, a set of specifications determined for each new trial would establish the working conditions for the corresponding director.

Although France is the only nation to have produced law on this matter, its initiative nonetheless falls in line with the sequence of innovations begun at Nuremberg and pursued in Jerusalem. Yet despite his having attended the Eichmann trial, Badinter makes no reference to it when he revisits the subject of his law a few years later. This is a bit surprising given the centrality of questions regarding the criteria for filming: "One must keep in mind that we film trials in which substantial matters are at stake, but the cameras could perturb the course of the proceedings. . . . It has been agreed upon that no camera movement should ever hinder a hearing. Camera placement has been determined precisely to avoid any disruption or manipulation. In order to maintain the objectivity of the documents, the sessions should be recorded with a static shot. At most, maybe a zoom on the victim or on the person in the midst of giving evidence, arguing his case, or presenting the charges."[23]

Several observations are called for here. The first concerns the fear that the cameras "perturb the course of the proceedings." In Nuremberg and Jerusalem judges had already examined whether the visible presence in court of a camera or its operator could cause practical or symbolic dysfunction. The intrusion of a recording apparatus into a space as ritualized as a courtroom could justifiably be perceived as dispossessing presiding judges of part of their control over the spatiotemporal facets of the proceedings. Those facets would no longer be confined to the sole company of the trial's protagonists and the material presence of the evidentiary exhibits. The camera's eye would preserve for posterity what normally had been inscribed within the ephemeral duration of the trial and the oral character of the hearings. The filming would in fact serve as a means to supervise the judicial process, a "democratic monitoring," observed Antoine Garapon, "of an unprecedented type (in France, at least)."[24]

But France's famous legal mind is raising a more serious issue here, and one of a different order. In 1945 and 1961 the potentially distracting novelty of recording equipment in court was accepted as long as its presence proved discreet. In 1987, suggests Badinter, the problem is henceforth the opposite: people participating in trials have become all too accustomed to audiovisual media. Even if the protagonists cannot see the cameras, the knowledge that they are being filmed could lead them to modify their behavior and the form (if not the content) of the exchanges. Badinter's fear would be founded if the site where the filming occurred was neutral and empty of ceremonials, its procedures free of ritual. In this case, the camera eye would indeed be a magnet for attention. But this is not at all the reality of a courtroom. The workings of justice are displayed by means of a sharply delineated spatial organization in which competing points of view confront each other beneath the watchful eye of the centrally positioned judge; this theatrical dimension suffices largely to capture the attention of those present.[25] It is doubtless true that if the filmed proceedings were broadcast (in one format or another) every night for the duration of the trial, it could subject witnesses and the jury to bothersome public exposure. As the proceedings unfolded in Jerusalem, however, neither judge nor press remarked any anomalies (at least where witnesses were concerned), and this despite the fact that footage was viewable throughout, both live and on tape delay.

The second reserve put forward by the former minister of justice is the worry that certain camera positions or perspectives could give rise to "manipulation." It is true that directors can privilege a particular protagonist in the course of a trial by showing one more often than another. Some focal distances or shot-scales can also be detrimental to or valorize the person being filmed. On this count, though, it is simply the integrity of the director that is at issue, not a technological trait whose effects cannot be adequately controlled. The length of the trial also provides opportunities to compensate where necessary to reestablish an appropriate equilibrium.

All the same, this concern is spelled out in the proposal's third point: a stationary shot would guarantee objective filming. Indeed this static approach constitutes one of the basic constraints imposed on the director: the camera must follow discussions as they unfold without resorting to changes in perspective to accentuate or downplay the comments of a given speaker. A corollary to this first rule is that the director should never cut away from live testimony. Such editing would not be appropriate: if a camera operator cuts off a witness in mid-deposition in order to show a brief view of the defense lawyer ostentatiously displaying disinterest in or disagreement with what is being said, this behavior could influence spectators' reactions and modify their impression of the proceedings. Once again, it is the professionalism of those assigned to film the trial that is really at stake here.

Objectivity is not, at any rate, the best term for characterizing what the courts can hope to achieve through the filming of a trial (regardless of the nature of the trial). At the end of each session, judges should be able to review the day's film and assess its technical quality. As we have already seen with the Nuremberg and Jerusalem trials, the director is expected to demonstrate a variety of skills (sustained concentration, an alert eye, a systematic mind). While directors are not legal experts, their role cannot be limited simply to recording passively each turn of speech as the judge authorizes one witness after another to take the stand. Rather a director should always be a half-move ahead of the trial's events since he alone, thanks to the gift of ubiquity the cameras provide him, is able to watch every person react to the matters at hand. This element of anticipation is facilitated by the fact that the director is provided with a program the night before each session, complete with the names of each witness to be called and the object of the hearing. Once the question is settled of where to place the cameras, the director's editing artistry must come to the fore. This artistry must tackle a space quite different from that found in a theater, insofar as the director is not confined to the fixed viewpoint of the spectators, front and center. He has the possibility of setting up his cameras to obtain a line of sight on each of the trial's participants. This ubiquity enables spectators to place themselves in the exchanges organized by the ceremonial of the court. If "pictures as proof" create a form of visible evidence, the filming of the trial reveals the exchanges that shape the judges' ultimate convictions.

When the first trial ever held in France for crimes against humanity opened in Lyon in 1987, twenty-five years had already passed since the Eichmann trial and more than forty since Nuremberg. The crimes of which Klaus Barbie was accused could be pursued in court only because of their imprescriptibility. As with those that would follow (Touvier and Papon), the temporality of this trial is paradoxical. Yan Thomas reminds us that criminal acts "can be judged in court today because their specific set of legal statutes renders them contemporary for us." The system of imprescriptibility in essence allows everyone to be the "contemporary of crimes past whose perpetrators are still alive."[26] Once the latter are deceased, what happens when this initial temporality is joined several years later by a second one, that of a television broadcast? Such was the case when the Barbie trial aired, for instance, after the convicted Nazi criminal had died in prison on September 25, 1991, and most of his surviving victims had passed away. What type of temporal relation would spectators foster with this series in thirty-seven installments, *The Barbie Trial*, which was shown to them on television in the form of two-hour daily episodes?

One of the historians who helped edit these programs for France's History Channel, David Schreiber, reports that the committee charged with creating the series decided that it would follow the chronological thread of the trial and that no extraneous archival images would be used. The program did include, however, the on-set presence of a historian (Henry Rousso) and a legal expert (Assistant Prosecutor Pierre-Olivier Viout), whose role was to contribute explanations useful for comprehending the stakes and stages of the trial. Another organizational point agreed upon was that the number of episodes would equal the number of trial sessions. As Schreiber explains, "This rule carried out a sort of 'temporal homothetic transformation' between trial and television broadcasts. In our opinion, it had the advantage of respecting the temporality of the event while also providing a straightforward working principle."[27] Broken up by the two specialists' commentary, abridged by reediting, the trial footage was also recentered in order to allow the addition of a time stamp placed in a corner of the screen; spectators could thus see at every moment the date of the hearing and the exact hour of its recording.

These modifications appreciably altered the original archive and engendered effects that merit analysis in how their use impacts reception. Superimposing the various staggered temporalities of the event, trial, and television broadcast (itself subject to a system of multiple retransmissions) doubtless creates new perceptions of a history whose contemporariness is, in a sense, constantly reactivated.[28] And, in any event, this is not the archive Badinter called for—and which no one to date has viewed in its entirety—and it is not the trial edited live by the director.[29]

CHAPTER 11

Hearings on Film, Film in Hearings

"Composure and Patience": The "Straight Thread" of the Touvier Trial

Guy Saguez, an accomplished director with considerable experience in live recording, was selected to film the Touvier trial.[1] Compared to the 1985 law, the set of specifications he was given are rather precise in its technical detail. These requests nevertheless seem to oscillate between satisfying the magistrates' demands and those of the curators charged with handling the audiovisual recording intended for the judicial archives:

> Article 9. Recording method.
>
> The shoots will be done using the courtroom's available lighting; no additional projectors will be allowed. Three cameras manned by operators will record the proceedings: the first is to be a stationary installation on a mezzanine at the back of the hall while the two others will be placed around the room and have a radial movement of one meter.
>
> The mixing will be handled by an on-site control man, under the supervision of a judicial advisor as established by Article 3.
>
> The presiding judge will have a screen monitor at his disposal.
>
> Shot selection will be as neutral as possible.
>
> The sound-feed will also be recorded on videotape. The production switcher will be able to modulate it via the microphone output line and via the sound console's input line for the three extra microphones.[2]

In addition to establishing working agreements with the presiding judge, Saguez was thus also obliged to collaborate with a judge advocate, namely,

Andrée Chauleur, general secretary of the Ministry of Justice's Audiovisual Archives Commission.[3] She was, in fact, to be the director's principal interlocutor. Saguez kept a trial journal in which he made notes on these negotiations: "I have to make [Ms.] Chauleur understand that we must go beyond simply following the 'straight thread' of speeches—that we must also be the visual witness of what transpires and that the 'secondary shots' will perhaps be as useful to historians as the transcript itself, *in extenso*. . . . Otherwise, an audio recording would have sufficed."[4]

The greatest constraint was being limited to ambient light, a condition contrary to the requirements for high-quality recording. Video was not yet digital, and thus it was necessary to install additional illumination if, for instance, one wished to obtain any real depth to the visual field. If dark shadows were an obvious problem, sudden partial changes in brightness were even more detrimental. At the Barbie trial, an inopportune ray of sunlight shot through the glass ceiling of the Lyon courthouse during Pierre Truche's indictment speech and overexposed part of the lead prosecutor's face.

The most noteworthy innovation in this operation was the installation of a control monitor in front of the presiding judge. Previously judges organized the sessions on sight and opened the floor to persons authorized to speak by turning on their microphone. Henceforth presiding magistrates had available a visual relay allowing them to see the mix being performed in the control room. Though it hardly came into play in the trial, the generalization of this system of internal television broadcast is one of the major characteristics of the evolution not only of filmed trials but of the court's very functioning. For example, at the International Criminal Tribunal for the former Yugoslavia, the protagonists depended mostly on their personal monitors to observe the actions of others. This new apparatus has no impact on the accuracy of the justice dispensed; on the contrary, it is relieved of elements that burdened it in the past. Henceforth robed lawyers are less likely to resort to arm-waving gesticulations that are a holdover from rituals of the aristocratic days.

Saguez realized the technical obstacles facing him from the moment he set foot in the Versailles courthouse. First and foremost, the defendant was seated at a height that made him difficult to film:

I wonder if yesterday's difficult bargaining was successful: Will they agree to place Touvier's chair on a rostrum in order to raise it up a bit? In our current visual frame, his lawyers have their heads right in the middle of the defendant's stomach. . . .

The adjustments have been made; they have "elevated" Touvier. Now we will see him better. So as not to forget him. We will bolt down his chair so that, even in the minute space granted him, he will not be able to evade the eyes of the Presiding Judge or those of the cameras.[5]

In order to improve the sound pickup, Saguez also obtained authorization to double the court's microphones with better quality equipment. He soon became aware, however, that this improvement had a regrettable by-product: confidential exchanges between the defendant and his lawyer were now clearly audible, when in fact these are not public communications. Only the mixing table could hear them, however, and the remarks were not preserved in the archival version.

When the opportunity presented itself, Saguez occasionally reminded the plaintiffs' lawyers to be careful not to block the line of view for shots featuring witness testimony and to be attentive to their physical posture. While political cartoonists are allowed to sketch people dozing off, sneaking peaks at their datebook, or chatting with a neighbor in total disregard of the trial, the director cannot indulge in such atmosphere shots, even if they are part of the life of a trial, whose length can be trying on all. In a memo written for his film crew, Saguez put to paper some crucial instructions: "Resist the monotony. Raise your concentration level. COMPOSURE AND PATIENCE."

All in all, it is pretty straightforward. The cameras must be discreet, so as not to disrupt the course of the trial, but not too discreet, in order that their presence serve to remind everyone of an obligation—simple enough, but not always easy to observe: being a member of the audience presupposes a constant watchfulness, regardless of whether one is directly concerned by or involved in all phases of the proceedings. What is demanded of the presiding judge is henceforth expected of everyone since, in the relatively private (closed) space of the court, the trial's unfolding is *exposed* to the camera's watchful eye. "Everyone played their part, beginning with the lawyers who agreed to wear small transmitter microphones while pleading their case," reported the newspaper *Ouest-France*. "But the knowledge that they were being filmed at all times had to impact the behavior of the trial's key actors, who were tenser in the early-going. Just a matter of time before they forgot about the cameras, which was exactly what the film crew wanted."[6]

But, in point of fact, one cannot simply "forget about the cameras," as was demonstrated on April 20, 1993, when the head judge of the Paris Court of Appeals decided in what was known as the "Contaminated Blood Trial" to forgo the visual archive and authorize only conservation of an audio recording of the proceedings.[7] Leaving aside the extrajudiciary aspects of such a decision and the extremely delicate matter of displaying political figures in the witness box, the judge's decision raises the question of what belongs to the realm of hearing and what to that of seeing. Especially in the era of "reality" television, there is a real risk of succumbing to voyeuristic desires in all kinds of circumstance, public or private. People in the limelight now learn how to carry themselves on camera to convey a favorable image. They are coached on public speaking, often oversimplifying argumentation that is supposed to reach the greatest number possible. Faced with unforeseen events, political officials have to come up with the right phrase for the moment or the most telegenic approach. The courts must shelter themselves from such "buzzword politics" by guaranteeing all the trial's protagonists time sufficient for developing their own contradicting truth.

Up until now, a proper balance had been for the most part preserved between verbal exchanges inside the halls of justice and their media echo outside on the courthouse steps. A useful mediation could occur in the passage from one discourse to another, since at the time the recording and broadcast of the proceedings was not permissible. Now, however, audiovisual taping allows the public to see and hear for themselves what transpires: the trial's protagonists are subjected to greater exposure, but they retain control of their intervention, both length and content.

In the Touvier trial, the obligation to follow the "straight thread" of the speeches was not respected, the director Saguez having succeeded in convincing the judicial advisors of the need to capture in the best manner possible the dynamics and distribution of the proceedings' exchanges. The ritual of the trial itself has hardly been modified by the demands of audiovisual archiving. The cameras have melted discreetly into the decor of the courtroom floor—and even then, on an exceptional basis only.[8] For Saguez's purposes, then, he simply needed to anticipate slightly during certain phases of the trial people's reactions in order to capture those brief moments of truth. For example, during Touvier's character examination, the accused started out on the defensive. This kind of exercise is old hat for a magistrate but not for the defendant. The camera rendered Touvier's anxiety by jumping back and forth between him and the presiding judge. For this trip back in time, to the era of World War II, Touvier was expecting only a discussion of Historical context (with a capital "H"); instead he was treated to the tale of his own (personal) history. The surprise on his face is plainly visible as his private life is exposed to all. The presiding judge continually prods him to confirm the veracity of his account, or even to flesh it out with further recollections. Little by little, Touvier becomes party to this look back on his family's social milieu, his upbringing. When he is questioned about his father—visibly, still a sensitive subject—he seems to feel some satisfaction at hearing the latter deemed "authoritarian," a judgment the accused had probably never formulated quite so explicitly for himself. Situated a ways back from the scene, the camera places the audience in the middle of this exchange, allowing viewers to imagine what cannot be said but is expressed by gestures, grimaces, and pauses. A narrative thus comes together, containing and exceeding the judicial proceeding, benefiting from the court's scenography yet simultaneously reorganizing it via the control room editing.

Saguez's recording of the Touvier trial was reworked into a television series but could not be programmed on France's History Channel until eight years later. This situation had changed by the time of the Papon trial, which was shown fairly promptly thanks to the law of July 13, 1990, which reduced the regulations by authorizing television broadcasts as soon as a conviction without possibility of appeal was obtained. In the French daily *Libération*, Jean-Michel Thénard expresses his approval of this film, "done without bad cinema and [which] confirms—if it still needed to be—how useful cameras can be in court. Not to produce the truth but to show it in the process of emerging."[9] Built on a certain number of invariables, solid due to the results obtained by the judicial investigation, the trial can stay on track. Viewers, on the other hand, will be struck by these micro-events as well, which enter into the formation of their opinions of the main personalities of the trial.

In this way, over the course of the first few days of the Papon trial, the presiding judge, Jean-Louis Castagnède, gradually finds his bearings. He agreed to allow a camera installation behind him, elevated and in line with the witness stand. Another, in the auditorium, allows a full-frame front view. Not a single detail can escape this camera. What disappears in the stenography of the proceedings is not only recorded but contributes to the creation of a full temporality with its dramatic ebbs and flows. This perspective favors an empathic perception of the interventions, not to the advantage of any one individual in particular but improving everyone's chances of being heard. Where the presiding judge is concerned, everyone expects him to be ready to face the unexpected, even when it pops up very early in the trial, in the form of a motion filed by the defense for the accused to be released on bail. On the third day of the trial (Friday, October 10, 1997), Judge Castagnède reads the court's ruling: "The court orders the accused released on bail." His discomfort is quite visible when he explains what brought him to his decision. Knowing full well what the plaintiffs' reaction will be, he slows the pace of his speech, progressively unveiling his argumentation, as if to moderate its tenor. For a moment (which seems quite long on film), the surprise is so complete that nothing happens in the auditorium. The president judge hesitates, looks down at his files, while one of his assessors tries to signal to him that a lawyer is requesting the floor. The camera is a step ahead of him and has already turned toward Arno Klarsfeld (the lawyer representing the Association for the Sons and Daughters of the Deported Jews of France), who declares right off the bat that he is withdrawing from a room "where the trial has no more meaning." The camera swings back to Castagnède: caught off-guard by a reaction that no doubt strikes him (as it does many television viewers) as rather cavalier, the presiding judge courteously asks him to stay. But the younger Klarsfeld, having already put on his navy blue backpack, leaves the court.

In front of the cameras, Castagnède is not undermined by this incident. His function obliges him to maintain a certain reserve, so what he restrains himself from declaring publicly—most certainly commentary critical of the lawyer's behavior—is nonetheless legible in his facial expression. This is not merely a visual effect, to the extent that in that moment time almost seems to drag out; the scene takes too long to develop for the rhythm of today's television shows.

Moving Toward "Open" Courts

The audiovisual experimentations begun in Nuremberg have been taken up and renewed by the majority of judicial authorities put in place during periods of transition or the establishment of constitutional democratic regimes, as was seen, for instance, in South Africa and Argentina. In this type of trial, the tribunal discovers a new form of solidarity that Mark Osiel describes as springing from "civil *dissensus*."[10]

In breaking with existing courts and their legal options, South Africa's Truth and Reconciliation Commission made it possible for victims and criminals to meet face-to-face. Rolling throughout the entire process, the cameras occasionally captured a timid—and always painful—gesture of reconciliation.[11] The television broadcast that relayed these scenes to the general population was beneficial to the dialogue. The entirety of the Commission's filmed archives has been preserved and will soon be available for consultation at a foundation created for this very purpose.

The same cannot be said of the court cases brought in the 1980s against members of the Argentine military who had been charged with human rights violations for their actions during the 1976–83 dictatorship which resulted in ten thousand murders and nearly thirty thousand missing. Despite the fact that these trials too were the object of unabridged recording, they have yielded only a few very short excerpts shown on television, in which the audio of the witnesses' voices were systematically edited out so as to minimize their importance.[12] Activist groups formed by children of the missing ensured the preservation of these audiovisual cassettes, which were sent to Norway for safekeeping. One of the magistrates who was the most active in the judicial investigations of the junta, Luis Moreno Ocampo, has since become a prosecutor at the International Criminal Court.[13]

The legacy of Nuremberg has also spread to everyday courtroom justice. Given the wealth of examples, one can now draw some initial conclusions about how the presence of cameras or screening of movies impacts the course of trials.

In France as elsewhere, most examples since the 1980s where the prosecution has had recourse to video evidence belong to the category of *faits divers*. The footage in question often comes from bystanders or surveillance devices. Rarely of good quality, these films record the acts and gestures of people who are unaware that they are on camera. The screening in court of a filmed document that was recorded unbeknown to a defendant in the midst of committing his criminal action generally produces a strong effect on all of the trial's participants, beginning, of course, with the perpetrator of the offense himself.[14]

The example of Denis Lortie, a young corporal in the Canadian Army, is a good illustration. On May 8, 1984, he burst into the National Assembly of Québec with the intention of killing the entire government. As he ran through the hallways, he fired an automatic weapon at those who crossed his path. In an analysis of Lortie's reaction at trial, Pierre Legendre recounts

the moment when the former solider was confronted with the visual recording of his acts: "The exhibit thus screened . . . stages Lortie in the Theater of
Death. On the one hand, there is his screen incarnation and, on the other, he
is obliged to join the ranks of the audience, himself now a spectator of himself.
From the position of actor (who does not know that he is playing a role), he
shifts to that of contemplator of the film that kills, that is, he becomes that
other of himself, the alienated person whom he is watching. In other words,
Lortie peels off from the murderous footage."[15] According to a court journalist, the accused "cracked" on seeing the video of his shooting spree.

In France on March 26, 2000, Kamel ben Salah is also unable to bear
looking at the film clip documenting the massacre he was accused of committing. Two Dutch couples had been murdered in their Montfort vacation
home on May 20, 1999:

> In the dusky light of the wood-paneled courtroom whose windows
> had been curtained to improve visibility of the screening, the ac-
> cused Kamel ben Salah sits facing the members of the jury who in
> turn are staring at [images of] the deceased. . . . He lowers his eyes
> and shrinks further down into his chair with each passing image,
> both hands placed over his mouth. . . . When a close-up appears on
> the screen of the disfigured face of fifty-year-old Marianne van
> Hulst, her mouth squished flat by a broad strip of adhesive tape and
> a gaping wound in her throat, her linens soaked with blood, the ac-
> cused plunges his head into the dock.[16]

Even when the defendant does not admit to his crimes, his reactions when
confronted with the footage constitute a sort of avowal that jeopardizes his
chances of acquittal.

We can thus better appreciate the foresight of Fritz Lang's early intuition,
that the judicial pertinence of motion picture screenings lies in their impact
in the court's staged space of confrontation for the parties involved. They
can undermine spurious arguments from the defense as well as serve as an
instrument for elucidating the truth. The footage's probative value depends
in part on its degree of professionalism; in the instance of *Fury*, the film
evidence was shot by a news reporter and later shown in movie theaters.

With the recent proliferation of amateur cameras, the availability of
filmed evidence has increased substantially. Hayat el-Alami, a young woman

roughed up by a policeman during a traffic stop, had initially been accused of "insulting a police officer" and charged with "resisting" a member of the forces of order. The incident was taped by a bystander, however, and this amateur film disproved the officer's account. The footage was admitted as evidence and turned accuser into accused: "Watching it twice on Tuesday, September 26, during an exceptionally long hearing (eleven hours), the Évry tribunal sought to clarify the scene recorded on the night of March 25 in Ris-Orangis (Essonne county). The court wanted to situate it in its original (unfilmed) context and understand the mechanisms that turned a routine traffic stop into a flashpoint of police aggression."[17]

This footage operates on two levels. The first is purely informational and stems from an analysis that seeks to reconstruct the chain of events; it is simply a summary report. The second consists in confronting the accused with his offense (when it is a matter of a particularly atrocious crime) or himself (when the camera puts his image on the screen). The violence of the footage shown in court is a rejoinder to the violence of the criminals and their offenses; it can contribute to the confrontations and mediations organized in session by the magistrates.

In recent times presiding judges have begun authorizing the filming of trials. In *L'Appel aux assises* (2002), Joëlle and Michèle Loncol filmed the forty-eight hours when jurors deliberate on their decision before moving on to sentencing. In 2004 France 3's documentary magazine *3,600 Seconds* dedicated a program to *comparutions immédiates* (immediate arraignments) in Lyon's Superior Court. That same year movie theaters carried Raymond Depardon's documentary, *10ᵉ chambre, instants d'audience* (10th District Court, 2004).[18] Benefiting from an authorization granted by the head of the court of appeals (Jean-Marie Coulon), Depardon and his crew of three camera operators and two sound technicians compiled footage over a three-month period (May to July 2003) using a 16mm camera equipped with special twenty-two-minute magazines and five state-of-the-art microphones. Depardon attended approximately five hundred trials in the Paris courtroom but could only film a hundred or so. Commented the director, "To me, the camera acts as a magnifying glass. It re-centers and re-dramatizes what in reality is hazy and diluted." On the issue of whether hearings were disrupted by the presence of a television crew, Depardon remarked, "Time and fatigue really play in our favor. After a certain point, the protagonists forget all about us."[19]

In the end, Presiding Judge Michèle Bernard-Requin, with whom Depardon worked ten years earlier for *Délits flagrants* (Caught in the Acts,
1994), is the only one who remains cognizant throughout that she is being
filmed. It shows, for instance, when she overdoes some of her reactions, especially in response to lawyers whose cavalier preparation probably owes
much to the relatively insignificant offenses being tried. (It should be noted,
however that this impression is due in part to the fact that Depardon elected
to focus attention on the power relations that structure exchanges between
court authorities and defendants.) The presiding judge is filmed more or less
from the perspective of the prisoner, whereas the latter is systematically
captured in a high-angle shot, thus signaling symbolic markers of the judicial ritual. With respect to a disruptive factor, all of the defendants appearing in these sequences (selected by the director to illustrate the diversity of
their crimes and demeanors) are too busy struggling with their words and
arguments to take notice of the camera; not a single one of them ever looks
directly into it. One of *10th District Court*'s merits is that it brings home the
realization that the majority of the infractions that landed these people in
the dock are ones that could potentially be committed by any of us.

In Europe film projects of a similar nature diverge significantly depending on the country. German law forbids filming or recording hearings with
a view toward their eventual television broadcast, while Italy practices more
flexible regulations. (Judges there can authorize audiovisual coverage if they
feel it benefits freedom of information.) In Great Britain, despite a 1989 official report in favor of such filming, the Contempt of Court Act 1981 has
remained dissuasive, insofar as it endows judicial authorities with the power
to sanction media accounts that treat jailed or indicted individuals as if
their guilt had already been established. In July 2004, however, the British
government did announce a pilot program installing remote-controlled cameras in appellate courts.[20] And Scotland had already constituted something
of an exception, since its less stringent regulations enabled the BBC to broadcast trials on occasion in the early 1990s.[21]

As for the United States, most states have adopted arrangements for
conditionally permitting the filming and broadcast of civil and penal trials.
Federal policy remains much more conservative in this domain, however. It
is true that the first attempts were hardly encouraging. In 1932 the prime
suspect (Bruno Richard Hauptmann) in the famous Lindbergh baby kidnapping was arrested and tried two years later. Tipped off to his imminent
arrest, the theater newsreel companies sent teams to cover the event. They

were authorized to film the ensuing interrogations in New York's Greenwich Street police station. As Raymond Fielding reports, "Newsreel men were allowed to shoot both silent and sound footage within the courtroom between sessions, by means of a rota pool system whereby the footage produced from two cameras was made available to all the newsreel companies."[22] Even more disruptive than the media circus surrounding Hauptmann's arrest was the presence in court of 141 press writers and photographers, 125 telegraph operators, and forty messengers. "The disturbances were so egregious that in 1938 the American Bar Association added a measure (Canon 35) to the *Canons of Professional Ethics* banning photographers from the halls of justice."[23]

Consequently it is not until the 1950s, in Colorado, that a camera reenters an American tribunal. By the 1970s and 1980s, though, the practice regains broad acceptance. The creation in July 1991 of the cable channel Court TV further underlines this re-"opening" of the courts—at the same time as it signals the arrival of a powerful lobby pushing to convince the relevant authorities of its subscribers' "demand" for such programming.

Inspired by CNN (twenty-four-hour reporting) and C-Span (broadcasts of legislative sessions), Court TV made a niche for itself in an audiovisual landscape already offering a smattering of shows featuring filmed excerpts from trials. In these early days of "reality programming," the major networks had several new formats on the air: NBC's *Trial Watch* showed selected court footage in the morning; *People's Court* on Fox brought the legal disputes of ordinary citizens to the small screen in the afternoon; and CBS's half-hour show *Verdict* used images from within and outside the courtroom to reconstruct trials in a primetime slot.[24] The staggering attention generated by the O. J. Simpson trial built up Court TV's audience considerably (in addition to being broadcast live on CNN), but the shoddy handling of the case—on the part of both the prosecution and the media—once again risked jeopardizing jurisprudence, whose justification lay in an ethics of showing the general public the serene workings of justice. Would the efforts of John Ford's team at Nuremberg, or those of Saguez and of Hurwitz, be undone? Sylvie Kauffmann notes the harm done to the American justice system by the prosecution's failure to keep control of the trial: "It was as if it was not a double murder that was being tried but a certain police force (Los Angeles's was hardly irreproachable), a certain society (Can one make it to the top without being knocked back down if one is born black and poor?), and a certain version of justice (Does the jury system require reform?)."[25]

Far removed from all this excess, the state of New York created a committee in 1987 charged with gathering data on the effects of filming and
broadcasting trials. It first canvassed onsite observations and polled the
principal figures concerned. The second phase (1995–97) was completed in
collaboration with the Fordham University School of Law, which generated
an invaluable report.[26] The question of the desirability of audiovisual coverage of trials was first asked of judges who had never been confronted with
the experience. The 351 responses split evenly, 47 percent for and 47 percent
against. While 46 percent agreed that this practice could have educational
benefits, a vast majority—80 percent—feared that it could turn the courtroom into an entertainment hall. If cameras were indeed to be admitted, 63
percent of the judges endorsed taping the proceedings from gavel to gavel.
Again, though, 80 percent worried about the commercial motivations driving television stations to cover the work of justice. Somewhat surprisingly,
the judges were equally divided about whether live or delayed broadcasts
were best. One might have anticipated a strong preference for deferred programming in light of the judges' inexperience in this domain and their fear
of seeing hearings turned into spectacles. This distrust of tape delay is probably owed to impressions founded on their knowledge of network news, that
it would be impossible for them to maintain any control over the footage if
it was in the hands of local and especially national TV studios. Direct feeds
are thus attractive because they possess two safeguards: the possibility of
putting a halt to recording instantaneously (72 percent favor a "kill-switch")
and the ten-second lapse on live transmission (77 percent in favor).

Concern with being in charge of their courtroom seems to be the priority for the judges amenable to filmed trials. In turning our attention to the
226 respondents who had already presided over hearings involving audiovisual coverage, we come across different sources of worry. For criminal trials,
the major reservation concerns eventual objections from its participants (74
percent, versus only 32 percent for civil proceedings). Judges are especially
sensitive about the issue of jurors; 76 percent feel that the latter should be
alerted from the very outset if the hearings are to be preserved on film. With
respect to the accused, their rights are understood to be included under the
procedures that seek to provide a fair trial, even though care of the accused
is never specifically mentioned.[27]

In line with the thinking of the majority of the judges questioned, the
committee formulates the opinion in its conclusion that the presence of television cameras in a courtroom "enhances public scrutiny of judicial pro-

ceedings."[28] Opinions are more mixed—more than 50 percent declined to answer—on the effects of cameras on the jurors and, to a lesser extent, on witnesses. If those testifying do not wish to be taped, 28 percent of the magistrates feel the court should inquire about the reasons. Another 34 percent believe the presiding judge should respect this objection and immediately order the film crew to blur the witnesses' faces.

CHAPTER 12

The Face of History

Marie-Claude Vaillant-Couturier's Inaugural Speech

For a magistrate, a witness has seen all or part of the facts tied to the object of the trial and, having been sworn in, stands before the court to speak to that effect. These depositions do not have the same status as that of evidence. In the legal system in place throughout continental Europe, witnesses for the prosecution are usually heard during the preliminary investigation and their remarks are recorded. As mentioned in Chapter 4, in 1945 the IMT preceded with a certain number of pretrial interviews (with surviving victims) and interrogations (of individuals believed to have committed atrocities). These were recorded in writing and often accompanied by other documents, such as photographs. Moreover even if they rarely cited them in court, Justice Jackson's team also had at their disposal the interviews carried out by the UNWCC, JAG, and OSS, as well as the accounts cited in the Polish and Soviet investigative committee reports. Finally, they consulted summaries drafted by the Signal Corps and FPB, in particular the note cards authenticating the still and motion pictures taken to document the discovery of Nazi crimes. These collected sources of "testimony" figure extensively in the dossier's mass of documents. In other words, the fact that few people were called to testify (per Jackson's decision) does not mean that such testimony did not have its importance. One can even argue the contrary. In the course of a trial lasting nearly a year, the appearance of a surviving witness of the genocide, one whose deposition is only a couple months removed from the experience endured, has every chance to make a very strong impression, like that produced by unprecedented acts.

When Marie-Claude Vaillant-Couturier arrived in Nuremberg to testify, she had already prepared her remarks, but she memorized them since she was not allowed to read from a text in the hearing. Despite the very short amount of time since her return from Auschwitz, she had sought to distance herself from the events. Instead of a personal speech, she preferred to use a collective "we," speaking in the name of those comrades who did not return. Deported for political reasons, she was an activist used to public appearances. However, Vaillant-Couturier discussed not only what directly involved her co-detainees and her. The judges posed a series of questions pertaining to the fate of the Jewish women deportees, then broadened the scope of their inquiry to ask if she considered the policies enacted in the camps as constituting a "system." Below we have transcribed some of the questions posed by French deputy prosecutor Charles Dubost and Justice Geoffrey Lawrence but have omitted Vaillant-Couturier's answers (except for her last one) in order to demonstrate how they led the witness to move from a descriptive register in a personal narrative to the formulation of a general analysis.

Dubost:
—What do you know about the trains carrying Jews, which arrived [at Auschwitz] at almost the same time as you, coming from Romainville?
—Are you a direct witness of the selection process transpiring at the arrival of the convoys?
—Can you talk to us about the selection processes—if you don't mind—that were carried out at the onset of winter?
—A moment ago, madame, you told us that the deportees were sent to the gas chamber as soon as they stepped down from the train, without even being counted. What happened to their clothes, their luggage?
—Would you be willing to speak to us about the Gypsy camps?
—Madame, have you seen SS leaders or members of the Wehrmacht visit the Ravensbrück or Auschwitz camps while you were there?
—Do you testify, consequently, that the Germany army was involved in the atrocities you have described on orders from their main headquarters?
—You are absolutely certain, your testimony implicates both the SS and the [German] Army?

—Madame, would you tell me if you are able to answer the following question? Did the SS doctors who took charge of the selections act on their own ideas or according to orders received?

—Did you personally witness these acts?

—Could you provide us with information about the living conditions of the men in the neighboring camp at Ravensbrück, from when you saw them the day after their liberation?

Judicial President Lawrence:

—The conditions in the Ravensbrück camp seem to be the same as at Auschwitz. Having heard these details, could we now address the issue in a more general manner—unless there was a substantial difference between Ravensbrück and Auschwitz?

—Was the situation in this camp an exception? Or do you believe that it was part of a system?

Vaillant-Couturier responded to the preceding question in the following manner: "Our only goal, for months and years, was for a few of us to get out of there alive so that we could tell the world what the Nazi jails really were: In Auschwitz as in Ravensbrück—and everywhere else, as my companions who were interned in other camps also report—there was a systematic and implacable determination to use men as slaves and, when they can't work any longer, to kill them." While the question is seeking to work up to a level of general fact ("Do you believe that it was part of a system?") to reach what one could term a historical judgment, Vaillant-Couturier remains in the register of testifying, offering what she (and others) witnessed. When defense lawyer Hanns Marx asks whether these statements stem from her own observation or from "communications" to her "by other individuals," she answers, "Every time that this was the case, I noted it in my statement. I have never cited anything that has not been verified at its source and by several people, but the majority of my statement comes from what I personally witnessed."

We can still appreciate today the conditions and impact of this deposition thanks to its recording, whereas, if we had access only to the stenographer's text of this testimony, it would lose much of its force, abstracted, as it were, from the context in which it was given.[1] Because of the audiovisual archive, we see how the witness constantly maintains the dignity and exactitude of her account and her efforts to preserve the coherence of a narrative being reconstructed on the spot in the face of constant interruptions from the judges, asking her to slow down (in order to facilitate the simultaneous translation of her testimony), to repeat what she just said (due to the difficulties of hearing properly in an auditorium where the translators' booths had not been soundproofed), or correct errors of factual comprehension (caused by lapses in the judges' attention, strained by presiding for nine months running). Through variations in frame scale, the camera can pull in tight on Vaillant-Couturier's face or, by adopting a broader frame, show her under the judges' watchful eyes. Instead of flattening the perspective opened by the initial shot selection (that of the courtroom itself), these changes allow spectators to follow it via the succession of visual segments, without ever losing track of the thread of the discussion. Years later this Auschwitz survivor explained in an interview that she was impatiently waiting for the moment when, her deposition completed, she would walk past the bench where the accused were seated. She wanted to look them in the eye and see if they had the courage not to lower their own eyes.[2] The entire group of people seated close to the witness dock—stenographers, translators, judges, and prosecutor—seemed at the instant to hold their breath and follow the witness's steps as she moved across the room. The power of that brief scene, captured on camera, is one of the numerous relays that enable the film of that trial and of its reconstitution of the incriminated acts to re-create today something of its presence and empathy, without, however, erasing the temporal distance that separates us from Nuremberg and its stakes (Figures 58–61).

In her appearance at the IMT, Vaillant-Couturier found a way to make the best of the constraints imposed by the judicial framework. Preserved for us because cameras were allowed to record it, this moment constitutes one of the highlights of the trials against the Nazi officials.

Gideon Hausner and the Holocaust Survivors

After having been confronted with the Nazi camps by way of archival footage for the production of *Strange Victory*, and then having gone to Auschwitz in order to film *The Museum and the Fury* (1956), Leo T. Hurwitz was unable to hide his emotion when, just a few days before the Eichmann trial began, he met for the first time a future colleague, Yacov Yanolowicz.[3] The director described the moment in a letter to his son:

He is foremost [an] Israeli cameraman, president of the union; and he will be a member of my television crew. He himself was in a concentration camp—working as a slave laborer in the Messerschmitt factory. He told me such stories of the imprisonment and liberation that—as much as I have seen and read—it is difficult to realize how the human animal can come through it to normal living. Here is a man about my age, with a smiling, pleasant sensitive face, clearly a man of real depth and strong character, alive to his world—and this man was once a stick of bones as he describes it, unable to recognize, by its feel, his own body when he washed himself. He says his ribs felt like the keys of a piano. . . . This man sat across my table this evening, a man full of life, mature and positive—and it is almost impossible to grasp how he could have made the transition from then to now.[4]

It is well known that the Eichmann trial encouraged the presence and decision to speak of the genocide survivors by offering them a public stage.[5] The mediatization of this trial, which helped give exposure to their speeches, was neither an innovation nor specific to this trial itself. This trait had already been a priority for Justice Jackson, who wanted to make available to the IMT the audiovisual equipment necessary for publicizing the debates and guaranteeing their historical lasting presence: "Since but few visitors could be accommodated in the ruined city of Nuernberg and fewer spectators in the courtroom, the contemporary world also must learn of these proceedings at second hand. . . . The architect, the OSS presentation branch, the Army engineers and Signal Corps, and the lawyers cooperated in the effort to put to use every scientific means of perpetuating an accurate visual record of the events of the trial."[6]

Where witnesses are concerned, they were undeniably better represented in Jerusalem than in Nuremberg, where only thirty-three were called by the prosecution. This figure does not include, however, the sixty-one individuals brought to the stand by the defense, the 143 people who were questioned, or the nineteen who took advantage of the option open to the accused of testifying on their own behalf. (Göring, in particular, seized every occasion to launch into long arguments pleading in his favor.)

During the preliminary investigation, prosecutor Gideon Hausner stuck to the IMT's example in adopting a resolutely documentary approach. Fifteen years after the end of World War II, though, the context had changed: in light of the mass of archives made available by the IMT, establishing Eichmann's guilt would not require the mobilization of teams (film crews,

researchers) or exceptional resources.[7] Under questioning from the chief of
Israeli police in charge of the preliminary investigation, Avner Less, the defendant himself would provide them with a detailed narrative of his activities.[8] Hausner's worries were, in fact, elsewhere: he had decided to delegate
to witnesses, through the succession of their personal accounts, the task of
composing the lived narrative of the extermination of Europe's Jews.

Just prior to the trial's opening, Hausner gave the judges a list on April
11, 1961, of thirty-nine people he wanted to call to the stand: "For I wanted
people to testify on the various stages of the destruction process from the
beginning of the war, on the great Jewish centers and what had gone on in
them, on the way big communities had hoped to ward off disaster and, finally,
on the extermination camps themselves in their different phases. Above all,
I wanted people who would tell what they had seen with their own eyes and
what they had experienced on their own bodies."[9]

As the hearings went along, he had dozens of others appear on the stand
in front of an audience that was nothing like that of the opening days. Two
weeks into the trial, a great many of the international press correspondents
left Jerusalem to cover other events. As a result, it became much easier for
the public to attend the trial, and this noticeably modified its atmosphere:
"Now, their seats are filled with a colorful crowd of spectators—bearded
Orthodox Jews wearing their flat-brimmed hats right in court, plump shawl-
costumed Oriental women, lithe young men in for a day from a kibbutz,
curvaceous and intense-looking young Sabra [native-born] girls, American
tourists, and Jerusalem merchants."[10]

Having come to be part of something unprecedented, these spectators
were struck by the august judicial rituals and the tribunal's austere decor.
It was, of course, within the logic of the trial that their attention turn first to
the accused. Harry Mulisch astutely observes that one of the reasons for this
attraction was owed to the fact that up until then Eichmann had in essence
been "invisible."[11] The defendant will again occupy a central place later on,
in the final sessions, but in the meantime, the audience next turns its eyes to
the witness's faces (faces more than words, since the interpreter's simultaneous translations are reserved for the media and honorary guests): "The
whole courtroom is stilled and all faces appear absorbed in thought when
these witnesses testify in voices which reveal in the overtones the power of
the memories welling up in them."[12]

Only a minute minority of the public attended more than one session.
Thus, given that there was a new batch of spectators each day, the presence

of numerous witnesses must also be interpreted as a means of increasing the chances that viewers would get to see such testimony, regardless of the day. That said, only those viewers who remained for several weeks—or better yet, for the entire trial—could come away with the impression that Hausner was seeking to produce. As to the television relay, especially for the United States, an opinion poll would be necessary to form an idea of viewers' reactions. Did the multiplication of witnesses produce a lesser effect in the end? The question comes to mind in light of the Nuremberg precedent, where the demand made by Jewish associations to be represented in court settled on the notion that a *single* speaker would have the greatest impact. Jacob Robinson was quite explicit on this point: "The trial will be a public one; press and radio from the entire world will be represented there; the unique opportunity of pronouncing an earth-shattering *J'accuse* presents itself and should certainly be taken advantage of. . . . It must indeed be an historic occasion as, for instance, Weizman[n]'s appearance before the Peel Commission, which should appeal to both the emotions and the reason of mankind."[13]

From the video control room, Hurwitz took care to alternate between shots isolating witnesses testifying on the stand and others showing Hausner's gestures and attentive glance (filmed from behind or at a three-quarter angle). Television viewers could thus observe quite clearly how the prosecutor oversaw their deposition, at times even standing at their side (Figures 62 and 63). He had given them a mission, one which they needed to complete as well as possible. Moreover television stations from around the world began almost immediately to demand footage showing the faces of the survivors, such shots being more likely to guarantee a large audience than the ordinary workings of the trial, weighed down by its dead time, long stretches, and procedural baggage.

It would be a mistake to reduce this matter to an opposition between the spectacle of human emotion and the rigors of a "documentary" trial. In the last article he wrote for the *Spectator*, Telford Taylor was severely critical of one of the foundations justifying the presence of witnesses at the Jerusalem trial, that is, the first count of Eichmann's indictment defined as his "crime against the Jewish people": "The dangerous historical implication of the 'crime against the Jewish people' is that it is not a crime against everyone else. In the modern, and it is to be hoped enlightened, view, crimes are committed not so much against victims as against the community from which emanates the law that is broken."[14]

Taylor renews this argument fifteen years later in the interview he grants Marcel Ophuls for *The Memory of Justice*. In a long and detailed review of the film, a then-youthful Michael Walzer considers that the director paid too much attention to the justice of the "victors," while rarely (or poorly) addressing that of the "victims." The philosopher goes on to state acerbically, "Taylor is his hero. At Nuremberg, Taylor called the victims of Nazism to the witness stand and spoke to the court, at least in part, in their name. But in the film, he seems to speak only for that stone-cold goddess with whom we are all familiar: scales in one hand, sword in the other, eyes covered."[15] In Walzer's opinion, it was extremely inappropriate to draw any comparisons between the respective guilt of those responsible for the genocide of the Jews and that of the authors of crimes committed in Algeria and Indochina.[16] In any case, if it was a matter of applying the principles used at Nuremberg, these should not be invoked in the name of "abstract moralizing and harsh impersonal judgments"; otherwise one risks failing to "recognize in justice the human effort *to be just*."[17]

In the course of their discussion, Ophuls asked Taylor if he was in favor of the death penalty. The former chief counsel answered that he supported it at Nuremberg, but that he was opposed to the manner in which it was used in the United States. "What about for Eichmann in Jerusalem?" asks Ophuls. Walzer summarizes the exchange between the two: "He [Taylor] was uneasy about it in the Eichmann case, he says, because Israeli law rules out the death penalty except for crimes against the Jews, 'which is not a rational basis for administering punishment.' Ophuls (off-camera) says: 'It seems like a racist basis.' And then the camera moves on to something else. Now 'racist' is an accurate description of Nazi law. Applied to Israel, it is an example of that easy and dishonest comparison that the film otherwise so strenuously avoids."

Taylor is mistaken in his belief that the Israeli death penalty is applicable only to crimes committed against "the Jewish people." Israel's penal code calls for the same punishment in the instances of "war crimes" and "crimes against humanity" (committed under the Third Reich or during World War II) as it does for crimes against "the Jewish people." These are, in fact, precisely the three charges on which Eichmann is tried and convicted. At any rate, Walzer failed to see how Israel was "racist" in adding a new category, albeit specific, to those already applied in Nuremberg as a means to address the legal status of the Holocaust: "Jews must be expected to have special feelings about it and about justice with regard to it."[18]

Asked to explain himself about this accusation of racism on September 27, 1976, by the American Jewish Congress's director Julius Schatz, Ophuls reversed course after having discussed the matter with Taylor and read Walzer's article. In a letter dated October 28, the German-born Franco-Swiss filmmaker wrote, "I agree with you and others that the statement of the actual provisions in the Israeli law under which Eichmann was tried, is just not accurate enough in the context of my casual conversation with Prof. Taylor, to be a fair reflection of our views, even though I still agree with the overall assessment that it reflects. That's why I cut the entire reference to the Eichmann case out of my film some ten days ago."[19]

Thus by the time Taylor received a copy of the Walzer piece and prepared to respond, the incident had been closed. But the criticism also called his integrity into question, so Taylor felt obliged to answer, which he did on November 19. A bit annoyed by the condescending tone of his junior colleague, he willingly recognized his mistake, owed to the constraints, he explained, of an interview that did not allow him to be as precise as he had been fifteen years earlier in a series of articles for *Time*, in which he did in fact refer correctly to the provisions of Israeli civil code. Taylor's "oversight" was nevertheless not entirely unconscious. Stung by Walzer's critique, Taylor reiterated his argument all the more forcefully in his rejoinder to the American intellectual: "But 'Special feelings about justice' with regards to crimes against Jews is another matter. If you are saying that it is justifiable to make criminal liability or the severity of punishment turn on whether or not the victims of the prohibited conduct are Jewish, then, with all respect, you are defending racism in the administration of justice."[20]

In the midst of finishing his book on "just and unjust" wars, Walzer was slow to reply. But in doing so, he sought to tone down the polemics, which Taylor appreciated. Walzer referred back to the former chief counsel's 1961 book, reminding him that, at the time, the author had spoken of religion and nationality where the Jews were concerned, and not of "race." With this "linguistic" clarification out of the way, Walzer stuck to his position that it was not unreasonable for one to feel bound to the "experience of the holocaust," given the scale of the crime committed. In the philosopher's opinion, the witnesses first and foremost had the right to speak about this. Walzer had been quite explicit on this point in his review of Ophuls's film: "Justice is the indignation of the victims, purged of merely personal feeling, expressed in universal terms."[21] Embodied by its survivors, the memory of the crime is not superimposed on the judicial process via some legal injunction;

it is part and parcel of that very process. It is for this reason that the gradual construction, from witness to witness, of this narrative is problematic, though it may seem to others to be prejudicial to its complete and proper expression. For his part, though, Walzer is ultimately more interested in the fact of witnesses being heard than in that of letting them speak.

The practical problem here is that the Jerusalem judges were faced with what they considered to be a desire on the part of the general advocate to obstruct justice by assembling this parade of witnesses. As a result, when the time came to render their verdict, they reacted in the opposite direction: "the verdict was handed down in December. It was concise, almost dry, noticeably different from the prosecutor's style. The judges based themselves largely on the documents and made little use of the witnesses' testimony. They seldom cited the suffering of the victims, concentrating instead on the crimes themselves. They were more methodical than the prosecution, more matter-of-fact, careful to avoid emotion and ideology."[22]

The Issue of Witness Credibility at the Klaus Barbie Trial

None of the witnesses called by Hausner had been granted access to the dossier, and none of them had taken part in Eichmann's arrest or the decision to try him.[23] An entirely different situation held sway in the French trials. When Barbie appeared in court, some of the victims present were members of Serge Klarsfeld's Association for the Sons and Daughters of the Deported Jews of France and had played active roles in demanding that he be brought back from his Bolivian hideaway and put on trial. Others were activists for memory (*militants de la mémoire*) whose protests and judicial efforts succeeded in obtaining the opening of legal proceedings, the right to be named plaintiffs at the trial and to appear as "judicial witnesses" (to borrow Henry Rousso's phrase).[24]

In 1994 Anne Grynberg and I were charged with producing three films for the Musée-Mémorial des enfants d'Izieu, dedicated to Jewish children exterminated during World War II, in particular those from Izieu who featured prominently in the Klaus Barbie trial.

One of the motion pictures comprised excerpts from the court proceedings themselves, so we were constrained to work with the filming and editing performed for the initial audiovisual archive. Twenty-five minutes long, *La Rafle des enfants d'Izieu: Extraits filmés du procès Barbie* (The

Roundup of the Izieu Children: Film Excerpts from the Barbie Trial) was to
be placed in the final part of the museum's permanent circuit, in a room set
off on its own.[25] In preparation for our own film, we assembled a small group
(Sabine Zlatin's lawyer, Roland Rappaport; a judicial sociologist, Alain Ban-
caud; and the film's production chief, Vincent Guigueno) and watched in
their entirety all of the trial sessions dealing with the children of Izieu. In
our first exchanges, we did not concern ourselves with selecting footage.
Instead we tackled a novel experience: What are the effects produced by
viewing a trial, seven years after the fact, one that itself treats events that took
place forty years earlier? Based on our experience, the witnesses produce the
strongest impact (and this despite the diversity of those present at the trial,
whose different personalities and roles should have helped prevent their being completely swept up by the emotion of seeing and hearing the witnesses).
In the end, we settled on a sample of five: the former director of the summer
camp, Sabine Zlatin, whose husband, Miron, was executed by firing squad in
Reval, Estonia, a few weeks after his arrest with two Izieu teens; Dr. Léon
Reifman, the only person to have escaped the roundup (he jumped out of a
window), but whose sister, nephew, and parents perished in the Auschwitz-
Birkenau gas chambers; Ita Halaunbrenner, whose husband and one of their
children were deported and gassed at Auschwitz-Birkenau; a camp survivor,
Édith Klebinder, deported for being at the wrong place at the wrong time, in
the same convoy as most of the children of Izieu; another survivor, Léa Feldblum, also sent, along with her children, to Auschwitz-Birkenau; and Julien
Favet, the roundup's only eyewitness.

A written description would not permit one to appreciate the differences
among these depositions. For example, Ita Halaunbrenner, whose role was
so important in the pretrial phases, had her children with her on the stand.
In listening to her account, one notices that initially they are holding her
hands and, so great is the tension in the hall, by the end are propping her up
in their arms. Having told how her husband and one of their children were
arrested, she suddenly changes registers and demands of the court: "How is
it that this man [Barbie], is still alive? He's still alive?" (Figure 64).

Dr. Reifman's demeanor was entirely different. He spoke first of what
he did the morning of the roundup, then of what he had seen, and finally of
what he thought about the defendant. His slow, gentle diction and the extremely nonconfrontational tenor of his observations were striking. But under-
neath this seeming serenity lay certain feelings of guilt. On April 6 he drove his
children from Bellay to Izieu to drop them off for their school holidays and was

forced to watch helplessly as they were arrested. He alone managed to escape. In his remarks, he first takes on the guise of narrator. Soon, however, as we see clearly in this scene, numerous slight changes to his demeanor occur. Most frequently he lowers his eyes and pauses (Figure 65). On two occasions, he discreetly returns to the circumstances that allowed him to escape being captured with the others (emphasis added to mark these moments):

On reaching Izieu, I just had time to greet my parents and then went up to the infirmary to see my sister. We chatted for a few minutes. Then the dining hall bell rang to summon the children to breakfast. My sister came down, I followed along; when I reached the middle of the stairs, I saw three plainclothes men head into the hallway leading to the refectory. In the middle, a short man, in a gabardine and hat. Two others, much taller, flanked him. *So, of course, I stopped.* The first man, to the right of the short one, spotted me and said, "Sir, please come down, we need your assistance." In proper French, moreover, without accent. And then they headed off down the hall. *I stopped.* At that point, I saw my sister who signaled to me, "It's the Germans, get out of here!"[26]

Changing topics, Dr. Reifman next shares a few of his reflections:

I haven't come here bound and determined to have an expiatory victim, and the person of the defendant seems to me of little significance in relation to the immense tragedy that Nazi ideology produced. I expected—and it was my hope—that I would find myself in the presence of a man who expressed regrets, some remorse, for all of the atrocities committed. I have not heard that and my hope has been disappointed. I must be very naïve. So what I hope for now, not so much out of a desire for vengeance but, rather, as a lesson for history, is that through the man before us this whole ideology be condemned—it dishonors humankind.

When it was Julien Favet's turn to testify (as the only eyewitness of the Izieu roundup), we were a bit uneasy. He was employed on the Perticoz family farm, next-door to his children's house. Favet had been trephined after an accident and, with cap doffed for his court appearance, a large wound was quite visible (Figure 66). The photographer Marc Riboud recalls, "During this trial, I took pictures of another important figure. . . . An illiterate farm hand, [Favet] is physically hideous; his plunging red eyes and deformed mouth would frighten anyone. I spent two hours at his home and discovered a man of extraordinary purity in his sentiments. Revolted by injustice, he is totally committed to truth, even down to details like the stone on which he sat when he saw Barbie. He remembers everything like it happened yesterday, with the visual memory of those possessing uncluttered minds. It was indeed a fascinating visual experience for me."[27]

Even if Favet knew the children, he had no family ties to any of them. The Izieu roundup was no threat to him either. In the strictest judicial sense, he was well and truly the only eyewitness of the principal actions for which Barbie was being tried.[28] Though Serge Klarsfeld had already provided conclusive written proof (the telex that Barbie sent to Paris on April 6, 1944), Favet's deposition was going to be an important visual confirmation.[29] The farmer's recollection of the facts was intact:

> The eldest among them—ten, twelve years old—got set to jump out of the truck but right away two Germans put them back down like old sacks of potatoes. I saw the summer camp director, Mr. Zlatin. He stuck his head up over the truck siding and yelled to my boss who was standing in his doorway: "Mr. Perticoz, don't come out! Stay safe and sound at home!" A German soldier intervened at that point, jamming his machine gun into [Mr. Zlatin's] stomach and giving him a good solid kick in the shins. The blow from the machine gun doubled him over and he had to lie down in the truck bed and then I didn't see him any more.

Next, the presiding judge asked Julien Favet about the accused:

> "Have you recognized Barbie?"
> "Yes. It's true, I swear it. I recognized him by his expression." A pause. "I recognized him as if he was you, Judge, sir. With all due respect."[30]

When Marcel Ophuls asked about this testimony in *Hotel Terminus: The Life and Times of Klaus Barbie* (dir. Ophuls, 1988), chief prosecutor Pierre Truche explained why he did not consider it reliable: "Julien Favet is a good, honest man and he lives as he speaks. But I myself cannot say, 'I'm going to convict for very serious crimes based on the deposition of one person who saw another person, just for *a couple seconds*, forty years ago.'"

The credibility problem encountered here does not concern the truth of the facts being reported but the social persona or linguistic expression of the person articulating them. French not being Léa Feldblum's native tongue, her testimony is labored, with the result that she too saw her court deposition slightly discounted. Roland Rappaport stepped in to correct this negative effect: "Judge, sir, with great emotion we have heard the convoy's sole survivor tell her story. We understand her difficulties perfectly well. I would like to add something: you should know that Madame Léa Feldblum, who was carrying false papers naming her a French citizen, revealed her true identity when she understood the fate that awaited the children and adults that were there, in order not to be separated from them."

If Favet's testimony had been communicated to the judges only in the form of a written deposition, one that the legal team had sorted through, it would have been granted consideration much more easily. Moreover edited testimony of this sort was a common enough practice, as we saw in our analysis of the woman doctor at Belsen in Chapter 6. On film, though, Favet probably inspires confidence more than anything else, because spectators can sense his sincerity. The very fact that he is filmed in a judicial setting reinforces this impression. As for Léa Feldblum, while it is true that her remarks are not easy to follow, the sudden break in her deposition, itself recounted in a halting rhythm, also makes an impact on the audience, for she pauses to recall that the color of the sky appeared reddened by the smoke issuing from the gas chambers.

These witnesses had lived through traumatic experiences, and their facial expressions and their gestures, as well as their words, provoked an empathy that was magnified by the effect of proximity produced by the camera. It is their presence that wins us over (or not); it is a matter of personal conviction, even if it is not the deep, intimate conviction asked of jurors. French historian François Hartog understandably expresses concern over this phenomenon of "witnesses today [who] are first and foremost victims or the descendants of victims. This status as victim is the basis of their authority and feeds the sort of reverential fear that sometimes accompanies it. It creates a risk of confusing authenticity and truth or, worse, identifying the latter with the former, when in fact what separates veracity from reliability, on the one hand, and truth from proof, on the other, is a distinction to be preserved."[31] This authority based on victimhood can even play against judicial witnesses who end up being unfairly regarded with some suspicion.

At Nuremberg the victims present at trial were able to inscribe their testimony within a judicial frame where memory, history, and justice all combined in an inaugural record. Over time historians have gradually freed themselves of their long dependence upon the archives and themes developed by the IMT. The collection of witness accounts now occurs outside of the courtroom (even if they still take an audiovisual form inspired by Nuremberg practices).

In their approach to establishing trial conclusions, judges have often leaned in the direction of the defense's objections, by minimizing the role of witnesses. The chief prosecutor of the Barbie trial thus adopted the same position as the Eichmann judges, insisting in his indictment that he would found his demonstration more on evidentiary exhibits than on depositions from the stand.

CHAPTER 13

The Spectator's Place

Footage Shown in Closed Session: A "Trying Experience" in Jerusalem

In performing its dual functions—pedagogic and therapeutic—the Eichmann trial only briefly fell under the sway of powerful emotions. After the living witnesses on the stand, Gideon Hausner still had one other means at his disposal for conveying such testimony. On April 15, 1961, shortly after the hearings began, journalist Robert S. Bird noted with near astonishment that the court did not seem willing to allow recourse to exhibits or films that would present Nazi crimes in their spectacular horror: "The fact is, the basic case of the Israeli government against Eichmann is to be presented through documentary evidence, along with some eyewitness and camp-survivor testimony. But primarily the case will rest on documents. The government is holding firm [to] the decision to present a strictly legal, decorous, and non-sensational trial against Eichmann."[1]

Just as at Nuremberg, footage had, of course, been presented, but always in the context of tightly focused debates, and its screening never made any real impact. The general arrangements were quite different, as a matter of fact. At Nuremberg the film on the camps was moved up to November 29 and thus was screened in the first days of the trial. In Jerusalem the exhibit was not a documentary but rather a collection of archival images strung together, whose screening (June 8) came almost two months into the trial, in a hall emptied of public spectators. (For security reasons, only journalists and special guests were allowed to attend that morning's hearing.) Also, the room's spatial configuration hardly favored dynamic mediation: only the accused had a direct frontal view, the screen having been installed next to the witness stand. The invited viewers and judges were perpendicular to it and could not, as had been possible at Nuremberg, take in the defendant and the footage at the same time (Figure 67). Eichmann's reactions were not being monitored in any special way, a departure from how the twenty-one Nazi officials tried in 1945 were handled.[2]

The first debate for the judges, the advocate general, and the defense took place on May 26. On this occasion, Hausner reminded those present that he planned to present footage as evidence and sought the Court's opinion on this matter: "It is our intention to exhibit in Court a number of documentary films in order to illustrate certain events about which evidence had already been led, and other events on which evidence will be produced next week. Naturally we will ensure suitable authentication of the incidents contained in these films. We shall produce witnesses who will be asked to testify under oath that this is how matters looked in fact."

The presiding judge asked two questions of Hausner: Had this type of presentation been done previously, and, if so, was there any record kept of the procedure adopted? Hausner replied by citing the precedent of the Bergen-Belsen and Nuremberg trials. He gave the appearance of wanting to mark himself off from a simplistic, primary approach to the footage. His object was not to use it for the identification of such and such a place but rather to "illustrate certain events." As for the IMT discussions on this issue, the advocate general reminded the Court that these were in the written transcription of the Nuremberg proceedings.

Hausner then detailed the content of the films that he had chosen.[3] Going in order, he named Auschwitz survivors, the Warsaw Ghetto, a train transporting Jews to Ravensbruck, and the Mauthausen camp. The presiding judge asked when the footage had been shot: Had it been before or after the liberation of the camps? Hausner's explanation was fairly confused, revealing spotty knowledge about the provenance of these archives and their prior legal qualification as evidence. The Court was in fact right to insist on this question of dates. In 1945 it had not really been an issue. The Allies had direct links to their materials, either locating motion pictures shot by the Nazis themselves (*Original German Film [8 mm] on the Atrocities Committed against the Jews*, projected December 13, 1945) or presenting their own movies on the liberation of the camps. In both cases, the screenings were accompanied by affidavits guaranteeing the authenticity of the documents taken from the enemy or the circumstances surrounding those recorded by the Allies.

In 1961 Yad Vashem's archival center was still in the fledgling stages of its policy of collecting and publicizing camp footage. Presumably it was under these haphazard conditions that the Israeli prosecution assembled its cinematic evidence. Whereas the jurists on Jackson's team imposed strict rules for the selection of source footage, Hausner mixed raw clips with edited sequences or even uncaptioned archival scenes found in recent movies. Thus it was that they did track down the Soviet movie on Auschwitz, but with Czech commentary. The advocate general deduced from the commentary that the film had been made in Czechoslovakia, which shows that he was unaware of the existence of Karmen's documentary—a significant lapse in that it was the Soviet screening of excerpts from their director's work in the spring of 1945 in New York that led Eisenhower to speed up production of the American film on the camps. The prosecution had turned up other archives in commercial cinema storerooms, which caused Hausner to think that private directors had worked alongside the Allies' camera crews in 1945 (which was not the case). Finally, one of the documents selected by the prosecution was a segment pulled from a German TV film, *In the Steps of the Hangman*, made at the time of the Eichmann trial.[4]

Conscious of the uncertain provenance of all of these audiovisual archives, Hausner explained how he planned to authenticate them: "At any rate we shall not exhibit anything which cannot be substantiated by witnesses."

In truth, though, the best he could provide would be the "authenticating witness" encountered above (see Chapter 1) in American jurisprudence establishing the probative status of motion pictures. It seems hard to imagine, however, that anyone would have ended up recognizing themselves by viewing this footage of deportees taken during the liberation of the camps. The "witnesses" in question are thus those that Hausner wanted to call for the hearings and whose narrative would treat their personal experience more than it would serve to confirm their presence during the Allies' film shoot.

All that to say that the set of instructions imposed at Nuremberg was not followed at Jerusalem. The defense was justified in demanding the opportunity to look at the films prior to their screening in court in order to "evaluate" them. Yet rather than raising the problems tied to identifying the content of the footage or pointing out the absence of professional witnesses having participated in the filming, Robert Servatius merely asked permission for his client to watch the clips in his company (which was granted). On the day of the in-court projection (Thursday, June 8), Israeli poet, novelist, and documentary filmmaker Haïm Gouri wrote:

> [These films] are being screened at a closed session of the Jerusalem District Court, where Adolf Eichmann is on trial.
>
> He is not seeing these films for the first time. Clips were shown to him during his interrogation by Section 06. Through the defense attorney, he was asked to be present at this showing as well, so that he could identify the military units by their uniforms.
>
> He is still playing games, and Servatius follows his lead. He sees great significance to the fact that, after twenty years, one of the witnesses is unable to remember what color uniform the murderers of his children wore. Was it black? Green? Brown?
>
> Some reporters thought the films would "break" Eichmann. They thought, for some reason, that seeing things with his own eyes would affect him more than witnesses had. He had many opportunities to break down. But so far he has not done so.[5]

Did journalists truly believe that the footage would end up competing with the witnesses and not with the written documents? Whatever the case, under pressure from the judges to produce affidavits for his footage, Hausner reversed course. He had in fact provided the Court with a list of nine people who could authenticate these films (at least partially), but, since the defense did not issue any requests of this type, the names simply remained available at the judges' discretion. Hausner thus decided to go forward with the presentation of the documents and to provide the commentary himself: "There will be no evidence running with the screening. I shall announce before the screening of each section what is being shown." Servatius did intervene at this juncture to express reservations. He was not calling the films' authenticity into question, but he had concerns about the impact on interpretations of their meaning stemming from the editing performed after the fact in the instance of the documentaries produced by the Allies or in that of the newsreels.

Servatius chose an example that allowed him to block Hausner on this issue: the infamous sequence filmed by the British at Bergen-Belsen. The advocate general had not mentioned it during the initial discussion on

May 26. Eichmann's lawyer felt that the shot of the pile of corpses being bulldozed into a pit was misleading: "My feeling is that whoever prepared the report aimed less at a factual description than at the impression made." Although Servatius had already seen this document at Nuremberg, he acted as if he knew nothing of its circumstances. It is indeed the case that this footage, used extensively after the war to demonstrate the savagery of the camp authorities, had been subject to mistaken interpretations; some had assumed that the soldier driving the bulldozer was German and that this brutal manner of carrying out the summary burial of deceased deportees was typical of the methods employed by the Nazi executioners.

The problem was that Hausner too was bothered by this scene, but for different reasons: "To my regret, graves were opened in this process, and bodies were dragged along. I am not saying that the accused, or his subordinates, or [those] in whose name he operated, committed this act. This film was taken after the liberation of Bergen-Belsen. But this is what such a burial looked like."

At Nuremberg this segment was not shown on its own. On the contrary, it was a rare example of footage being situated through testimony—in this instance, from the woman doctor analyzed in Chapter 6 and an interview with a British officer. This clip lent itself to confusion when shown in isolation by Hausner, which enabled Servatius to extend his remark and ask what connection existed between what was being shown and the role of his client. What had already transpired several times with witnesses—the judges lost patience listening to long depositions made by witnesses without any direct imputation of the accused's responsibility—thus ended up happening with the showing of this footage as well.

The projection was thus broken up by commentary to provide information about the events reported in the films and contradictory debates on the origin and pertinence of the archives selected. At the end of the clip, Hausner took a dramatic tone in addressing the judges: "I regret that it was necessary to subject the Court to such a harrowing experience. That is the end of the screening."

It is not possible today to compare this mass of footage strung together (and which no one preserved in this form) to the American prosecution's movie presented in 1945. Hausner recalls this projection as a "particularly trying" moment. Doubtless it was, for still today the viewing of such documents never fails to produce a shock. Having failed in his attempt to get the footage admitted as evidence, he foisted it upon the court as a sort of argument by authority, the films being explained by his own commentary.

Rony Brauman and Éyal Sivan, authors of *A Specialist*, the 1999 documentary based on filmed archives of the Eichmann trial, consider the contrary to be true.[6] Of the opinion that these images have been "a thousand times seen, a thousand times discussed," they preferred to center their attention on Eichmann watching the screen: "We bet on . . . the power of imagination and against the rehashing of the imagery of misfortune."[7] Pierre Joffroy seemed struck by this aspect: "It was difficult, almost impossible, to tear one's glance away from this character, so dreary and prim in his blue suit, with his striped tie, receding hairline, and glasses. What did he think today? What did he grasp of his fate? Apparently, he was shown a film on the concentration camps at a screening inside Fort Iyar. He watched it attentively and then offered only one comment: 'That didn't concern me, my offices weren't in charge of that.' The idea that he could have used the occasion to express some feelings of regret never even crossed his mind."[8] An eyewitness account by *New York Times* reporter Homer Bigart reveals, however, a decidedly undemonstrative defendant: "Once, Eichmann opened his mouth as if to get more breath. Once, after a close-up of a startling corpse covered with flies, Eichmann coughed. During a change of film he watched the projector intently. During another interruption he scribbled a brief note to his counsel, Dr. Robert Servatius. This followed a shot of American officers forcing German officials of the town of Weimar to look at piles of dead Jews at Buchenwald."[9] From this perspective, focusing one's attention on a defendant who hardly budges over an entire hour might not be the best way to engage the viewer's imagination.

In taking into account the prosecution's difficulty in procuring these films, as well as their very limited exposure and diverse nature, they cannot be properly deemed clichés or icons of Nazi barbarity. At Nuremberg the very function of the screening arrangements had been to create the possibility of establishing some distance, in not forcing the judges, prosecution, or audience to confront the images head-on but rather in deflecting them spatially toward the accused, whose reactions were thus rendered visible.[10] To speak of them as "heady clichés" or a "spectacle of misfortune" seems an exaggeration. It serves no purpose to replace the ideological pressure exercised by Hausner with another form of distortion, one that leads to reducing the prosecution witnesses to a mere parade in *A Specialist*.[11]

A Public Event: The Screening of a Filmed Massacre at the International Criminal Tribunal for the Former Yugoslavia

At Nuremberg and even more so at Jerusalem, the in-session film projections drew their force from the relatively closed nature of the trials. The room's spatial disposition created unusual conditions for viewing and reacting in that it set up a legal confrontation organized around exhibits which at the time had received little public exposure. Installed in the center of the room, between the judges and the accused, the large screen was a symbolic marker indicating the entry into the courts of film footage, to be observed in darkened halls. Only the prosecution chose to employ this kind of evidence; the defense did not propose a "counter-projection" even though it could have asked for one.

At the time of the creation of the International Criminal Tribunal for the Former Yugoslavia (ICTY) in 1993, the circulation of such footage had increased substantially.[12] Its presence in court was becoming more prevalent but also more banal. Modeled especially after common law, ICTY procedures allow plaintiffs in attendance for introductory declarations to present right from the outset documents whose eventual admissibility would be determined later. More than ever, we see here the notion of the court as "workshop" described by Luigi Ferrajoli. Taking its cue from the standardized decor of international assembly halls, The Hague tribunal offers a space free of any symbolic materialization. Personalized installations enable the judges, defense team, and prosecution to have at their disposal a laptop computer and multifunction screen. Set up with several channels, it provides nonstop transmission of a teletext transcription of the proceedings, the edited mix of the trial recording executed from the control room, videos cited in session, and written or pictorial documents displayed as exhibits (Figure 68).

Most of the videotape selected was drawn from news programs and edited documentaries already aired on television in the former Yugoslavia or elsewhere in Europe. Some of the documents came from private sources; they had been shot in the presence of (or even at the behest of) those responsible for the incriminated acts. The mass of images, willingly displayed or hidden depending on the various interests at stake, played a significant role in shaping public opinion at the time when these acts were being judged by the ICTY. While journalists were summoned to appear before the International Criminal Tribunal for Rwanda (ICTR) created in Arusha in 1994, only one expert witness of this sort, Renaud de la Brosse, was called at The Hague.[13] De la Brosse's report covered the role of propaganda in the Serbian media.[14] Similarly, in her opening speech (February 12, 2002) of the trial of Slobodan Milosevic, prosecutor Carla del Ponte identified this subject as important, committing her team to analyzing "the sinister role of some in the media."[15] The prosecution carried this out during the proceedings by regularly including films conveying an orator's remarks or attesting to the "reality" of the facts mentioned.

In a preliminary declaration, British barrister and deputy prosecutor Geoffrey Nice referred to several videos previously shown that he added to other written and oral documents (intercepted phone calls, for instance) in order to build the indictment. The major novelty in this trial (with respect to Nuremberg) lay in the identity of the defendant: a head of state whose "common criminal enterprise sought to force, through crimes punishable under Articles 2, 3, 4, and 5 of the Statute of the Tribunal, the majority of non-Serbs—for the most part, Muslims and Croatians from Bosnia—to vacate permanently vast portions of the Republic of Bosnia and Herzegovina's territory."[16] It was thus appropriate during hearings to screen films, among other documents, proving the accused's declaration of the "objective of the common criminal enterprise" and the crimes that resulted from it as a "natural and foreseeable consequence—eventualities, in other words, of which he could not help but be aware. As at the IMT, the films projected belong to two distinct registers: those of political speeches, which assisted in the reconstruction of the stages leading up to the war; and those of the atrocities committed, putting on display the most extreme consequences of these criminal plans.

In the first category, it sufficed to state that the document was a "well-known video" to justify its screening as the opening excerpt, shown on February 12, 2002. The footage was a recording of a political rally held April 24, 1987, in Kosovo. Nice presented the clip in the following manner: "Can we get another snapshot of this accused at about this time? At the end of February or beginning of March of 1989, there was a demonstration. The subject was nationalism. We'll see the video in just a second. The accused spoke to a crowd of perhaps up to a million demonstrators in Belgrade. He spoke of settling accounts with Kosovo leaders and promised decisive action, but perhaps most interesting is this: he kept the crowd waiting for a full twenty-four hours and then only spoke to them for four minutes. Can we see the clip?"[17]

Another political rally, this one from June 28, 1989, was featured in footage described as "another . . . famous clip" which would "be entered into the evidence of this case."[18] On that day Milosevic gave a speech commemorating the June 28, 1389, Battle of Kosovo Polje (the Kosovar Blackbird's Field), a historic defeat at the hands of invading Turkish forces for a coalition of Balkan Christians led by Lazar of Serbia. In reviving Serbian nationalism, Milosevic galvanized a crowd of nearly a million people, essentially announcing (albeit implicitly) the end of Yugoslavia. The prosecution wanted to show when and how he had elaborated the project to create a "Great Serbia" that would assemble within a single nation all of the Serbs scattered across the former Yugoslavia. First indicted for his alleged role in the criminal acts of violence committed during the Kosovo conflict in 1999, he would also be charged for crimes committed during the wars in Bosnia (1992–95) and Croatia (1991–95). Advocate General del Ponte, having outlined the principal occasions on which Milosevic's plans were made public, now moved on to the second category of film. It was in this context that the screening took place of news clips on the fall of Vukovar, the expulsion of the non-Serbian populations, and the November 22, 1991, roundup and execution of civilians by soldiers in a warehouse.[19]

The technique of tying video excerpts to events already well-known by the trial's participants contributed significantly to the fluidity of the historical reviews. The footage is not required to "illustrate" a statement but stands rather on equal footing with it in the proposed critical narrative. It creates, for instance, effects of proximity that are at once spatial (it can be useful to break up a little of the courtroom's anonymity by transporting everyone to the places in the former Yugoslavia where the crimes occurred) and temporal (the grain of the image is that of archival footage; the presence of certain individuals in these clips is like the final trace of their life). One should hardly be surprised that Milosevic broke with the strategies favored by Eichmann and other Nazi officials. In deciding to appropriate video as a weapon, he was seeking to disrupt the reliability of this procedure or, in passing, del Ponte's project of counteracting the perverse effects wrought by the media during the war.

From the first moments in which he addressed the court, Milosevic went on the offensive, trying to challenge the prosecution on this very terrain: "I'd like to show a video first and then I'll continue speaking after that."[20] The film that he asks the control room to cue up is an investigative documentary, *Es begann mit einer Lüge* (It Began with a Lie), made in 2001 by journalists Jo Anger and Mathias Werth and shown on the prominent German channel ARD. Anger and Werth accused the German defense minister Rudolf Scharping of having distorted the facts in order to win public and parliamentary support for Germany's commitment to join the ranks of the multinational forces in Kosovo. The following excerpt from the program's narration reveals what value it had for the defendant seeking to prove that no massacre took place at Racak:

> [The village] is known as Racak. The Serbs suffered a terrible massacre here, a massacre which led to the attack by the NATO aviation. It occurred in 1999. The head of the verification mission of the OSCE [Ambassador William G. Walker, director of the Organization for Security and Cooperation in Europe] arrived with a number of television crews. They found forty-four bodies. Walker said this is a massacre and the result of a civil war between the Serbs and the other inhabitants. Many people were also wounded. I need several minutes to gather my thoughts. But what did actually happen in Racak? Here at the university in Pristina, the pathologist [Finnish medical examiner Helen Ranta] examined the bodies, and there was doubt that what happened in Racak was indeed a massacre.[21]

Milosevic's goal is to refute the notion that the viewing of a news clip carries only one possible meaning. He will subject the prosecutor's films to a kind of cross-examination and will cite other clips, explicated by his own analysis, during a seventeen-hour-long intervention for which he had requested and received authorization to complete without interruption. Over the course of the trial, this system will occasionally work to his advantage. Joël Hubrecht notes that the ex-president had his speech of June 29, 1989, shown a second time in order to minimize its bellicose character: "Milosevic never gave public speeches as hateful as those given by a Seselj or a Karadzic. . . . But no one in the Serbian community (or any other) ever understood them as a call to calm; quite the contrary, in fact."[22] Outside the courtroom, Milosevic could also count on Serbia's national media (RTS,

Serbian radio and television) to relay his message. As a result, as Antoine Garapon stresses, "Serbs and Bosnians don't see the same trial. Serbian news programs manage to select trial excerpts that make Milosevic into a glorious being who is lifting his head up once again. All the segments which go badly for him are scrambled so that the average Serbian viewer does not see them, unless they look on the internet."[23]

The prosecution also scored points in this battle of images, however. A "crucial piece of evidence" (in Hubrecht's words) was shown in February 2003; it consisted of a handheld sequence shot with a camcorder on May 4, 1997, that placed Milosevic at a celebration for the sixth anniversary of the Red Berets. Even more damning, though, was the June 1, 2005, session, during which never-before-seen footage of atrocities committed ten years earlier was projected. One witness, Obrad Stevanovic, was cross-examined by the deputy prosecutor, who was trying to get him to admit that as the assistant to the minister of the interior he had to be aware of the movements of Serbian paramilitary troops heading toward Bosnia and Herzegovina to commit crimes. The massacres near Srebrenica produced nearly eight thousand victims, most of whom were Bosnian Muslims killed and thrown into mass graves.

On the screen, six members of the Scorpions (a paramilitary group with ties to the Serbian Ministry of the Interior and the Supreme Command in Belgrade) force six young Muslims out of a truck. Initially the Scorpions make them lie down next to one another on the ground at the side of the road and lead them to believe that they are going to be executed. The militia men then have them get back to their feet and walk into the middle of a field, where they are shot in the back. "The killers untie the hands of the last two [so] that they bury their companions in death before being executed themselves. The last words that they hear are those of the cameraman: 'Hurry up with the last two, I'm almost out of battery.'"[24]

The brutality of this document viewed in the hearing shocked the judges:

Judge Patrick Robinson: Mr. Nice, can you tell us about that film?
Deputy prosecutor Nice: Yes, to a degree I will. But if I can just deal with—
Defense counsel Steven Kay: —We haven't established any foundation for this. To my mind, this looks like sensationalism. There are no questions directed to the witness on the content of that film in a way that he can deal with it. It's merely been a presentation by the

Prosecution of some sort of material they have in their possession that has not been disclosed to us and then it has been shown for the public viewing without any question attached to it. It's entire [*sic*] sensationalism. It's not cross-examination.

Judge Robinson: Mr. Nice, there is some merit in that. That's why I asked what are we going to be told about the film. Who made it, in what circumstances, and what questions are you putting to the witness in relation to it?

Deputy prosecutor Nice: Certainly. I'm coming to that. As to the—as to the film, my suggestion to the witness is that this is a film showing, as it happens, Scorpions executing prisoners from Srebrenica.[25]

This document was obtained through the efforts of a nongovernmental organization (NGO), the Humanitarian Law Center.[26] One of the killers filmed the executions to keep as a trophy. He then had copies made for the five others, and it is one of these copies that ended up in the possession of the NGO. The deputy prosecutor was in fact performing his duty in subjecting the witness to factual questioning. However, Nice was trying to do it in such a way as to provoke a reaction as well, in the hopes of discovering something like a chink in Stevanovic's self-assurance. We had already seen this approach employed at Nuremberg, when the Allies imposed screenings on the Germans. At The Hague, Defense Counsel Kay is not wrong in stating that one of the effects sought here is to sway public opinion. Judging from the reactions of the Serbian officials, the prosecution probably succeeded far beyond its expectations, despite the fact that a majority of the media correspondents had long since deserted the courthouse.

The film was broadcast the following night on two Serbian television stations, including the national station RTS, a notable occurrence given that it had previously been rejected when the Humanitarian Law Center proposed it for televised transmission. On this latter occasion, Prime Minister Vojislav Kostunica announced the arrest of eight suspects at a press conference that included Carla del Ponte in the audience (in Belgrade for a brief visit). Kostunica explained, "I feel that it is important for public opinion in our country that we react immediately and, based on this terrible and shocking document, make sure that those who are involved in this crime be arrested and answer for it in court."[27]

At The Hague the proceedings benefited significantly from jurisprudence developed at Nuremberg for the in-session presentation of filmed documents. This procedure has become a natural recourse, its growth occurring in tandem with the evolution of the role of televised media in contemporary societies. That said, it was never a case of trying to trade the rigor of a contradictory trial for tugging on emotional cords. With a great deal of agility and pertinence, the magistrates often shored up their remarks with specific references to still and motion pictures. Technological developments enabled them to produce exhibits whose power of conviction could hardly be contested. One noteworthy instance was their use of satellite photography to show very clearly the displacement or camouflaging of mass graves.[28] Even as the ICTY had already begun its work, criminals were trying to escape the most serious charge that could be brought against them, that of crimes against humanity.

CHAPTER 14

Court Settings and Movie Stagings: From Nuremberg to the Khmer Rouge Trials

Otto Ohlendorf's Confession

In reflecting on the trust that we should place in a "historical" witness's narrative account, both for its faithfulness and its truth value, Paul Ricoeur evokes the tragic solitude of those "whose extraordinary experience stymies the capacity for average, ordinary understanding. But there are also witnesses who never encounter an audience capable of listening to them or hearing what they have to say."[1] The philosopher was doubtless thinking of those who survived the Nazi policy of extermination of the Jews of Europe during World War II. It is not certain, however, that he was including those on the side of the criminals, be they decision makers or only executors of these mass murders. And yet these latter shared the same space for witness deposition in the heart of the IMT as their victims and their words were made available to be assessed according to the same spatial and technical arrangements. The "tragic solitude" evoked by Ricoeur belongs only to the survivors. As to the Nazis, the expression of words attesting to their crimes, regardless of the mechanisms of dissimulation or claims made, constitutes an exceptional case as well. For those in attendance at Nuremberg, the confessions of the guilty were not necessarily easier to listen to than the depositions of the victims.

This entire mass of testimony marked a major innovation, preceding the collective development of historical research for this period as well as the workings of personal memory. It was carried out in the courtroom and under the eye of the cameras, ensuring that they would receive significant exposure already in 1945, but also a lasting place in the annals, making it possible for later generations to have access to a vivid memory like no other.

These advantages, undeniable though they may be, do not prevent us from wondering whether the witness stand is the most appropriate place for the encounter between the bearer of the experience of war's violence and a receptive audience.[2] But this also entails examining how the entire group of participants managed (or not) to achieve their respective aims. First, there are the victims, who are trying to construct a narrative and to socialize it. Second, there are the criminals, whose behavior in court can permit them to finagle a lesser sanction for themselves (as was the case for Albert Speer). Third, there are the investigating magistrates and the judges, whose responsibilities, given the historic scale of the acts being tried, far exceed the stakes of ordinary criminal courts. Fourth, as a corollary to the preceding, the Nuremberg Trial was seeking to reach a planetary audience, in the short term as in the longer duration of its legacy.

Most notably with respect to the filming of the trial and the presentation of motion pictures as evidence, the experiments inaugurated by the IMT have not remained confined to the judicial realm.[3] Survivors of mass crimes committed after 1945 have taken their inspiration from the precedent of Nuremberg. In anticipation of a trial endlessly put off, Cambodian filmmaker Rithy Panh brought to light, in a specifically cinematic setting, testimonial speech and gestures (of both victims and perpetrators, moreover). Having established a bond of trust, he was able to obtain from those willing to speak on camera what never emerged with the same force in Phnom Penh, once the hearings did finally open on February 17, 2009, at the tribunal charged with hearing the Khmer Rouge cases.[4]

Over time, in tandem with the evolving and diverse modes of writing the history of the Shoah and other war-related cataclysms, audiovisual mediation has imposed itself as the dominant characteristic of these massive enterprises of gathering witness testimony, from the opening of the camps by the Allies in 1944–45 to the construction of the recent museums conceived as memorials. In the Nuremberg courthouse, the policy of establishing the crimes committed during World War II and their presentation at trial were thought out and organized with constant regard to the limitations of film recording, thus revolutionizing the practices common to the world of justice. More recently the tendency to inscribe the quest for survivors' narratives under the aegis of "the duty to remember," out of fear that witnesses might die without having had the opportunity to leave a trace of their history for the generations to come, has led to a situation in which the specificities of the making (and reception) of films have too often been taken for granted.[5] This paradox can be explained by the intersection of several different registers of truth—historical, judicial, anthropological, and memorial—that characterize this type of ongoing work with memory.

From the very outset of their trial before the IMT, the twenty-one Nazi officials present pled not guilty. Since they seemed to have adopted an attitude of systematic denial toward their criminal policies, the chief prosecutor decided to turn to visual proof of their atrocities much earlier than planned. Accompanying the footage was the reading on January 2, 1946, by Executive Trial Counsel Col. Robert Storey of a report drawn up by Hermann Graebe, manager of a civil construction company who had worked for the German army in occupied Ukraine and was present at the mass execution of Jews that took place on October 5, 1942, near Dubno. In both cases—the screening of a movie conceived by the American prosecution team and the reading of a deposition from a witness not implicated in the acts reported—the mediation was indirect between the crime and its evidentiary exhibition. It was only on the following day (January 3) that, for the first time, a witness took the stand who was a front-line participant in what is known today as the "Shoah by Bullets." SS Maj.-Gen. Otto Ohlendorf would later be tried and hanged, but for the moment he was being called only as a witness. As he readied himself to speak, he was facing the prosecutor, but also the benches of the prosecution and the audience packed into the mezzanine.

This situation turned out to be doubly unprecedented: Ohlendorf was going to talk and he was going to do so "facing" his accusers. Normally, for crimes tried in ordinary venues, perpetrators and victims alike are placed with their backs to the audience. Thus situated, they have to address the Court, surrounded by the jury, which represents society. But while they are on the witness stand, they are not supposed to be offered up to the eyes or passions of the audience and press. The judges occupy the center of the courtroom, flanked on its left and right by the defense and the prosecution. In Nuremberg, however, the young American architect (Dan Kiley) in charge of redesigning the Hall of Justice to house the IMT completely disrupted the traditional judicial setting, primarily in displacing the judges from the middle and putting in their stead a movie screen and the witness stand, both aligned to face flush the hall's spectators.

In light of these arrangements, one could wonder whether the Allies were giving in to the temptation of a "show trial," siding with spectacle over the serene unfolding of the court's proceedings. During trial preparation, Robert H. Jackson deliberately sought to build what he termed a "documentary" case. The evidence presented in court had to be exhibits drawn for the greater part from archives, preferably those of the Germans themselves, tokens of the prosecution's fairness. It was for this reason that the prosecution lawyers only rarely called on victims, who had not been permitted to be named as plaintiffs in the case, partly because Jackson feared that emotions would get the better of them. With regard to the criminals, would there be anyone else, outside of those seated in the defendants' dock, perhaps less important but at least more talkative, who might take the stand?

Ohlendorf had been head of the SD Inland, the Nazi bureau of domestic intelligence. He had directed Einsatzgruppe D, which was charged with mobile massacre operations in the Crimea. After having offered his racial "expertise" to the Nazi government and participated in the "Germanizing" of the East, he was one of those who made possible the passage from political notions to criminal applications. Aspects of his presentation would surprise the audience: his relative youth (thirty-nine), his unflinching answers to questions impugning his responsibilities, his chilling apparent precision, all grounded in a rational defense of orders received and acts performed (Figure 69). His demeanor had nothing in common with Göring's gesticulations or Speer's false bravado. It seemed evident—at least in retrospect—that the Nazi major general had elaborated a very shrewd strategy for his testimony.

During interrogations following his arrest, again during his testimony before the IMT, and then finally at his own trial, Ohlendorf provided a certain amount of information, including on items unrelated to his own charges.[6] This established him first of all as an "expert witness" for the American investigators. He also evokes memories of World War I stamped with the trappings of "total war." And as Christian Ingrao has demonstrated, Ohlendorf displays "an unchanged Nazi fervor in its de-dramatizing function, a defensive rhetoric that leads him to understand the genocide as inevitable."[7]

Today the principal stages and modalities of the execution of the Jews of Europe are known and have been established by scholars, which was not the case when the SS major general testified before the IMT. Without necessarily realizing the importance of the full details implied by the question that he asks Ohlendorf, American prosecutor John H. Amen highlights one of the key moments in the evolution of the Einsatzgruppen's murderous practices, the point precisely at which they cross the line to genocide (Figures 70 and 71):

> *Amen*: Will you explain to the Tribunal why you . . . believe that the type of execution ordered by you, namely, military, was preferable to the shooting-in-the-neck procedure adopted by the other *Einsatz* groups?
>
> *Ohlendorf*: On the one hand, the aim was that the individual leaders and men should be able to carry out the executions in a military manner acting on orders and should not have to make a decision of their own; it was, to all intents and purposes, an order which they were to carry out. On the other hand, it was known to me that through the emotional excitement of the executions ill-treatment could not be avoided, since the victims discovered too soon that they were to be executed and could not therefore endure prolonged nervous strain. And it seemed intolerable to me that individual leaders and men should in consequence be forced to kill a large number of people on their own decision.[8]

Ohlendorf wants to lead the Court to believe that he ordered only executions of a military type and not summary ones with a bullet in the back of the head. The latter did in fact occur, however, and they marked a change in the scale of the killing, henceforth carried out at a much faster pace and soon performed in gassing trucks, in which it was considered easier to murder women and children (a major transgression for the assassins):

> *Amen*: Did you receive reports from those who were working on the vans?
>
> *Ohlendorf*: I received the report that the *Einsatz* commandos did not willingly use the vans.
>
> *Amen*: Why not?
>
> *Ohlendorf*: Because the burial of the victims was a great ordeal for the members of the *Einsatz* commandos.[9]

Yet here too the "emotional excitement" was too great for the killers. The extermination camps, with their gas chambers and crematoria, will enable these units to eliminate without facing the violence inflicted.

This attention on the part of the IMT to the internal difficulties of the executioners is far removed from the frequent reproach claiming that the trials amounted to little more than "victor's justice." We should also stress that another criticism still heard today—that the Allied tribunal failed to build a prosecution case befitting the charges of the crime of genocide—does not seem justified either. If the chief prosecutor's primary objective was indeed to bring to justice the "Conspiracy," he never hesitates to draw extensively on Ohlendorf's testimony in order to displace the trial's center of gravity from the twenty-one defendants present in court to the "organizations" charged with carrying out the mass crimes:

> *Robert H. Jackson*: The flowering of this system is represented in the fanatical SS General Ohlendorf, who told this Tribunal without shame or trace of pity how he personally directed the putting to death of 90,000 men, women, and children. No tribunal ever listened to a recital of such wholesale murder as this Tribunal heard from him and from Wisliceny, a fellow officer of the SS. Their own testimony shows the SS responsibility for the extermination program which took the lives of five million Jews—a responsibility that that organization welcomed and discharged methodically, remorselessly, and thoroughly. These crimes with which we deal are unprecedented, first because of the shocking number of victims. They are even more shocking and unprecedented because of the large number of people who united their efforts to perpetrate them. . . . In administering preventive justice with a view to forestalling repetition of the Crimes against Peace, Crimes against Humanity, and War Crimes, it would be a greater catastrophe to acquit these organizations than it would be to acquit the entire twenty-two individuals in the box.[10]

While giving his testimony, Ohlendorf was thus facing the entire group of protagonists assembled in the Hall of Justice. The passage from his testimony quoted earlier is included among the moments that were filmed by the proceedings' official film crew. Normally Jackson should have been placed so that he faced the camera and the audience; here, however, he was seen from the back, thus accentuating the empathetic position of those in attendance, who represented in this sense the community of the United Nations in the war and its victory against Nazism. Whereas Ohlendorf's deposition immediately grabbed—and has continued to attract—people's attention, most commentators have not sufficiently stressed the importance of Jackson's intervention. In the long run, the continued audiovisual exposure that this scene has received has allowed it to emerge into public awareness more easily than from its place buried within the twenty-two-volume trial transcript. Since 1946 portions of these two passages have been shown in several films, reaching millions of viewers around the world.[11]

Avrom Sutzkever's Silence

On February 27, 1946, prosecutor Ernst Smirnov called Avrom Sutzkever to the stand.[12] Another poet, but also an advisor to the Soviet prosecution, Ilya Ehrenburg, had put Sutzkever at the top of a witness list he drew up. Sutzkever was born in 1913 in Smarhon, near Vilnius (or Vilna, in a Lithuania forcibly incorporated into the Russian Empire). During World War I his family sought refuge in Siberia, then in "Wilno" (now under Polish control). At the time of the trial, Vilnius was the capital of the Soviet Socialist Republic of Lithuania. Sutzkever would have preferred to give his identity as a Yiddish poet. Though his nationality of birth was Polish, the prosecutor Smirnov introduced him as a "Soviet citizen" and asked him to cite this during the proceedings. At a meeting in Moscow on February 16, 1946, it took five hours to write up the protocol of his deposition.

What was his frame of mind as he readied himself for his appearance before the Tribunal? Many years later he recalled, "I didn't get a moment's sleep the last two nights before my deposition. I saw my mother before me, running naked across a field of snow, and the warm blood flowing from her bullet-riddled body began to stream down the walls of my room and encircled me. . . . It was difficult for me to assess my feelings. Which was stronger, the affliction or the desire for vengeance?"[13]

Now comes the moment for him to take the stand under the eye of the cameras (Figure 72). The first imposition that he must deal with is being forced to express himself in Russian; he had wanted to speak in Yiddish, but both Smirnov and the Court refused this. Presiding Judge Geoffrey Lawrence politely invites him to take a seat, but now it is Sutzkever's turn to refuse. Having asked the poet his name and nationality, Lawrence once again entreats him to be seated (Figure 73).

Sutzkever states his identity and then grumbles a bit at the bailiff standing next to him. Sutzkever recollects, "I told the Marshall twice that I did not want to sit down, as one normally would. I spoke standing, as one does for the recitation of the Kaddish for the missing." Smirnov asks him where he was during the German Occupation, to which the poet answers, "Vilna." The Russian prosecutor then asks, "You witnessed the persecution of the Jews in that city?"[14] Sutzkever responds in the affirmative. The Court now awaits his narrative—but the witness does not speak. He seems to be backtracking from this commitment, which was long in coming and for which he had prepared himself. He observes a silence that lasts exactly eleven seconds. The trial's routine grinds to a halt. No further translation is coming through the headsets, reinforcing the audience's visual attention on what is transpiring before them.[15]

This blank lasting eleven seconds is not mentioned in the official transcript of the hearing. It is preserved only in the audiovisual recording. For scholars who have already pored through the voluminous transcript in search of the most noteworthy sessions, the discovery of this scene with Sutzkever is a surprise rich in meaning for the status and place of witnesses on film. For those who learn of the trial through this filmic trace, it constitutes an incomparable entry into the concrete reality of what took place at Nuremberg.[16]

In watching, then in listening to Avrom Sutzkever, we are not led into single-minded lamenting over the victims or pure resentment toward the criminals. His testimony is like that of Marie-Claude Vaillant-Couturier insofar as it inscribes itself in several registers. The testimony comes from a *survivor* as well as from an *eyewitness* of the alleged acts. It has been subjected to a mediation that is at once collective (the five-hour meeting to draw up the protocol) and personal (the choices in self-expression are those of a poet, attuned to how writing works with and on language). His deposition is in conformity with judicial procedure at the same time as it seeks to set itself off from it. Last, this testimony, via the physical presence of the witness, is anchored in material evidence. Indeed spectators cannot help but notice that Sutzkever is holding something in his hand as he testifies. In this instance, however, no visual image has been preserved of the moment when this document emerges from anonymity into the light of public debate; we are forced to consult the official transcript to uncover this information. A back-and-forth movement is thus established between the trial's recorded accounts, written and audiovisual.

Sutzkever begins by telling the story of what happened in Vilna: "When the Germans seized my city, Vilna, about 80,000 Jews lived in the town.

Immediately, the so-called *Sonderkommando* was set up at 12 Vilenskaïa Street, under the command of Schweichenberg and Martin Weiss. The manhunters of the *Sonderkommandos*, or as the Jews called them, the *Khapun*, broke into the Jewish houses at any time of day or night, dragged away the men, instructing them to take a piece of soap and a towel, and herded them into certain buildings near the village of Ponary, about 8 kilometers [4.8 miles] from Vilna. From there hardly one returned."[17]

Then, having described how his wife's newborn child was murdered, he speaks of his mother: "On the next day I went to my mother in the ghetto, and I found her room empty. A prayer book was still open on the table and a glass of tea, not yet touched. . . . In the last days of December 1941, Muhrer [*sic*] gave a present to the ghetto. A carload of shoes belonging to the Jews executed at Ponary was brought into the ghetto. . . . Among them I recognized my mother's."[18]

After the liberation of Vilna, in July 1944, Sutzkever discovered a German document concerning the clothes of Ponary's Jews. It was this paper that he was grasping in the Nuremberg courtroom and whose contents he eventually communicated to the judges and prosecution: "To the District Commissioner at Vilna: Pursuant to your order, the old Jewish clothing from Ponary is at present being disinfected by this establishment and delivered to the administration of Vilna."[19]

Even though it was thus directly introduced into the hearing, the document was classed as evidence. In this way, Sutzkever wound up his testimony by adding a written proof to the oral character of his witness account. Without giving in to his emotions (as Jackson had feared he might), the Yiddish poet showed himself fully up to the task of responding to the chief prosecutor's desire to valorize this intervention, given under oath, with the addition of a document originating with the Nazi authorities. By holding it in his hand without immediately revealing its contents, he provoked a curiosity in the audience that still arises today with each new viewing of the audiovisual recording.

The Nuremberg experience is unique. The justice system began the endeavor of historical inquiry and the collection of testimony before historians had set to work on it and witnesses provided their accounts. When the laws lag behind and the courts are prevented by international circumstance from intervening, those who endured and survived the tragic events sometimes take charge. This was the case for Cambodia and the initiative shown by Rithy Panh, a filmmaker and witness of the Khmer Rouge's criminal politics.

Rithy Panh and His Documentary Techniques:
Putting Criminals as Well as Victims on Camera

The youngest of nine children at eleven years old when the Khmer Rouge arrived in Phnom Penh, Panh was incorporated into a mobile youth brigade before working in a hospital as a nurse's aide. He escaped from Cambodia in 1979 and ended up at a refugee camp in Mairut, Thailand. He went into exile in France a year later, where he enrolled in the Institut des Hautes Études Cinématographiques. All of his subsequent films as director owe their subject matter to the history of his native country.[20]

In *S21: The Khmer Rouge Killing Machine* (2003), Panh shows victims and guards returning to the prison set up by the Khmer Rouge in the heart of Phnom Penh in the hopes of stirring up their memories of what happened there and to encourage the verbalization of their witness accounts.[21] How did the Franco-Cambodian filmmaker convince these respective figures to speak on camera? The director explains: "I told them that I was not a prosecutor and that my movie was not a tribunal. That if they came to the shoot at peace, they would leave at peace. That talking could help them feel better about themselves. But, that said, where the victims and their families are concerned, my work would not cleanse criminals of crimes committed."[22]

While the Nuremberg precedent is not really an important source for Panh's work, there can be no doubt that the crimes against humanity trials filmed in France and South Africa's Truth and Reconciliation Committee serve as major inspirations.[23] In the absence of any due process in his own country, the filmmaker felt it was necessary that he take on the cinematic responsibility for addressing it, including devising how best to forefront the words of his interviewees, at times at cross-purposes to their visions of events. The fact that Panh considered naming his movie *Anatomy of a Trial* speaks volumes about his intentions.

The Cambodian director's initial selection (or, at least, the one settled on at the editing stage) takes place in an intimate setting. He presents S21's former deputy chief of security, Him Huy, who is shown in the company of his wife and their infant, soon joined by his own mother and father. Huy was in charge of the guards and of busing the prisoners to their executions. Panh's sequence begins with Huy's mother; her words are addressed to her son, even though her regard is fixed on the interviewer throughout (Figure 74):

> *Huy's mother*: You didn't go there of your own free will. But that's all that people see. [pause] You have to tell the truth. Be it 100, 200—it doesn't matter who killed who—you killed.
> . . .
> *Huy*: I'm ill all day long, I can't eat anything.
> *Huy's mother*: When I think about it—regardless of whether it's another woman or me, another son or mine—I ask myself why he did it. I feel pity for the dead and pity for my son. My son stayed at home, he never behaved badly, never insulted elders. And they indoctrinated him, turned him into a thug who killed people. I gave my son a good education. When I think about the Khmer Rouge, who killed without hesitation—what cruelty!
> *Huy's father*: The Khmer say, "Bones cry out, the flesh calls out." It's a matter of bad karma. You, what do you think?
> *Huy*: If we had killed people—as indeed I did—of our own free will, that would be evil. But they gave us orders. They terrorized me with weapons and their power. [I'm] not where the evil lay; the evil was the leaders who gave the orders. In my heart, I fear evil. I feared dying. I still fear it even now.

This is not the first time that Huy has discussed his role at S21. He had already given numerous interviews when the American Peter Maguire met him a few years before the filming of the documentary *S21*. Maguire recalls, "So, here he was, the man whose name appears at the top of the execution lists at S21. There was a sort of feral innocence to Huy's demeanor that took me by surprise, but his eyes were hard."[24]

Huy did have time over the years to prepare arguments in defense of his actions, but it nevertheless remains the case that the presence at his side of his parents is probably unprecedented in footage of this sort. In this instance, the words spoken or exchanged are made possible by the third parties that the camera and director constitute. Panh does not ask any questions, but he has prepared the way for this confrontation; he has, in a certain sense, brought it about. Although Huy and his mother are seated quite close, they hardly ever look at each other while they are speaking. It is partly out of modesty (since they are conscious of being filmed), but also because the camera represents a sort of safety net, a support that leads Huy to open up. His mother addresses him directly ("You have to tell the truth"), speaks of him in the third person ("They indoctrinated him"), or draws from elements of his own defense ("Who was killing who? I didn't know").

As philosopher Ricoeur has pointed out, "a patient does not access his repressed memories by himself; he needs something like the authorization of another person in order to remember." At the same time as it is unfolding in Huy's mental space, this memory finds a linguistic mediation that offers it up to others. In this sense, to borrow Ricoeur's words again, it is correlative of a "process of socialization," which makes it possible to reach a larger audience (through the film's release) yet still find its articulation in the protected space of the family home.[25]

In the relationship of trust that directors build with those being filmed, be they victims or criminals, does the absence of police or judicial constraints favor the emergence of a larger truth? Even in personal asides, Panh does not judge the criminals that he films. This does not prevent him from pointing it out when he catches his interlocutors in a lie, even suggesting on occasion that they start a sequence over: "I talked with them about the subjects I wanted to discuss, then I confronted them with the evidence: the photo of a prisoner who committed suicide, the execution or infirmary logbooks, testimony from former comrades, or a survivor's account. . . . But it was a battle every time. I had to alternate techniques, trying to catch them off-guard, then lapsing into moments of reflection, and avoid falling into a pattern that would allow them to reconstitute their system of defense. When one of them denied his actions or downplayed their significance, he knew that he was running the risk of being confronted with his own contradictions."[26] All the same, when the Khmer Rouge Tribunal approached Panh about providing it with a copy of the hundreds of hours of footage that he had shot, the filmmaker refused, arguing that he had made an accomplished personal work. Barring a judge's decision declaring the rushes as evidence, Panh did not feel that they could be exploited as autonomous documentary material.

One has only to consult another interview with Huy, this one recently shot and produced by the Documentation Center of Cambodia (DC-Cam), to see the extent to which the former prison guard, no longer hemmed in by Panh's staging for *S21*, ends up presenting himself as a victim, forced by his "job" to obey the orders he was given: "I think every day about those who died. . . . I didn't want to work there. I asked to be transferred. They refused.

I'm not the one to blame." In the estimation of DC-Cam director Chhang Youk, "People from the [Cambodian] countryside get bored when a movie is too long or has complicated Western-style editing. We made this other documentary [*Derrière les murs de S21*; Behind the Walls of S21] in order to help people understand what happened at Tuol Sleng."[27] It was in fact the case that many former criminals returned to their villages without being threatened with any charges. Indeed even today it can be hard to tell if it is they who fear their fellow citizens or the reverse.[28]

The second staging designed by Panh consisted of having former guards return to the halls of S21. These scenes are some of the movie's most powerful, possessing considerable visual and verbal impact. One of those appearing in the film, Khiew "Poev" Ches, is seen entering an empty room that used to serve as a group cell. He recreates his duties for the camera:

I start my shift, I check the padlock four times. I shake the padlock and the iron bar. I check them, everything's fine. I move on to the next row. I shake the padlock and bar, everything's fine. I come to the middle. Here, in the middle. "This row, on your feet! Hands up!" I start searching them. I pat down their pockets. I look everywhere. They can't have a pen that could be used to open their veins, nor bolts and screws which they could use to kill themselves by swallowing them. I come back to the middle. "Sit down! Nobody moves!" I move on to this row. "Get up! On your feet! Put your hands up!" I start searching them. I look, I pat them down, the pockets, their waist, I pat them down, I'm searching to make sure they don't have a pen for opening their veins, or bolts and screws they could swallow. I come to the middle. "Sit down! Nobody moves!" I turn around. "You! Where's your shirt? Without a guard's authorization? You dare take off your shirt, to hang yourself with? Give it here!" I tear it from his hands and leave with it.

In another scene, a former guard falls almost automatically into repeating the same series of gestures he used to perform twenty years earlier, when he gave orders to the prisoners under his care (Figures 75 and 76):

"You, too, you're tossing and turning, why aren't you asleep? Don't budge while you sleep, whore-of-your-mother!" [At the bars of another cell window.] "You have to go? I'll bring the box." The box . . . I open the door. . . . "Here, go ahead and go. Make sure you don't miss. It stinks, and I have to clean it up by myself! If you spill any, you'll get a beating!" I re-lock the cell door. [From the bars of another window.] "You, why are you moving around? If you don't listen up, I'm coming in and you'll get a beating. Here, have some water!" They draw it here . . . there. . . . I hit them on the back. "Wait your turn to drink! You fight over it, you get nothing! No discipline, whore-of-your-mother!" [He comes back out.] I re-lock the door.

Last, there is a night scene in which Huy himself returns to the "killing fields" of Choeung Ek. He recounts the last stages of the prisoners being led to their place of execution. (They had been told that they were going to be sent home.) Huy remembers that Duch personally attended the sessions where prisoners were beaten with batons and had their throats cut:

We would put the prisoner on his knees. He would have his hands cuffed behind his back and *kramar* over his eyes.[29] [Huy gets to his feet and acts out the scene using an iron bar.] We'd take an iron bar and aim for the nape of the neck. He'd fall face down. We'd cut his throat open with a knife. Then we'd take off the handcuffs. If his clothes weren't stained, we'd take those, too. But not if they were bloodstained. We put them in a corner. Then we dragged the body over and threw it in the pit. After the execution, we checked the logbook. If any prisoners were missing from it, we'd have to bring the bodies back up and recount. When the tally was right, we threw them in the pit, buried them, took care to fill the pit back up.

Once again the power of this "testimony" is owed to the fact that Huy is speaking at the very scene of the crime, in a sort of reenactment of the conditions under which the prisoners were executed. This replay produces something like exaltation in Huy; shot in profile, his expression is impressive as the narrative works through the minutiae of his actions. Even with Panh's presence there as a reminder, Huy is wrapped up in this moment, without any awareness that he is being filmed and will soon be seen by millions of people.

Caught unawares by the Vietnamese arrival in Cambodia in 1979, S21 prison director Duch did not have time to destroy their archives, which included thousands of handwritten documents, identity photos, and undeveloped negatives. There were also hundreds of notebooks belonging to the regime leadership and stacks of government publications. The Vietnamese immediately gathered up these documents in order to reveal to the public the crimes committed by the Khmer Rouge. Secure in their position as invader-liberator, they hastily threw together a trial that found Pol Pot and his foreign minister, Ieng Sary, guilty in absentia of genocide.

It had nevertheless proven difficult to demonstrate the existence of direct links between these leaders and the orders to torture and execute prisoners at S21. Given that Pol Pot had died in 1998 and Sary's trial was still to come, this responsibility was imputed to Duch during the trial, whose preliminary hearings began on February 17, 2009, in Phnom Penh. The case against him revolved around S21, as both the central bureau of Kampuchea's security services and as a place of torture and execution. This necessarily required a general presentation on the Khmer Rouge and the conditions under which 1.5 million died as a result of deportation, forced marches, hard labor, or deliberate malnutrition, as well as 200,000 victims of summary executions. This history had already been documented, in writing and on film, well before the Extraordinary Chambers in the Courts of Cambodia (ECCC) began to assemble such evidence for its files in the preliminary investigations.

A team of historians led by Ben Kiernan at Yale University was the first to begin compiling the history of the Cambodian genocide.[30] Their work led to the creation in 1995 of the DC-Cam, which collected over a million documents of various sorts on the history of the Khmer Rouge, including most of S21's archives. Cornell University digitized these documents at the behest of the Cambodian government, which then entrusted them to the DC-Cam.[31] Last, as we saw earlier, Panh dedicated the majority of his films to an attempt to understand what took place between 1975 and 1979.

There was one all-important figure that Panh could not manage to bring back to Tuol Sleng for the filming of *S21*, and that was Duch. Since he had been in prison since 1999, such an initiative could come only from a judicial body. This finally occurred in February 2008. In an intentionally laconic public statement, the ECCC announced that it was organizing "reconstitutions" at Choeung Ek and Tuol Sleng. This decision was presented as "routine," "part of the judicial investigation, which is confidential." The sites in question and their surrounding vicinities were closed on these occasions to the public (including the press).

Duch was then led through the same rooms filmed seven years earlier by Panh. The former prison director was accompanied, of course, by magistrates, but also by survivors who had come to ask him what they had been guilty of. A French journalist relayed a summary account of the end of Duch's visit as described by an eyewitness: "Standing at the entryway to the prison, [Duch] joined his hands in prayer and apologized to his victims, claiming that he had blindly obeyed orders from his superiors telling him to kill his own people." The reporter added, this time in his own words, "On Tuesday, in the middle of the 'killing fields,' the torturer cried before the collected remains of some 15,000 victims of the Khmer Rouge."[32]

Quite unexpectedly, Rithy Panh was granted permission to visit Duch in prison, where he was awaiting trial and planning to plead guilty.[33] The filmmaker recorded nearly three hundred hours of interviews with the accused and used the footage to produce a film, *Duch: Master of the Forges of Hell* (2011), which was accompanied by a book cowritten with novelist Christophe Bataille.[34] Panh has indicated that he conceived this extended confrontation between a criminal and a survivor not only as a means to entice the accused to speak outside of the courtroom but also in the hope—ultimately disappointed—of getting the defendant to explain himself: "I had to give Duch the opportunity to speak since he had not been able to in *S21: The Khmer Rouge Death Machine*—at the time, I had not been granted permission to meet him. It was necessary that Cambodians film this historic trial. And I had the very, very naïve idea that Duch, whose criminal activity in the 70s went extremely deep, could only take the opposite path from that taken in his trial—a step towards us, towards humanity."[35] However, instead of showing only footage from the interview with Duch, Panh chose—doubtless in order to reestablish some distance from remarks he found unbearable—to include archival images and clips from his own films. Moreover this was not limited to the editing stage; he also did this during the interview with Duch, whom we see reacting as a spectator. While the director himself is never present on camera, this technique enables Panh to oppose his films to Duch's comments, as a sort of defense against the latter's lies, half-truths, and deliberate omissions. In doing so, Panh gives these inserted excerpts a historical value, something close to evidence, insofar as they consist of the victims' words and the reenactments of the daily violence carried out by the former tormentors at S21 Prison. They are presented in an accusatory mode, as in a cross-examination.

After the investigation and the reconstitutions, the trial put on display "the charges intending to portray them beyond their pure efficacy and to foreground the offense committed."[36] Nevertheless it was only due to DC-Cam's collection of visual documents that the Tribunal could refer, when it so desired, to film exhibits of crimes committed at S21; Vietnam had provided these motion pictures to the historical association, which in turn agreed to the ECCC prosecutors' request for access to them. These films show the corpses of prisoners, some of them decapitated, in addition to different types of prison cell, torture instruments, and irons. One document shows a Vietnamese soldier holding an enfeebled infant in his arms and carrying it out of the prison.

A Mixed Tribunal for the Khmer Rouge

From Nuremberg to Phnom Penh, the judicial setting of the great historical trials reinforced its punitive and symbolic powers without encroaching upon the autonomy of the nations involved. Let us examine first the matter of sovereignty. It is important not to lose sight of the fact that while Nazi leaders were being brought before international courts, other trials were organized for military tribunals in Allied nations or in national courts hearing cases of crimes committed on their territory. Today a permanent international criminal court exists and has hosted its first trials.[37] It is reasonable to suppose that its most active opponents—first among them, the United States—will at the very least become more moderate in the pressure they apply to the countries inclined to recognize this court as competent to treat such matters.

The status of the Khmer Rouge Tribunal is especially interesting in this respect given that it is mixed. This is not new in itself, except when one considers the scale of the crimes and the foreign and domestic political stakes for the future of Cambodian society. In the end, the Cambodian government's lack of enthusiasm for pursuing the prosecution of the Khmer Rouge and its desire to downplay its eventual political effects (particularly in terms of democracy and transparency) led to the Tribunal's half-national, half-international composition. Moreover the preservation of its sovereignty in these trials did not prevent the Cambodian prime minister from allowing foreign countries to finance most of Phnom Penh's scheduled contribution, despite the fact that these same countries were also largely funding the

United Nations' participation. It is quite remarkable that the two countries judged in Nuremberg and in Tokyo after 1945, Germany and Japan, figure among the largest contributors. The Japanese government has already transferred via the United Nations $40 million for the Tribunal, and in 2008 alone it donated almost $3 million toward the host's portion of the expenses. Japan even committed substantial aid to Cambodian economic development.[38] For its part, the United States, having long refused to participate in the Tribunal, took a step toward acknowledging its legitimacy by contributing, albeit modestly, to the project since the fall of 2008.[39]

Even though Cambodia, in essence, sought to gain control of the ECCC through its negotiations with the UN over the distribution of judicial responsibilities between local magistrates and international judges, its government largely saw its maneuvers backfire. The Tribunal is situated in the capital, halfway between the downtown center and the airport; thus rather than an *hors sol* justice (to borrow Garapon's expression)—that is, an "uprooted" justice, one produced artificially, outside of its natural environment— the Tribunal provided a fair trial in an auditorium able to seat more than five hundred people in its main hall, and its proceedings were guaranteed the exposure they deserve thanks to the presence of the international press.[40]

While the technical setup for the hearings was modeled after that of The Hague's courtrooms (individual screens for all participants providing live feed of the proceedings and consultation of trial exhibits), the presence of large numbers of spectators constitutes a real difference. One should recall that Cambodia's population had grown from 5.6 million in 1979 to more than 14 million at the time of the trials, the majority of whom are under eighteen years old. As a result, the persistence or the reactivation of a vivid memory of crimes committed in 1975–79, on the one hand, and the knowledge and teaching of the history of the Khmer Rouge, on the other, was not a simple matter. Eighty-five percent of Cambodia's inhabitants live in rural areas, and the country is also one of the poorest and least developed in the region, with 35 percent in 2004 listed as living below poverty level. A brutally fast transition to a market economy has only exacerbated this situation. Even though the school system has not actively encouraged the study of the history of the Khmer Rouge's crimes, the high death rate among children as a result of the landmines still strewn across Cambodian soil is a cruel daily reminder of the geopolitical situation during the 1970s.[41]

Though the building housing the Cambodian Tribunal is modern in structure, the court's floor plan maintains traditional judicial scenography in situating the trial's protagonists (Figure 77). The defendant Duch has his back to the spectators, as do the witnesses representing the plaintiffs. Some of the latter are even completely shielded from public view in order to protect their anonymity. A glass wall has been installed in order to provide a physical separation between the judicial stage and the amphitheater's public seating. While the pretext was to ensure the defendant's security, this measure served also to render more indirect any interaction between the trials' main figures and the audience, in anticipation of potential outbursts of anger or emotion on the part of survivors present in the crowd.

Nuremberg and the more recent example of the ICTY have nevertheless convinced judges of the usefulness of filming trial proceedings. At Nuremberg the Allied tribunal shaped the early phase of collective memory through the orientations it gave to initial historical research on the war years, if only through the archives it made available to scholars. Although Chief Prosecutor Jackson used his opening remarks to appeal to universal conscience, and despite the fact that footage from trial sessions figured widely in international newsreels, one is forced to admit that the German population paid little heed to the hearings. In Phnom Penh justice was served via the contact with the Cambodian people. Have the means of disseminating the trial footage been sufficient to convey the stakes and facilitate understanding of these judicial events? There is reason to doubt, given that too few Cambodian citizens had access to a computer to benefit from the Tribunal's official website, still the primary venue housing the recorded proceedings. That said, that the trial has been archived online in its entirety promises future roles for these documents, especially at the Bophana Center directed by Panh. A concerted effort has also been made to show trial footage in rural Cambodia and engage in discussions with villagers.[42]

Within the self-contained space of the courthouse, at once near to and removed from the Cambodian countryside's "killing fields," the presence of cameras did not impose any "media-driven" demand for transparency upon the trial sessions. On the contrary, the filming made it possible to expand the spatial and temporal frame of this judicial narrative, which it is the judges' and prosecutors' responsibility to render audible to the greatest number possible, all the while having determined beforehand which charges appear representative of the events to be judged and afterward the sentences and reparations to be requested.[43] The dual presence of judges and filmmakers unquestionably marks a key stage in the evolution of the work of memory and the figuration of the history of mass crimes.

Conclusion

From the outset, bringing the Nazi criminals to justice was a stated goal included in the Allies' military engagement. But the clash between the United States and Nazi Germany was also played out on another terrain: a war of films. While Hollywood reigned supreme in the art of circulating founding myths in the form of fiction films, the Nazis put the professionalism of their news cameramen and documentary directors to brilliant use throughout occupied Europe. With mixed results, the major American studios did their best to welcome into their midst Fritz Lang, whom Joseph Goebbels had been counting on to oversee German cinema. On the East Coast, MoMA discovered in the person of Siegfried Kracauer a knowledgeable scholar of German newsreels (whose production had fallen into Nazi hands thanks to the efforts of Alfred Hugenberg in the last days of the Weimar Republic). However, it took the attack on Pearl Harbor for Americans to resolve themselves finally to giving a famous director free rein in filming the war. From the Pacific arena to the Nuremberg trials, John Ford was a valuable trump card as Hollywood and the Pentagon played out their hands. While working with Maj. Gen. William J. Donovan in the secret services, Ford made it possible for Justice Robert H. Jackson to bring motion pictures into the courtroom and to allow the IMT proceedings to be filmed. In concert with other filmmakers (e.g., George Stevens) and other camera crews (the Signal Corps), Ford was able to assemble on extremely short notice in the spring of 1945 the right camera operators and an adequate procedural plan for composing an account of what the Allies had discovered in the Nazi camps.

Given his knowledge of the events, we can doubtless take Budd Schulberg at his word when he claims that the teams sent by Ford into central Europe to uncover what films may have been made in the concentration camps by the Germans themselves always arrived on the scene only to find that the documents had just been destroyed. Schulberg's detailed recounting of this ill-fated quest attests to the importance that the mission had in Jackson's eyes. Whereas the Nazis had done everything in their power to destroy evidence of their mass crimes, the Allies gave top priority to collecting whatever proof still existed. The movies produced by the Germans in the framework of elaborating and executing the plan that would lead to the war and the mass crimes were easily found and shown in the instance of establishing the charge of conspiracy. For the camps, the Allies were forced to substitute their own testimonial accounts for the missing movies that the Germans had probably made and then destroyed.

This approach contained a double risk. First, in order to bring before a court the crimes committed against the Jews, the IMT had to invent a new legal charge—crime against humanity—which by definition could be applied to the Nazis only retroactively, in violation of the foundations of legal principles. Second, the evidentiary exhibits prepared by Jackson took the form of accounts that, albeit firsthand, were necessarily produced by the victors. The Nuremburg court had tremendous difficulties while drafting its written decision in distinguishing between the charge of war crimes and that of crimes against humanity. Determining what sentences to impose on the accused also posed real dilemmas. This was not at all the case for their use of film footage, however, which unquestionably made a big impact in the course of the trial and which produced jurisprudence whose influence we can still see today in the handling of cases brought before The Hague's International Criminal Tribunal.

Film's entry into the courtroom is thus marked by a series of infringements on common law. To our mind, the most spectacular is certainly the dual status of evidence and testimony accorded to the movies that the Allies shot in the camps. Jacques Derrida draws on the example of the amateur video that revealed the acts of police brutality committed against Rodney King in order to highlight the problem posed here: "the videographic recording may have served as an archive, perhaps as an exhibit, perhaps as evidence, but it did not replace testimony. Proof or evidence—evidence!—of this fact is that the young man who shot the footage was asked to come himself and attest, swearing before the living persons . . . that it was really he who held the camera, that he was present at the scene, that he saw what he shot, etc. There is therefore a heterogeneity of testimony to evidence and, consequently, to all technical recording. Technics will never produce a testimony."[1] The witness, as discussed here by Derrida, is precisely the "authenticating witness" who, as we showed in Chapter 1, determines in American jurisprudence the admissibility of film footage in court proceedings, which allows for the document in question to be deemed eventually as "evidence."

Projected in the Nuremberg courtroom on November 29, 1945, *The Nazi Concentration Camps* includes in its credits the producer's and director's affidavits for the footage filmed by the Americans and British during the liberation or discovery of the camps. That said, these segments were not chosen by chance but rather were taken in response to instructions and for the express purpose of endowing the clips with a judicial status should they ever come to be needed. Moreover the cameramen did not merely authenticate their footage by signature; they physically inscribed themselves into the film by standing within the visual frame, near corpses of the deportees scattered across the ground. The crew then got back behind the camera to record the narratives of available survivors. In sum, they stacked several levels of attestation of a reality that they were seeking to document in the most "objective" manner possible.

In Nuremberg's Hall of Justice, the film on the camps presented itself as a trace of the mass crime committed by the Nazis and as the representative of the dead and surviving filmed in 1945. In Ricoeur's words, "Between the trace and that of which it is the trace," there exists "a curate function of place-holding."[2] This function was all the more important since the victims had not been allowed to participate as plaintiffs in the trial. There exists a sort of structural parallel between the way the projection of the movie mediates among the trial's protagonists and the tertiary position occupied by the court between crime and punishment. In both instances, it is a matter of containing the thirst for vengeance that arises from the violence endured.

The evidentiary value of movies has parallels to the filmed trial as archive in another important aspect, which is its reproducibility. The document thus receives greater public exposure and remains available for future generations. The justice system is now able to assure that, well after the trial arguments have ended and the verdict has been rendered, people in another time and place will benefit from the possibility of watching both the films shown during the trial and the audiovisual recording of its complete proceedings. The courts can thus further extend the "narrative transactions" that it initiated in the societies in question with the end of combat and the reestablishment of social solidarity.[3]

The footage circulating henceforth inside and outside the courtroom is not a threat to the demand for truth, serenity, and fairness in the proceedings. The effects of a movie screened in session do not at all cancel out the necessary effort of imagination that must kick in when the crime being tried exceeds the limits of representation. As to trials on film, in addition to their value as archives, they ensure the necessary transmission of the democratic values that inspire public debate, both at the time of the case and after. Attempts to mislead the public cannot long withstand careful analysis of the images, and this regardless of the degree of manipulation at issue. Of course, television media also need to be vigilant in order to avoid leaving their viewers defenseless. In the instance of Rumania's 1989 trial of Nicolae Ceaușescu, the event largely owed its considerable exposure to the live television broadcast, but in no way was the filming responsible for the parody of justice that was staged. On the contrary, the footage reveals its brutality, even if viewers may catch themselves feeling some satisfaction at seeing the fear in the eyes of a tyrant who realizes his preprogrammed death is drawing near.[4]

Beyond its immediate objectives of earning convictions and making reparations, the IMT that presided in Nuremberg from October 20, 1945, to October 1, 1946, undertook innovations whose stakes are still operative today. In the face of war's violence, the civility of the proceedings must be maintained during the trial's contradictory phases. Regardless of whether it has a slightly theatricalized feel (the IMT) or has become completely banal (the ICTY), the presence in court of filmic traces of the acts being tried before the judges lends to the reconstitution of the past a powerful effect of cinematic realism tinted with the foreignness of time gone by.

Introduction

1. In chronological order: Mark Osiel, *Mass Atrocity, Collective Memory, and the Law* (New Brunswick, N.J.: Transaction, 1997); Florent Brayard, ed., *Le Génocide des Juifs entre procès et histoire, 1943–2000* (Paris: Complexe, 2000); Peter Maguire, *Law and War: An American Story* (New York: Columbia University Press, 2001); Donald Bloxham, *Genocide on Trial: War Crimes Trials and the Formation of Holocaust History and Memory* (Oxford: Oxford University Press, 2001); Stéphane Audoin-Rouzeau, Annette Becker, Christian Ingrao, and Henry Rousso, eds., *La Violence de guerre 1914–1945* (Paris: Complexe, 2002); Omer Bartov, Atina Grossman, and Mary Nolan, *Crimes of War: Guilt and Denial in the Twentieth Century* (New York: New Press, 2002); Ronald Smelser, ed., *Lessons and Legacies*, vol. 5, *The Holocaust and Justice* (Evanston, Ill.: Northwestern University Press, 2002); Antoine Garapon, *Des Crimes qu'on ne peut ni punir ni pardonner: Pour une justice internationale* (Paris: Odile Jacob, 2002); William A. Schabas, *The UN International Criminal Tribunals: The Former Yugoslavia, Rwanda and Sierra Leone* (Cambridge: Cambridge University Press, 2006); Madoka Futamura, *War Crimes Trials and Transitional Justice: The Tokyo Trials and the Nuremberg Legacy* (New York: Routledge, 2008); Daniel Joyce, "Photography and the Image-Making of International Justice," *Law and Humanities* 4, no. 2 (2010): 229–49; "In Flagrante Depicto: Film In/On Trial," special issue, *Cardozo Law Review* 31, no. 4 (2010).

2. "Report from Mr. Justice Jackson, Chief Counsel for the United States in the prosecution of Axis War Criminals" (NARA, RG226, E90, B12, F126, 3).

3. Even though she recognizes Nuremberg's inadequacies, Martha L. Minow still believes in the historical and ethical value of the Nazi criminal trials: "Nonetheless, or perhaps, precisely in the face of potential cynicism and despair, Nuremberg launched a remarkable international movement for human rights founded in the rule of law; inspired by the development of the United Nations and of nongovernmental organizations around the world; encouraged national trials for human rights violations; and etched a set of ground rules about human entitlement that circulate in local, national, and international settings." Minow, *Between Vengeance and Forgiveness: Facing History*

After Genocide and Mass Violence, foreword by Richard J. Goldstone (Boston: Beacon, 1998), 47.

4. See New York State Committee to Review Audio-Visual Coverage of Court Proceedings, *An Open Courtroom: Cameras in New York Courts* (New York: Fordham University Press, 1997).

5. Georges Didi-Huberman, *Images in Spite of All: Four Photographs from Auschwitz*, trans. Shane B. Lillis (2003; Chicago: University of Chicago Press, 2008), 82.

6. This was done primarily at the National Archives and Records Administration (NARA) in Maryland and the Centre de Documentation Juive Contemporaine (CDJC) in Paris. We also took an inventory of what was available at the film library at the Établissement de Communication et de Production Audiovisuelle de la Défense in Ivry-sur-Seine, at the Bundesarchiv-Filmarchiv in Berlin, and at London's Imperial War Museum. To situate the screening of films in the course of courtroom debates, we referred to twenty-two debates and to IMT documents: *Trial of the Major War Criminals Before the International Military Tribunal, 14 November 1945–1 October 1946*, 22 vols.; *Documents*, 20 vols. (Nuremberg: IMT, 1947). We therefore consulted the archives of the Office of Strategic Services, in particular the files of the Field Photographic Branch (NARA), then the John Ford archives at the Lilly Library, Bloomington, Indiana.

7. NARA (in particular, record groups [RGs] 153, 208, and 226).

8. Primarily at the Library of Congress, Washington, D.C., and the Oral History Department, Columbia University, but also at the American Jewish Historical Society, New York, the University of Southern California, Los Angeles, and the CDJC.

9. Arthur W. Diamond Law Library, Columbia University Law School, New York.

10. For Kracauer, the Film Study Center, Museum of Modern Art, New York; for Hurwitz, the George Eastman House in Rochester, New York; and, for Saguez, private collection.

11. We initiated this project, which is now completed thanks to a partnership between the United States Holocaust Memorial Museum and the Compagnie des Phares et Balises of Paris.

Chapter 1. The Filmmaker, the Judge, and the Evidence

1. On Lang's early American career, see "Fritz Lang Bows to Mammon," *New York Times*, June 14, 1936, 10, 2.

2. Lotte H. Eisner, *Fritz Lang*, ed. David Robinson, trans. Gertrud Mander (London: Secker and Warburg, 1976), 161.

3. Born in 1909, Krasna was under contract with MGM as a scriptwriter and producer.

4. On the functioning of the code, see Richard Maltby, "The Production Code and the Hays Office," in Tino Balio, ed., *Grand Design: Hollywood as a Modern Business Enterprise, 1930–1939* (New York: Scribner's, 1993), 37–72.

5. From the *Fury* file, Margaret Herrick Library, Academy of Motion Picture Arts and Sciences, Los Angeles, cited in Rolf Aurich, Wolfgang Jacobsen, and Cornelius Schnauber, eds., *Fritz Lang: Leben und Werk, Bilder und Dokumente* (Berlin: Jovis, 2001), 251.

6. Arthur F. Raper, *The Tragedy of Lynching* (Chapel Hill: University of North Carolina Press, 1933). Raper's work has been republished several times (e.g., New York: Dover, 1970, 2003).

7. "The Tragedy of Lynching," Fritz Lang Archives, Bibliothèque du Film (BiFi), Paris.

8. Perhaps he also knew of William Faulkner's short story "Dry September" in *Scribner's Magazine* (1931), a story of the hours leading up to and following a lynching.

9. Files 2752, 2751, and 2791, Lang Archives, BiFi.

10. Jean Douchet, "Dix-sept plans," in Raymond Bellour, ed., *Le Cinéma américain: Analyses de films* (Paris: Flammarion, 1980), 200–232, 228–29.

11. Anne Chaon, "Le Lynchage comme art photographique," *Le Monde Diplomatique* 555 (June 2000): 24. See also James Allen, ed., *Without Sanctuary: Lynching Photography in America* (Santa Fe, N.M.: Twin Palms, 2000). In a foreword, Representative John Lewis of Georgia writes, "These photographs bear witness to the hangings, burnings, castrations, and torture of an American holocaust" (7).

12. Fritz Lang, with Peter Bogdanovich, "No Copyright for the Director," in Bogdanovich, *Fritz Lang in America* (New York: Praeger, 1967), 15–117, 18–19.

13. "The first screening—to which MGM had invited no-one of any importance—was an enormous success.... The studio was astonished with the success.... Lang (who had been forbidden to touch the film at a late stage of the editing) went to the opening with Marlene Dietrich, and left during the applause" (Eisner, *Fritz Lang*, 176).

14. Lavine worked for MGM as a legal specialist and in 1933 participated in the writing of a "prison" movie, *Day of Reckoning* (dir. Charles Brabin).

15. A sign of the importance Lang gave to the probative value of newsreels is that he uses the same idea in two other films, *You Only Live Once* (1937) and *The Woman in the Window* (1944). See Stella Bruzzi, "Imperfect Justice: Fritz Lang's *Fury* (1936) and Cinema's Use of the Trial," *Law & Humanities* 4, no. 1 (2010): 1–19.

16. In "L'Image accusatrice," special issue, *Cahiers de la Photographie* (1985): 80.

17. Boleslaw Matuszewski, *Une nouvelle source de l'histoire: Création d'un dépôt de cinématographie historique* ([Paris]: [n.p.], 1898), 8–9. See also the work appearing several years later by H. D. Gower, L. Stanley Jast, and W. W. Topley, *The Camera as Historian: A Handbook to Photographic Record Work for Those Who Use a Camera and for Survey or Record Societies* (London: Sampson Low, 1916).

18. Thomas Grimm, "La Cinématographie historique," *Le Petit Journal*, July 15, 1898. See also Raymond Borde, *Les Cinémathèques* (Paris: Ramsay Poche Cinéma,

1983), 30–32; Magdalena Mazaraki, "Boleslaw Matuszewski: Photographe et opéra-teur de cinéma," *1895* 44 (December 2004): 47–65.

19. By the end of the nineteenth century, it was in fact recognized that when pho-tographic shots "derive all their value from the taste, intelligence and technical skill of the cameraman, they are protected, just like art works, by the law of July 19, 1793." E[mmanuel] N[apoléon] Santini, *La Photographie devant les tribunaux: Recueil des jugements et arrêts rendus par les Tribunaux de 1ère instance, Cours d'appel, Cour de cassation et intéressant les photographes amateurs et professionnels* (Paris: Charles Mendel, ca. 1898).

20. Fernand Izouard, "Le Cinématographe et le droit d'auteur," *Annales de la Pro-priété Industrielle, Artistique et Littéraire* 1 (1908): 155–61, quoted in Alain Carou, *Le Cinéma français et les écrivains: Histoire d'une rencontre, 1906–1914* (Paris: École Na-tionale des Chartes/AFRHC, 2002), 61.

21. Édouard Herriot, "Discussion de l'interpellation de M. Brenier sur l'utilisation du cinéma dans l'enseignement et dans l'éducation sociale," *Journal Oficiel*, Novem-ber 9, 1928, 1069–81, quoted in Dimitri Vezyroglou, *Le cinéma en France à la veille du parlant: Un essai d'histoire culturelle* (Paris: CNRS, 2011), 310.

22. Austin Abbott, *A Brief on the Modes of Proving the Facts Most Frequently in Issue or Collaterally in Question on the Trial of Civil or Criminal Cases* (Rochester, N.Y.: Lawyers' Cooperative, 1901), 266.

23. Richard Lea Kennedy, *Trial Evidence: A Synopsis of the Law of Evidence Gener-ally Applicable to Trials*, 2nd ed. (Kansas City: Vernon Law Book, 1935), 190–91. This probative category is not unlike the idea of "necessary and indubitable" proof estab-lished under France's ancien régime. As Christian Biet reminds us, "The first evidence is the *notorium facti* (notorious fact) perceptible by the sense organs: the obvious no-torious fact is the best evidence, the *probation probatissima* (supreme proof), and al-lows for knowing the truth about the crime. Thanks to it, the judge has no need for a demonstration." Biet, *Droit et littérature sous l'Ancien Régime: Le jeu de la valeur et de la loi*, Lumière classique (Paris: Champion, 2002), 129.

24. Kennedy, *Trial Evidence*, 192–94.

25. Pierre R. Paradis, "The Celluloid Witness," *University of Colorado Law Review* 37 (1965): 235–68.

26. In this latter case, one must give the name of the person, type of camera, cir-cumstances of the shoot, and certify that "the pictures were a true and correct likeness of the things which [the witness] saw at the time they were taken" (Paradis, "The Cel-luloid Witness," 237).

27. Paradis, "The Celluloid Witness," 239.

28. Peter Burke cites the remark of art critic John Ruskin, who thought that pho-tographic evidence "presents a great interest if you know how to counter-interrogate it." Burke, *Eyewitnessing: The Uses of Images as Historical Evidence* (Ithaca, N.Y.: Cor-nell University Press, 2001), 25). See also Paul Hughes, "The Evaluation of Film as

Evidence," in Paul Smith, ed., *The Historian and Film* (Cambridge: Cambridge University Press, 1976), 47–79.

29. "Police Use Cine-Camera to Convict Speedsters," *World Film News*, May 1936, quoted in Don Macpherson, ed., *Traditions of Independence: British Cinema in the Thirties* (London: BFI, 1980), 125. *Editor's note*: The article reprinted in its entirety in Macpherson gives the mistaken impression that the events occurred in 1936.

30. "FBI Filmed Nazis with a Telephoto," *New York Times*, September 13, 1945. It was thanks to the systematic placement of surveillance cameras in London that the perpetrators of the terrorist bombings on July 7 and 21, 2005, were quickly identified.

31. 108 Ohio App. 241, 161 N.E.2d 413 (1959), quoted in Paradis, "The Celluloid Witness," 267–68.

Chapter 2. The Camera

1. On immigrants' exposure to American films, see Douglas Gomery, *Shared Pleasures: A History of Movie Presentation in the United States* (Madison: University of Wisconsin Press, 1992). With regard to these conservative attacks on Hollywood, see Christian-Marc Bosséno, "La Place du spectateur," "Cinéma, le Temps de l'Histoire," special issue, *Vingtième Siècle: Revue d'Histoire* 46 (1995): 145.

2. William J. Perlman, ed., *The Movies on Trial: The Views and Opinions of Outstanding Personalities Anent Screen Entertainment Past and Present* (New York: Macmillan, 1936), 242. Another study, dealing with filmmakers' internalization of the censorship code was published under the title *Decency in Motion Pictures* (1937); see Gerald Mast, ed., *The Movies in Our Midst: Documents in the Cultural History of Film in America* (Chicago: University of Chicago Press, 1982), 340–44.

3. Thomas Doherty, "Documenting the 1940s," in Thomas Schatz, ed., *Boom and Bust: American Cinema in the 1940s* (Berkeley: University of California Press, 1999), 397.

4. The rise of Nazism was, for example, the subject of a special edition called *Inside Nazi Germany—1938* (see below, p. 41). See also the debate between George Dangerfield and John Grierson, which appeared in 1936 in *World Film News* and is cited in Don Macpherson, ed., *Traditions of Independence: British Cinema in the Thirties* (London: BFI, 1980), 120–22.

5. V. I. Pudovkin's texts were an important source of inspiration for members of the Workers' Film and Photo League; they were translated into English at the time as Pudovkin, *On Film Technique: Three Essays and an Address*, trans. Ivor Montagu (London: Gallancz, 1929). Vertov's works were just as instrumental; see Vertov, *Kino-Eye: The Writings of Dziga Vertov*, ed. Annette Michelson, trans. Kevin O'Brien (Berkeley: University of California Press, 1984).

6. See Mason Klein and Catherine Evans, with Maurice Berger, Michael Lesy, and Anne Wilkes Tucker, *The Radical Camera: New York's Photo League, 1936–1951* (New Haven, Conn.: Yale University Press, 2011).

7. As of 1927, the Eyemo, a portable 35 mm camera weighing approximately six and a half pounds, was developed by the Bell and Howell Company and used throughout the 1930s to film domestic news events and then World War II.

8. William F. Kruse, "Workers' Conquest of the Films," *Workers Monthly* 4, no. 11 (1925): 526, quoted in Russell Campbell, *Cinema Strikes Back: Radical Filmmaking in the United States, 1930–1942* (Ann Arbor, Mich.: UMI Research Press, 1982), 33.

9. Jean Heffer, *La Grande dépression: Les États-Unis en crise (1929–1933)*, Collection Archives 64 (Paris: Gallimard/Julliard, 1976), 195–96.

10. "Film and Photo League: Report of Left Book Club Conference," *Left News*, August 1937, quoted in Macpherson, ed., *Traditions of Independence*, 159.

11. Similar experiences had just occurred in Germany, including that which brought together Bertolt Brecht, Slatan Dudow, and Hans Eisler for the making of *Kuhle Wampe* (1932). See Brecht, "The Sound Film *Kuhle Wampe or Who Owns the World?*" (1933), in *Brecht on Film and Radio*, ed. and trans. Marc Silberman (London: Methuen, 2000), 204–6.

12. Leo T. Hurwitz, "The Revolutionary Film—Next Step" (1934), in Lewis Jacobs, ed., *The Documentary Tradition* (New York: Norton, 1979), 91.

13. Hurwitz, "The Revolutionary Film," 92. Gilles Deleuze, in showing what separates Sergei Eisenstein's dialectical vision from D. W. Griffith's, states, "Griffith is oblivious to the fact that rich and poor are not given as independent phenomena, but are dependent on a single general cause, which is social exploitation. . . . These objections which condemn Griffith's 'bourgeois' view do not merely relate to his way of telling a story or of understanding History. They relate directly to parallel (and also convergent) montage." Deleuze, *Cinema 1: The Movement-Image*, trans. Hugh Tomlinson and Barbara Habberjam (Minneapolis: University of Minnesota Press, 1986), 32.

14. Hurwitz, The Revolutionary Film," 16. Here again, beyond the strictly ideological stakes and the WFPL's own production, the question arose about shaping the reading of news pictures shown in flux.

15. Ralph Steiner, "Revolutionary Movie Production," *New Theatre*, September 1934, 22.

16. Lev Koulechov [Kuleshov], "L'Écran aujourd'hui," *Navy Lef* 4 (1927), in *Écrits (1917–1934)*, trans. Valérie Pozner (Lausanne: L'Âge d'Homme, 1994), 142.

17. Ralph Steiner and Leo Hurwitz, "A New Approach to Film Making," *New Theatre*, September 1935, 22. Hurwitz wrote, "It was clear that the question of *truth or lie* lay not in the stuff you were using but in the thoughts, responsibility, empathy of the film maker and his capacity to shape a form which could tell . . . how much of the truth? This responsibility and empathy were not different from the truth or lie of the fiction film or any other art." Hurwitz, "One Man's Voyage: Ideas and Films in the 1930s," *Cinema*

Journal 15, no. 1 (1975): 12. As for the Group Theatre, directed by Strasberg and Harold Clurman, it extrapolated the lessons of Stanislavsky and the Art Theater of Moscow, before inspiring Elia Kazan, Robert Lewis, and Cheryl Crawford at the time of the creation of the Actors Studio in 1947, whose direction Strasberg took on in 1951. In a 1977 interview, Hurwitz also mentions the importance of Brecht's theater, whose first performances Hurwitz situates in 1933–34 (Hurwitz Papers, Motion Picture Department, George Eastman House; henceforth Hurwitz Archives, GEH).

18. Lugon tells about it in an account drawn from extensive archival research, in which he refuses to separate the historicity of the notion of "documentary" from the specificities of the medium, its uses, its reception, and its heritage. Olivier Lugon, *Le Style documentaire: D'August Sandler à Walker Evans, 1920–1945* (Paris: Macula, 2001).

19. James Agee and Walker Evans, *Let Us Now Praise Famous Men* (1941; Boston: Houghton Mifflin, 1960), xiv.

20. Dorothea Lange and Paul Schuster Taylor, *An American Exodus: A Record of Human Erosion*, ed. Sam Stourdzé, Histoire figurée (1939; Paris: Jean-Michel Place, 1999), 6.

21. "Lange to Roy Stryker, 19 January 1940," quoted in Henry Mayer, "The Making of a Documentary Book," in Lange and Taylor, *An American Exodus*, ccxx.

22. With Morris L. Ernst, Lorentz published a book entitled *Censored: The Private Life of the Movies* (New York: Cape and Smith, 1929), in which he defended the idea that documentaries could surpass theater, journalism, and literature in influence.

23. *The River* was produced by the Farm Security Administration, which succeeded the Resettlement Administration.

24. In 1939 the U.S. Film Service commissioned Robert J. Flaherty to direct a documentary, *The Land* (1942), while Lorentz himself directed an attempt at documentary fiction, *The Fight for Life* (1940).

25. The association also garnered support from figures like Elia Kazan, Lewis Milestone, and John Dos Passos. See William Alexander, "Frontier Films, 1936–1941: The Aesthetics of Impact," *Cinema Journal* 1 (Fall 1975): 16–28. Among the principal productions of Frontier Films were *Heart of Spain* (1937), first undertaken by American journalist Herbert Kline and Hungarian photographer Geza Karpathi and scripted and edited in the United States by Hurwitz and Strand; *China Strikes Back* (dir. Harry Dunham, 1937); *People of the Cumberland* (dirs. Sidney Meyers and Jay Leyda, 1938), with assistance from Kazan and William Watts and making use of the collaborations of Steiner on screen image and Erskine Caldwell for the commentary; and *Native Land* (dirs. Hurwitz and Strand, 1942).

26. Russell Campbell notes, "The mise-en-scène, too, adhered to conventional patterns of spatial-temporal continuity, and was evolved in terms of ordinary dramatic tension and climax. The result was that, in the compromise Hurwitz hoped to effect between Stanislavsky and Brecht, Stanislavsky won out" (*Cinema Strikes Back*, 282–83).

27. Stuart Liebman, "Documenting the Left," *October* 23 (Winter 1982): 66.

28. Poet Archibald MacLeish and novelist and Pulitzer Prize–winner John Dos Passos were the spokespersons for *History Today*, which became *Contemporary Historians, Inc.*

29. Dos Passos and Orson Welles were involved in directing the film, as well; see Erik Barnouw, *Documentary: A History of the Non-Fiction Film*, rev. ed. (Oxford: Oxford University Press, 1983), 135–37.

30. In June 1942 Frank Capra took charge of the 834th Photo Signal Detachment, the source of, among others, the series *Why We Fight*, comprising seven films produced between 1942 and 1945: *Prelude to War, The Nazis Strike, Divide and Conquer, The Battle of Britain, The Battle of Russia, The Battle of China*, and *War Comes to America*.

Chapter 3. Learning to Read Enemy Films

1. Raymond Fielding, *The March of Time, 1935–1981* (New York: Oxford University Press, 1978), 198.

2. Fielding, *The March of Time*, 197. Fielding reports that Jack Warner refused to show *Inside Nazi Germany* in Warner Brothers' two hundred movie theaters, whereas David Selznick considered it "one of the greatest and most important reels in the history of pictures" (199).

3. Julien Bryan was on the German-Polish border when German troops crossed over in September 1939, thus providing the only pictures not filmed by the Nazis themselves (see *Siege*, 1939).

4. Peter Decherney, *Hollywood and the Culture Elite: How the Movies Became American* (New York: Columbia University Press, 2005), 129.

5. Alfred Barr, "Nationalism in German Film," *Hound and Horn* 7, no. 2 (1934): 278.

6. Barr, "Nationalism in German Film," 279.

7. Barr, "Nationalism in German Film," 281. As examples of anti-Napoleonic films, Barr cites *Der Choral von Leuthen* (The Hymn of Leuthen, dirs. Carl Froelich, Aren von Cserépy, Walter Supper, 1933), *Yorck* (dir. Gustav Ucicky, 1931), *Marschall Vorwärts* (dir. Heinz Paul, 1932), *Schinderhannes* (The Prince of Rogues, dir. Curtis Bernhardt, 1928), *Der elf Schill'schen Offiziere* (dir. Rudolf Meinert, 1932), and *Der Rebel* (The Rebel, dir. Luis Trenker, 1932) (280). *Editor's note*: Having become a media magnate in the interwar years, Alfred Hugenberg used his resources to promote extremist right-wing politics and inadvertently helped Hitler accede to power. Der Stahlhelm, Bund der Frontsoldaten (Steel Helmet, League of Frontline Soldiers) was a veterans' group formed after World War I. By the end of the 1920s, its membership had reached half a million, making it the largest paramilitary organization in Germany. In 1929 Der Stahlhelm threw its weight behind Hugenberg's attacks on the Weimar Republic.

8. Iris Barry, "Hunting Film in Germany," *American German Review*, June 1937, 40–43.

9. Reporting on the international film conference, the *New York Times* on April 25, 1935, asserted that Germany's entire movie industry was controlled by the government.

10. Leni Riefenstahl, *Hinter den Kulissen des Reichsparteitagfilms* (Munich: Zentralverlag der NSDAP, 1935), 176, quoted in Glenn B. Infield, *Leni Riefenstahl: The Fallen Film Goddess* (New York: Thomas Cromwell, 1976), 230–31.

11. Infield, *Leni Riefenstahl*, 179.

12. The translator jotted marginal notes on the transcription of the film about people appearing on screen (e.g., Alfred Rosenberg and Julius Streicher) and the political context at the time (e.g., the purge of the Sturmabteilung [SA, or Stormtroopers]); see "*Triumph of the Will*: Typescript copy with handwritten notations by Iris Barry," FSC/MoMA Archives.

13. *Editor's note*: *Heimat* has no equivalent in English but refers to home and hearth, a lifestyle anchored in one's birthplace and the objects associated with it.

14. "Notes on Portions of Three Nazi Propaganda Films Screened at the Museum of Modern Art, Monday, September 29, 1941," 6 (File OIAA-025, FSC/MoMA Archives).

15. Cover copy, *The Triumph of the Will*, FSC/MoMA Archives. With respect to the purge, an entire sequence is dedicated to the SA and their leader, Viktor Lutze, who is literally carried in triumph by his men in the style Ernst Röhm so enjoyed. It is Heinrich Himmler, however, at the head of the SS procession, who interrupts the parade to shake the Führer's hand.

16. Luis Buñuel, *My Last Sigh*, trans. Abigail Israel (New York: Knopf, 1983), 179, 180. Chaplin was familiar enough with *Triumph of the Will* to be inspired by it in directing *The Dictator*, but it was above all Adenoid Hynkel's acting that allowed him to appreciate the artifice of Hitler's gestures and public performances; see Christian Delage, *Chaplin, la grande histoire* (Paris: Jean-Michel Place, 2002).

17. Ron Magliozzi, current head of MoMA's Film Study Center, sees above all Barry's imprint on the reediting of *Triumph of the Will*; see Magliozzi, "On Luis Buñuel and *Triumph of the Will*," report, October 4, 2000 (FSC/MoMA Archives).

18. Luis Buñuel, *Entretiens avec Max Aub*, 1984, trans. Lucien Mercier (Paris: Belfond, 1991), 95. For Carlo Ginzburg, the Riefenstahl film "is extraordinarily effective. What's more, it's one of the most disturbing movies I've ever seen. As a spectator, I react negatively to its content, yet at the same time am fascinated by the formal power with which this propaganda discourse is expressed." Ginzburg, "Di tutti i doni che porto a Kaisare . . . Leggere il film scrivere la storia," in Stefano Pivato, ed., *Storie et storia* (Rimini) 9 (April 1983): 4–17. (Claire Bustarret assisted with this source.)

19. It is only after meeting Erwin Panofsky that Kracauer publishes the essay, "Supplement. Propaganda and Nazi War Films." Kracauer, *From Caligari to Hitler: A Psychological History of German Film*, ed. Leonardo Quaresima (Princeton, N.J.: Princeton University Press, 1947, 2013), 275–308.

20. Prior to leaving Berlin, Kracauer had hardly ever reviewed American films. Once in the United States, he devoted slightly more attention to doing so, but not at all as comprehensively as, for instance, James Agee did. Kracauer expressed appreciation for the plastic quality of the narrative of the U.S. Film Service's inaugural film, *The River*, but he was not impressed by its dialogue, which he considered artificially subordinated to the screen images. Among the filmmakers he covered at this time, one finds Preston Sturges (nine films cited from 1941 to 1944), Frank Capra, Alfred Hitchcock, Walt Disney, Orson Welles, and George Cukor, as well as a few from the avant-garde (Maya Deren, Hans Richter, Whitney).

21. Enzo Traverso, *Siegfried Kracauer: Itinéraire d'un intellectuel nomade*, rev. ed. (Paris: La Découverte, 2006), 151.

22. "Siegfried Kracauer to John Marshall," May 9, 1941 (Archives of the Rockefeller Archive Center, 250/2989; hereafter RAC), quoted in David Culbert, "The Rockefeller Foundation, the Museum of Modern Art Film Library, and Siegfried Kracauer, 1941," *Historical Journal of Film, Radio and Television* 13, no. 4 (1933): 495–511. Philippe Despoix writes, "Among the objects left by Kracauer, there are several boxes full of thousands of tiny note cards. They are the cards on which he noted the films he saw. Their number is mindboggling. Between 1924 and 1933, he published 700 critiques in the *FZ* [*Frankfurter Zeitung*]." Despoix, "Siegfried Kracauer, essayiste et critique de cinéma," *Critique* 539 (April 1992): 313.

23. Siegfried Kracauer, "The Task of the Film Critic" (1932), rep. in Anton Kaes, Martin Jay, and Edward Dimendberg, eds., *The Weimar Republic Sourcebook* (Berkeley: University of California Press, 1994), 634–65, 634.

24. Kracauer is referring here to news produced by Fox or Paramount as well as that by the UFA. See Siegfried Kracauer, "Die Filmwochenschau" (1931), in *Kino: Essays, Studien, Glossen zum Film*, ed. Karsten Witte (Frankfurt am Main: Suhrkamp, 1974), 11.

25. Kracauer, *From Caligari to Hitler*, 206. See Christian Delage, "L'Enjeu du film documentaire," in *La Vision nazie de l'histoire à travers le cinéma documentaire du Troisième Reich* (Lausanne: L'Âge d'Homme, 1989), 109–16.

26. When Kracauer's book on Caligari came out in France in the 1970s, the reproach often made—that the theorist sees German films only as a "reflection" of society or of collective mentality—underestimates how difficult it was from abroad for Kracauer to understand the extent to which Germany had fallen under the Nazi sway (and thus to operate a similar distancing with regard to his own critical work).

27. "Kracauer to Marshall," RAC.

28. "Barry to Marshall, May 14, 1941" (RA-250, 2989), RAC. Concerning the role played by Soviet film, Rudolf Arnheim wrote in 1925, "We had learned primarily through the influence of the Russians that film, taken as a means of photographic expression, best fulfilled its role when it observed men captured in action, in the midst

of their everyday occupations." Arnheim, "Erinnerung an Wilfried Basse," in *Wilfried Basse: Notizen zu einem fast vergessenen Klassiker des deutschen Dokumentarfilms* (Berlin: Volker Spiess, 1977), 81.

29. Sidney Bernstein had come to the United States in June 1942 on an official mission to present his politics of audiovisual wartime communication to Hollywood's industry leaders; see Bernstein, "The War Job of Motion Pictures," *Film Daily*, June 26, 1942, NARA, RG 208, E1, B3, Motion Pictures, August 1942.

30. For the excerpt relating to Kracauer, see "Kris and Speier, Directors, Research Project on Totalitarian Communication, New York, NY, to Marshall" (May 19, 1941), RAC-260, 3101.

31. In the words of Pvt. Richard Griffith, "As in all good, 'constructive' criticism, Dr. Kracauer's reviews are more interesting than the films he writes about.... It seems to me that someone in Washington might be interested in Dr. Kracauer's reviews of such fragmentary material—perhaps Lasswell, whose recent letter of praise to Kracauer has sent the good doctor into ecstasy" ("Griffith, War Department, Office of the Chief of Special Service, to Capt. Leonard Spielgass, Film Production Section," War Department, Archives FSC/MoMA). Griffith, as assistant curator of MoMA's film library, later published *A Report on the Film Library, 1941–1956* (New York: MoMA, 1956).

32. See Ernst Kris, "The Imagery of War," *Dayton Art Institute Bulletin* 15, no. 1 (1942).

33. Kracauer wrote two studies for MoMA: *Propaganda and the Nazi War Film* (1942, 100 pages) and *The Conquest of Europe on the Screen: The Nazi Newsreel 1939–1940* (1943, 50 pages) (FSC/MoMA Archives).

34. Siegfried Kracauer, "Bibliography. Propaganda and the Nazi War Film," in *De Caligari à Hitler*, 385–400. *Editor's note*: The essay is included in the English-language edition of *From Caligari to Hitler*, but the thematic bibliography mentioned here is incorporated into a general bibliography.

35. Kracauer also cites the article by Ilya Ehrenburg reprinted by MoMA: Ehrenburg, "Protest gegen UFA," *Frankfurter Zeitung*, February 29, 1928; a text by Horkheimer, "Theoretische Entwürfe über Autorität und Familie," in *Studieren über Autorität und Familie* (Lüneburg: Dietrich zu Klampen, 1936); Franz Neumann, *Behemoth: The Structure and Practice of National Socialism* (Oxford: Oxford University Press, 1942); Erwin Panofsky, "Style and Medium in Moving Pictures," *Transition* 26 (1937); Meyer Schapiro, "Nature of Abstract Art," *Marxist Quarterly* 1 (January–March 1937); and Schapiro, "A Note on Max Weber's Politics," *Politics* 2 (February 1945).

36. Siegfried Kracauer, "Propaganda and the Nazi War Film," in *From Caligari to Hitler*, 278–79.

37. Kracauer, "Propaganda and the Nazi War Film," 297, 294. The study by Speier is "Magic Geography," *Social Research* 8, no. 3 (1941): 310–30.

38. Kracauer, "Propaganda and the Nazi War Film," 308.

39. Kracauer, "Propaganda and the Nazi War Film," 309, 310.

40. Kracauer, "Propaganda and the Nazi War Film," 298. Hitler, for instance, defines the function of propaganda in these terms: "The task of propaganda lies not in a scientific training of the individual, but rather in directing the masses towards certain facts, events, necessities, etc., the purpose being to move their importance into the masses' field of vision. The art now is exclusively to attack this so skillfully that a general conviction of the reality of a fact, of the necessity of an event, that something that is necessary is also right, etc., is created." Hitler, *Mein Kampf,* ed. John Chamberlain et al. (New York: Reynal & Hitchcock, 1940), 231–32. *Target for Tonight* was directed by Harry Watt in 1941 and shows the preparation and unfolding of an air raid over Germany.

41. Erwin Panofsky, "Style and Medium in the Motion Pictures," in *Three Essays on Style,* ed. Irving Lavin (Cambridge, Mass.: The MIT Press, 1997), 122.

42. Richard Griffith, "A Big Year for Fact Films," *New York Times,* September 17, 1939; Iris Barry and Richard Griffith, *The Films of Fact* (New York: MoMA Film Library, 1942).

43. Decherney, *Hollywood and the Culture Elite,* 142–43.

44. Walter Benjamin, "The Work of Art in the Age of Mechanical Reproduction," in *Illuminations: Essays and Reflections,* ed. Hannah Arendt, trans. Harry Zorn (New York: Schocken Books, 1968), 251n21.

45. "Kracauer to Barry" (Oct. 23, 1942), Archives FSC/MoMA.

46. Kracauer, "Propaganda and the Nazi War Film," 304–5.

47. The NSDAP produced two films tending to legitimize extermination of the physically and mentally handicapped because of the cost to society of caring for them, the costs of their care under the Weimar Republic being attributed to the Jews: *Erbkrank* (Hereditary Defect, dir. Herbert Gerdes, 1936) and *Alles Leben ist Kampf* (Every Life Is a Struggle, dirs. Gerdes and W. Hüttig, 1937).

48. Kracauer, "Propaganda and the Nazi War Film," 305–6.

49. Kracauer, Archives FSC/MoMA.

50. Kracauer, "Propaganda and the Nazi War Film," 277.

Chapter 4. Face-to-Face with Nazi Atrocities

1. In regard to World War I on this topic, see Laurent Veray, *Les Films d'actualité français de la Grande Guerre* (Paris: SIRPA/AFRHC, 1995); Jean-Baptiste Péretié, "Vrai comme au cinéma: Persuasion et démonstration dans les actualités françaises," in Christophe Prochasson and Anne Rasmussen, eds., *Vrai et faux dans la Grande Guerre* (Paris: Découverte, 2004), 112–29.

2. Tomasz Kizny, *Gulag: Life and Death Inside the Soviet Concentration Camps, 1917–1990* (Tonawanda, N.Y.: Firefly Books, 2004).

3. Kizny, *Gulag*, 72–73.

4. Kizny, *Gulag*, 136–37. A few images in Kizny's book are taken from films, like *Solovki* (Labor Camps in Solovki, dir. A. A. Cherkasov, prod. Sovkino, 1928). The quality of the photo strips presented (see 42–43, 46–47) leads one to believe that this film document was not released, as is probably the case for the sequences from the Kolyma region in the 1930s (see 306, 314–15).

5. Ernst Friedrich, *War Against War*, introduction by Douglas Kellner (Seattle, Wa.: Real Comet Press, 1987).

6. On this subject, see Bernd Hüppauf, "Emptying the Gaze: Framing Violence Through the Viewfinder," *New German Critique* 72 (Fall 1997): 3–44. The author proposes dealing with the images made by the executioners by considering them not as expressing their point of view only but as actually sharing a common space: "Even a brutal act of separation produced at the same time a situation of implication, tearing down the invisible walls of separation. The photographers who were spatially distanced from the killing, hidden behind their cameras, produced a world of signs shared by actors and victims" (41).

7. Quoted in the documentary, *Das Auge des Dritten Reiches, Hitlers Kameramann und Fotograf, Walter Frentz* (The Eye of the Third Reich [Walter Frentz], written, dir. Jürgen Stumpfhaus, Arte, 1992). Himmler's notebook confirms this visit: "15 August 1941. Morning: present during an execution of Jews and [Russian] partisans on the outskirts of Minsk." *Der Dienstkalender Heinrich Himmlers 1941/42*, ed. Peter Witte et al. (Hamburg: Christian, 1999), 195.

8. Quoted in *The Eye of the Third Reich (Walter Frentz)*.

9. Ilsen About, "La Photographie au service du système concentrationnaire national-socialiste (1933–1945)," in Clément Chéroux, ed., *Mémoire des camps: Photographies des camps de concentration et d'extermination nazis (1933–1999)* (Paris: Marval, 2001), 28–53.

10. Sybil Milton, "Photography as Evidence of the Holocaust," in Milton and Genya Markon, eds., "Photography and the Holocaust," special issue, *History of Photography* 23, no. 4 (1999): 303.

11. Polish cameraman Stanislaw Wohl explains his discovery of the Majdanek camp this way: "We entered Majdanek a few minutes after the Nazis left. Hitler's crematoria still smoldered. Live prisoners, in their state of extreme biological and psychological exhaustion, wanted to greet us. But they had no strength to raise their hands or cross themselves." "W Chelmie i Lubline," *Film* 28, no. 9 (1969), quoted in Stanislaw Ozimek, "The Polish Newsreel in 1945: The Bitter Victory," in K. R. M. Short and Stephan Dolezel, eds., *Hitler's Fall: The Newsreel Witness* (London: Croom Helm, 1988), 72.

12. Filmed testimony of Alexander Vorontsov, *The Liberation of Auschwitz, 1945* (Chronos UK, 1994). According to Primo Levi, when they arrived the Soviet soldiers "did not greet us, nor did they smile; they seemed oppressed not only by compassion but by a confused restraint, which sealed their lips and bound their eyes to the funereal

scene." Levi, *The Reawakening*, trans. Stuart Woolf (1963; New York: Touchstone, 1995), 16.

13. Reported in *Contre l'oubli* (Against Forgetting), written by William Karel, Jean-Charles Deniau, and Philippe Alfonsi, dir. Karel (Taxi Productions, 1995).

14. In France an eighteen-minute expurgated version of the Soviet film on the liberation of the Majdanek camp was initially banned by the Ministry of Prisoners, Deportees and Refugees. Although it had been issued a distribution visa on April 30, 1945, the film was not incorporated into French news magazines; see Claudine Drame, "Représenter l'irreprésentable: Les camps nazis dans les actualités françaises de 1945," *Cinémathèque* 10 (Fall 1996): 12–27.

15. "Un film anti-hitlérien réalisé à Hollywood," *Cinématographie Française* 775 (September 9, 1933): 13. I am grateful to Jean-François Cornu for this information.

16. "Will Hays empêche la production d'un film anti-allemand," *Cinématographie Française* 783 (November 4, 1933): 7.

17. "Report of Samuel W. Honaker, American Consul General, to U.S. Ambassador Hugh R. Wilson, Berlin. Date: 12 November 1938. Subject: Antisemitic Persecution in the Stuttgart Consular District," PS-2604, Office of the U.S. Chief of Counsel, Archives du Procès de Nuremberg, CDJC, Paris.

18. See John Horne and Alan Kramer, *German Atrocities: A History of Denial* (New Haven, Conn.: Yale University Press, 2001); Christophe Prochasson, "Sur les atrocités allemandes: La guerre comme représentation," *Annales Histoire et Sciences Sociales* 4 (July–August 2003): 879–94.

19. See John Horne, "Les Mains coupées, 'atrocités allemandes' et opinion française en 1914," in Jean-Jacques Becker et al., eds. *Guerre et cultures, 1914–1918* (Paris: Armand Colin, 1994), 133–46; Prochasson and Rasmussen, eds., *Vrai et faux dans la Grande Guerre.*

20. Alan Kramer cites the case of the American historian Ralph H. Lutz, who in 1933 considered "the accusations leveled against the German army during the war as fabrications conceived to demonize the German nation for propaganda purposes." Kramer, "Les 'atrocités allemandes': Mythologie populaire, propagande et manipulations dans l'armée allemande," in Becker et al., *Guerre et cultures*, 147.

21. Raul Hilberg thus cites the extension of the camp of Bergen-Belsen in the fall of 1943, "which started out as a model camp, [but] it could not afford an inspection by a foreign government even in its early days." Hilberg, *The Destruction of the European Jews*, 3rd ed. (1961; New Haven, Conn.: Yale University Press, 2003), 2:632–33. Such inspections did take place—successfully—at Theresienstadt; see Karel Margry, "Theresienstadt (1944–1945): The Nazi Propaganda Film Depicting the Concentration Camp as Paradise," *Historical Journal of Film, Radio and Television* 12, no. 2 (1992): 145–62.

22. Robert H. Jackson, opening speech, in "Second Day, Wednesday, 21 November 1945," *Proceedings: 14 November 1945–30 November 1945*, vol. 2 of *Trial of the Major*

War Criminals Before the International Military Tribunal. Nuremberg 14 November 1945–1 October 1946 (Nuremberg: IMT, 1947), 130.

23. "The Atrocity Stories," *Collier's*, January 6, 1945.

24. "Supreme Headquarters. Allied Expeditionary Force. Public Relations Division, K. B. Lawton, Colonel, Signal Corps to Signal Officer, Sixth Army Group, Signal Officer, Twelfth Army Group, Special Motion Picture Coverage Unit. Subject: Motion Pictures of Concentration Camps" (Apr. 26, 1945), NARA, RG 226, E148, B73, F1038.

25. See Thomas Doherty, *Projections of War: Hollywood, American Culture, and World War II* (New York: Columbia University Press, 1993), 247–50.

26. "Camp Horror Films Are Exhibited Here," *New York Times*, May 2, 1945. Oscar Doob, head of public relations for the Loew circuit, reports that the news was shown without garnering any particular reaction from the audience, even though the theater directors felt some nervousness before showing it.

27. "Camp Horror Films Are Exhibited Here."

28. Dwight D. Eisenhower, "To George Catlett Marshall, 15 April 1945," in *The Papers of Dwight David Eisenhower. The War Years*, ed. Alfred D. Chandler (Baltimore: Johns Hopkins University Press, 1970), 2616.

29. "Congress, Press to View Horrors," *New York Times*, April 22, 1945.

30. Renée Poznanski, "Que savait-on dans le monde?," in Stéphane Courtois and Adam Rayski, eds., *Qui savait quoi? L'extermination des Juifs, 1941–1945* (Paris: La Découverte, 1987), 42.

31. This film was also preceded by a warning: "You have just seen some of the atrocities committed by the Germans. The motion picture you are about to see is a training film prepared by the War Dept. for the U.S. Army of Occupation in Germany, so that they will be fully instructed and advised concerning their all-important mission."

32. Jack Warner made a fourth version, *Hitler Lives*, which won the Oscar for best short documentary in 1945; see David Holbrook Culbert, "American Film Policy in the Re-Education of Germany After 1945," in Nicholas Pronay and Keith Wilson, eds., *The Political Re-education of Germany and Her Allies After World War II* (London: Croom Helm, 1985), 175–76.

33. James Agee, "Atrocity Films," *The Nation* 60 (May 19, 1945): 54.

34. The subject would have been of interest locally, since St. Louis had a significant German American community (including the Pulitzers). The publisher (1885–1955) chose to take over and develop the newspaper his father had started in St. Louis rather than the one he bought himself (the *New York World*); see Daniel W. Pfaff, *Joseph Pulitzer II and the Post-Dispatch: A Newspaperman's Life* (University Park: Pennsylvania State University Press, 1991).

35. Alvin H. Goldstein, "Public Showing of Nazi Atrocity Film Urged," *St. Louis Post-Dispatch*, May 12, 1945.

36. Goldstein, "Public Showing of Nazi Atrocity Film Urged."

37. "Public Reaction to Army Signal Corps Film," *St. Louis Post-Dispatch*, May 31, 1945.

38. Polls about Americans' knowledge of the Nazi camps show progress in awareness between 1944 and 1945. In early May 1945, to the question "What do you think of information that the Nazis killed a great number of people in concentration camps or let them die of hunger: is it true or false?," 84 percent answered, "true"; see Robert A. Abzug, *Inside the Vicious Heart: Americans and the Liberation of Nazi Concentration Camps* (New York: Oxford University Press, 1985), 135–40.

39. Philippe Despoix, "Mémoires berlinoises, ou l'heure zéro chez Billy Wilder," *CiNéMaS* 15, no. 1 (2004): 29–42.

40. The British arrived in the region late on the afternoon of May 19. Headquarters were set in Burgsteinfurt and placed under the command of the 3rd Division. A film montage of the camps had been made to be incorporated into a series of news items intended for a German public; see, for this film of Ohrdruf, Ziegenheim, Kaunitz, Holzen, Schwarzenfeld, Göttingen, Hadamar, Arnstadt, Bergen-Belsen, Gardelegen, Thekla, Nordhausen, and Buchenwald, *Welt im Film* 5 (June 15, 1945).

41. The Feldherrnhalle was constructed by Friedrich von Gärnter and inaugurated in 1844. Statues were erected there in memory of Generals Jean t'Serclaes de Tilly and Carl Philipp von Wrede. In 1923, at the time of his unsuccessful putsch, Hitler went there. During the Third Reich, an honor guard kept watch in front of the commemorative plaque displayed in remembrance of the putsch attempt.

42. As Michael Pollak rightly observes, "These depositions bear . . . the marks of the principles of the administration of judicial proof: restriction to the issue in the trial, eliminating all elements considered not germane." Pollak, *L'Expérience concentrationnaire: Essai sur le maintien de l'identité sociale* (1990; Paris: Métailié, 2000), 188.

43. Jorge Semprún, *Literature or Life* (1994), trans. Linda Coverdale (New York: Penguin, 1998), 198.

44. Semprún, *Literature or Life*, 199–200.

45. Semprún, *Literature or Life*, 200.

46. See Chéroux, "Margaret Bourke-White," in *Mémoire des camps*, 134–39.

47. The gesture would thereby correspond to what Eisenhower wanted: *firsthand* evidence.

48. Jean Breschand, *Le Documentaire: L'autre face du cinéma* (Paris: Cahiers du Cinéma, 2002), 77.

49. To this day the first prints of the camp films offer a brilliance and contrast completely lacking in those copies that have long been in circulation. Hence the value of going back to the source of these films, to the U.S. National Archives, if only to appreciate and at the same time discover the set of color films of the camps made in 1945 by the U.S. Air Force; see the bibliography compiled in Charles Lawrence Gellert, ed., *The Holocaust, Israel and the Jews: Motion Pictures in the National Archives* (Washington, D.C.: NARA, 1989).

50. Color can also have the opposite effect of de-realization: Ilsen About recounts how, for the camp commandant and military engineers of Dora-Mittelbau, who wanted to reassure Nazi officials about their factory's ability to build V2 missiles, the choice of assigning cameraman Walter Frentz to do a color report on the site was supposed to seem like "evidence of technical modernity. . . . This iconographic ensemble, which erases the camp's repressive dimension (no SS or Kapo appears in the visual field) helps give the picture of an effective machinery functioning thanks to the collective efforts of the detainees and their apparent cohesion." About, "Le Reportage photographique de Walter Frentz à Dora," in Chéroux, *Mémoire des camps*, 64.

51. See Stewart Binns, "The Second World War in Color," *History Today* 49, no. 9 (1999): 3.

52. See Jason G. McKahan, "Color in the Camps: Holocaust Memory in Color Archival Footage" and McKahan and Caroline Joan S. Picart, "Visualizing the Holocaust in Gothic Terms: The Ideology of U.S. Signal Corps Cinematography," in Caroline Joan Picart, ed., *The Holocaust Film Source Book*, vol. 2, *Documentary and Propaganda* (Westport, Conn.: Praeger, 2004).

53. In 1943, for the Office of Strategic Services, Ford directed a short subject in black and white and in color about the National Gallery in Washington, D.C. After footage of paintings by Vermeer, Rubens, Monet, Renoir, and Gauguin, the film commentary concludes, "The World and Man / These are the materials / From which great artists / Have created their revelations / Of Man's mind and soul" (NARA, RG 226, E 133, B 156, F 1323).

54. John Ford quoted in Peter Bogdanovich, *John Ford* (Berkeley: University of California Press, 1978), 74. This opinion did not prevent him from filming live and in color the shots compiled under the title *The Battle of Midway* (1942). William Wyler did the same for the movie *Thunderbolt* (1945).

55. Lawrence Douglas, *The Memory of Judgment: Making Law and History in the Trials of the Holocaust* (New Haven, Conn.: Yale University Press, 2001), 31.

56. McKahan, "Color in the Camps." We should also remember that, unlike with the advent of the talkies, which made the continuation of silent films impossible, some directors continued, in spite of commercial pressure, to work in black and white and still do.

57. George Raynor Thompson et al., *United States Army in World War II: The Technical Services. The Signal Corps: The Outcome, Mid-1943 Through 1945* (Washington, D.C.: Office of the Chief of Military History, U.S. Army, 1966), 565.

58. Stevens had made three films during the war (*Woman of the Year* and *Talk of the Town* in 1942 and *The More the Merrier* in 1943) before joining the army as a colonel and participating in the D-Day landing in 1944. See *From Hollywood to Nuremberg: John Ford, Samuel Fuller, George Stevens* (dir. Delage, 2012 [France]; DVD available in English).

59. The only reel Stevens ever showed was the one shot at Dachau, which he presented to his crew in preparation for filming *The Diary of Anne Frank* (U.S., 1959). A copy is available at NARA (USAF 18457).

60. Serge Daney, "Le Travelling de *Kapo*," *Trafic* 4 (November 1992): 10.

Chapter 5. "Establishing Incredible Events by Means of Credible Evidence"

1. Telford Taylor, *The Anatomy of the Nuremberg Trials: A Personal Memoir* (1949; Boston: Little, Brown, 1992), 39.

2. Taylor, *The Anatomy of the Nuremberg Trials*, 39.

3. John Q. Barrett, "Closing Reflections on Jackson and *Barnette*," in "Recollections of *West Virginia State Board of Education v. Barnette*," special issue, *St. John's Law Review* 81 (Fall 2007): 793–96.

4. See Willard B. Cowles, "Trial of War Criminals by Military Tribunals," *American Bar Association Journal* 30, no. 6 (1944): 330, cited from copy in the Jackson Papers, RHJ 43, Manuscripts Dept., Library of Congress, Washington, RHJ 43.

5. Woodrow Wilson, "Jusqu'à la remise à la délégation allemande des conditions de la paix" (March 28, 1919), quoted in Paul Mantoux, *Les Délibérations du Conseil des Quatre* (Paris: CNRS, 1955), 71, quoted in Stéphane Audoin-Rouzeau and Annette Becker, *14–18: Understanding the Great War* (New York: Hill and Wang, 2002), 228.

6. Robert H. Jackson, *Proceedings of the 39th Annual Meeting of the American Society of International Law, April 13–14, 1945* (Washington, D.C.: American Society of International Law, 1945), 13, 15.

7. Jackson, *Proceedings of the 39th Annual Meeting*, 18. The George W. Bush administration adopted the exact opposite position in refusing to participate in the 2002 founding of the International Criminal Court and in signing bilateral accords aimed at exempting U.S. citizens from all risk of legal action; see Antoine Garapon, *Des Crimes qu'on ne peut ni punir ni pardonner: Pour une justice internationale* (Paris: Odile Jacob, 2002), 334–37.

8. See Jean-Jacques Becker, "Les Procès de Leipzig," in Annette Wieviorka, ed., *Les Procès de Nuremberg et de Tokyo* (Paris Complexe, 1996), 51–60; Michael Marrus, *The Nuremberg War Crimes Trial, 1945–1946: A Documentary History* (Boston: Bedford, 1997), 1–14.

9. Robert H. Jackson, opening speech, in "Second Day, Wednesday, 21 November 1945," *Proceedings: 14 November 1945–30 November 1945*, vol. 2 of *Trial of the Major War Criminals Before the International Military Tribunal. Nuremberg 14 November 1945–1 October 1946* (Nuremberg: IMT, 1947), 101.

10. On the basis of lists of these defendants that were made public, the Germans then methodically proceeded with countertrials in which the accused were all acquit-

ted. John Horne and Alan Kramer, *German Atrocities, 1914: A History of Denial* (New Haven, Conn.: Yale University Press, 2001), 345–55.

11. On the evolution of war jurisprudence, see Peter Maguire, *Law and War: An American Story* (New York: Columbia University Press, 2001); Michael Walzer, *Just and Unjust Wars* (New York: Basic Books, 1977).

12. Besides Stimson, Bernays, Chanler, and Jackson, this group of New York jurists included Judge Rosenman and John J. McCloy.

13. Composed originally of a small group of close collaborators, Jackson's team would bring together nearly 650 people in November 1945, when the trial opened.

14. *The Battle of Midway* (1942) and *December 7th* (1943) would each win an Oscar.

15. Lord Wright of Durley, "Record of Conference Held on May 6, 1945, between Members of the UNWCC and Members of the United States Senate and House of Representatives, United Nations War Crimes Commission, C. 115, 24 May 1945," 2 (NARA, RG153, 3 135, B76, F148).

16. "Robert H. Jackson, May 7, 1945," 4 (Jackson Papers, RHJ 95).

17. "John A. Hall, Colonel, JAGD, War Crimes Branch Office, to Colonel Claude B. Mickelwait, Staff Judge Advocate, Headquarters, 12th Army Group, U.S. Army, 27 April 1945" (NARA, RG226, E148, B73, F1038).

18. Field Photographic Branch, Office of Strategic Services, *Monthly Report for Period 1–31 May, 1945*, 8 (NARA, RG226, E148, B73, F1038).

19. "Memorandum to Monthly Report, 9 June 1945," FPB (NARA, RG226, E148, B73, F1038).

20. *Justice Jackson's Story*, transcript of tape recording by Harlan B. Phillips, Oral History Research, Columbia University, 1952–1953, Jackson Papers, RHJ 190, 1082.

21. There remained the problem of the multiple definitions attributed to *war crimes*. As the OSS report argues, "The time is here to say whether it has precise meaning or not. No difficulty can come from the use of the term if the user, when he speaks of cases, has clearly in mind the categories of war crimes which he is speaking of and does not confuse the tribunals and the agencies which would be employed." "The Trial of War Criminals," n.d. (NARA, RG226, E148, B76, L1087).

22. "Report from Mr. Justice Jackson, Chief Counsel for the United States in the prosecution of Axis War Criminals" (NARA, RG226, E90, B12, F126, 3). In a brief note sent to Jackson to congratulate him on his nomination as head of the IMT, Judge J. F. T. O'Connor justifies the need to preserve carefully the documents of the future trial: "The Memory of man is short—even now much of the horror, such as the poisonous gas attacks of World War I, have faded from memory" (Jackson Papers, May 17, 1945, RHJ 95).

23. Jackson underscores, "These hearings, however, must not be regarded in the same light as a trial under our system, where defense is a matter of constitutional right. Fair hearings for the accused are, of course, required to make sure that we punish only the right man for the right reasons. But the procedure of these hearings may

properly bar obstructive and dilatory tactics resorted to by the defendants in our ordinary criminal trials" ("Report from Mr. Justice Jackson," NARA, RG226, E90, B12, F126, 3).

24. On the first term, see Antoine Garapon, *Bien juger: Essai sur le rituel judiciaire*, Opus (Paris: Odile Jacob, 1997), 152. As for the second, Luigi Ferrajoli observes that trials become the site of "historiographic experimentation" in the sense that "the sources are forced to interact *de vivo*, not only because they are heard directly, but also because they are forced to confront one another, subjected to cross-examination and prompted to reproduce, as in a psychodrama, the adjudicated event." Ferrajoli, *Dritto e ragione: Teoria del garantismo penale* (Bari: Laterza, 1989), 32, quoted in Carlo Ginzburg, *The Judge and the Historian: Marginal Notes on a Late-Twentieth-Century Miscarriage of Justice*, trans. Antony Shugaar (London: Verso, 1999), 18.

25. Jackson Papers, RHJ 95.

26. "Memorandum on Trial Preparation, Approved by Chief of Counsel, 16 May 1945," 5 (NARA, RG153, E135, B87, L481).

27. "Minutes of a Meeting with Justice Robert H. Jackson Held at the Federal Court House, N.Y.C., Tuesday, June 12, 1945, from 10 to 11:30 A.M.," P-66, Nathan D. Perlman Collection, n.d. (Archives of the American Jewish Historical Society, hereafter AJHS).

28. In the summary of the meeting recorded in his journal, Jackson seems to have been more open at the time to the notion of granting specific consideration to the case of the Jews of Europe than he indicated that he was in the oral interview he gave later at Columbia University: "Their fear has been that the easier route of convicting for some minor offenses would prevail and the Jewish problem be submerged, i.e., they want a decision on the Jewish mistreatment—which they say has been passed by in all trials so far. [As one of their requests] they want a court in the main trial based on the persecution of the Jews. This I agree should be done" (Robert H. Jackson, "Tuesday, June 11, 1945," *Diary Kept by Robert H. Jackson, 27 April–10 November 1945*, Jackson Papers, RHJ 95).

29. *Jews in Nazi Europe, February 1933 to November 1941: A Study Prepared by the Institute of Jewish Affairs*, New York, November 1941 (Archives of the AJHS).

30. *Institute of Jewish Affairs: Its Aims and Methods*, New York, February 1942 (Archives of the AJHS).

31. *Institute of Jewish Affairs*, 15–16. The mood nevertheless leans toward optimism, as shown by the titles of contributions by Beryl Harold Levy ("Winning the Peace") and Paul Tillich ("Three Solutions to the Jewish Problem").

32. Jacob Robinson, preface to *Hitler's Ten Years War on the Jews*, IJA, New York, 1943 (Archives of the AJHS).

33. Sydney S. Alderman, transcript of tape recording by Harlan B. Phillips, Oral History Research, Columbia University, 1953, 935. Alderman was Jackson's top assistant on the team preparing the IMT trial.

34. In 1936 Glueck published a pioneering study showing the importance of the social sciences—anthropology and psychiatry in particular—in understanding common law crime, its genesis, judicial treatment, and eventual prevention; see Glueck, *Crime and Justice* (Boston: Little, Brown, 1936). On June 23 Jackson also solicited Glueck to present a method of documentary indexing for the forms used to present evidence collected by the IMT.

35. Sheldon Glueck, "Trial and Punishment of Axis War Criminals," *New Republic* 109 (November 22, 1943): 706–9; Sheldon Glueck, *War Criminals, Their Prosecution and Punishment* (New York: Knopf, 1944); Sheldon Glueck, *The Nuremberg Trial and Aggressive War* (New York: Knopf, 1946).

36. According to Tom Segev, these calculations proved more judicious than the assessments arrived at by David Ben-Gurion during the same period. Shortly after May 8, 1945, Ben-Gurion attempted a "postwar Zionist reckoning." His entry for that day "looks like a page from an accountant's ledger, all numbers: so many Jews lived in Europe before the war, so many were murdered, so many remained alive. Ben-Gurion listed them by country; not a single one of the sums he recorded was correct." Segev, *The Seventh Million: The Israelis and the Holocaust*, trans. Haim Watzman (New York: Hill and Wang, 1993), 114. If one compares the IJA figures with those established by Raul Hilberg, some are very close (Poland, Lithuania, Czechoslovakia, France), others are high (USSR, Rumania, Germany, Austria), and some low (Hungary, the Netherlands).

37. *Statistics on Jewish Casualties During Axis Domination*, June 1945, IJA; *Statistics on Jewish Casualties During Axis Domination*, August 1945, IJA (Archives of the AJHS). In the two tables, the total is 5.7 million Jewish victims.

38. Jackson reports on July 7, 1945, that one of his special envoys in Europe, Col. John Amen, had discovered a copy of the "Hossbach Protocol," which explicitly connected the plan of aggression and the intent to exterminate the Jews. Robert H. Jackson, *Justice Jackson's Story*, transcript of tape recording by Harlan B. Phillips, Oral History Research, Columbia University, 1952–1953, Jackson Papers, RHJ 190, 1153–54.

39. Donald Bloxham, *Genocide on Trial: War Crimes Trials and the Formation of Holocaust History and Memory* (Oxford: Oxford University Press, 2001), 89. Jackson was not the first to emphasize this charge; Stimson, the secretary of war, claims to have convinced Roosevelt in fall 1944; see Lord Shawcross [Hartley William Shawcross], "Robert H. Jackson's Contributions During the Nuremberg Trial," in Charles Desmond, Paul A. Freund, Potter Stewart, and Lord Shawcross, *Mr. Justice Jackson: Four Lectures in His Honor* (New York: Columbia University Press, 1969), 95.

40. "Letter of the League of American Writers to Robert H. Jackson," November 22, 1938 (Jackson Papers, RHJ 54).

41. States Jackson, "Every American of understanding, instead of being possessed by a power complex, is minority-conscious, for neither in faith, class nor party can he say he is of an *assured* majority." Robert H. Jackson, *We Hold These Truths: Statements*

on Anti-Semitism by 54 Leading American Writers, Statesmen, Educators, Clergymen and Trade-Unionists (New York: League of American Writers, 1939).

42. Robert H. Jackson, "The Challenge of the Christian Conscience," Jackson Papers, RHJ 54.

43. Novick observes, "A handful of Christian Americans made general references to a Jewish state as recompense for the guilt of Christendom for anti-Semitism . . . but there is no reason to believe that these scattered remarks had any broad resonance." Peter Novick, *The Holocaust in American Life* (New York: Mariner Books, 2000), 72.

44. *Editor's note*: The Évian Conference was organized at the behest of President Roosevelt and held July 6–13, 1938, in Évian-les-Bains, France, to discuss the plight of Jewish refugees fleeing Nazi Germany.

45. Brandeis (1856–1941) and Cardozo (1870–1938) were both Supreme Court justices, Brandeis from 1916 to 1939 and Cardozo from 1932 to 1938. In the 1930s Brandeis was one of the few judges who supported the fundamental aims of the New Deal legislation. As for Cardozo, he was an ardent propagator of a more social view of economics.

46. "Statement of President Roosevelt, 7 October 1942," and "Statement of President Roosevelt, 24 March 1944," in *The United States and the Peace, Part I: A Collection of Documents, August 14, 1941–March 5, 1945* (Jackson Papers, RHJ 95).

47. War Crimes Office document (NARA, RG153, E135, B82, L445).

48. War Crimes Office document.

49. "Genocide," *Washington Post*, December 3, 1944.

50. Raphael Lemkin, *Axis Rule in Occupied Europe: Laws of Occupation. Analysis of Government Proposals for Redress* (Washington, D.C.: Carnegie Endowment for International Peace, Division of International Law, 1944).

51. Raphael Lemkin, "Genocide," *Free World*, April 1945, in "Letter from Raphael Lemkin to Robert H. Jackson," May 4, 1945 (Jackson Papers, RHJ 95). Colonel Donovan had already consulted Lemkin for investigations expedited by the OSS.

52. "Les Actes constituant un danger général (interétatique) considérés comme délits de droit de gens," in *Rapport spécial présenté à la cinquième conférence pour l'unification du droit pénal à Madrid (14–20 déc. 1933), explications additionnelles* (Paris: A. Pedone, 1934).

53. "The plan of genocide had to be adapted to political considerations in different countries. It could not be implemented in full force in all the conquered states, and hence the plan varies as to subject modalities, and degree of intensity in each occupied country. Some groups—such as the Jews—are to be destroyed completely." Lemkin, *Axis Rule in Occupied Europe*, 81. See also Olivier Beauvallet, *Lemkin, face au génocide* (Paris: Michalon, 2011).

54. Charles Herbert Stember et al., *Jews in the Mind of America* (New York: Basic Books, 1966), 141, cited in Novick, *The Holocaust in American Life*, 113n39.

55. See Michael Marrus, "A Jewish Lobby at Nuremberg: Jacob Robinson and the Institute of Jewish Affairs, 1945–1946," *The Nuremberg Trials: A Reappraisal and Their Legacy*, special issue of *Cardozo Law Review* 27, 4 (February 2006): 1651–65.

56. Jackson, *Justice Jackson's Story*, 1075–76.

57. He adds parenthetically, "Strangely enough, later, that is exactly the position that [Hermann] Göring took on the stand" (Alderman, transcript of tape recording by Harlan B. Phillips, 1261).

58. Léon Poliakov, *Le Procès de Jérusalem: Juger Adolf Eichmann* (Paris: Calmann-Lévy, 1963), 376–77. See also Michael Marrus, "The Holocaust in Nuremberg," in David Silberklang, ed., *Yad Vashem Studies* (Jerusalem: Yad Vashem, Holocaust Martyrs' and Heroes Remembrance Authority, 1988), 13–14.

59. Jackson, *Justice Jackson's Story*; Poliakov, *Le Procès de Jérusalem*, 377–78.

60. Jackson, *Justice Jackson's Story*, 1077.

61. Cmdr. James B. Donovan, legal counsel of the OSS, was head of the IMT teams responsible for war crimes. On June 7 Jackson had already written to Col. William J. Donovan, head of the OSS, asking him to help with "The collection, evaluation, integration, and presentation of evidence of all types (including photographic), with such assistance from other Departments and agencies of the Government as may be required" (NARA, RG226, E148, B76, F1087).

62. In Paris a film crew was supposed to handle the audiovisual recording of interrogations, as per Jackson's request.

63. "Memorandum from General Counsel to Chief, Field Photographic Branch, OSS," June 12, 1945 (NARA, RG226, E133, B124, F1077). The crew assembled by Ford included Budd Schulberg, Jack Munroe (a former reporter from Fox), John Bott, Karl Jacoby (a technical expert and former prosecutor in Berlin exiled in the United States since 1941), Maga Policek (an Austrian refugee who spoke many languages), Susan Shestopel (formerly in Soviet news reporting in Moscow), Joe Zigman, Robert Parrish, and Robert Webb (film editors), Robert Hiden (promoted to "cross-filer"), Stuart Schulberg (brother of Budd), and an expert in speed writing ("Sgt. Smith"); see Budd Schulberg, "The Celluloid Noose," *Screen Writer: A Publication of the Screen Writers' Guild, Inc.*, August 1946, 5. Parrish shares his recollections of this period with famed French director Bertrand Tavernier in Thierry Frémaux, ed., *Amis américains: Entretiens avec les grands auteurs d'Hollywood* (Lyon: Institut Lumière, Actes Sud, 1993), 314–17.

64. Before and after the Nuremberg Trial, Budd Schulberg published two works on Hollywood: *What Makes Sammy Run?* (New York: Random House, 1941) and *Moving Pictures: Memories of a Hollywood Prince* (New York: Stein and Day, 1981).

65. Metronome News was created in 1929 by press tycoon William Randolph Hearst, the main competitor of the Pulitzer group. Orson Welles drew his inspiration for *Citizen Kane* (1941) from Hearst.

66. Schulberg, "The Celluloid Noose," 6–7.

67. See Lucas Delattre, *Un Espion au cœur du Troisième Reich* (Paris: Denoël, 2003).

68. Jackson, *Justice Jackson's Story*, 1155.

69. Jackson, *Justice Jackson's Story*, 1239. François Hartog recalls, "In the 19th century, once history became a science, the science of the past, all that was left for it to do was to declare that it is made up of documents, though with the proviso that it be understood, to echo [Charles-Victor] Langlois and [Charles] Seignobos, that *authentic*, 'borrowed from judicial language[,] refers only to the provenance and not the content of the document,' and to remember that a science thus constructed can accept only 'written transmission.'" Hartog, "Le Témoin et l'historien," *Gradhiva* 27 (2000): 11. We will see later that labeling a film as evidence steers the question away from authenticity toward content.

70. See Antoine Garapon, "De Nuremberg au TPI: Naissance d'une justice universelle?," *Critique Internationale* 5 (Fall 1999): 167–80.

71. See Michael Salter, *Nazi War Crimes, U.S. Intelligence and Selective Prosecution at Nuremberg: Controversies Regarding the Role of the Office of Strategic Services* (New York: Routledge-Cavendish, 2007).

72. Telford Taylor, "Memorandum for Mr. Justice Jackson, and the Board of Review. Subject: Order of proof, use of witnesses, use of motion pictures and related subjects," November 3, 1945 (Jackson Papers, RHJ 111).

73. Taylor, "Memorandum for Mr. Justice Jackson," 1.

74. We return later to the role of witnesses in the Nuremberg trial through a concrete analysis of Marie-Claude Vaillant-Couturier's appearance on the stand. In the meantime, let us simply recall that victims were not allowed to act jointly with the prosecutor to obtain redress as civil plaintiffs (*parties civiles*).

75. Taylor, "Memorandum for Mr. Justice Jackson," 1.

76. Taylor, "Memorandum for Mr. Justice Jackson," 1–2.

77. Taylor, "Memorandum for Mr. Justice Jackson," 1–2.

Chapter 6. Getting Film into the Courtroom

1. In reporting the experience of his first encounter with film of the Nazi camps, sociologist Michael Pollak writes, "I was 13 when, in 1961, I saw film of the Nazi extermination camps for the first time. It was the documentary *Mein Kampf* by Erwin Leiser, a movie I have never again seen since. But those images of horror are still with me. They rendered even more haunting the questions that the immediate postwar generation continually asked their parents' generation." Pollak, *L'Expérience concentrationnaire: Essai sur le maintien de l'identité sociale* (1990; Paris: Métailié, 2000), 16.

2. François Hartog, *The Mirror of Herodotus: The Representation of the Other in the Writing of History*, trans. Janet Lloyd (Berkeley: University of California Press, 1988), 251.

3. As Yan Thomas recalled in a lecture for the seminar series "L'Espace de la procédure: Acteurs, confrontations, pouvoir," École des Hautes Études en Sciences Sociales, December 13, 2004.

4. Michel Foucault, *Discipline and Punish: The Birth of the Prison*, trans. Alan Sheridan (New York: Random House, 1975), 37.

5. Denis Salas, *Du procès pénal: Éléments pour une théorie interdisciplinaire du procès* (Paris: PUF, 1992), 86, quoted in Marc Olivier Baruch, "Procès Papon: Impressions d'audience," *Le Débat* 102 (November–December 1998): 15.

6. Dulany Terrett, *United States Army in World War II: The Technical Services. The Signal Corps: The Emergency (To December 1941)*(Washington, D.C.: Washington Office of the Chief of Military History/Dept. of the Army, 1956); George Raynor Thompson et al., *United States Army in World War II: The Technical Services. The Signal Corps: The Test (December 1941 to July 1943)* (Washington, D.C. Office of the Chief of Military History/U.S. Army, 1957); and George Raynor Thompson et al., *United States Army in World War II: The Technical Services. The Signal Corps: The Outcome (Mid-1943 Through 1945)*(Washington, D.C.: Office of the Chief Military History/U.S. Army, 1966). On the role of the Office of War Information, see Allan M. Winkler, *The Politics of Propaganda: The Office of War Information, 1942–1945* (New Haven, Conn.: Yale University Press, 1978).

7. Terrett, *United States Army in World War II*, 228.

8. *Government Information Manual for the Motion Picture Industry*, Washington, D.C., June 1942 (NARA, RG208, E6A, Box 3).

9. See "Film as Social Connection" in Chapter 2.

10. See K. R. M. Short, "Washington's Information Manual for Hollywood, 1942," *Historical Journal of Film, Radio and Television* 3, no. 2 (1983): 171–80.

11. For a general view, see Clayton R. Koppes and Gregory Black, *Hollywood Goes to War: How Politics, Profits, and Propaganda Shaped World War II Movies* (Berkeley: University of California Press, 1987); Thomas Doherty, *Projections of War: Hollywood, American Culture, and World War II* (New York: Columbia University Press, 1993).

12. [*Instruction*], n.d., OSS Archives, NARA, RG226, E133, B124, F1077, 1. This unpublished document appears to be from one of the later editions, since it refers to the international tribunal that was going to be set up by the Allies.

13. In other official documents, such as those issued by the USWCO, the case of concentration camps is taken up more specifically: "If the crime scene is a concentration camp, the investigator should try to decide just what happened. Determine the facts: first, what had happened; second, choose a starting point—whether it be an examination of the interior or exterior of a room, building, camp, etc. Do not enter a place and run here and there in an aimless and haphazard manner. Evidence has often been destroyed by people running around in circles." Lt. Cmdr. George H. Brereton, "War Crime Investigation Methods and Techniques" (lecture), June 18, 1945, 6–7 (NARA, RG153, E135, B82, L445).

14. Pierre R. Paradis, "The Celluloid Witness," *University of Colorado Law Review* 37 (1965): 235–68.

15. Its being a question of Nazi political leaders who had agreed to testify, the manual states, "There is a possibility that the international tribunal for trial of war criminals will specifically rule that defendants may be compelled to give self-incriminating testimony in Court. However, on the chance that the ruling will be to the contrary, and, in the interest of fair procedure, such a witness should be warned that whatever he says may be used against him later." *Government Information Manual for the Motion Picture Industry*, Washington, D.C., June 1942 (NARA, RG-208, E-6A, Box 3).

16. On July 2, 1945, the FPB worried about how the search for films to show William J. Donovan and Jackson was progressing in Germany: "It was suggested that weekly or bi-weekly screenings of atrocities and other film evidence, taking one subject at a time, would be of value." "Field Photographic Branch, Report of John Sutton," July 10, 1945 (NARA, RG226, E148, B73, F1078).

17. The shortening postediting of the duration of the filmed images will be questioned later, when the movie is shown during the trial of Holocaust denier Ernst Zündel. Robert A. Kahn reports, "For the jury to view the film, it [the film] would have to survive two hearsay objections. First, the film itself was hearsay. In a sense, this objection is a formality, one that can be made against all written documents. In the case of *Nazi Concentration Camps,* however, this objection had a substantive bite. The troops who liberated the camp shot more than 80,000 feet of film, of which only 6,000 made it in the final version. Were the scenes included in the film representative? This was a substantive question, [one] that deserved an answer.... Second, the narrative did more than simply describe the pictures." Kahn, *Holocaust Denial and the Law: A Comparative Study* (New York: Palgrave Macmillan, 2004), 51.

18. Robert H. Jackson, "Second Day, Wednesday, 21 November 1945," *Proceedings: 14 November 1945–30 November 1945*, vol. 2 of *Trial of the Major War Criminals Before the International Military Tribunal. Nuremberg 14 November 1945–1 October 1946* (Nuremberg: IMT, 1947), 123.

19. Jackson, "Second Day, Wednesday, 21 November 1945," 130.

20. "PS-2430" refers to the designation of the film as it was entered into evidence by Commander Donovan; see Donovan, "Eighth Day, Thursday, 29 November 1945," *Proceedings: 14 November 1945–30 November 1945*, vol. 2 of *Trial of the Major War Criminals Before the International Military Tribunal. Nuremberg 14 November 1945–1 October 1946* (Nuremberg: IMT, 1947), 432. Regarding this film, Lawrence Douglas writes, "Although *Nazi Concentration Camps* displays many of the virtues that distinguished Stevens' filmmaking—classically framed panoramas that dissolve into fastidiously composed close-ups, arresting stills, unsettling juxtapositions—this technique found itself enlisted to create a work that exploded the very filmic universe his Hollywood career had served to build." Douglas, *The Memory of Judgment: Making Law and History in the Trials of the Holocaust* (New Haven, Conn.: Yale University Press,

2001), 28. Stevens was, in fact, responsible only for the footage of Nordhausen, Dachau, and Mauthausen presented in the film, which was edited by Kellogg and the FPB teams.

21. Citations are from the film's commentary.

22. *Editor's note*: The documentary misidentifies these figures: they are Dr. Adolf Wahlmann and Karl Willig.

23. Though the FPB eventually cut this conclusion, the woman doctor announces at the end of her story, "In the name of all prisoners who are still here and alive, I can only express great thanks to the British Army that the day of our liberation has finally come."

24. See, for example, the memorandum of November 30, 1944, to which a list of war crimes considered to be the most serious was attached (NARA, RG266, E148, B76, F1087).

25. See testimony of Navy Lt. Jack H. Taylor, "Mauthausen Concentration Camp," in "Complete Text of Narration in *Nazi Concentration Camps*" (2430-PS), *Official Text. Documents and Other Material in Evidence. Numbers 2239-PS to 2582-PS*, vol. 30, *Trial of the Major War Criminals Before the International Military Tribunal, Nuremberg, 14 November 1945–1 October 1946* (Nuremberg, 1948), 467–68.

26. "Speech of Woman Doctor at Concentration Camp, Belsen" (NARA, RG226, E90, B12, F126).

27. As can be seen by viewing the images frame by frame, the doctor starts her story after hearing or seeing a starting signal. Just prior to this moment, she is smiling, relaxed, as she waits for this exercise.

28. Marie-Anne Matard-Bonucci and Édouard Lynch, eds., *La Libération des camps et le retour des déportés* (Paris: Complexe, 1995), 76. See also Barbie Zelizer, *Remembering to Forget: Holocaust Memory Through the Camera's Eye* (Chicago: University of Chicago Press, 1998).

29. This document appears in the archives of the OSS, which shows that the FPB team had it at its disposal while making the film on the camps. The report specifies that upon the arrival of the British forces, "Work was immediately commenced of burying all corpses and the clearing up of the Camp. By the 19th of May 1945 the Prisoners' Camp was completely cleared and all its inmates had been moved to four Hospitals and Three Transit Camps in the Wehrmacht Barracks area above referred to. The 13,000 corpses found and the 13,000 who died subsequent to the 15th April had been buried and the final hut in the Concentration Camp was burned down on the 21st May 1945, at 1800 hours." "Interim Report No. 1 of the War Crimes Investigation Team, re War Crimes and Atrocities by the Germans at Bergen-Belsen Concentration Camp, from 1st December 1944–15th April 1945 and other Concentration Camps from 1940–1945," June 22, 1945 (NARA, RG238, E190, B98, WC3163-3170, 8.

30. See Elizabeth Sussex, "The Fate of F 3080," *Sight and Sound* 53, no. 2 (1984): 97; Benedetta Guerzoni, *"The Memory of the Camps,* un film inachevé," in Christian Delage and Anne Grynberg, eds., "La Shoah: Images témoins, images preuves," special

issue, *Cahiers du Judaïsme* 15 (2003): 61–70. After consulting the film archives at the Imperial War Museum, it appears that the current copy corresponds to the montage and commentary established in 1946. However, one reel (the fifth, showing Majdanek and Auschwitz) is missing.

31. Sidney Bernstein, "Material Needed for Proposed Motion Picture on German Atrocities," Supreme Headquarters Allied Expeditionary Force, Psychological Warfare Division (Textual Record F 3080, Imperial War Museum, London).

32. Peter Tanner, *A Painful Reminder* (documentary, Granada TV, 1985).

33. London Headquarters, "War Diary, Preamble . . . to January 1944" (NARA, RG226, microfilm 1623).

34. This raw footage can be viewed at the film library of the Établissement de Communication et de Production Audiovisuelle de la Défense (Ivry-sur-Seine, France), call number SA 612. See also Samuel Fuller's unreleased and untitled film shot at Falkenau; Christian Delage and Vincent Guigueno, "Samuel Fuller à Falkenau: L'événement fondateur," *L'Historien et le film* (Paris: Gallimard, 2004), 46–58.

35. *Proposed Line of Commentary for Film on Concentration Camps* (Textual Record F 3080, Imperial War Museum, London).

36. Budd Schulberg himself thought *Nazi Concentration Camps* "reached its unbelievable climax, with corpses piled so high at Belsen that a bulldozer had to be driven through them to clear a path." Schulberg, "The Celluloid Noose," *Screen Writer: A Publication of the Screen Writers' Guild, Inc.*, August 1946, 14. Airey Neave writes in 1978, "Scenes familiar to the present generations of television viewers, like the piles of corpses at Belsen, were an unheralded shock to many. Those who had survived the camps had their memories re-awakened." Neave, *Nuremberg: A Personal Record of the Trial of the Major Nazi War Criminals in 1945–1946* (London: Hodder and Stoughton, 1978), 247. Joseph E. Persico has the same memory: "Later generations might become harder by repeated exposure of these sights, but scenes of bulldozers shoving moon-white corpses into mass graves were being seen for the first time by this audience." Persico, *Nuremberg: Infamy on Trial* (New York: Penguin, 1994), 143.

37. French author Georges Perec remarked, "This is what you see today, and the one thing we know is that this is not the way it was at the turn of the century but this is what is left for us to see and we have nothing to exhibit." Perec, with Robert Bober, *Ellis Island*, trans. Harry Mathews (New York: New Press, 1995), 47; see Christian Delage and Vincent Guigueno, "'Ce qui est donné à voir, ce que nous pouvons montrer': Georges Perec, Robert Bober et la Rue Vilin," *Études Photographiques* 3 (November 1997): 121–40.

38. Read the useful clarification by Bernard Genton, "'A Sea of Shoes . . .': La perception de la Shoah aux États-Unis (1941–1945)," *Sources* 6 (Spring 1999): 99–136.

39. Another film document made by the Germans was shown on February 22, 1946. This one featured a series of photographs taken at the sites of various crimes, filmed with a caption stand and turned into an evidentiary document (USSR-442) to be shown at trial.

40. A copy of this film, as well as the description of its contents made for the trial (Document CCCLIX-1, incomplete), can be found at the Centre de Documentation Juive Contemporaine housed at the Mémorial de la Shoah (Paris, France). The title of the film as cited by Colonel Smirnov (*The Atrocities by the German Fascist Aggressors in the USSR*) is different from the original, mentioned correctly in CCCLIX-1. The Soviets also presented a film called *Destruction of Lidice* (USSR-370) on February 22, 1946.

41. Telford Taylor, *The Anatomy of the Nuremberg Trials: A Personal Memoir* (1949; Boston; Little, Brown, 1992), 316. *Editor's note*: While the reference to Strock is correct, Taylor confuses the Austrian-born Wehrmacht major general *Artur* Gebauer with the SS Hauptsturmführer mentioned by Smirnov, *Fritz* Gebauer, commander of the Janowska camp in occupied Poland; see "Sixty-First Day, Monday, 18th February 1946," *Proceedings: 5 February 1946–19 February 1946*, vol. 7 of *Trials of the Major War Criminals Before the International Military Tribunal, Nuremberg 14 November 1945–1 October 1946* (Nuremberg, 1947), 548–59.

42. L. N. Smirnov, "Sixty-Second Day, Tuesday, 19th February 1946," *Proceedings*, vol. 7, 601.

43. Roman Rudenko, "Fifty-Fourth Day, Friday, 8 February 1946," *Proceedings*, vol. 7, 192–93. (*Editor's note*: Krakow, Warsaw, and Radom are now part of Poland; Lvov is in the Ukraine, and Lublin is in the Czech Republic.)

44. For a summary of the career of the Soviet Union's most famous reporter, read Dominique Chapuis and Patrick Barbéris, *Roman Karmen, une légende rouge* (Paris: Seuil, 2002). On the Soviet politics of film production (newsreels, documentaries, fictional movies during the war), see also Jay Leyda, "Test: 1941–1947," in *Kino: A History of Russian and Soviet Film* (1960; Princeton, N.J.: Princeton University Press, 1983), 365–97. Most of the prominent Soviet photographers and cameramen assigned by the Stalinist state to record the visual story of the Holocaust (with a marked tendency toward minimizing the Jewish identity of victims) happened to be Jewish; see David Shneer, *Through Soviet Jewish Eyes: Photography, War, and the Holocaust* (New Brunswick, N.J.: Rutgers University Press, 2011).

45. L. N. Smirnov, "Sixty-Second Day, Tuesday, 19 February 1946," *Proceedings*, vol. 7, 576. Smirnov will use the same terms in speaking of the extermination camps: "I pass on to the presentation of evidence on the camps of extermination, the so-called *Vernichtungslager*. Numerous proofs on this subject have already been presented to the Tribunal and therefore I shall limit myself to the presentation of evidence which is connected with the documentary films which are to be shown to the Tribunal today" (583).

46. See Stuart Liebman, "Les Premières constellations du discours sur l'Holocauste dans le cinéma polonais," in Antoine de Baecque and Christian Delage, eds., *De l'histoire au cinéma* (Paris: Complexe, 1998), 193–216; Stuart Liebman, "La Libération des camps vue par le cinéma: L'exemple de *Vernichtungslager Majdanek—Cmentarzysko Europy* d'Aleksander Ford (1944)," in Delage and Grynberg, "La Shoah: Images témoins, images preuves," 49–59; Stuart Liebman, "Les Premiers films sur la

Shoah: Les Juifs sous le signe de la Croix," "Les Écrans de la Shoah: La Shoah au regard du cinéma," special issue, *Revue d'Histoire de la Shoah* 195 (July–December 2011): 145–79.

47. Pierre Legendre, "Lortie à la rencontre de son image: Note sur la diffusion de l'enregistrement vidéo pendant le procès," in *Le Crime du caporal Lortie: Traité sur le père* (Paris: Fayard, 1989), 102.

48. Renaud Dulong, *Le Témoin oculaire: Les conditions sociales de l'attestation personnelle* (Paris: EHESS, 1998), 30.

49. "Kellogg to Ford, Nov. 20, 1945," 3, John Ford Papers, Manuscripts Department, Lilly Library (Bloomington, Indiana).

50. Bruce M. Stave and Michele Palmer, eds., with Leslie Frank, "The Courtroom's Architect. Dan Kiley: Architect of Palace of Justice Renovations," *Witnesses to Nuremberg: An Oral History of American Participants at the War Crimes Trial* (New York: Twayne, 1998), 15. An example of the integration of Kiley's work in the Nuremberg team is given in the document "War Crimes. Documentary Research Unit," n.d. (NARA, RG226, E99, B9, F8).

51. John Dos Passos, "Report from Nürnberg: Nazis Mope and Fidget in the Prisoners' Dock as They Hear Themselves Arraigned at Trial," *Life*, December 10, 1945, 29.

52. Stuart Schulberg mentions this decision in a short piece that appeared in 1946: "An Eyewitness Reports," *Hollywood Quarterly* 2 (July 1947): 413.

53. Joseph Kessel, "Nuremberg," *France-Soir*, December 3, 1945.

54. "Atrocity Films in Court Upset Nazis' Aplomb," *New York Herald Tribune*, November 30, 1945, 11.

55. Thomas J. Dodd, quoted in "Nazis on Trial See Horror Camp Film," *Washington Post*, November 30, 1945, 2.

56. Ilsen About, "Les Photographies du camp de concentration de Mauthausen: Approches pour une étude de l'iconographie photographique des camps de concentration," M.A. thesis, Université de Paris-VII, 1997, 89.

57. Yan Thomas, "La Vérité, le temps, le juge et l'historien," *Le Débat* 102 (November–December 1998): 22. For Geoffrey Robertson, Nuremberg successfully met this challenge: "Its charter defined crimes against humanity and its procedures proved by acceptable and credible evidence that such crimes had been instigated by some of the defendants. . . . When the prosecutor showed newsreels of Auschwitz and Belsen . . . the defendants, spot-lit for security in the dock, averted their eyes in horror from the ghastly screen images of the emaciated inmates of their concentration camps." Robertson, *Crimes Against Humanity: The Struggle for Global Justice* (New York: New Press, 2002), 231.

58. Dos Passos, "Report from Nürnberg," 30.

59. G. M. Gilbert, *Nuremberg Diary* (New York: Farrar, Straus, 1947), 4.

60. Gilbert, *Nuremberg Diary*, 46.

61. Edmund Jan Osmańczyk, *Dokumenty pruskie* (Warsaw: Czytelnik, 1947), 32–53. The author thanks Krystyna Prendowska for translating this Polish text.

62. Gilbert, *Nuremberg Diary*, 162.

63. Gilbert concluded his account of February 19 by quoting these few words of Hans Fritzsche: "I have had the feeling—of getting buried in a growing pile of filth—piling up week after week—up to my neck in it—and now—I am choking in it" (*Nuremberg Diary*, 164).

64. Gilbert, *Nuremberg Diary*, 162.

65. *Editor's note*: The Soviet Union secret police (NKVD) assassinated more than twenty thousand Poles in the Katyn Forest during April and May 1940; some eight thousand of these were from the Polish Officer Corps. The Duma, Russia's lower parliamentary house, finally officially recognized Stalin's responsibility for the Katyn massacre on November 26, 2010.

66. *Amtliches Material zum Massenmord von Katyn* (Berlin: Zentral Verlag der NSDAP, 1943).

67. Other films were shown during the Nuremberg Trial: on February 5, 1946, an excerpt of the French film *Forces occultes* (entered as evidentiary items RF 1152 and 1152b); on February 21, a piece entitled *Destruction of the Art and Museums of National Culture Perpetrated on the Territory of the USSR* (USSR-98); on May 3, a newsreel showing Hitler's return to Germany after the defeat of France; and on May 7, the Americans presented footage entitled *U.S. Army Film of Materials That Were Found in the Reichsbank Vaults, Taken in Frankfurt When the Allied Forces Captured That City* (US-845).

68. Siegfried Kracauer, *Theory of Film: The Redemption of Physical Reality* (1960; New York: Oxford University Press, 1997), 305–6 quoted and analyzed in Enzo Traverso, *Siegfried Kracauer: Itinéraire d'un intellectuel nomade*, rev. ed. (Paris: La Découverte, 2006), 177.

69. Telford Taylor, "Memorandum for Mr. Justice Jackson, and the Board of Review. Subject: Order of proof, use of witnesses, use of motion pictures and related subjects," November 3, 1945 (Jackson Papers, RHJ 111), 1. There is no written trace of internal debate by the judges of the IMT concerning the validity of using audiovisual evidence. Curiously it is only during the Eichmann trial that the jurists, some of whom had already participated in the Nuremberg Trials, discuss arguments for and against it.

70. Robert H. Jackson, *Justice Jackson's Story*, transcript of tape recording by Harlan B. Phillips, Oral History Research, Columbia University, 1952–1953, Jackson Papers, RHJ 190, 1259–60.

71. It seems excessive to say, as Gary Jonathan Bass does, that only after evoking "nightmarish reports from the liberation of Dachau and Belsen," were the Allies finally confronted "with some of the reality of the Holocaust, shocking them into including it in their trial plans as they had not in their military plans. This flush of empathy came long after America had settled on a legalistic policy, in October 1944."

Bass, *Stay the Hand of Vengeance: The Politics of War Crimes Tribunals* (Princeton, N.J.: Princeton University Press, 2000), 180.

72. *Elaboration* is employed here in the sense of "working through" (*Durcharbeiten* in German, *perlaboration* in French) analyzed by Freud, which can be understood as the process by which analysis integrates an interpretation and overcomes the resistance it creates. See Jean Laplanche and J.-B. Pontalis, *The Language of Psycho-Analysis*, 1967, trans. Donald Nicholson-Smith (London: Hogarth Press and Institute of Psycho-Analysis, 1973), 366.

Chapter 7. Catching the Enemy with Its Own Pictures

1. Telford Taylor, *The Anatomy of the Nuremberg Trials: A Personal Memoir* (Boston: Little, Brown, 1992), 150–51.

2. In their 1946 film on the Nuremberg Trial, the Soviets evoke this moment on a much more prosaic note: "Step by step, the prosecution reestablished in factual events the damning Nazi conspiracy against peace and humanity. The early stages of Nazism and the first SA's. Rudolf Hess seems to have forgotten everything. He suffers from memory loss. These images will help him, no doubt. That bestial ceremony, those nocturnal festivities, those demonstrations of force: ridiculous and pompous! Now Hess is remembering!" *Nuremberg Trials*, dir. C[arl] Svilov, prod. Roman Karmen, USSR, 1946.

3. Christian Gerlach sees the influence of the conspiracy theory at work here, particularly in the way Rudolf Höss and Dieter Wisliceny were questioned: "Investigations and judges tended to date certain phases as early as possible. The statements themselves both reinforced and reflected prevailing notions of the decision-making process in, and the political structure of, the Nazi regime." Gerlach, "The Eichmann Interrogations in Holocaust Historiography," *Holocaust and Genocide Studies* 15, no. 3 (2001): 429.

4. Regardless of the authors reviled, these images could not help but shock the German population. Hitler let Goebbels know that he had not found this mise-en-scène very appropriate and the document was never shown again. It was better to take the symbolic power of the book and use it to make Nazi thought sacred, which is what the propaganda did in the twenty-five-minute film, *Das Buch der Deutschen ("Mein Kampf")* (NSDAP, 1936).

5. The footage of this meeting is incorrectly situated in 1941; see Christian Delage and Vincent Guigueno, "L'Actualité, la mémoire, l'histoire: Montoire, un événement médiatique?," *L'Historien et le film* (Paris: Gallimard, 2004), 131–58.

6. "Let the *enemy* prove to our soldiers the enormity of his cause—and the justness of ours," argued Capra. "Use the enemy's own films to expose their enslaving ends. Let our boys hear the Nazis and the Japs about their own claims of master-race crud—and our fighting men will *know* why they're in uniform." Frank Capra, *The Name Above the Title: An Autobiography* (1971; New York: Da Capo, 1997), 331, 332.

7. The list of Nazi personalities filmed in this series is included in Peter Bucher, *Wochenschauen und Dokumentarfilme, 1895–1950 im Bundesarchiv-Filmarchiv* (1984; Coblenz: Bundesarchiv, 2000).

8. Robert H. Jackson, opening speech, in "Second Day, Wednesday, 21 November 1945," *Proceedings: 14 November 1945–30 November 1945*, vol. 2 of *Trial of the Major War Criminals Before the International Military Tribunal. Nuremberg 14 November 1945–1 October 1946* (Nuremberg: IMT, 1947), 102.

9. *The Nazi Plan* (item 6), February 1933.

10. *The Nazi Plan* (item 10), April 1933. These initial actions against the Jews of Germany were brought up in France in a newsreel from *Pathé-Journal* dated April 5, 1933. Titled "Manifestation des anciens combattants juifs" (Jewish Veterans Protest), the news story allowed one to hear excerpts of speeches by several orators. One explained, "We constantly see Jews being arrested, paraded through the city in supposedly funny costumes, led to the prefect's office and then taken away in trucks. But taken away where? To so-called reprisal camps. None of this can be denied by Hitler's government, American consuls have written it down in their reports. It is not for some jingoistic purpose, for some nationalistic purpose that we are demonstrating, that we are fighting Hitler. We are distinguishing between two cultures: we are against Hitler's Germany, we are for Albert Einstein's Germany."

11. *The Nazi Plan* (item 12), May 10, 1933.

12. Ley was also a defendant but escaped trial by committing suicide in October 1945, just prior to the Nuremberg proceedings.

13. Ian Kershaw, *Hitler* (London: Longman, 1991), 96. See also Saul Friedländer, *Reflections of Nazism: An Essay on Kitsch and Death* (New York: Harper & Row, 1984); Norbert, *National Socialist Rule in Germany: The Führer State, 1933–1945*, trans. Simon B. Steyne (Cambridge, Mass.: Blackwell, 1993). The relatively minor presence of Goebbels, despite the fact that he appears frequently in German newsreels, can be explained by the job assigned him: to put Hitler's actions in a good light and, more generally, to ensure a system of two-pronged propaganda, one aimed at the Nazis and the other at the German populace.

14. Footage includes scenes from Nuremberg in 1927 (item 2); 5th Congress, 1933 (17); 6th Congress, 1934 (21); 7th Congress, 1935 (24); 8th Congress, 1936 (31); 9th Congress, 1937 (34); 10th Congress, 1938 (40).

15. There was not, however, any footage showing the invasion of France. This was probably done to avoid rubbing salt in the still fresh wounds of a member of the IMT prosecution. One can surmise that similar reasoning leads to the omission of the German-Soviet Non-Aggression Pact.

16. Philippe Burrin, "Charisma and Radicalism in the Nazi Regime," trans. Peter S. Rogers, in Henry Rousso, ed., *Nazism and Stalinism: History and Memory Compared*, trans. and ed. Richard J. Golsan (Lincoln: University of Nebraska Press, 2004), 56.

17. Burrin, "Charisma and Radicalism," 70. However, one must not forget that other trials would follow on the heels of Nuremberg's prosecution of the principal

Nazi war criminals. There were twelve in all, targeting doctors, judges, upper-echelon SS officers, and high-ranking civilian and military government officials.

18. Victor Klemperer, *The Language of the Third Reich: LTI, Lingua Tertii Imperii: A Philologist's Notebooks*, 1957, trans. Martin Brady (London: Athlone, 2006), 15–16.

19. Burrin writes, "There is no possible doubt about the significance of this threat: Hitler had in mind the physical extermination of the Jews." Philippe Burrin, *Hitler and the Jews: The Genesis of the Holocaust*, 1989, trans. Patsy Southgate (London: Edward Arnold, 1994), 62.

20. "War Crimes Film Procurement Project. Method of Procedure" (NARA, RG226, E148, B76, L1087). This document enumerates the full set of twelve charges approved and retained against the defendants. Although centered on the conspiracy, they refer several times to the plight of the Jews, either generally (point 8 concerns "The destruction of all resistance to the defendants' plans. Film on the destruction of the opposition—democrats, pacifists, Jews, Catholics, etc. would be important") or specifically (point 9: "The division of German citizenry into those having rights [Aryans] and those without [Jews]. Film reports on speeches dealing with the internal Jewish problem would be of value here"). Fiction films designed for commercial use are also considered useful examples: "A picture like *The Jew Suss*, for instance, . . . should be carefully viewed and recorded." (*Editor's note*: directed in 1940 by Veit Harlan, *The Jew Suss* was an anti-Semitic betrayal of its literary sources commissioned by Goebbels.)

21. Budd Schulberg, "The Celluloid Noose," *Screen Writer: A Publication of the Screen Writers' Guild, Inc.*, August 1946, 7–8.

22. An expurgated version was produced under the title *Verräter vor dem Volksgericht* (Betrayer of the People's Court, 1944–1945), of which a copy is available at the Bundesarchiv-Filmarchiv (call number 3179); see Johann Chapoutot, "The Nazi People's Court (1944) or the Failure of 'Total Justice,'" in Christian Delage and Peter Goodrich, eds., *The Scene of the Mass Crime: History, Film, and International Tribunals* (London: Routledge, 2012), 101–12.

23. Joel G. Sayre, "Letter from Nuremberg," *New Yorker*, December 1, 1945, 110. Born in 1900, Sayre was a journalist, scriptwriter, and novelist. After covering several phases of World War II, he was a special correspondent for the *New Yorker* in Germany in 1945. From this experience he wrote a book about a Jewish family living under the Third Reich, *The House Without a Roof* (New York: Farrar, Strauss, 1948).

24. *Editor's note*: In Malmédy on December 17, 1944, members of an SS Panzer division massacred eighty-four American prisoners of war.

25. Schulberg, "The Celluloid Noose," 14–15.

26. Speaking of the news item filmed at the Sporthalle in Munich, where Goebbels calls for total war, Olivier Lévy-Dumoulin shows through a small incident just how omnipresent the desire to control the film image is, even during live taping: "After a reverse shot of an enraptured audience, the film comes back to a low angle shot of the orator and then the furtive hand of someone near Goebbels appears and snatches

from the Reichminister's lectern the bottle of beer Goebbels had drunk to quench his thirst. This is an effect of unchecked authentication that the editing cannot erase for lack of another close shot of Goebbels at the moment he resumes his speech. This singular error shows the degree to which other *mises en abyme*, this cinema within cinema, are a result of a disposition that is well-defined, fully-embraced, even demanded." Dumoulin, "Et le *Reichsminister* inventa la réalité semaine après semaine (L'authenticité selon les *Deutsche Wochenschauen*)," in Sylvie Crogiez-Pétrequin, ed., *Dieu(x) et hommes: Histoire et iconographie des sociétés païennes et chrétiennes de l'Antiquité à nos jours* (Rouen: Publications des Universités de Rouen et du Havre, 2005), 670.

27. G. M. Gilbert, *Nuremberg Diary* (New York: Farrar, Straus, 1947), 68.

28. Henry Rousso with Philippe Petit, *The Haunting Past: History, Memory, and Justice in Contemporary France*, trans. Ralph Schoolcraft (1998; Philadelphia: University of Pennsylvania Press, 2002), 66.

29. Thus, as Taylor reports, Jackson one day asked a defendant, Schacht, "to confirm a declaration he had made privately in 1938, namely that he had fallen 'into criminal hands,' and then to name 'the criminals in question.' Schacht gave only the names Göring and von Ribbentrop, present in the dock, and Himmler, Bormann, and Heydrich. Who were dead or absent. He claimed he was unable to name any others. . . . Jackson lessened the effect of Schacht's response by producing several photographs showing Schacht in public with, among others, Bormann, Ley, Streicher, Frick, Goebbels, von Papen, Göring, and Hitler. Important officials like group photographs. The physical presence of Schacht in these documents did not prove he had been involved with any one of them in particular and Jackson's stratagem was at his own expense" (Taylor, *Anatomy of the Nuremberg Trials*, 388).

30. Donald Bloxham rightly observes that "Nuremberg was the theatre in which to create the full sweep of the Nazi drama." Bloxham, *Genocide on Trial: War Crimes Trials and the Formation of Holocaust History and Memory* (Oxford: Oxford University Press, 2001), 69.

31. "Cmdr. Kellogg to Justice Jackson, February 28, 1946" (Jackson Papers, RHJ 102).

Chapter 8. The Un-United Nations and the Ideal of a Universal Justice

1. "President Franklin D. Roosevelt Statement of War Crimes," White House press release, October 7, 1942, Washington, D.C.

2. "Declaration by United Nations Subscribing to the Principles of the Atlantic Charter," January 1, 1942, Washington, D.C.

3. On the role of Lester Cole in adapting Neumann and Than's proposal, see Vincent Lowy, "Les Premières images de fiction de la déportation: *None Shall Escape* (1944) d'André de Toth," *International Journal on Audio-Visual Testimony* 8 (June 2002): 7–30. Neumann and Than were nominated in 1945 for the Academy Award for Best Original Story; for more on these two actors, consult Mieczyslaw B. Biskupski,

Hollywood's War with Poland, 1939–1945 (Lexington: University Press of Kentucky, 2010), 111–18.

4. See Neal Gabler, *An Empire of Their Own: How the Jews Invented Hollywood* (New York: Anchor, 1989).

5. This information is culled from the file established on procedures for movie theater owners who were going to show the film. Especially helpful is "*None Shall Escape* Presages Film Trend: Timely Drama Pictures Post-War Trial" (Margaret Herrick Library, Los Angeles). Some of this information was made known to the press in the form of dispatches while the film was being made and when it came out; see two articles in the *New York Herald Tribune* (October 10, 1943, and April 2, 1944).

6. NBC said it was interested in showing all or part of the film, but this never occurred. "R. L. Morgan, Major, General Staff Corps Executive, Washington Branch, to Ted Mills, NBC Television, New York" (September 28, 1946), Jackson Papers (RHJ 102).

7. The film's subtitle was "A Report to the People of the United States on the Forthcoming Trial of International Criminals."

8. On October 22–23, 1941, after the assassination of German officers, including the Feldkommandant of Nantes, ninety-eight hostages (mostly communist militants) were executed at Mont-Valérien (in the western Paris suburb of Suresnes), Châteaubriant, Nantes, and at the camp of Souges (near Bordeaux).

9. Antoine Garapon reminds us that "the American imprint" on Nuremberg justice "is important, for it originates in a conception of law different from that of continental Europe. Law is not opposed to politics but can be an instrument of it; hence the idea of a strategic legalism rather than a clear-cut separation between law and diplomacy." Garapon, *Des Crimes qu'on ne peut ni punir ni pardonner: Pour une justice internationale* (Paris: Odile Jacob, 2002), 40; see also Peter Maguire, *Law and War: An American Story* (New York: Columbia University Press, 2000).

10. "Lt. Budd Schulberg, USNR, Project Supervisor, Cmdr. John Ford, USNR, Chief, Field Photo Branch, OSS, to Mr. Harry Cohn, Columbia St. Sudios, 4 August 1945" (NARA, RG226, E90, B12, F124).

11. See Diane Morel, "La Liberté est trop précieuse pour rester enfouie dans les livres d'histoire *M. Smith au Sénat*," "Le Cinéma face à l'histoire," special issue, *Vertigo* 16 (1997): 24–32.

12. The OSS shooting script for *That Justice Be Done* indicates, "Shot from Revolutionary War; shot from Civil War; shot from this war; series of courtroom shots; German people being shown exhibit of Nazi horrors." Commentary: "Public trial, equality before the law, the right of defendants to prepare their own defense—a trial so orderly, so thorough, so free from passion that no would-be martyrs will ever be able to point to themselves as victims of enemy lynch law—so that the guilt of the accused can be convincingly brought home to the German people who benefited from their crimes—that is the kind of justice we are setting up" (NARA, RG226, E90, B124, PO158).

13. Robert H. Jackson, "September 6, 1945," *Diary Kept by Robert H. Jackson, 27 April–10 November 1945*, Jackson Papers, RHJ 95.

14. The JAG efforts combined with Jackson's in making Lewis Allen's movie, *Sealed Verdict* (1948). The main character, Commander Lawson, belonged to the JAG office, and the opening sequence used excerpts from Jackson's filmed speech. The press file announced, "Film affords inside views of famed war crimes trials"; see the *New York Times* review, November 3, 1948.

15. Mark Osiel, *Mass Atrocity, Collective Memory, and the Law* (New Brunswick, N.J.: Transaction, 1997), 33–34.

16. No doubt to demonstrate that the sentence had been the object of deliberations and that it had taken time to reach a decision, the day and time of the verdict were indicated with great precision ("18 December 1943, 2340 hours"). After seeing the film in July 1945, Jackson wrote in his journal, "In the evening, substantially the entire staff attended a showing of the moving picture released by the Russian Government showing the Karkhov Trials, a very interesting exposition of the Russian method of proving a case by the defendants themselves" ("May 17, 1945," *Diary*).

17. Jackson Papers, RHJ 95.

18. According to our sources, neither the French nor the British had cameramen present at Nuremberg. In any case, neither the Service Cinématographique des Armées Françaises (now Établissement de Communication et de Production Audiovisuelle de la Défense) nor the Imperial War Museum film library hold specific materials on Nuremberg.

19. "Notes to the subject: Nuremberg trial picture, Carl Zuckmayer, 27 September 1948, to Pare Lorentz, CAD [Civil Affairs Division], War Dept., 292 Madison Avenue, New York City" (NARA, RG153, E135, B95). The film dossier, referred to hereafter as "NARA, Trial Film," can be found in files 527 and 528.

20. "*Nuremberg Trial.* Documentary Film. First Rough Draft. Treatment," 53 pp. (typed ms), in NARA, Trial Film.

21. These maps were based on those seen in the movie produced by Walt Disney and directed by Perce Pearce and James Algar, *Victory Through Air Power* (1943), an animated documentary extolling the merits of strategic aerial bombardments during the war (available as sixty-five-minute DVD under the title, *Walt Disney Treasures: On the Front Lines*).

22. "Nuremberg Trial Documentary Film, comments made by Mr. Rockwell, Chief Legal advisor, OMGUS" (NARA, Trial Film).

23. Osiel, *Mass Atrocity*, 91.

24. A sign of the confusion surrounding this project is that, in a letter dated December 16, 1946, to Ray Kellogg, James B. Donovan believes he is right when he tells Kellogg that Schulberg and Lorentz are in the process of leaving for Germany "to make a propaganda film on the trial," when in fact they were in Los Angeles and New York, respectively. "James B. Donovan, National Bureau of Casualty and Surety Underwriters, New York, to E. Ray Kellogg, 825 South Wooster Street, Los Angeles, December 16, 1946" (Jackson Papers, RHJ 102).

25. "*The Nuremberg Trial* (First Draft—Legal Script). Prepared by Stuart Schulberg for the Films and Theatre Section, Reorientation Branch, Civil Affairs Division, War Department. Approved by Pare Lorentz, Chief, Films and Theatre Section, 20 January 1947" (Jackson Papers, RHJ 115, 51 pp.).

26. "*The Nuremberg Trial* (First Draft—Legal Script)," 50–51.

27. "Nuremberg Judgment. Preliminary script, 7 January 1947," 70 pp. (NARA, Trial Film). Schulberg informed Lorentz of his critical reading of this new project on February 26, 1947: "I believe this script is at worst unproduceable and at best dull and repetitious." Lorentz then wrote a three-page memo on March 3, 1947, addressed to Col. R. B. McRae of the War Department in which he outlines and expands upon Schulberg's remarks.

28. "Claim Internal U.S. Army Snarl Let Reds Beat Yanks on Nuremberg Film," *Variety*, June 11, 1947. A review appearing on May 28, 1947, stated, "*Nuremberg Trials* is a grim if slightly disjointed Soviet newsreel-documentary version of the trial of top Nazi war criminals. U.S. exhibitors long have contended that documentaries must be topflight if [they are to be] able to serve as regular screen fare. This [film] hardly measures up to this classification. Furthermore, [it] gives the Russians too much credit for winning the war." The famous critic Bosley Crowther was less negative: "Except for an obvious partiality toward the Soviets among the prosecutors and a predominance of reference to the victimization of Russians during the war, the film might have been assembled by competent craftsmen of any of the Allies." Crowther, "Goering, with Swagger Lacking, in *Nuremberg Trials* at Stanley," *New York Times*, May 26, 1947.

29. "Robert H. Jackson to Honorable Kenneth C. Royall, Secretary of War, the Pentagon, Washington, D.C., October 21, 1948" (NARA, Trial Film).

30. The taking of Berlin alone cost the Red Army nearly 300,000 soldiers, equivalent to the number of American soldiers killed on the European and Japanese fronts from 1941 to 1945; see Pieter Lagrou, "Les Guerres, les morts et le deuil: Bilan chiffré de la Seconde Guerre mondiale," in Stéphane Audoin-Rouzeau et al., eds., *La Violence de guerre, 1914–1945: Approches comparées des deux conflits mondiaux* (Paris: Complexe, 2002), 313–27.

31. "Robert H. Jackson to Maj. Gen. Daniel Noce, Director, Civil Affairs Division, the Pentagon, Washington, D.C., November 17, 1947" (NARA, Trial Film).

32. With the probable exception of François de Menthon, notes Marrus, which he attributes to "the unease in postwar France and elsewhere on Jewish issues, and to distortions of the popular memory having to do with wartime collaboration and popular anti-Semitism." Michael Marrus, "The Holocaust at Nuremberg," *Yad Vashem Studies* 26 (1998): 16.

33. Recalling the November 26 toast made in the Russian's honor during a visit to Nuremberg that caused "a big stir," Telford Taylor writes in his memoirs, "For most of us, the role played by Wychinsky [*sic*] as prosecutor, during the infamous trials of the

Soviet purges of 1936–1938 which had resulted in the execution of thousands of political and military leaders, made him a fearsome character." Taylor, *The Anatomy of the Nuremberg Trials: A Personal Memoir* (Boston: Little, Brown, 1992), 211. *Editor's note*: Vyshinsky, Stalin's chief prosecutor for the infamous "Moscow Trials," also helped lead the Soviet legal team at Nuremberg.

34. Lorentz and Schulberg's film nevertheless evokes the Molotov-Ribbentrop Pact by calling the invasion of the USSR a "violation of the non-aggression pact." The Soviet documentary was hardly kind to the French. Speaking about the invasion of Western Europe, the film states, "For the Germans, it was a walk in the park. The Wehrmacht paraded about in Paris thanks to the incompetence of [successive French prime ministers Paul] Reynaud and [Édouard] Daladier."

35. *Editor's note*: Hjalmar Schacht, Franz von Papen, and Hans Fritzsche were acquitted. Nikitchenko also relented on Hess, eventually settling on a life sentence for fear that the former Nazi Deputy Führer would benefit from further clemency.

36. See the chapter, "Nuremberg: A Cold War Conflict of Interest," in Peter Maguire, *Law and War: An American Story* (New York: Columbia University Press, 2000), 203–34.

37. "Robert H. Jackson to Pare Lorentz, May 27, 1947" (NARA, Trial Film).

38. Nevertheless Stuart Schulberg notes that the Berlin release was delayed several months, until May 1949, given the likelihood "that 2,200,000 blockaded Berliners already had enough on their minds." S. Schulberg, "Nürnberg," *Information Bulletin: Magazine of U.S. Military Government in Germany* 164 (June 28, 1949): 9–12.

39. "Nuernberg Reaction to the Film *Nuernberg und seine Lehren*: A Survey of Audience Reaction," OMGUS Information Control Division Surveys Branch (NARA, B 147, F 5/233-2/6).

40. In the American film, the commentary stresses that "the greatest crime was against the Jews." Nazi leaders are accused of having committed "genocide," labeled a "crime against humanity." The adoption of these notions during the trial was far from unanimous, and they did not, as a matter of fact, appear in the judgment rendered. However, Hannah Arendt is correct in underscoring that "The notion that aggression is 'the supreme international crime' was silently abandoned when a number of men were sentenced to death who had never been convicted of a 'conspiracy' against peace." Arendt, *Eichmann in Jerusalem: A Report on the Banality of Evil* (New York: Viking, 1963), 120.

41. "Robert H. Jackson to Pare Lorentz, May 27, 1947" (NARA, Trial Film).

42. "George S. Eyster, Colonel, GSC, Deputy Chief, Public Information Service, Department of the Army, Washington, D.C., to Robert H. Jackson, The Supreme Court, 4 January 1949" (NARA, Trial Film).

43. "William Shirer to Justice Jackson, January 8, 1949" (NARA, Trial Film).

44. "Robert H. Jackson to Pare Lorentz, March 11, 1949" (NARA, Trial Film).

45. See "Remarks before a showing of the film *Nuremberg: Its Lesson for Today*," 6 pp. (NARA, Trial Film). It was finally this original version, with no modification other than its translation into English, that became the documentary's American edition. Recently restored, the film had a limited U.S. run in 2010; see A. O. Scott, "Rare Scenes Re-Emerge from Nuremberg Trials," *New York Times*, September 29, 2010, C6.

46. Leo T. Hurwitz, *Account of Career*, n.d. (1970s), 4 (Hurwitz Archives, GEH).

47. "Dialogue Sheets: *Native Land*," 1 (Hurwitz Archives, GEH).

48. "Joris Ivens to Leo T. Hurwitz, April 1, 1943" (Hurwitz Archives, GEH).

49. After seeing the film, Charles Chaplin proposed that it be shown to American soldiers in conjunction with *Shoulder Arms* (dir. Chaplin, 1918) so that they would "know why they fight," but Hurwitz refused. "Leo T. Hurwitz to William Morris, November 5, 1943" (Hurwitz Archives, GEH).

50. Among the organizations targeted were the Communist Party, KKK, Civil Rights Congress, Joint Anti-Fascist Refugee Committee, and Veterans of the Abraham Lincoln Brigade.

51. "Photo-Notes," special issue, *Official Publication of the Photo League*, January 1948, 1–2. Harking back to the history of the League, Rosenblum recalled how it had been able to give an honest rendering of the crisis that had struck the country in the 1930s: "Historians of the future will be grateful indeed to such League filmmakers as Hurwitz, Sidney Meyers, and Julian Roffman. The history of the Photo League is the history of its members. We have developed a tradition based on social realism because our members concern themselves deeply with the world they live in" (New York Public Library, special collections).

52. In a preparatory note to the film project, the tone was set: "What's the subject? What are we talking about? The subject is Fascism. Some men, white, protestant, are deemed privileged above others, Negroes, Jews, Mexicans, etc." (Hurwitz Archives, GEH).

53. Herb Tank, "Movies: *Strange Victory*," *Daily Worker*, September 27, 1948, 12.

54. Stanley Gontarski, "Barney Rosset's *Strange Victory*: Race Relations and Political Resistance in Postwar America," *Irish Journal of American Studies* 8 (1999): 61–77.

55. See Christian Delage and Vincent Guigueno, "Les Contraintes d'une expérience collective: *Nuit et Brouillard*," in *L'Historien et le film* (Paris: Gallimard, 2004), 59–78.

56. "Leo T. Hurwitz to Mr. Jacques Ledoux, Cinémathèque de Belgique, March 5, 1958" (Hurwitz Archives, GEH).

57. MoMA's film library catalogue presents Hurwitz's work in the following manner: "Its skillful pacing and complex weave of information combine in an effective tribute to the war's victims and in the threat to survival of art and memory posed by the postwar world of nuclear arms. So forceful is its view of the Cold War era, the film was apparently never released in Poland, and is only now being released in the U.S. for

the first time." Eileen Bowser, "The Museum and the Fury," in *Circulating Library Catalog* (New York: Museum of Modern Art, 1984), 134. Christian Delage helped organize a special showing of the movie at the Mémorial de la Shoah in France on March 2, 2005, thanks to the loan of a copy from the MoMA.

Chapter 9. Documentary Archives and Fictional Film Narratives

1. Natasha Fraser-Cavassoni, *Sam Spiegel* (New York: Simon & Schuster, 2003), 72.

2. The chief camera operator for *Citizen Kane*, Gregg Toland, was one of John Ford's main collaborators in the Field Photographic Branch.

3. Welles accepted all these conditions and even made himself finish a day early, in the hope that International Pictures would honor its commitment to assign him several movies afterward—which it did not.

4. Trivas first worked as a set designer, in particular for Alexis Granovsky's Jewish Theater. After directing several films in Berlin, one of which was set in the trenches of World War I (*Niemansland* [No Man's Land], 1931), Trivas emigrated to the United States in 1941 and became a scriptwriter.

5. *Editor's note*: Frank Capra was the uncredited director of *Your Job in Germany* and Theodor Geisel—later famous in the United States as the children's author Dr. Seuss—its uncredited screenwriter.

6. Michael Denning, *The Cultural Front: The Laboring of American Culture in the Twentieth Century* (New York: Verso, 1996), 376. See also, in an essay inspired by Welles's film, Siegfried Kracauer, "Hollywood's Terror Films: Do They Reflect an American State of Mind?," *Commentary* 2, no. 2 (1946): 132–36.

7. According to some, Nims cut thirty-two pages of the script written by Veiler prior to beginning the shoots. Whatever the case, Nims accepted the cuts Spiegel sought from Welles during the editing, which mostly concerned the opening sequence in South America.

8. Orson Welles and Peter Bogdanovich, *This Is Orson Welles*, ed. Jonathan Rosenbaum (New York: Da Capo, 1998), 187.

9. Welles had a personal and professional relationship with Roosevelt. In addition to the numerous speeches he wrote during the war, the director worked in the Armed Forces Radio Service, which earned him a letter of appreciation: "The War Department and the Navy Department express to Orson Welles their appreciation for patriotic service in recognition of outstanding devotion and distinguished performance rendered servicemen overseas in cooperation with the Armed Forces Radio Service" (Welles manuscripts, Manuscript Department, Lilly Library, Bloomington, Indiana; hereafter Welles Manuscripts).

10. Bernard Genton reports, "Kurt Weill wrote the music, well-known playwright and screenwriter Ben Hecht wrote the text, actors Paul Muni and Edward G. Robinson did the narration. This show, also performed in Washington, Philadelphia, Chicago,

Boston, and Los Angeles, reached a total of more than 100,000 people. But it was financed chiefly by the Bergson Group, which was linked to the Committee for a Jewish Army, a radical Zionist organization that was spurned in leading Jewish American circles. Genton, "'A Sea of Shoes . . .': La perception de la Shoah aux États-Unis (1941–1945)," *Sources* 6 (Spring 1999): 117. A film report on the show is included in the Paramount News of March 16, 1943 (seven mins., copy available at NARA).

11. Welles Manuscripts. Its U.S. release was May 25, 1946.

12. Writes Karr, "When the trial begins, it will not go too rapid although the court can review evidence before it is submitted so that the defendants cannot bring in extraneous material to take up time and becloud the issue" ("Madeline Karr to Orson Welles, October 1945," Welles Manuscripts).

13. Welles and Bogdanovich, *This Is Orson Welles*, 189.

14. See the chapter "*Citizen Kane*'s Anti-Fascist Newsreels" in Michael Denning, *The Cultural Front: The Laboring of American Culture in the Twentieth Century* (New York: Verso, 1996), 384–94.

15. *Editor's note*: The term *Werwolf* has multiple uses in the Nazi era; in this instance, it refers to a member of the unit loyal to Himmler that deliberately stayed behind enemy lines to engage in subversive attacks.

16. Falkenau was a subcamp belonging to the larger complex of the Flossenbürg concentration camp. A U.S. military tribunal sentenced twenty-five of the torturers from Flossenbürg and its satellites to the death penalty; see Christian Delage and Vincent Guigueno, "Samuel Fuller à Falkenau: L'événement fondateur," in *L'Historien et le film* (Paris: Gallimard, 2004), 46–58.

17. Isabelle Poudevigne, film editor for my film, *De Hollywood à Nuremberg: John Ford, Samuel Fuller, George Stevens* (dir. Christian Delage, 2012), has identified a number of splices that appear at the beginning of Fuller's film on Falkenau, and which reveal that he doubtless began editing it anew before changing his mind and deciding that it was best to leave it in its 1945 version.

18. The film, released in France on April 29, 1959, appeared in the United States as *Hitler's Executioners*.

19. *Tell Me, Sam* (dir. Emil Weiss, 1989).

20. The film was reedited and issued as a DVD in 2005 in its long version.

21. For an overall view of the "trial film" genre in connection with the Holocaust, see Hanno Loewy, "Zwischen *Judgment* und *Twilight*, Schulddiskurse, Holocaust und das Courtroom Drama," in Sven Kramer, ed., *Die Shoah im Bild* (Munich: Text + Kritik, 2003), 133–69.

22. The television project was an episode for the CBS series *Playhouse 90*, broadcast on April 16, 1959.

23. "Memorandum for Abby Mann from Telford Taylor. Re: Structural Elements and Background of the Nuremberg 'Subsequent' Trials," October 22, 1957 (Telford Taylor Papers, Arthur W. Diamond Law Library, Columbia University Law School, Series 9, Subseries 3, box 3, folder 64, hereafter TTP-CLS). The memo was drafted in

ten sections: "Courts, Prosecution Counsel, Defense Counsel, Administrative Staff, Simultaneous Interpretation, the Jail, Chain of Command, Foreign Delegations, Pictorial Background, Atmosphere."

24. "Benjamin B. Ferencz to Arnost Horlick[-Hochwald], January 10, 1961" (TTP-CLS, 9-3-4-76).

25. "Telford Taylor to Hon. Lucius Clay, United States Command, Berlin, APO 742, December 8, 1961" (TTP-CLS, 9-3-4-76).

26. Remarks reported by Hy Gardner, *Herald Tribune*, December 15, 1961.

27. Kramer confessed, "The film was totally rejected: it never did three cents' business in Germany. It played so many empty houses it just stopped." Donald Spoto, *Stanley Kramer: Film Maker* (New York: Putnam's Sons, 1978), 229.

28. At the time, the press emphasized the serious nature of the movie. For the *Times* (London), it was not the affective impact but the argumentative dimension that characterized it: "While it appeals, as it cannot help doing, to the emotions, [the film] is primarily a matter of intellectual argument—and the argument, of vital importance then, is still of vital importance today" (December 15, 1961). Bosley Crowther also lauds the work: "[Mann and Kramer] have cut through the specious arguments, the sentiments for mercy, and the reasonings for compromise, and have accomplished a fine dramatic statement of moral probity. They have used the motion picture to clarify and communicate a stirring, sobering message to the world." Crowther, "Judgment at Nuremberg," *New York Times*, December 20, 1961. In France, Louis Marcorelles alludes to the polemicist Julien Benda's *La Trahison des clercs*, playing off its original intent (a perceived intellectuals' betrayal) to call into question the "clerks" of the court, that is, the lawyers and judges. Marcorelles, "La Trahison des clercs," *Cahiers du Cinéma* 128 (February 1962): 46–50.

29. Kramer explains, "We took some measurements and carefully recreated [the courtroom] on the soundstage in Hollywood, although we finally had to scale down some of the dimensions for some of the camera movements" (Spoto, *Stanley Kramer*, 229).

30. As Annette Wieviorka recalls, however, it is true that at Birkenau "the term 'crematorium' designates installations in which gas chambers and crematoria are both present." Wieviorka, *Déportation et génocide: Entre la mémoire et l'oubli* (Paris: Plon, 1992), 53.

31. Judith E. Doneson, *The Holocaust in American Film*, 2nd ed. (Syracuse, N.Y.: Syracuse University Press, 2002), 99–100.

Chapter 10. Trials of the Present or the Past?

1. Tom Segev, *The Seventh Million: The Israelis and the Holocaust* (New York: Hill and Wang, 1993), 327. The youthfulness of the Israeli population is one of the first things that struck Telford Taylor, in Jerusalem for the trial as a special correspondent.

Taylor, "Adolf Eichmann's Third Life," *Spectator* 206 (April 21, 1961): 550, 552–53, 552. See also David Cesarini, *Eichmann: His Life and Crimes* (London: Heinemann, 2004); David Cesarini, *Becoming Eichmann: Rethinking the Life, Crimes, and Trial of a "Desk Murderer"* (Cambridge, Mass.: Da Capo, 2006); Henry Rousso, "Réflexions sur un procès historique," in *Juger Eichmann, Jérusalem, 1961*, ed. Henry Rousso (Paris: Mémorial de la Shoah, 2011), 8–27, http://www.ihtp.cnrs.fr/spip.php%3Farticle1111.html; Deborah Lipstadt, *The Eichmann Trial* (New York: Nextbook, Schocken, 2011); Claude Klein, *Le Cas Eichmann: Vu de Jérusalem* (Paris: Gallimard, 2012).

2. David Ben-Gurion, "The Eichmann Case as Seen by Ben-Gurion," *New York Times Magazine*, December 18, 1960, SM7.

3. Peter Kihss, "Eichmann Trial to Be Seen on TV," *New York Times*, November 14, 1960, 13.

4. Fruchtman was married to an Israeli, Hava Sternberg, the niece of Israeli Justice Minister Pinchas Rosen. Fruchtman and Sternberg met in 1952 while Fruchtman was working on the outskirts of Jerusalem for the production of *Salome: The Dance of the Seven Veils* (dir. William Dieterle, 1953).

5. Biroc and Hamilton were in fact members of George Stevens's Special Coverage Unit, created initially by Eisenhower to film the D-Day landings in Normandy; see *From Hollywood to Nuremberg: John Ford, Samuel Fuller, George Stevens* (written and directed by Christian Delage, 2012).

6. Murray Schumach, "Critics of the Motives Behind Films Based on Headlines Answered by Producer," *New York Times*, January 24, 1961.

7. Richard F. Shepard, "U.S. TV Networks Irked at Coverage of Eichmann Trial," *New York Times*, February 2, 1961, 45.

8. Moshe Landau (presiding judge), Benjamin Halevi (judge), and Yitzhak Raveh (judge), "The Trial of Adolf Eichmann: Recording of the Proceedings. Decision" (March 10, 1961). The Nizkor Project has made available the complete trial transcript compiled by Dr. Daniel Fraenkel of the Israel State Archives, http://www.nizkor.org/hweb/people/e/eichmann-adolf/transcripts/Sessions/decision-to-record.html.

9. John Henry Wigmore, *A Treatise on the System of Evidence in Trials at Common Law: Including the Statutes and Judicial Decisions of all Jurisdictions of the United States* (Boston: Little, Brown, 1904), 3:2377n3.

10. Macabee Dean, "Invisible Electronic Eye to Film Eichmann Trial," *Jerusalem Post*, March 12, 1961.

11. This technique is known as "mixing" ("Switch"), a delicate operation because done on the fly with no possibility of subsequent corrections. It was in fact impossible (and pointless) to record what each of the cameras was filming live because often, when camera operators know the director has chosen another feed for the Recorder, they take advantage of the break to adjust their visual frame and focus or even wait while a tape reel is changed.

12. "Forum & Questions—Thoughts" (Hurwitz Archives, GEH). Persona non grata in the film industry, Hurwitz turned to television, where he was active in its earliest days. He created the news and special events format and produced a sixty-minute talk show, *An Evening with Richard Rodgers*, for CBS.

13. Journalist Alvin Rosenfeld, observed, "A small number of the viewers seemed to be attracted by the novelty of television, Israel having no TV as yet. But the great majority were deadly serious and watched the proceedings with an almost eerie intensity. Some viewers were moved to tears as the indictment droned out the terrible statistics of death and destruction." Rosenfeld, *New York Herald Tribune*, April 12, 1961.

14. "Leo T. Hurwitz to Jack Gould" (n.d., Hurwitz Archives, GEH). Gould picks up Hurwitz's hint (though without mentioning Hurwitz by name) when he writes that the camera operators' work is "lively and competent overall." Jack Gould, "TV: Live Court Drama," *New York Times*, April 13, 1961, 71.

15. Leo T. Hurwitz, "Videotaping the Eichmann Trial" (January 4, 1962, Hurwitz Archives, GEH).

16. *La Gazette cinématographique* 11 (November 1935). The author thanks Priska Morrissey for pointing out this article.

17. *Editor's note*: In fall 1952 three members of a British family were murdered on French soil. Gaston Dominici, owner of a neighboring property, was controversially convicted after an investigation and trial that drew intense coverage in France and abroad.

18. Robert Badinter and Annette Wieviorka, interviewed by Jérôme Burtin, Béatrice Fleury-Vilatte, and Jacques Walter, "Justice, image, mémoire," *Questions de Communication* 1 (March 2002): 98. *Editor's note*: After the Liberation of France, Marshal Pétain was tried and convicted in 1945 under the Provisional Government of the French Republic. Though Pierre Laval had been named by Pétain to head his administration, the two had a difficult relationship, and Laval would testify against the former Vichy head of state.

19. The notorious "Butcher of Lyon," Klaus Barbie, was charged with crimes against humanity for his activities as regional Gestapo chief in southeastern France; he was convicted in 1987. Frenchman Paul Touvier, a mid-level member of the collaborationist *Milice* (militia police), was also brought to trial for crimes against humanity committed in the Lyon region; he was found guilty in 1994. His compatriot Maurice Papon was a high-ranking bureaucrat, tried for complicity in crimes against humanity occurring in his role in organizing deportations from Bordeaux; Papon was sentenced to ten years in prison.

20. Élisabeth Linden, *Rapport de la Commission d'enquête sur l'enregistrement et la diffusion des débats judiciaires* (Paris: Ministère de la Justice, February 2005).

21. "Law 85-699 of July 11, 1985, concerning the establishment of historical archives for the courts."

22. "Decree 86–74 of January 15, 1986, issued for the application of Law 85-699 of July 11, 1985, concerning the establishment of historical archives for the courts."

23. Badinter interviewed by Jérôme Burtin, Béatrice Fleury-Vilatte, and Jacques Walter, "Justice, image, mémoire," *Questions de Communication* 1 (March 2002): 99.

24. Garapon situates the significance of this opportunity in the following manner: "The notion of *accountability* [English in the original], which has no equivalent in our [France's] political vocabulary, is usually reduced either to its disciplinary aspect (and thus relates simply to the threat of deontological sanctions) or to its political version whereby a new name is given to the control that the political powers can exert over the nomination of judges—or demands for their reprimand. In a democracy where popular sentiment dictates the politics of its leaders, however, pictures confer a new meaning to the term: the former sense of 'to be accountable' (as in the instance of a financial 'accountant') is enriched with another one, that of being exposed to the public eye." Antoine Garapon, "Mise en images de la justice: À défis nouveaux, garanties nouvelles," *Images Documentaires* 54, 2nd trimester (2005): 88–89.

25. On the "sovereign" space of the halls of justice, see Katherine Fischer Taylor, *In the Theater of Criminal Justice: The Palais de Justice in Second Empire Paris* (Princeton, N.J.: Princeton University Press, 1993); Jean-Louis Halpérin, "La Visualisation des différentes procédures en Europe, XVIIIᵉ–XXᵉ siècles," "La Justice en images," special issue, *Sociétés & Représentations* 18 (October 2004): 63–73.

26. Yan Thomas, "La Vérité, le temps, le juge et l'historien," *Le Débat* 102 (November–December 1998): 25, 29.

27. David Schreiber, "Histoire, justice et télévision: *Le Procès Barbie* sur la chaîne *Histoire*," in Christian Delage and Anne Grynberg, eds., "La Shoah: Images témoins, images preuves," special issue, *Cahiers du Judaïsme* 15 (2003): 102.

28. Inaugurated in France by the prominent cable channel Canal+, this system of multiple rebroadcasts allows one to see a prerecorded presentation of a program that occurred live or to catch up, out of sequential order, on an episode one missed. Fans of a particular television series now go back and forth constantly among a variety of viewing contexts: a chance viewing of the original broadcast, a home-recorded version, or not-yet-broadcast episodes downloaded in order to know before the designated day what is going to happen.

29. Another step facilitating consultation of these materials recently occurred in France with the production of a DVD box set about the Barbie trial, composed of edited footage from the archives. *Le Procès Barbie: Lyon, 11 mai/4 juillet 1987*, six DVDs (Paris: Arte Éditions, 2011).

Chapter 11. Hearings on Film, Film in Hearings

1. Saguez has worked in a variety of formats. He directed former newscaster Christine Ockrent's show *France Europe Express* on France 3 and *Le Forum des euro-*

péens on the Franco-German station Arte, as well as programming featuring major news coverage (*24 heures*), music (*Rapido,* with Antoine de Caunes), and literature (Jean-Michel Mariou, *Mais qu'est-ce qu'elle dit, Zazie?*). He also dreamed up Arte's well-known nightly going-off-air credits depicting sheep to be counted.

2. "Cahier des clauses administratives particulières, janvier 1994," Ministère de la Justice, Direction de l'administration générale et de l'équipement (Archives Guy Saguez). Article 3 specifies that a magistrate representing the Ministry of Justice be designated "to monitor that the proper course of operations is followed." His mission is "to verify that the present set of specifications, the above-named clauses, and the application of the agreed-upon recording methods are all respected, under the presiding judge's supervision, in concert with the director. It will be his responsibility to advise the director throughout and to serve as liaison with the session's presiding judge."

3. Andrée Chauleur, "La Constitution d'archives audiovisuelles de la justice: Législation et premiers enregistrements, 1985–1995," in *Mettre l'homme au cœur de la justice: Hommage à André Braunschweig* (Paris: Association Française pour l'Histoire de la Justice, Litec, 1997), 185–216.

4. Saguez also requested permission to focus on the table intended for evidentiary exhibits.

5. Guy Saguez, "Notes de tournage, 16 mars–23 avril 1994" (Archives Guy Saguez).

6. "'Une Filmation' pour l'histoire," *Ouest-France*, April 21, 1994.

7. *Editor's note*: In 1991 journalist Anne-Marie Casteret established that France's national blood bank (Centre National de Transfusion Sanguine) had knowingly distributed HIV-contaminated samples to hemophiliacs in 1984–85, as a result of which some two thousand people contracted the disease. While former socialist government ministers Laurent Fabius, Georgina Dufoix, and Edmond Hervé were cleared of charges of involuntary manslaughter, Drs. Michel Garretta, Jean-Pierre Allain, Jacques Roux, and Robert Netter were convicted of a variety of offenses. In 2012 Fabius was named minister of foreign affairs in President François Hollande's administration.

8. This is not the case outside the courtroom, where the press is free to film the arrival of the trial's main parties and record their statements. During the Touvier trial, the Association for the Sons and Daughters of the Deported Jews of France used the Palace of Justice steps as a platform for communicating their activist messages. On the machinations of the press and some of the trial's participants, see Rafaël Lewandowski's subtle documentary, *Audiences: Des journalistes au procès Papon* (Hearings: Journalists at the Papon trial, 2000).

9. Michel Thénard, "Caméra témoin," *Libération*, February 2, 2005.

10. Mark Osiel, *Mass Atrocity, Collective Memory, and the Law* (New Brunswick, N.J.: Transaction, 1997), 41–48.

11. See Andrea Lollini, "Le Rôle (pré)constituant de la Commission vérité et réconciliation," Ph.D. diss., École des Hautes Études en Sciences Sociales, Paris, 2003;

Barbara Cassin, Olivier Cayla, and Philippe-Joseph Salazar, eds., *Vérité, réconcilia-tion, réparation*, Le Genre Humain (Paris: Seuil, 2004).

12. See Claudia Feld, "La Télévision comme 'scène de la mémoire': Les images du *Procès des dictateurs argentins*," in Gilles Delavaud, ed., *Télévision: La part de l'art* (Paris: L'Harmattan, 2002), 171–86.

13. The proceedings of the International Criminal Court are filmed. Live audio and video feeds issue from the courtrooms, including broadcasts in translation, with a thirty-minute deferred video link accessed from each table in the hot-desk area. Broadcast-quality videos can be freely used by members of the press, who may quote or excerpt the most relevant proceedings.

14. An extraordinary example occurred in 1960. The Central Committee of the Romanian Communist Party produced a movie called *Reconstitution*, in which a group that had been arrested by the regime's secret police (the Securitate) and accused of rob-bing the national bank performed a filmed reenactment of the holdup. The individuals in question cooperated in the hopes of winning clemency from the court, but the five men (all Jewish and communist) were condemned to death and executed, and the one woman assigned to forced labor. See *L'Incroyable hold-up de la banque communiste* (The Incredible Holdup of the Communist Bank, dir. Alexandru Solomon, 2005).

15. Pierre Legendre, *Le Crime du caporal Lortie: Traité sur le père* (Paris: Fayard, 1989), 101.

16. Patricia Tourancheau, "Kamel ben Salah détourne les yeux," *Libération*, March 27, 2002. The novelty here was the use of animation. On crime scene photography (whose history is, of course, much longer), consult Luc Sante, *Evidence: NYPD Crime Scene Photographs, 1914–1918* (New York: Farrar, Straus and Giroux, 1992); Sandra S. Phillips, Carol Squiers, and Mark Haworth-Booth, *Police Pictures: The Photograph as Evidence* (San Francisco: Chronicle, 1997).

17. Jean-Michel Dumay, "Sévère réquisitoire contre le policier impliqué dans l'interpellation de Ris-Orangis," *Le Monde*, September 28, 2000. The Rodney King case (March 3, 1991) remains emblematic in the mediatization of filmed images as evidence in trials opposing ordinary citizens and the members of the police force. Consult Frank P. Tomasulo, "I'll See It When I Believe It: Rodney King and the Prison-House of Video," in Vivian Sobchack, ed., *The Persistence of History: Cinema, Television and the Modern Event* (New York: Routledge, 1996), 69–88. See also the documentary films *The Rodney King Case: What the Jury Saw in California v. Powell* (dir. Dominic Palumbo, 1992); *The Rodney King Incident: Race and Justice in America* (dir. Michael Pack, 1998).

18. See Michael Da Silva, "*The 10th District Court: Moments of Trials*," online movie review, http://sensesofcinema.com/2010/cteq/the-10th-district-court-moments -of-trials/.

19. Raymond Depardon, with Jacques Mandelbaum, "Images d'exception d'une justice ordinaire," *Le Monde*, May 16, 2004, 20.

20. The program has been limited to the courtrooms of two figures from the ju-diciary's upper spheres, the lord chief justice and the master of rolls. As Élisabeth Lin-

den notes, "Ministers, judges, and jurists will watch screenings of trials in their entirety before reaching a determination about allowing a more widespread use of this experience." Linden, "Annexes," in *Rapport de la Commission d'enquête sur l'enregistrement et la diffusion des débats judiciaires* (Paris: Ministère de la Justice, 2005), 10.

21. Sheriff Noel McPartlin lectured on his experience in Scotland at a conference organized in 2003 by the Institut des Hautes Études sur la Justice, whose website provides further information on the Images and Representations research group, http://www.ihej.org/programmes/images-et-representations-de-la-justice/.

22. Raymond Fielding, *The American Newsreel, 1911–1967* (Norman: University of Oklahoma Press, 1972), 211.

23. General Council of the Bar (England and Wales) Public Affairs Committee, *Televising the Courts: Report of a Working Party of the Public Affairs Committee of the General Council of the Bar* (1989); see also Paul Mason, *The Impact of Electronic Media Coverage of Court Proceedings at the International Criminal Tribunal for the Former Yugoslavia* (The Hague: Centre for Media and Justice, 2000).

24. Claudine Mulard, "États-Unis: Justice en direct," *Le Monde*, August 18, 1991. Steven Brill, founder of the judicial publisher American Lawyer Media, created Court TV in association with Time-Warner, NBC, and Cablevision.

25. Sylvie Kauffmann, "Le Procès O. J. Simpson, miroir de l'Amérique," *Le Monde*, July 12, 1995. More recently, in the 2005 California trial of Michael Jackson (accused principally—and acquitted—of molesting a minor), the judge forbade any filming to protect the proceedings from media pandemonium. The E! Channel responded by contriving daily reenactments of the key occurrences, selecting actors—especially where Jackson's role was concerned—based on their resemblance to the trial protagonists.

26. New York State Committee to Review Audio-Visual Coverage of Court Proceedings [NYSC], *An Open Courtroom: Cameras in New York Courts* (New York: Fordham University Press, 1997).

27. A notable departure from this pattern is the state of New York, which has, in fact, taken deliberate steps in this direction. Where two types of preliminary hearing are concerned, permission to film requires the accused's approval: "Under Section 218 of the Judiciary Law, neither arraignments nor suppression hearings may be covered by cameras unless the defendant consents to the coverage. Of the thirty-seven states which permit camera coverage in criminal proceedings without the consent of the defendant at trial, it appears that New York is the only one to explicitly limit coverage of arraignments" (NYSC, *An Open Courtroom*, 81).

28. NYSC, *An Open Courtroom*, 69.

Chapter 12. The Face of History

1. See *Nuremberg: The Nazis Facing Their Crimes* (dir. Delage, 2007), DVD (Lionsgate).

2. Marie-Claude Vaillant-Couturier, in *The Memory of Justice* (dir. Marcel Ophuls, 1976).

3. Hurwitz edited *The Museum and the Fury* during a seminar bringing together Israeli filmmakers and writers in Tel-Aviv in late April 1961.

4. "Leo T. Hurwitz to Tom Hurwitz, Wednesday, March 22, 1961" (Hurwitz Archives, GEH).

5. See Annette Wieviorka, *The Era of the Witness*, 1998, trans. Jared Stark (Ithaca, N.Y.: Cornell University Press, 2006).

6. Robert H. Jackson, preface to Charles W. Alexander (photographs) and Anne Keeshan (text), *Justice at Nuernberg: A Pictorial Record of the Trial of Nazi War Criminals by the International Military Tribunal, at Nuernberg, Germany, 1945–46* (Chicago: Marvel Press, 1946). Alexander was the director of photography for the Nuremberg Trial.

7. In the days before the trial, Yad Vashem published a few of the written documents that could demonstrate Eichmann's guilt, insisting on positivistic, self-explanatory nature ("The document speaks for itself") in a manner similar to that employed by Jackson's team. "Towards the Eichmann Trial," special issue, *Yad Vashem Bulletin* 10 (April 1961).

8. *Eichmann par Eichmann*, ed. Pierre Joffroy and Karin Königseder, preface by Avner W. Less, postface by Joffroy (Paris: Grasset, 1970). Since the Jerusalem District Court applied common law principles to its proceedings, Eichmann was heard as a witness during the trial, and excerpts from his deposition with Less were read in court.

9. Gideon Hausner, *Justice in Jerusalem* (New York: Holocaust Library, Schocken, 1962), 292–93. Claude Lanzmann was motivated by the same aims when he directed *Shoah* (1985); see Michel Deguy, ed., *Au sujet de* Shoah: *Le film de Claude Lanzmann* (Paris: Belin, 1990).

10. Robert S. Bird, "Portrait of a Courtroom: Horror Brings a Stillness," *New York Times*, April 30, 1961. According to Jacob Robinson, eighty-five thousand people attended the 121 sessions of the trial. A minority of those would have attended more than once, but one may safely assume that overall the audience changed from day to day, with spectators coming not just from Jerusalem but from all over the country and beyond. Robinson, *And the Crooked Shall Be Made Straight: The Eichmann Trial, the Jewish Catastrophe, and Harrah Arendt's Narrative* (New York: Macmillan, 1965), 137.

11. Mulisch wryly notes, "The image of Satan that the press had created out of Eichmann in the last few months can be more easily approached theologically than psychologically. . . . But with Eichmann the theological effect has disappeared with his apparition. He turns out to be human: a somewhat grubby man with a cold, wearing glasses." Harry Mulisch, *Criminal Case 40/61: The Trial of Adolf Eichmann: An Eyewitness Account*, trans. Robert Naborn (Philadelphia: University of Pennsylvania Press, 2005), 36–37.

12. Mulisch, *Criminal Case 40/61*, 36–37.

13. Jacob Robinson, "Some Basic Ideas with Regard to the Appearance of a Jewish Witness at the International Military Tribunal," September 5, 1945 (Records of the World Jewish Congress, Jacob Rader Marcus Center of the American Jewish Archives, Cincinnati, Ohio). *Editor's note:* After violent clashes erupted in 1936 between Arabs and Jews in Palestine, the British Peel Commission sought to understand the causes and recommend a solution; Chaim Weizmann spoke on behalf of the Jewish population.

14. Telford Taylor, "The Faces of Justice in Jerusalem," *Spectator* 208 (January 5, 1962): 10.

15. Michael Walzer, "The Memory of Justice," *New Republic*, October 9, 1976, 22.

16. Taylor published a book in 1970 in which he voiced the opinion that the American crimes committed in Vietnam should be subject to judicial judgments inspired by the principles of Nuremberg. Telford Taylor, *Nuremberg and Vietnam: An American Tragedy* (Chicago: Quadrangle, 1970). The accusation that he pays more attention to the butchers than the victims has little basis, however; he had just coedited with Alan Dershowitz a collection entitled *Courts of Terror: Soviet Criminal Justice and Jewish Emigration* (New York: Knopf, 1976).

17. Walzer, "The Memory of Justice," 22.

18. Walzer, "The Memory of Justice," 22.

19. "Marcel Ophuls to Mr. Julius Schatz, Director, American Jewish Congress, October 28th, 1976" (TTP-CLS 9-3-5-100).

20. "Telford Taylor to Mr. Michael Walzer, November 19, 1976" (TTP-CLS 9-3-5-100).

21. Walzer, "The Memory of Justice," 22.

22. Tom Segev, *The Seventh Million: The Israelis and the Holocaust*, trans. Haim Watzman (New York: Hill and Wang, 1993), 356. An example confirming this tendency is the short documentary *Verdict for Tomorrow* (dir. Hurwitz, 1961), produced by Capital Cities toward the end of the trial but edited in Albany by Robert Braveman using video filmed by Hurwitz (who received a contract on November 3, 1961, informing him that he was a "consultant" on this movie). A quick examination establishes that witnesses are featured scarcely 15 percent of the time in this twenty-eight-minute motion picture. The host of the program (broadcast by the Anti-Defamation League) was Lowell Thomas, who bracketed trial footage with clips filmed in Germany of Kristallnacht that he himself had narrated at the time for Twentieth Century Fox Movietone Newsreels. See Lawrence Douglas, "Trial as Documentary: Images of Eichmann," in Dagmar Herzog, ed., *Lessons and Legacies*, vol. 7, *The Holocaust in International Perspective* (Evanston, Ill.: Northwestern University Press, 2006), 369–84.

23. This is true as well of the historians who were called to testify. At Nuremberg their interventions were pretrial in the capacity of expert witness, whereas in Jerusalem the first to appear was Salo Baron, who failed to convince Taylor of his judicial relevance: "The enormously erudite Dr. Salo Baron . . . lectured for several hours on

Jewish demography (urbanization and population movements), characteristics (adaptability and cohesiveness), and social organization in the various countries occupied by the Germans. . . . All this was most enlightening, but had little enough to do with the guilt or innocence of Adolf Eichmann." Telford Taylor, "Mirror, Mirror, on the Wall," *Spectator* 206 (May 19, 1961): 706, 708.

24. Rousso notes that, of the 111 people called to testify as witnesses in the Barbie trial, twenty-nine appeared for "general interest" testimony, while those giving depositions as direct victims (or relatives of victims) numbered eighty-two (forty-three survivors, twenty-six former members of the Resistance, and thirteen eyewitnesses). Henry Rousso, "Vichy, Crimes against Humanity, and the Trials for Memory," lecture, University of Texas at Austin, September 11, 2003. Slightly displacing the emphasis, Marie-Bénédicte Dembour and Emily Haslam speak instead of "victim-witnesses." Dembour and Haslam, "Silencing Hearings? Victim-Witnesses at War Crimes Trials," *European Journal of International Law* 15, no. 1 (2004): 151–77.

25. See Christian Delage and Vincent Guigueno, "Le Film dans le parcours muséographique," *L'Historien et le film* (Paris: Gallimard, 2004), 159–69. The film was installed at the end of the visit, along with one of the other three, *Avec les enfants?* (With the Children?), which presents the fate of the Jewish children deported from France. Questions directed at young visitors to the Izieu exhibit reveal that the shot in which we are confronted with Barbie's image in court makes a most striking impression on them. Pierre-Jérôme Biscarrat, lecture, March 2005, Musée d'Art et d'Histoire du Judaïsme, on view in the Médiathèque de la Maison d'Izieu.

26. Barbie trial, 13th day, May 27, 1987.

27. Frank Horvat, "Entretien avec Marc Riboud," in *Entre Vues* (Paris: Nathan, 1990), horvatland.com/pages/entrevues/09-riboud-fr_en.htm.

28. In addition to the Izieu roundup, Barbie was also being called to account for the roundup at the offices of the Union Générale des Israélites de France (February 9, 1943) and the last convoy out of Lyon (August 11, 1944), in which six hundred people (for the most part Jews and members of the Resistance) were deported to Auschwitz.

29. The text of Barbie's memorandum reads, "An end was put this morning to the activities of the children's summer camp at Izieu-Ain. In all, forty-one children from the ages of three to thirteen were arrested, along with five adults. Neither cash nor objects of value were found. On April 7, 1944, they will be transferred to Drancy [a French internment camp in Paris's northeastern suburbs]."

30. Barbie trial, 13th day.

31. François Hartog, "Le Témoin et l'historien," *Gradhiva* 27 (2000): 14.

Chapter 13. The Spectator's Place

1. Robert S. Bird, "Israel Restricts Display of Eichmann's Horrors," *International Herald Tribune*, April 16, 1961.

2. In spite of the procedural changes, the psychologist Capt. Gilbert did make the trip to Jerusalem in order to present a summary of his analytical observations of the Nuremberg defendants (discussed in Chapter 6).

3. The footage shown included Resnais's *Night and Fog* (1955), with English subtitles. During the screening, Hurwitz filmed Eichmann watching the movie (see *Eichmann Trial—Session 70—Screening of films*, story RG-60.2100*84, tape 2084, http://resources.ushmm.org/film/display/detail.php?file_num=2297&clip_id=72B9B7D4-9184-461E-A102-1DB48EA1E55A). On Resnais's documentary, read Christian Delage, "Alain Resnais's *Night and Fog*: A Turning Point in the History of the Holocaust in France," in Dagmar Herzog, ed., *Lessons and Legacies*, vol. 7, *The Holocaust in International Perspective* (Evanston, Ill.: Northwestern University Press, 2006), 352–68.

4. Faced with the dilemma of how to cull a segment from this edited work, Hausner explained that he preferred not to show the movie in its entirety "because it adopts a moralizing tone in order to arrive at certain conclusions and clearly it would not be proper for us to ask the Court to view all of it." For the introduction of this telefilm, see http://www.nizkor.org/hweb/people/e/eichmann-adolf/transcripts/Sessions/Session-054-06.html.

5. Haïm Gouri, *Facing the Glass Booth: The Jerusalem Trial of Adolf Eichmann*, trans. Michael Swirsky (Detroit: Wayne State University Press, 2004), 134–35. *Editor's note*: Headed by police commander Avraham Selinger, Israel's Section 06 (more commonly known as Bureau 06) was created specifically to investigate and prepare the prosecution of Eichmann.

6. Brauman and Sivan should be commended for their reconstitution of this archive. Rony Brauman and Éyal Sivan, *Éloge de la désobéissance: À propos d'un "spécialiste," Adolf Eichmann* (Paris: Le Pommier, 1999), 41–47. For an extremely critical perspective on Brauman and Sivan's work, consult the remarks made by the former director of the Steven Spielberg Jewish Film Archive, Stewart Tryster, as reported in *Ha'aretz*, January 31, 2005. Tryster provided us with a copy of a lecture he presented at the Berlin conference organized by Ronny Loewy in January 2005 at the Deutsches Historisches Museum. Tryster, "We Have Ways of Making You Believe: The Eichmann Trial as Seen in *The Specialist*." See also Christian Delage, "*Un Spécialiste*, de Rony Brauman et Éyal Sivan," *Esprit*, May 1999, 185–90; Stuart Liebman, "If This Be a Man . . . Eichmann on Trial in *The Specialist*," *Cineaste* 27, no. 2 (2002): 40–42.

7. Brauman and Sivan, *Éloge de la désobéissance*, 100.

8. Pierre Joffroy, in *Eichmann par Eichmann*, ed. Pierre Joffroy and Karin Königseder, preface by Avner W. Less, postface by Joffroy (Paris: Grasset, 1970), 445.

9. Homer Bigart, "Eichmann Is Unmoved in Court as Judges Pale at Death Films," *New York Times*, June 9, 1961, 16.

10. For a comparison of the two trials, see Michael Patrick Murray, "A Study in Public International Law: Comparing the Trial of Adolf Eichmann in Jerusalem with the Trial of the Major German War Criminals at Nuremberg," J.S.D. thesis, George Washington University, 1973.

11. Of the 113 witnesses called by the prosecution, forty-eight appear in *A Specialist*, forty of whom are shown in the five-minute stretch preceding Abba Kovner's remarks.

12. See Antoine Garapon and Joël Hubrecht, "La Justice pénale internationale entre la balance et le sablier: Réflexions sur le procès Milosevic," *Esprit* 7 (July 2002): 33.

13. Ferdinand Nahimana (founder and former director of Radio-télévision libre des Mille collines [Thousand Hills Free Radio-Television, or RTLM]), Jean-Bosco Barayagwiza (another founding member of RTLM), and Hassan Ngeze (editor in chief of the extremist journal *Kangura* [Wake Others Up]) were indicted in 2003 for "genocide, conspiracy, and incitation to commit genocide, and crimes against humanity." The ICTR condemned Nahimana and Ngeze to life in prison and Barayagwiza to thirty-five years in prison in what are often referred to as the "Media Trial of Hate."

14. A "Special United Nations Report" on this topic published in 1992 concluded that "the rumors and disinformation are not only widespread but also constitute a crucial element of the current situation in the former Yugoslavia, contributing substantially to stirring up ethnic hatred and spurring a desire for revenge which is one of the principal causes of the atrocities committed." See also Tim Allen and Jean Seaton, eds., *The Media of Conflict: War Reporting and Representations of Ethnic Violence* (New York: Zed, 1999); Philip Hammond and Edward S. Herman, eds., *Degraded Capability: The Media and the Kosovo Crisis* (London: Pluto Press, 2000).

15. "Transcript, Tuesday, February 12, 2002," in *Milošević, Slobodan (IT-02-54): Kosovo, Croatia and Bosnia* (The Hague: ICTY), 10.

16. Del Ponte, Nov. 22, 2001, The Hague.

17. Geoffrey Nice, "Transcript, Tuesday, February 12, 2002," in *Milošević, Slobodan*, 18, 20–21.

18. Nice, "Transcript, Tuesday, February 12, 2002," in *Milošević, Slobodan*, 26.

19. Some other protagonists were shown as well, such as the Serbian paramilitary leader Arkan, the former president of the Republic of Serbian Krajina Goran Hadzic, and various officers of the Yugoslav National Army.

20. Milosevic, "Transcript, Thursday, February 14, 2002," in *Milošević, Slobodan*, 225.

21. *Es begann mit einer Lüge*, quoted in "Transcript, Thursday, February 14, 2002," in *Milošević, Slobodan*, 226.

22. Joël Hubrecht, "Procès Milosevic: Regard sur un 'interminable' procès," www.ihej.org. *Editor's note*: Indicted for war crimes by the ICTY, Radovan Karadzic is, of course, the Bosnian Serb politician captured in 2008, while Vojislav Seselj, founder of the Serbian Radical Party, transformed his ICTY trial for war crimes into a lengthy saga.

23. Antoine Garapon, "Mise en images de la justice: À défis nouveaux, garanties nouvelles," *Images Documentaires* 54, 2nd trimester (2005): 75. See also Joël Hubrecht, "Le Procès Milosevic: Une communication 'virtuelle,'" *Esprit* 6 (June 2004): 37. On the filming of the trial, see Paul Mason, *The Impact of Electronic Media Coverage of Court Proceedings at the International Criminal Tribunal for the Former Yugoslavia* (The Hague: Centre for Media and Justice, 2000).

24. Sylvie Matton, *Srebrenica: Un génocide annoncé* (Paris: Flammarion, 2005), 384.

25. "Transcript, Wednesday, June 1, 2005," in *Milošević, Slobodan*, 40, 278–79.

26. According to the director of the Humanitarian Law Center, Natasa Kandic, the Scorpions operated beginning in 1991–92 as a unit of Serbian state security. Quoted in Hélène Despic-Popovic, "Dix ans après, les Serbes voient l'horreur de Srebrenica en face," *Libération*, June 4, 2005.

27. Quoted in Stéphanie Maupas, "Des paramilitaires serbes sont arrêtés après la diffusion d'une vidéo au procès Milosevic," *Le Monde*, June 3, 2005.

28. Clea Koff, *The Bone Woman: Among the Dead in Rwanda, Bosnia, Croatia, and Kosovo* (New York: Random House, 2004).

Chapter 14. Court Settings and Movie Stagings

1. Paul Ricoeur, *Memory, History, Forgetting*, trans. Kathleen Blamey and David Pellauer (2000; Chicago: University of Chicago Press, 2004), 166.

2. For Michael Pollak, courtroom testimony bears "the marks of the principles of administering judicial proof: sticking to the object under judgment and eliminating all of the elements considered as off-topic." Pollak, *L'Expérience concentrationnaire: Essai sur le maintien de l'identité sociale* (1990; Paris: Métailié, 2000), 188. See also Régine Waintrater, *Sortir du génocide: Témoigner pour réapprendre à vivre* (Paris: Payot, 2003).

3. See Lawrence Douglas, *The Memory of Judgment: Making Law and History in the Trials of the Holocaust* (New Haven, Conn.: Yale University Press, 2001); Michael Salter, *Nazi War Crimes, U.S. Intelligence, and Selective Prosecution at Nuremberg: Controversies Regarding the Role of the Office of Strategic Services* (New York: Routledge-Cavendish, 2007).

4. The Former head of Tuol Sleng (or S-21, an interrogation center where torture was widely used), Kaing Guek Eav, a.k.a. "Duch," was finally convicted in 2010 of crimes against humanity and war crimes at age sixty-seven, having been held in prison since 1999 awaiting trial.

5. See the overview provided by Olivier Lalieu, "L'Invention du 'Devoir de mémoire,'" *Vingtième siècle: Revue d'histoire* 69 (January–March 2001): 83–94.

6. This is particularly true of his final intervention prior to the rendering of the verdict on February 3, 1948, in the American court at Nuremberg. Ohlendorf was found guilty and executed in Landsberg in 1951.

7. Christian Ingrao, "Les Intellectuels SS du Service de Renseignement (1900–1945)," Ph.D. diss., Université d'Amiens, 2001.

8. "Twenty-Sixth Day, Thursday, 3 January 1946," in *Proceedings: 17 December 1945–8 January 1946*, vol. 4 of *Trials of the Major War Criminals Before the International Military Tribunal, Nuremberg 14 November 1945–1 October 1946* (Nuremberg, 1947), 324.

9. "Twenty-Sixth Day, Thursday, 3 January 1946," in *Proceedings*, vol. 4, 323.

10. "Seventieth Day, Thursday, 28 February 1946," in *Proceedings: 20 February 1946–7 March 1946*, vol. 8 of *Trials of the Major War Criminals Before the International Military Tribunal, Nuremberg 14 November 1945–1 October 1946* (Nuremberg, 1947), 355, 376. The charge of conspiracy targeted "the directors, organizers, inducers or accomplices who took part in elaborating or executing a concerted plan or plot in order to commit any one of the crimes defined above" and who "are responsible for all of the acts accomplished by all of the people involved in the execution of this plan." The discrepancy between twenty-one and twenty-two defendants is owed to the fact that Martin Bormann had fled and was thus tried in absentia.

11. One such example is Marcel Ophuls's previously cited master work, *Memory of Justice*.

12. On the life and works of Sutzkever, see Justin Cammy with Anne-Gerard Flynn, "Smith College Professor Justin Cammy Remembers Abraham Sutzkever, the Most Important Yiddish Poet of the Holocaust," *Massachusetts Republican*, April 9, 2010, http://blog.masslive.com/nie/2010/04/smith_college_professor_justin.html.

13. Avrom Sutzkever, "Mon témoignage au procès de Nuremberg," trans. Gilles Rozier, "Les Écrivains et la guerre," special issue, *Europe* 796–97 (August–September 1995): 150.

14. "Sixty-Ninth Day, Wednesday, 27 February 1946," in *Proceedings*, vol. 8, 302.

15. Another text complements his account of the events witnessed: Avrom Sutskever, "The Vilna Ghetto," trans. M. Shambadal and B. Chernyak, in Vasily Grossman and Ilya Ehrenburg, eds., *The Complete Black Book of Russian Jewry*, 1970, ed. and trans. David Patterson (New Brunswick, N.J.: Transaction, 2009), 241–93.

16. The audiovisual recording of Sutzkever's deposition is available at the website of the United States Holocaust Memorial Museum, but the moment when he takes the stand and the eleven-second silence have both been cut to hasten the clip's presentation. My own documentary, *Nuremberg: The Nazis Facing Their Crimes*, shows these two scenes in their entirety.

17. "Sixty-Ninth Day, Wednesday, 27 February 1946," 302.

18. "Sixty-Ninth Day, Wednesday, 27 February 1946," 307. *Editor's note*: SS officer and head of the *Sonderkommando* unit in Vilnius Franz Murer established and administered the ghetto with virtually no checks on his power.

19. "Sixty-Ninth Day, Wednesday, 27 February 1946," 308.

20. A partial filmography includes *Cambodge, entre guerre et paix* (Cambodia, Between War and Peace; 1991), *Bophana, une tragédie cambodgienne* (Bophana, a Cambodian Tragedy, 1996), *Lumières sur un massacre* (Shedding Light on a Massacre; 1996), *S21: The Khmer Rouge Killing Machine* (2003), *The Burnt Theater* (2005), *Paper Cannot Wrap Up Embers* (2007), and *Duch, Master of the Forges of Hell* (2011). On this period of Cambodian history, see Ariane Mathieu, "Une Plongée au cœur du système génocidaire," in "Images, représentations, histoire: La tragédie cambodgienne des années soixante-dix," D.E.A. thesis, Université de Paris X-Nanterre, 2005, 128–56.

21. David Chandler, *Voices from S21: Terror and History in Pol Pot's Secret Prison* (Berkeley: University of California Press, 2000); Rithy Panh and Christine Chaumeau, *La Machine khmère rouge: Monti Santésok S-21* (Paris: Flammarion, 2009).

22. Press release, *S21: The Khmer Rouge Killing Machine.*

23. See David Schreiber, "Histoire, justice et télévision: *Le Procès Barbie* sur la chaîne *Histoire*," in Christian Delage and Anne Grynberg, eds., "La Shoah: Images témoins, images preuves," special issue, *Cahiers du Judaïsme* 15 (2003): 100–111; and Barbara Cassin, Olivier Cayla, and Philippe-Joseph Salazar, eds., *Vérité, réconciliation, réparation*, Le Genre Humain (Paris: Seuil, 2004).

24. Peter Maguire, *Facing Death in Cambodia* (New York: Columbia University Press, 2005), 125.

25. Ricoeur, *Memory, History, Forgetting*, 166; Paul Ricoeur, "Histoire et mémoire," in Antoine de Baecque and Christian Delage, eds., *De l'histoire au cinéma* (Paris: Complexe, 1998), 20.

26. Press release, *S21: The Khmer Rouge Killing Machine.*

27. Chheang Bopha, "Un Film du DC-Cam sur S-21 indigne Van[n] Nath, un des survivants," *Cambodge Soir*, March 9, 2007.

28. A similar situation occurred in Rwanda during the trials held in community courts known as *Gacaca*. It would be interesting to compare in this case as well the various approaches to obtaining accurate testimony and communicating it to the public; one would begin with the activities of the International Criminal Tribunal for Rwanda in Arusha, those of the Gacaca, and the work of a filmmaker who kept track over a ten-year period of the survivors and criminals of the Rwandan genocide living on a single hillside (*My Neighbor, My Killer*, dir. Anne Aghion, 2009). On the Gacaca experience, see Hélène Dumas, "*Gacaca* Courts in Rwanda: A Local Justice for a Local Genocide History?," in Christian Delage and Peter Goodrich, eds., *The Scene of the Mass Crime. History, Film, and International Trials* (London: Routledge, 2012), 57–73.

29. *Editor's note*: A *kramar* is a plaid scarf worn throughout Cambodia.

30. See Ben Kiernan, *The Pol Pot Regime: Race, Power and Genocide in Cambodia Under the Khmer Rouge, 1975–1979*, 2nd ed. (New Haven, Conn.: Yale University Press, 2002).

31. DC-Cam has drawn on this material for the publication of a number of books, including, most notably, Meng-Try Ea and Sorya Sim, *Victims and Perpetrators: The Testimony of Young Khmer Rouge Cadres at S21* (Phnom Penh: DC-Cam, 2001).

32. François Deroin, "'Douch' et ses juges sur les lieux de mort khmers rouges," *Le Monde*, February 28, 2008.

33. Late in the trial, Duch abandoned the initial strategy recommended by his French defense lawyer, François Roux, of pleading guilty. In the end, he pled not guilty on the advice of a second lawyer, Cambodian Kar Savuth. First sentenced to thirty-five years imprisonment (reduced immediately to nineteen for time served and illegal incarceration), Duch saw this extended—much to general surprise—on February 3, 2012, to life in prison when the plaintiffs successfully appealed a punishment deemed

insufficient. See Roux, "Pleading Guilty: The Case of Duch in the Khmer Rouge Trials," in Delage and Goodrich, *The Scene of the Mass Crime*, 155–66.

34. Rithy Panh with Christophe Bataille, *The Elimination: A Survivor of the Khmer Rouge Confronts His Past and the Commandant of the Killing Fields*, trans. John Cullen (New York: Other Press, 2013).

35. Rithy Panh, interviewed by Arnaud Vaulerin, "Je pensais que le bourreau dirait la vérité," *Libération*, January 7, 2012.

36. Ricoeur, *Memory, History, Forgetting*, 418.

37. Stéphanie Maupas, "Le Premier procès devant la CPI a valeur de test pour la justice internationale," *Le Monde*, January 27, 2009.

38. "$21 Million Pledged for Khmer Rouge Trial," *Japan Times*, January 12, 2009.

39. Seth Mydans, "Cambodia: U.S. Pledges Funds to Khmer Rouge Tribunal," *New York Times*, September 17, 2008, A12.

40. On the notion of "extraterritorial justice," see Antoine Garapon, "Projet universel ou justice des vainqueurs?," in *Des Crimes qu'on ne peut ni punir ni pardonner: Pour une justice internationale* (Paris: Odile Jacob, 2002), 46–83.

41. Reuters reports that the first textbook presenting the Khmer Rouge's crimes to Cambodian schoolchildren was distributed to classrooms in 2009. "Premier manuel sur le génocide khmer rouge publié au Cambodge," *LExpress.fr*, February 12, 2009.

42. For example, *Duch on Trial: Time for Justice* is a series of documentaries produced by Khmer Mekong Films showing the efforts of two journalists, Neth Pheaktra of the *Phnom Penh Post* and Ung Chan Sophea of *Cambodge Soir*, to provide summary accounts of the trial to local populations.

43. See Mark Osiel, *Mass Atrocity, Collective Memory, and the Law* (New Brunswick, N.J.: Transaction, 1997).

Conclusion

1. Jacques Derrida, with Bernard Stiegler, "The Archive Market: Truth, Testimony, Evidence," in *Echographies of Television*, trans. Jennifer Dajorek (Cambridge, Mass.: Polity Press, 2002), 94.

2. Paul Ricoeur, "Histoire et rhétorique," *Diogène* 168 (October–December 1994): 25.

3. Mark Osiel, *Mass Atrocity, Collective Memory, and the Law* (New Brunswick, N.J.: Transaction, 1997), 39.

4. Film always preserves the mark of the intentions that oversaw its production. On the eve of a European Parliamentary Council meeting that promised to be delicate for them, the Russians screened a movie in London that contained scenes of decapitations and torture of individuals held hostage by "Chechen bandits." Sophie Shihab notes that the film "did not obtain the desired media success." In her opinion, "the

attempt to manipulate public opinion was too obvious, even for those who refuse to believe the Chechen version of events, namely, that the scenes were filmed by members of their population working (knowingly or not) for the Russians who ordered the footage." Shihab, "Les Tchétchènes protestent contre la 'désinformation' orchestrée par Moscou," *Le Monde*, August 4, 2000.

BIBLIOGRAPHY

History and Justice

Association Française pour l'Histoire de la Justice. *La Justice des années sombres, 1940–1994*. Pref. Pierre Truche. Paris: Documentation Française, 2001.

Bensaïd, Daniel. *Qui est le juge? Pour en finir avec le tribunal de l'histoire*. Paris: Fayard, 1999.

Garapon, Antoine. *Bien juger: Essai sur le rituel judiciaire*. Paris: Odile Jacob, 1997.

Ginzburg, Carlo. *The Judge and the Historian: Marginal Notes on a Late-Twentieth-Century Miscarriage of Justice*. Trans. Antony Shugaar. London: Verso, 2002.

Hartog, François. "Le Témoin et l'historien." *Gradhiva* 27 (2000): 1–14.

Jeanneney, Jean-Noël. *Le Passé dans le prétoire: L'historien, le juge et le journaliste*. Paris: Le Seuil, 1998.

Koselleck, Reinhart. "Histoire, droit et justice." 1986. In *L'Expérience de l'histoire*. Trans. Alexandre Escudier. Ed. Michael Werner. 161–80. Paris: Gallimard/Le Seuil, 1997.

Le Crom, Jean-Pierre, and Jean-Clément Martin, eds. "Vérité historique, vérité judiciaire." Special issue, *Droit et Société* 38 (1998).

Ricoeur, Paul. *Memory, History, Forgetting*. Trans. Kathleen Blamey and David Pellauer. Chicago: University of Chicago Press, 2000.

Rousso, Henry, with Philippe Petit. *The Haunting Past: History, Memory, and Justice in Contemporary France*. 1998. Trans. Ralph Schoolcraft. Philadelphia: University of Pennsylvania Press, 2002.

Rousso, Henry, with Philippe Petit. *Vichy, l'événement, la mémoire, l'histoire*. Paris: Gallimard, 2001.

"Vérité judiciaire, vérité historique." Special issue, *Le Débat* 102 (November–December 1998).

Wieviorka, Annette. *The Era of the Witness*. 1998. Trans. Jared Stark. Ithaca, N.Y.: Cornell University Press, 2006.

Justice and Film

Cassiday, Julie A. *The Enemy on Trial: Early Soviet Courts on Stage and Screen*. DeKalb: Northern Illinois University Press, 2000.

Denvir, John, ed. *Legal Reelism: Movies as Legal Texts*. Urbana: University of Illinois Press, 1996.

Douzinas, Costas, and Lynda Nead, eds. *Law and Image: The Authority of Art and the Aesthetics of Law*. Chicago: University of Chicago Press, 1999.

Dulong, Renaud. *Le Témoin oculaire: Les conditions sociales de l'attestation personnelle*. Paris: EHESS, 1998.

Greenfield, Steve, Guy Osborn, and Peter Robson, eds. *Film and the Law*. London: Cavendish, 2001.

Kennedy, Richard Lea. *Trial Evidence: A Synopsis of the Law of Evidence Generally Applicable to Trials*. 2nd ed. Kansas City, Mo.: Vernon Law Book, 1935.

Legendre, Pierre. *Le Crime du caporal Lortie: Traité sur le père*. Paris: Fayard, 1989.

New York State Committee to Review Audio-Visual Coverage of Court Proceedings. *An Open Courtroom: Cameras in New York Courts*. New York: Fordham University Press, 1997.

Osborn, Albert S. *The Problem of Proof, Especially as Exemplified in Disputed Document Trials*. New York: Matthew Bender, 1922.

Paradis, Pierre R. "The Celluloid Witness." *University of Colorado Law Review* 37 (1965): 235–68.

Seagle, William. *The Quest for Law*. New York: Knopf, 1941.

Films of Nazi Camps and of War Crimes

Abzug, Robert H. *Inside the Vicious Heart: Americans and the Liberation of Nazi Concentration Camps*. New York: Oxford University Press, 1985.

Bartov, Omer, Atina Grossmann, and Mary Nolan, eds. *Crimes of War: Guilt and Denial in the Twentieth Century*. New York: New Press, 2002.

Chéroux, Clément, ed. *Mémoire des camps: Photographies des camps de concentration et d'extermination nazis, 1933–1999*. Paris: Marval, 2001.

Delage, Christian, and Anne Grynberg, eds. "La Shoah: Images témoins, images preuves," Special issue, *Cahiers du Judaïsme* 15 (2003).

Doherty, Thomas. *Projections of War: Hollywood, American Culture, and World War II*. New York: Columbia University Press, 1993.

Genton, Bernard. "'A Sea of Shoes...': La perception de la Shoah aux États-Unis (1941–1945)." *Sources* 6 (Spring 1999): 99–136.

Hüppauf, Bernd. "Emptying the Gaze: Framing Violence Through the Viewfinder." *New German Critique* 72 (Fall 1997): 3–44.

Kessel, Joseph. "Nuremberg." *France-Soir*, December 3, 1945.

Lipstadt, Deborah E. *Beyond Belief: The American Press and the Coming of the Holocaust, 1933–1945.* New York: Free Press, 1986.

Margry, Karel. "*Theresienstadt* (1944–1945): The Nazi Propaganda Film Depicting the Concentration Camp as Paradise." *Historical Journal of Film, Radio and Television* 12, no. 2 (1992): 145–62.

Matard-Bonucci, Marie-Anne, and Édouard Lynch, eds. *La Libération des camps et le retour des déportés.* Paris: Éditions Complexe, 1995.

Milton, Sybil. "Photography as Evidence of the Holocaust." *History of Photography* 23, no. 4 (1999): 303–12.

Pulitzer, Joseph. *A Report to the American People.* St. Louis, Mo.: St. Louis Post-Dispatch, 1945.

Schulberg, Stuart. "An Eyewitness Reports." *Hollywood Quarterly* 2 (July 1947).

Sussex, Elizabeth. "The Fate of F3080." *Sight and Sound* 53, no. 2 (1984): 92–105.

Zelizer, Barbie. *Remembering to Forget: Holocaust Memory Through the Camera's Eye.* Chicago: University of Chicago Press, 1998.

The Nuremberg Trial

Alexander, Charles W., with Anne Keeshan. *Justice at Nuernberg: A Pictorial Record of the Trial of Nazi War Criminals by the International Military Tribunal, at Nuernberg, Germany, 1945–46.* Chicago: Marvel, 1946.

Bass, Gary Jonathan. *Stay the Hand of Vengeance: The Politics of War Crimes Tribunals.* Princeton, N.J.: Princeton University Press, 2000.

Bloxham, Donald. *War Crimes Trials and the Formation of Holocaust History and Memory.* Oxford: Oxford University Press, 2001.

Brayard, Florent, ed. *Le Génocide des Juifs entre procès et histoire, 1943–2000.* Paris: Éditions Complexe, 2000.

Calvocoressi, Peter. *Nuremberg: The Facts, the Law, and the Consequences.* New York: Macmillan, 1947.

Cowles, Willard B. "Trial of War Criminals by Military Tribunals." *American Bar Association Journal* 30, no. 6 (1944): 330–33.

Davidson, Eugene. *The Trial of the Germans: An Account of the Twenty-Two Defendants Before the International Military Tribunal at Nuremberg.* New York: Macmillan, 1966.

Desmond, Charles, Paul A. Freund, Potter Stewart, and Lord Shawcross. *Mr. Justice Jackson: Four Lectures in His Honor.* New York: Columbia University Press, 1969.

Douglas, Lawrence. *The Memory of Judgment: Making Law and History in the Trials of the Holocaust.* New Haven, Conn.: Yale University Press, 2001.

Garapon, Antoine. *Des crimes qu'on ne peut ni punir ni pardonner: Pour une justice internationale.* Paris: Odile Jacob, 2002.

————. "De Nuremberg au TPI: Naissance d'une justice universelle?" *Critique Internationale* 5 (Fall 1999): 167–81.

Gilbert, G. M. *Nuremberg Diary*. New York: Farrar, Straus, 1947.

Harris, Whitney R. *Tyranny on Trial: The Evidence at Nuremberg*. 1954. Introduction by Robert H. Jackson, Foreword by Robert G. Storey. Dallas: Southern Methodist University Press, 1999.

Hazan, Pierre. *La Justice face à la guerre: De Nuremberg à La Haye*. Paris: Stock, 2000.

Jackson, Robert H. *The Nürnberg Case, as Presented by Robert H. Jackson, Chief of Counsel for the United States Together with Other Documents*. New York: Knopf, 1947.

Maguire, Peter. *Law and War: An American Story*. New York: Columbia University Press, 2001.

Marrus, Michael M. "History and the Holocaust in the Courtroom." In Ronald Smelser, ed., *Lessons and Legacies of the Holocaust*, vol. 5, *The Holocaust and Justice*, 215–39. Evanston, Ill.: Northwestern University Press, 2002.

————. "The Holocaust at Nuremberg." *Yad Vashem Studies* 26 (1998): 4–45.

————. *The Nuremberg War Crimes Trial, 1945–1946: A Documentary History*. Boston: Bedford, 1997.

Osiel, Mark. *Mass Atrocity, Collective Memory, and the Law*. New Brunswick, N.J.: Transaction, 1997.

Phleger, Herman. "Nuremberg—A Fair Trial?" *Atlantic Monthly* 177, no. 4 (1946): 60–65.

Le Procès de Nuremberg: Conséquences et actualisation. Brussels: Université de Bruxelles, Bruylant, 1988.

Stave, Bruce M., and Michele Palmer with Leslie Frank. *Witnesses to Nuremberg: An Oral History of American Participants at the War Crimes Trial*. New York: Twayne, 1998.

Taylor, Telford. *The Anatomy of the Nuremberg Trials: A Personal Memoir*. 1949. Boston: Little, Brown, 1992.

Trial of the Major War Criminals Before the International Military Tribunal: Nuremberg 14 November 1945–1 October 1946. Nuremberg: IMT, 1947–49. *Proceedings*, 22 vols. *Documents*, 20 vols.

Wieviorka, Annette, ed. *Les Procès de Nuremberg et de Tokyo*. Paris: Éditions Complexe, 1996.

Wyzanski, Charles E., Jr. "Nuremberg—A Fair Trial? Dangerous Precedent." *Atlantic Monthly* 177, no. 4 (1946): 66–70.

————. "Nuremberg in Retrospect." *Atlantic Monthly* 178, no. 6 (1946): 56–59.

INDEX

ACKNOWLEDGMENTS

This book benefited from many sources of support without which it could not have been completed. It all began with a question back in 2000 from my colleague and friend Christian Ingrao, who asked whether the interrogations preceding the Nuremberg Trials had been filmed. It was in seeking the means to answer him that I started to delve into the matter; this quest led me to the present work.

Thanks to Karen Taieb's warm welcome at the Centre de Documentation Juive Contemporaine, I was soon able to watch some of the movies shown at Nuremberg in 1945–46. François Hartog then responded favorably to my application for a grant from the Centre National du Livre. I therefore went to Washington, D.C., for a first round of research at the National Archives and Records Administration (NARA) in May 2000. The massive amount of documents available there is such that without assistance it is impossible to navigate through them easily and efficiently. I had the good fortune to happen upon Larry McDonald, who intervened to speed up a procedure that could have taken significantly longer. After an initial explanation in the reference room of the chain of access to the archives through the descriptive catalogues, he decided to grant me direct access to the stacks so that I could retrieve documents on my own once I had identified the desired contents. I can hardly express how much this favor facilitated my research. Similarly the ease of access to photocopy machines at NARA was an invaluable aid.

At a conference held at London's Imperial War Museum in February 2001, its host and organizer, Toby Haggith, gave me access to the relevant British documents. Following a letter of support from John Ford's grandson, Dan Ford, the Lilly Library of the University of Indiana at Bloomington allowed me to consult the Ford archives in its possession. In addition, the library provided financial assistance so that I could make copies of the documents that I needed. I thank Francis Lapka, Christopher S. Harter, and

Sue Presnell for their aid. After a second visit to the NARA in May 2001, I succeeded in obtaining a Fulbright Fellowship in 2002, which made possible a lengthy stay in Washington, as well as visits to New York, where I consulted resources at the Yivo Institute, MoMA's library (thanks to Ron Magliozzi and Charles Silver), and the New York Public Library, which, in the aftermath of 9/11, tried valiantly (with the help of the local population) to continue serving as before its many readers.

Thanks to the Institut d'Histoire du Temps Présent and its director, Henry Rousso, another round at the NARA and a trip to the American Jewish History Society were made possible in 2003, whereas support from the Institut des Hautes Études sur la Justice (Antoine Garapon, director) allowed me to visit in the spring of 2004 the Leo T. Hurwitz archives held at the George Eastman House (Paolo Cherchi Usai and Anthony L'Abbate, directors). Finally, due to assistance from Christopher M. Laico, I was able to consult some of Telford Taylor's papers held at Columbia University Law School. During a final brief work session in the United States Holocaust Memorial Museum's Film Department in April 2005, I was able to contribute to the acquisition by the Mémorial de la Shoah (Paris) of the complete film archives of the Nuremberg Trials; I am grateful to Raye Farr's benevolence.

These trips to the United States would not have been nearly so agreeable without the welcome of my friends Vanessa Schwartz (Washington, D.C., then Los Angeles) and Stuart Liebman (New York); I am most appreciative. My thanks also go to Lois, Jesse, and Alex, as well as George Stone. I was also able to present my work in a number of North American universities thanks in part to support from the Ministère des Affaires Étrangères (Marie Bonnel, Annie-Sophie Hermil, and Sonia Naily): New York University (Frédéric Viguier); the University of Southern California (Vanessa Schwartz); the University of Pennsylvania (Maurice Samuels); Texas A&M University (Richard J. Golsan, Ralph Schoolcraft III); and the Université de Montréal (Philippe Despoix). I was also able to give papers at two international conferences: Lessons and Legacies VII: The Holocaust in International Perspective, hosted in 2002 by the University of Minnesota–Twin Cities, and the annual meeting of the Law and Society Association, which was held in Chicago in 2004.

I would also like to thank the Research Division of the Université de Paris-VIII for its support, the Institut d'Histoire du Temps Présent-Centre National de la Recherche Scientfique for welcoming me as a visiting scholar for two years (2002–4), and the École des Hautes Études en Sciences Sociales for enabling me to lead a seminar on the subject of my research (Olivier Abel, Marc Olivier Baruch, Nancy Green, André Gunthert, François Hartog, Sabina Loriga, Christophe Prochasson, and Jacques Revel). Thanks also to Jean Astruc for facilitating the loan of numerous books from the IHTP library, Guy Saguez for his trust and access to his personal archives, and Valérie Martin for introducing me to my future editors at the Éditions Denoël. I would also like to acknowledge Natalie Zemon Davis.

Finally, I would like to thank all those whose encouragement helped me complete this project: Stéphane Audoin-Rouzeau, Marc Olivier Baruch, Annette Becker, Christian Biet, Alain Blum, Florent Brayard, Clément Chéroux, Jim Damour, Georges Didi-Huberman, Gabrielle Drigeard, Béatrice Fraenkel, Antoine Garapon, Carlo Ginzburg, Anne Grynberg, André Gunthert, Joël Hubrecht, Christian Ingrao, Pieter Lagrou, Hanno and Ronny Loewy, Gaelle Loiseau, Marie-Claude Miquel, Pap Ndiaye, Henry Rousso, David Schreiber, Yan Thomas, Michael Werner, and Nicolas Werth. Among my friends on the editorial staff of the review *Vertigo*, Hervé Aubron, Christian-Marc Bosséno, Priska Morrissey, and Cyril Neyrat have been particularly supportive. My gratitude goes to François Prodromidès as well; his attentive and knowledgeable reading of this manuscript was extremely useful to me.

I am also indebted to Mary Byrd Kelly and Ralph Schoolcraft III, who spent much time and energy on the English translation and editing of this book.

This book was written in Paris and Montélimar and in New York City. My thoughts go to my hosts in France and in the United States, especially the Guigueno and Liebman families, and to the one who is no longer with us, my brother Jean-Philippe.